Under Mountain Shadows

Under Mountain Shadows

*Kay Kershaw, Lesbian Eco-Warrior
of the Pacific Northwest*

WILLIAM D. FRANK

McFarland & Company, Inc., Publishers
Jefferson, North Carolina

LIBRARY OF CONGRESS CATALOGUING-IN-PUBLICATION DATA

Names: Frank, William D., author.
Title: Under mountain shadows : Kay Kershaw, lesbian eco-warrior of the Pacific Northwest / William D. Frank.
Description: Jefferson, North Carolina : McFarland & Company, Inc., Publishers, 2024 | Includes bibliographical references and index.
Identifiers: LCCN 2024001974 | ISBN 9781476693927 (paperback : acid free paper) ∞
ISBN 9781476652405 (ebook)
Subjects: LCSH: Kershaw, Kathryn. | Lesbians—Northwest, Pacific—Biography. | Women conservationists—Northwest, Pacific—Biography. | Conservation of natural resources—Northwest, Pacific. | Gay rights—United States. | Ecofeminism—United States. | BISAC: POLITICAL SCIENCE / Public Policy / Environmental Policy | HISTORY / United States / State & Local / Pacific Northwest (OR, WA)
Classification: LCC HQ75.4.K47 F73 2024 | DDC 306.76/63092 [B]—dc23/eng/20240206
LC record available at https://lccn.loc.gov/2024001974

BRITISH LIBRARY CATALOGUING DATA ARE AVAILABLE

ISBN (print) 978-1-4766-9392-7
ISBN (ebook) 978-1-4766-5240-5

© 2024 William D. Frank. All rights reserved

No part of this book may be reproduced or transmitted in any form or by any means, electronic or mechanical, including photocopying or recording, or by any information storage and retrieval system, without permission in writing from the publisher.

Front cover: Kay poses with her favorite horse, Rusty, circa 1947. Kay used this image for her Double K Ranch Christmas card in 1956 and in advertisements placed jointly with Northern Pacific Railway throughout the 1950s (Kershaw Family Collection).

Printed in the United States of America

*McFarland & Company, Inc., Publishers
Box 611, Jefferson, North Carolina 28640
www.mcfarlandpub.com*

Robert C. Kershaw
1939–2019

"You should write something about my Aunt Kay."
Bob Kershaw to the author, Yakima, Washington, October 2018

Contents

Acknowledgments	ix
Acronyms, Abbreviations, Definitions, Names	xi
Introduction	1
1. An Overview of Yakima County	3
2. Kay Kershaw and "Homosexuality" in the Early 20th Century	20
3. Kay Kershaw and Women's Aeronautics	30
4. The Great Depression and World War II	40
5. The Double K Mountain Ranch	49
6. Interlude: Shifting Perceptions During the Cold War	74
7. Cougar Lakes Wilderness—The First Decade (1958–1968)	83
8. Interlude: Isabelle Lynn and Justice Douglas Help Kay at Goose Prairie	111
9. NEPA, RARE I and II, and Cougar Lakes Legislation (1969–1980)	122
10. How Cougar Lakes Became the William O. Douglas Wilderness	141
Epilogue	151
Appendix: The Literary Odyssey of Isabelle Lynn	155
Chapter Notes	173
Bibliography	209
Index	219

Acknowledgments

As luck would have it, my peripatetic parents—Herbert L. and Heather C. Frank—chose to settle in central Washington with my two siblings in the late 1940s. Thus, I was the first of my family born and raised in Yakima: many of the people, places, and circumstances described in the following pages have informed my life from day one. This book reflects my deep appreciation for such a fortuitous turn of events.

The idea for this book evolved from my association with Kay's two nephews, Bob and Ed Kershaw. A chance conversation with Bob in late 2018 piqued my curiosity about Kay's remarkable life, and Ed's follow-up delivery in March 2020 of her personal collection of letters and memorabilia, in addition to the Kershaw family's history files, provided the impetus to take on this project. Ed's enthusiasm and encouragement never wavered as I worked through the manuscript over the course of three years. During that time, Ed and I were fortunate to make the acquaintance of many members of Pat Kane's family who provided access to their voluminous collection of letters. My thanks to Pat's nieces Maria Centrella and Patricia Bradley for their support and interest and to the Richardson family—the current owners of the Double K Ranch—for allowing all of us to gather on premises in June 2022.

I am indebted to Barb Smith Gilbert and Cragg M. Gilbert who provided documentation from their family archives and gave valuable feedback as the manuscript progressed through myriad versions. I also received input and support from local readers Larry Frank, Jane Gutting, and Terry Martin. Because of the complex nature of this book, I sought help from others with expertise and personal experience in a variety of subjects outside my areas of specialization. I am grateful especially for the crucial insight provided by Gary Atkins; M. Rupert Cutler; Brock Evans; and Lillian Faderman.

From start to finish, I was privileged to receive aid, encouragement, and inordinate amounts of time and effort from my two devoted and trusted editors, Nadine Cohodas and Laurie Moshier. For invaluable research assistance and feedback, special thanks to John Baule at the Yakima Valley Museum, whose knowledge of local Yakima history is nothing less than encyclopedic. Thanks also to cartographer Daniel Huffman and my go-to person for all things related to photography, Gordon King.

In addition to many of those individuals mentioned above, I am grateful for interviews conducted in person, by telephone, or over Zoom with Leo Adams; John Barany; Charlie de La Chapelle; Thomas P. Ferguson, Jr.; Alex Frank; Tim Franklin; John Gasperetti; Marty Hall; Joel Heinzen; Ginger Hislop; Noel Kelley; Robert H. Kershaw; Ruby Montana; Brad Patterson; Dale Robinson; Mary Ann (Kershaw) Robinson; Tripp Robinson; Kristin (Kershaw) Snapp; C. Peter Sorenson; and Erik Splawn. Because so many chose not to answer email queries and pleas for help, I would like to express my appreciation for those who did: E. John B. Allen; Michael Biggins; Carolin Bigwood; Eric Boyd; Jamie Carmody; Marcia Coyle; Susan Cyr; Amy Farranto; Phil Fenner; Kian Flynn; Elon H. Gilbert; Dan Herman; Mike Hiler; Annette Hofmann; Mike Hoge; Mary Humberston; Anne Jenner; Yvonne Keller; Gary Koehler; Eben Lehman; Jeff Leich; James Lewis; Adam Liptak; Seth McCormick Lynn, Jr.; Sophia Lyons; Linda Manning; Mary Margaret McKeown; Ed Marquand; Kevin McCarthy; Phil Menashe; Jo Miles; Layla Milholen; Tiffany Miller; Allee Monheim; Sid Morrison; Warren Robins; Clémence Scouten; Mary St. Germain; Karen Schneider; Morrie Shore; Lowell Skoog; Cathy Douglas Stone; Ed Stover; Tom Sullivan; Christof Thöny; Nina Totenberg; Tim Whiton; Glennys Young; and Julie Ziegler.

As always, my gratitude extends to those unsung heroes of historical research, the staffers toiling out of the limelight, especially at Brooks Library (Central Washington University); McAllister Museum of Flight; Yakima Valley Genealogical Society Library; Yakima Valley Library; Yakima Valley Museum; University of Washington Libraries and Special Collections; and the Library of Congress.

Finally, I would be remiss if I did not acknowledge the late Johnson Meninick (1933–2020), Honored Elder of the Confederated Tribes and Bands of the Yakama Nation, with whom I maintained a cordial relationship for nearly three decades. His oral histories, narrated as I sat by his side in a variety of settings during the 1990s, enhanced my awareness of the Nation's close connection to the traditional tribal lands, ceded to the government in 1855, upon which the majority of events recounted in this book occurred.

Any errors, shortcomings, or misrepresentations within the text are my own responsibility and should not reflect on the integrity and sincerity of the contributors listed above.

Acronyms, Abbreviations, Definitions, Names

AFA: American Forestry Association
AP: Associated Press
ATV: all-terrain vehicle
CCC: Civilian Conservation Corps
CLWA: Cougar Lakes Wilderness Alliance
CRWP: Citizens for Responsible Water Projects
DEIS: draft environmental impact statement
DOB: Daughters of Bilitis, San Francisco–based lesbian advocacy organization (1955–1972)
EIS: environmental impact statement
ERA: Equal Rights Amendment
FTSW: Friends of the Three Sisters Wilderness
FWOC: Federation of Western Outdoor Clubs
JBS: John Birch Society (also: Birchers)
KKK: Ku Klux Klan (also: the Klan)
LGBTQ+: lesbian, gay, bisexual, transgender, questioning, and inclusive
LSP: Lyle Stuart Publishers of New York
MRNP: Mt. Rainier National Park
NCCC: North Cascades Conservation Council
NEPA: National Environmental Protection Act of 1969
NPS: National Park Service of the Department of the Interior (also: Park Service)
OMB: White House Office of Management and Budget
ORV: off-road vehicle
PCT: Pacific Crest Trail
RARE (I and II): Roadless Area Review and Evaluation (I and II)
SCW: State College of Washington in Pullman, Washington [Washington State University as of 1959]
SEC: United States Securities and Exchange Commission
USFS: United States Forest Service of the Department of Agriculture (also: Forest Service)
WARS: wilderness attribute rating system

WERA: Washington Emergency Relief Administration
WPSC: White Pass Ski Company
WSDPW: Washington State Department of Public Welfare

* * *

Board foot: a one-inch-thick square foot of wood.
Fourth Congressional District, Washington State: Includes all of Yakima, Douglas, Benton, Okanogan, Grant, and Klickitat Counties, plus parts of Adams and Franklin.
Gifford-Pinchot: Gifford Pinchot National Forest.
Mazamas: Portland, Oregon–based outdoor club founded in 1894.
The Mountaineers: Seattle, Washington–based outdoor club founded in 1906.
North Yakima: name of Yakima, Washington, prior to 1918.
Square mile: 640 acres.
The Triangle: an area of land in Yakima County lying within a triangle described by the Cascade Crest from Goat Rocks to Naches Pass, the Naches River Canyon, and the Tieton River Canyon with its eastern vertex at a point twenty miles northwest of Yakima, Washington, where the Naches and Tieton Rivers flow together.
The Y: the junction of the Tieton and Naches Rivers.
The Yakama Nation: The Confederated Tribes and Bands of the Yakama Nation (also: the Yakamas; prior to 1994, the Yakima Nation).
Yakima: largest city in Yakima County located at the junction of the Naches and Yakima Rivers (also city of Yakima).
Yakima City: name of Union Gap, Washington, prior to 1918.

* * *

Gilbert Family Members Referenced:

Francelia Amsden Gilbert (1840–1935): mother of H.M. Gilbert
May Gilbert (1861–1942): sister of H.M. Gilbert
Horace Mark (H.M.) Gilbert (1862–1934): Yakima County agriculturalist at the turn of the last century
Curtiss Richey Gilbert (1894–1947): son of H.M. Gilbert and Marion Richey Gilbert
Elon James (Elon J.) Gilbert (1897–1978): son of H.M. Gilbert and Marion Richey Gilbert
Joan (Joanna Sprague) Gilbert (1901–1981): wife of Elon J. Gilbert
Horace Nathaniel (Horace N.) Gilbert (1901–1990): son of H.M. Gilbert and Marion Richey Gilbert
Cragg Douglas (Cragg D.) Gilbert (1923–2007): son of Curtiss Richey Gilbert and Anne Seely Gilbert

Virginia (McCormick) Gilbert (1926–2012): wife of Cragg D. Gilbert

Bruce Renwick Gilbert (1931–2017): son of Curtiss Richey Gilbert and Anne Seely Gilbert

Elon Hamilton (Elon H.) Gilbert (1939–): son of Horace N. Gilbert and Anne Richardson Gilbert

Jennith Knowlton Gilbert (Knox) (1937–): daughter of Horace N. Gilbert and Anne Richardson Gilbert

Cragg McCormick (Cragg M.) Gilbert (1952–): son of Cragg D. Gilbert and Virginia McCormick Gilbert

* * *

Family Members of Kay Kershaw (1907–1996) Referenced:

Abraham (?–?) and Alice (Buckley) Kershaw (1793–1861): married in 1815; Kay's great-grandparents

Robert Kershaw (1831–1916) and Mary Ann (Harrison) Kershaw (1844–1894): Kay's grandparents

Edward (Edwin) Ambrose Kershaw (1877–1959) and Ora (Whitmore) Kershaw (1876–1963): Kay's parents

Robert Whitmore Kershaw (1912–1930): Kay's brother

Ronald Edward (1908–2003) and Elizabeth (Betty) Ann (Boone) Kershaw (1913–2003): Kay's brother and sister-in-law

Robert (Bob) Chester Kershaw (1938–2019): Kay's nephew

Edward (Ed) Ronald Kershaw (1939–): Kay's nephew

Mary Ann (Kershaw) Robinson (1944–): Kay's niece

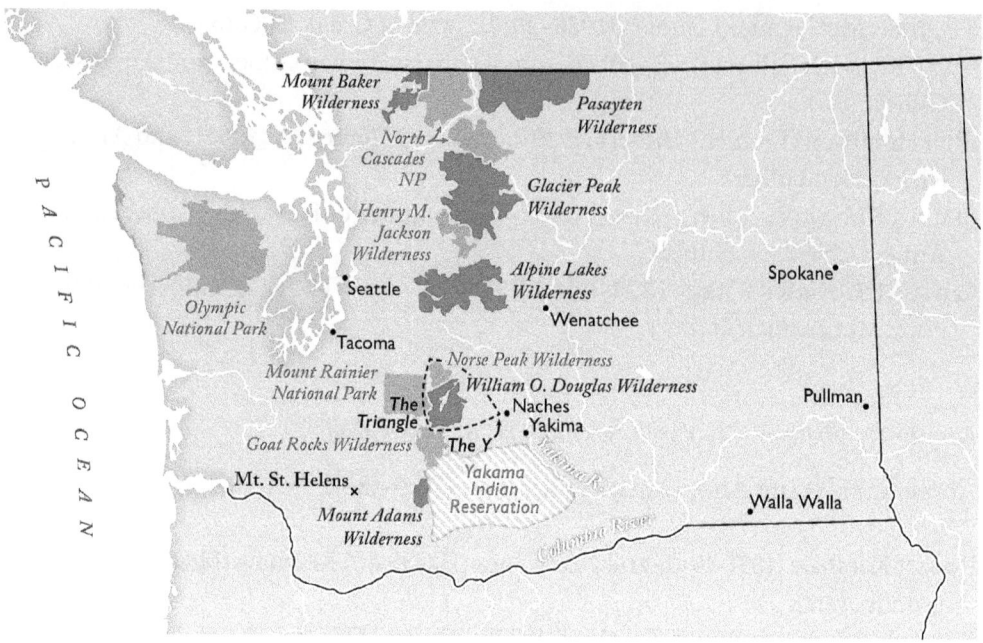

Map 1: Washington State (Daniel Huffman, cartographer).

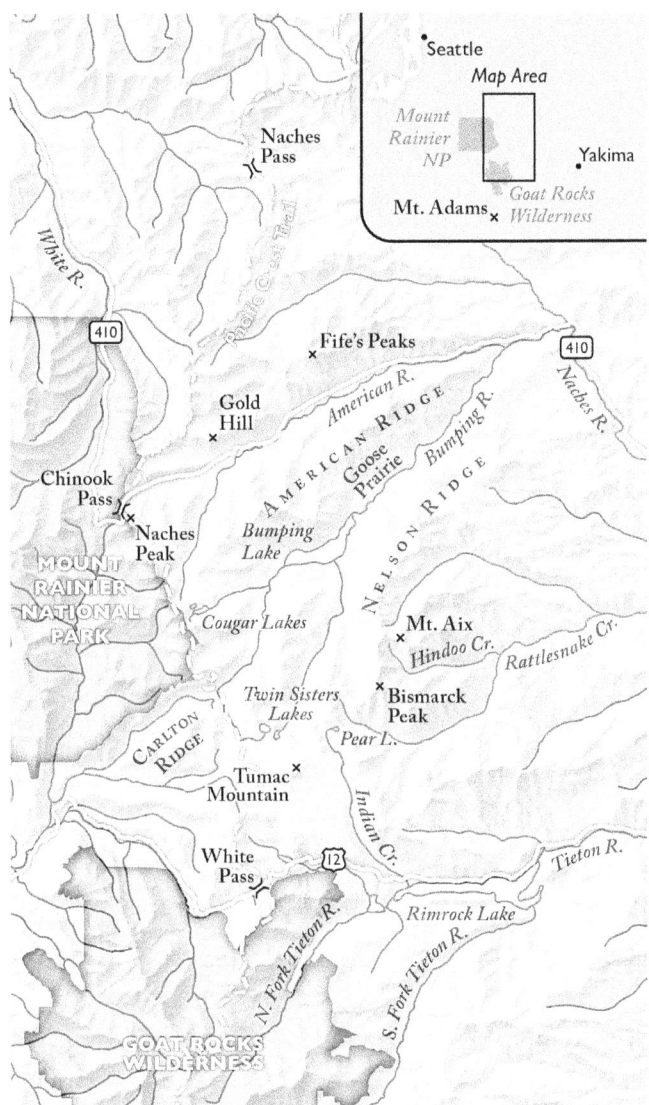

Map 2: Detail of the Triangle (Daniel Huffman, cartographer).

Introduction

"We get the feeling we are fighting shadows."[1]

Except for a stint as a Red Cross nurse during World War II, Kay Kershaw spent her entire life in the Pacific Northwest, most of it within Washington State's Yakima County, a region where the shadow metaphor looms large. The rain shadow created by the Cascade mountain range is prevalent here: warm, moisture-laden air moving inland from the Pacific Ocean rises up the west side of the mountains, drops the moisture as precipitation on the crest and, wrung dry, descends to the east. The result is a parched shrub-steppe on the east side of the state; this lack of water impacts all socio-economic aspects of life from the eastern foothills to the Idaho border. Similarly, residents of the city of Yakima live in the shadow of Mount Adams, the state's second highest volcano. In his 1950 book *Of Men and Mountains*, Supreme Court Justice William O. Douglas, Yakima's most renowned citizen of the twentieth century and a close friend of Kershaw's, writes, "[Mount Adams] was so legendary I might not have believed it existed had I not lived in its shadow and seen it in sun and storm for the past twenty years. The vision of it would come back to me in dusty law libraries as I searched for the elusive thing called law."[2] Perhaps it was this mental image of his "favorite snow-capped mountain"[3] overlooking the arid Yakima Valley that inspired Douglas's most famous and far-reaching words from his time on the bench. Writing for the majority in the Supreme Court's landmark decision in *Griswold v. Connecticut*—the 1965 case that delineated the privacy rights of married couples—Douglas states, "specific guarantees in the Bill of Rights have penumbras, formed by emanations from those guarantees that help give them life and substance. Various guarantees create zones of privacy."[4] Douglas's pithy summation of the principle of an individual's right to privacy and its introduction into the Bill of Rights paved the way for future ground-breaking Supreme Court decisions expanding gay rights in the twenty-first century. *Griswold v. Connecticut* formed the precedent for *Lawrence v. Texas* in 2003, which upheld the legality of sexual activity between same sex individuals, and for *Obergefell v. Hodges* in 2015, guaranteeing the right for same-sex marriages.[5] Each of these cases hinged on the right to privacy elucidated by Douglas in his *Griswold* opinion. As of this writing, the gamut of Supreme Court decisions stemming from Douglas's precedent-setting Griswold opinion is now under threat. Douglas's penumbra theory, once illuminating, has faded.[6]

For nearly twenty years prior to Douglas's 1965 deliberations on *Griswold v. Connecticut*, Kay Kershaw had been living in the shadows of American Ridge and Mount Rainier in Goose Prairie, the Justice's favorite haunt on Washington State's eastside. For her, these shadows and the Prairie's penumbra were more than mere metaphor. Kay was a lesbian. With Pat Kane, her first long-term romantic interest, she established the Double K Ranch, a dude ranch with an east coast clientele. From 1956 on, Kay continued the operation with her life-partner, Isabelle Lynn. The two of them became vociferous advocates for wilderness, gaining an ally and kindred spirit in Douglas. Their initial casual acquaintance blossomed into a profound and consequential friendship characterized by long visits and strategy sessions—dry martinis often included—over interests that ranged from world affairs to wildflowers, with more than the occasional dinner prepared from mutually-exchanged recipes.[7] Since his youth, Douglas had been infatuated with the mountains around his hometown of Yakima. Like Kershaw and Lynn, he was dismayed by the prodigious appetite of the United States Forest Service for timber sales on public land, road-building into pristine wilderness, and the issuance of multi-use permits for motorized vehicles on mountain trails. In promoting wilderness designation for the area surrounding Bumping Lake— the large reservoir near Goose Prairie and the Double K Ranch—Kershaw, Lynn, and Douglas formed a powerful triumvirate, enlisting the office of Washington's Senator Henry M. "Scoop" Jackson to champion their proposal for the Cougar Lakes area in the early 1960s. Four years after Douglas's death this entire region so beloved by the three of them became the William O. Douglas Wilderness in 1984.

In the mid–twentieth century, timber cutting, cattle-grazing on public lands, and driving jeeps through meadows in conservative eastern Washington were more in keeping with the norm than conservation and preservation of the wilderness. Much more fraught was living as a lesbian couple: the Ku Klux Klan infiltrated the area in the 1920s, virulent anti-communism filled the airwaves in the guise of the John Birch Society during the Cold War, and Christian fundamentalist interpretations of the Bible remained a constant right up to the end of the century. Justice Douglas knew that Kay and Isabelle were more than just business partners and friends, and paid it no mind. He admired and respected both of them—he and Kershaw shared Yakima Valley roots and Lynn acquired native bona fides after moving to the Pacific Northwest in her thirties. However unlikely in this era, an unabashed heterosexual eastern-educated lawyer, Yale law professor, Securities and Exchange commissioner, and finally a Supreme Court Justice found common cause with a rough-edged lesbian horse-packer and mountain guide. There is no doubt Douglas appreciated the down-to-earth Kershaw, whose conversation and opinions ranged far from the polished cocktail chatter current in the nation's capital. Simply put, Kay Kershaw led an unconventional life in surroundings that prized convention. Undaunted and undeterred, with Isabelle at her side, she made her mark on the land she loved.

1

An Overview of Yakima County

In 1911, when Kay Kershaw—born Kathryn Jane—was barely four years old, Jack and Kitty Nelson arrived in the Naches River canyon to serve as caretakers for a new dam at Bumping Lake. They stayed for over half a century. Kitty and Jack got to know just about everyone from the Naches area over the years, and Jack wrote about many of them in a memoir published in 1965. In a short section about Kay, Nelson depicts a lifestyle peculiar to their shared corner of eastern Washington:

> Kathryn we have known since she was a little girl … what a help she was to her father on the ranch. As she got older she could run a mower, a binder—all horse-drawn then. She could direct a pruning, picking or packing crew in their orchard operations…. Her real delight was when she could mount her saddle horse and take off at a gallop. It was only natural that as she grew older she acquired a pack horse so she could go on camping trips to the mountains.[1]

As Nelson points out, Kay's upbringing fit perfectly with farming practices current throughout the United States at the turn of the last century. However, the unique physical features of Yakima County not only influenced local socio-economic development but also played into the perceptions of local residents. This distinctive alchemy shaped Kay's compelling biography.

Geography

The terrain within the boundary lines of Yakima County is a study in contrasts. On the western side, the county's portion of the Cascade crest runs north from Mt. Adams to Naches Pass encompassing the Goat Rocks and White Pass while just skirting Mt. Rainier at Chinook Pass. This sixty-mile-long massif, one of the premier high alpine regions of North America, captures the bulk of the moisture carried from the Pacific Ocean as weather travels from the Washington coast to the state's interior. Precipitation here can be prodigious: annual snow accumulation at Chinook Pass, for example, regularly reaches a depth of fifteen feet. As the clouds release their moisture at this high elevation, a rain shadow develops all across the rest of the county resulting in lightly forested foothills that transition to flat shrub-steppe plains on the western outskirts of the city of Yakima. This arid landscape extends over the rest of the county and beyond, into the contiguous Klickitat, Kittitas, Grant, and Benton Counties.

From most vantage points in Yakima County, the Cascade crest is hidden from view by its low eastern foothills with their sparsely vegetated slopes. The one exception is Mt. Adams: at an elevation of 12,281 feet, this glaciated volcano looks over the city of Yakima (Yakima), the Yakama Indian Reservation, and the lower Yakima Valley. To the Confederated Tribes and Bands of the Yakama Nation (Yakama Nation), the mountain is a sacred place, known in the oral tradition as Pahto (or Klickitat), one of the three guardians of the Columbia River.[2] It has long been a focal point for exploration ever since the Lewis and Clark Expedition first saw it in the fall of 1805.[3] Pahto received the name Mt. Adams in 1839 as part of Hall J. Kelley's conception of naming the volcanic peaks from Mt. St. Helens to Mt. Shasta for early American presidents.

The other significant feature of Yakima County is the Yakima River, a major tributary of the Columbia River, flowing 215 miles from its source on the east of the Cascade crest at Keechelus Lake in Kittitas County through Yakima to its terminus at Richland in Benton County. Within Yakima County, the Yakima River has its own tributary, the Naches River, which flows around seventy-five miles from Naches Pass in the upper northwest corner of the county through the town of Naches to join the Yakima River in Yakima. Three important rivers feed the Naches from the county's western boundary high on the Cascade crest. Two of these join the Naches River within the Naches River Canyon: the American River flows east from the Chinook Pass region to its juncture with the Bumping River about four miles west of the latter's terminus at the Naches River. The Bumping River's source is Fish Lake situated northwest of Twin Sister Lakes, Blankenship Meadows, and Tumac Mountain: it flows down to Bumping Lake and past Goose Prairie to its juncture with the American River to join the Naches around thirty-five miles northwest of Yakima. Horseshoe Bend is a significant S-shaped kink in the river's course seven miles west of the town of Naches (Naches). The Naches River's third main tributary, the Tieton, flows thirty miles from the highest sections of the Goat Rocks through the Tieton Canyon to

Kay Kershaw (center) with Jack and Kitty Nelson skiing near Bumping Lake, Washington, ca. 1940 (Kershaw Family Collection).

join the Naches River at the junction of White Pass highway 12 and Chinook Pass highway 410, a point known locally as the Y, located five miles west of Naches. As the river runs along the Tieton Canyon it passes through Clear Lake and Rimrock Lake (formerly McAllister Meadow) and passes by local landmarks such as Spiral Butte, Kloochman Rock and Goose Egg Mountain. With the Cascade crest between Goat Rocks and Naches Pass as its base, these geographic features form an equilateral triangle of sorts as the Naches and Tieton drainages flow towards one another in an easterly direction culminating in a vertex at the Y. [See Map 2.]

Goose Prairie, the Double K Ranch, and Bumping Lake all lie some seven miles to the southwest of the Bumping and American Rivers' confluence. To the north, American Ridge extends from the American River to the Cascade crest between the nearly-parallel courses of the American and Bumping Rivers. Towering over the lake to the south are remnants of a volcanic caldera named for its 7,766' highpoint, Mt. Aix: this includes Nelson Ridge whose southernmost terminus is Bismarck Peak. West of the Mt. Aix caldera, the headwaters of the Bumping River flow northeast from Swamp Lake, Cougar Lakes, and Fish Lake at Carlton Pass, elevation 4,100', to meet at Bumping Lake. Further south, a broad plateau centered around another volcanic feature, Tumac Mountain, encompasses Apple and Pear Lakes, Blankenship Meadows, Twin Sisters Lakes, Indian Creek and Spiral Butte. Cowlitz Pass lies just a mile southwest of the Tumac cinder cone.[4] From the high points along American Ridge, Tumac Mountain, and the Mt. Aix group, the entire Cascade crest—Mt. Adams, the Goat Rocks, Chinook Pass, and Mt. Rainier—as well as the Stuart Range, Mt. Daniels, Mt. Hinman, and Bears Breast Mountain to the north and Oregon's Mt. Hood to the south are visible on a clear day. Such breathtaking views and varied terrain have inspired Yakima area mountaineers for nearly a century and a half. In the words of Justice William O. Douglas (quoting his own cobbled-together Russian proverb), "every devil loves the marshes where he was born."[5]

Mountain Travel

William O. Douglas and Kay Kershaw inherited a robust late-nineteenth-century tradition of traveling into the mountains from eastern Washington purely for pleasure and adventure. Well-documented exploits into the nearby mountains at the turn of the century featured quite a cast of characters, principal among them Claude Ewing Rusk (1871–1931) and Clarence Truitt (1893–1949), who established the precedent for mountain exploration in the central Cascades. Now a classic of mountaineering literature, Rusk's 1924 book *Tales of a Western Mountaineer* describes his numerous ascents of the Pacific Northwest's volcanic peaks. Truitt had a legendary capacity for extraordinary long-distance trekking and often accompanied Rusk on his excursions.[6] In 1920, both were the prime movers in organizing the Cascadians, a Yakima outdoors club. This group promoted all types of activities, often highlighted with an annual horse-packing trip within the Triangle: in 1923, for example, the Cascadians planned a two-week rambling jaunt through Mt. Rainier National Park (MRNP) from Lake Tipsoo to Longmire. The group finished the excursion through the Tieton River Canyon, returning to the Naches River via Indian Creek and Bumping Lake.[7]

Around the time of Rusk's well-documented ascents in the Cascades, another local climber made three mountaineering expeditions which would have far-reaching effects in the Yakima Valley during the latter half of the twentieth century. Curtiss Gilbert (1894–1947) was the son of Marion (Richey) and Horace (H.M.) Gilbert, a prominent fruit grower in the Yakima Valley at the turn of the century.[8] H.M. regularly had business out of town, and Marion often put Curtiss, as the eldest child, in charge of his younger siblings. Enthralled by the mountain adventures of a crafty bighorn sheep in Ernest Thompson Setton's book *Krag the Kootenay Ram and Other Animal Stories*, and exasperated by his onerous babysitting duties, he joined the local YMCA for an opportunity to escape into the Cascades.[9] For Gilbert, the tales of Kootenay Krag in Setton's book and the YMCA were a fortuitous combination. Between 1908 and 1912, Gilbert made two trips to Mt. Adams and one to Mt. Rainier from his home in North Yakima.[10]

Upon graduating from college as a ROTC lieutenant, Curtiss commanded an infantry company in France during World War I. Although he believed that his troops were brave under fire, Curtiss—inured to mountain life as a youngster—grew disconcerted by the incessant complaints from his fellow soldiers about the mud, rain, food, and general discomfort of life in the trenches. After he returned home from the war and reestablished himself in the fruit business in Yakima, Curtiss incorporated Boy Scout Troop 2 (later, Troop 9) in 1920, hoping to turn boys who had acquired basic outdoor skills in the mountains into young men with the ability to endure military service. Curtiss died prematurely at the age of 53 in 1947 after serving twenty-six years as a scoutmaster. The following year, Curtiss's son Cragg D. Gilbert (1923–2007)—named after Curtiss's childhood Kootenay hero—assumed leadership of Troop 9. A World War II veteran of the vaunted 10th Mountain Division, Cragg continued the climbing and skiing traditions of his father for thirty-two years, expanding them to include updated techniques acquired during his mountain warfare training.[11] The Gilberts—Curtiss, Cragg D., and Elon J., Curtiss's younger brother—were life-long friends of Kay Kershaw and William O. Douglas: they appear throughout the latter's articles, letters, and books. In 1949, Justice Douglas advocated to rename the highest peak in the Goat Rocks Mount Curtis [sic] Gilbert, a testament to the Gilbert family and the profound impact Curtiss had on mountaineering in eastern Washington.[12]

One other early-twentieth-century trip may have had an influence on a young Kathryn Kershaw. In *An X-Ray on the Naches Valley*, a handsome 1911 volume extolling the virtues of the Yakima region, author Henry A. McCormick praises Kay's father, Edwin Kershaw, and includes a picture of the family farmhouse on Rim

Curtiss R. Gilbert (left) and Elon J. Gilbert, 1919 (Gilbert Family Collection). As a young man, Curtiss Richey Gilbert made several extended horse-packing trips from Yakima into the Cascades in order to climb routes on Mt. Adams and Mt. Rainier. He served as a captain in the U.S. Army during World War I, then returned to Yakima to work in the fruit business with his father, H.M. Gilbert. He also founded Yakima Boy Scout Troop 9 which had a tremendous impact on the culture of mountaineering in central Washington during his lifetime and long after his premature death in 1947. His son, Cragg D. Gilbert, continued to lead Troop 9 through 1979. Cragg joined forces with William O. Douglas, Kay Kershaw, Isabelle Lynn, and Senator Henry M. Jackson to establish wilderness centered around Cougar Lakes. Curtiss's younger brother, Elon James, attended Harvard Business School, then returned to Yakima with his MBA in 1923 to work alongside Curtiss and his father in the Richey-Gilbert fruit enterprise. Elon was a high-school classmate and lifelong friend of William O. Douglas with whom he shared many adventures on trips into the Goat Rocks and along the Cascade Crest, often in the company of Kay Kershaw.

Rock Drive just outside of Naches: it is quite possible this book would have been inside the Kershaw home by the time Kay learned to read. In the back of the book is an eleven-page section titled "To the Mountains" with over a dozen black and white photographs. McCormick relates an engaging narrative about a group of visitors from the east coast who have come to vacation in Naches. Among them are two sisters, Margaret and Catherine, who are enthralled by Uncle Ruben, an old cow wrangler. Ruben regales them with exciting tales from his horse-packing trips up the Tieton River Canyon into the Goat Rocks, the text supplemented with photographs of horse and rider crossing meadows, high mountain lakes, and the glaciers and crevasses on the east and northeast sides of present-day Gilbert Peak. The girls are very keen to go exploring in the mountains, too, so Ruben arranges a tamer week-long trip up the Naches River Canyon that includes their parents and brother along with McCormick, his parents, and his cousin, Mary. Stopping for lunch on the first day at Horseshoe Bend, the girls clambered up several hundred feet on a nearby slope for a taste of mountaineering. The accompanying photograph shows three girls—surely Mary, Margaret, and Catherine—sitting in the rocks in their long dresses and sunhats with the caption "They enjoyed mountain climbing." During the week, the group spent one day riding up the Little Rattlesnake Creek drainage to Soda Springs and back, then passed by Hanging Rocks, Edgar Rocks, Spring Flats, Dead Horse Point, and Indian Flats on the way to Bumping Lake for several days of camping, fishing, hunting, and paddling in the water. After a visit to the Gold Hill mines on Morse Creek, the entourage returned home to Naches. The final illustration closing out "To the Mountains" is a small watercolor of the girls on horseback viewing the distant horizon.[13] One can imagine that such an adventure-filled travelogue about alluring terrain just outside the front door—featuring young girls (including Catherine, her very own namesake) and numerous pictures—had a significant effect on a horse-loving Naches farm girl.

Pioneers and Agriculture in Yakima County

In the middle of the nineteenth century, immigrant trains from Oregon passing through the Yakima Valley were intent on reaching Puget Sound via Naches Pass. Southern Yakima County's arid desert landscape discouraged most settlers whose prospects appeared more favorable in the verdant regions west of the Cascade crest. Although cattlemen arrived to take advantage of grazing on the wide-open plains, few pioneer families lingered until after the end of the Yakima War of 1855–58.[14] These early pioneers noticed that the Yakamas took advantage of the region's fertile volcanic soil by watering their crops with channels dug from nearby streams and creeks. In the late 1860s, a handful of enterprising horticulturalists introduced wheat and fruit trees to the Yakima Valley, transferring water to their fields by the same irrigation methods as the Yakamas. By the time the Northern Pacific Railroad had extended its line to North Yakima in 1885, hundreds of small irrigation ditches were already in place. Five years later, with the railroad well-established and the Selah Valley Ditch Company on the verge of completing a twenty-two-mile-long canal from the lower Naches to Selah, the population of Yakima County increased to 4,429 people.[15]

Edward (Edwin) Ambrose Kershaw (1877–1959), whose home is featured in *An X-Ray on the Naches Valley*, was a member of one of the pioneer families attracted to the rich farmland of the Yakima Valley during this period of agricultural expansion. His father, Robert Kershaw, was born in England in 1831. Robert arrived in the United States with his parents, Abraham and Alice, née Buckley (1793–1861), in 1845. Perhaps great-granddaughter Kay Kershaw inherited some of Alice's independent spirit. According to family letters and lore, at the age of fifty-six, Alice left her husband in the middle of the night, absconding with merchandise from their store near Philadelphia along with three of their nine children. They found refuge with some

Edward (Edwin) Ambrose Kershaw and Ora (Whitmore) Kershaw, ca. 1905 (Kershaw Family Collection). Edward (1877–1959) was born in Utah and came to the Yakima Valley in 1881. His parents established the Kershaw ranch near Gleed where Ed attended Lower Naches Grade School. As a youth, he enrolled in the Woodcock Academy at Ahtanum, Washington, a school for higher education founded in the late nineteenth century by the Ahtanum Congregational Church. He married Ora Whitmore in December 1904. Ora (1876–1963) was the daughter of the Reverend O.B. Whitmore, pastor of the Lower Naches Congregational Church. She moved to the Yakima Valley with her family in 1902 and married Edward Kershaw in her father's home in December 1904. Ora and Edward lived on the Kershaw ranch until retiring in 1945.

Mormon church members and joined the David Evans Company wagon train traveling from present-day Council Bluffs, Iowa, to Salt Lake City, Utah, in 1850. Selling a portion of the store merchandise, Alice's entourage—nineteen-year-old Robert, his older brother Samuel, and younger sister Esther Emily—purchased a wagon and team of oxen to haul the rest of their goods across the plains. They moved to Manti, Utah, in 1851, then Robert and Sam relocated to Beaver City in Beaver County, Utah, in 1856. While living in Beaver County, Robert testified in 1875 against John D. Lee, accused by the federal government of participating in a Mormon Church–approved massacre in 1857 of a party of California-bound settlers in Mountain Meadows.[16]

Robert married Mary Harrison in 1861 after the birth of their son William H. (1860–1898), with two children following: Robert H. (1861–1950) and Edward Ambrose. Perhaps set at odds with his Mormon neighbors after testifying in the Lee trial, Robert left Utah in 1880 to settle in the area now known as Naches; his family

Kay Kershaw and her brothers at the family farm house in Gleed, 1912 (Kershaw Family Collection). From left: Kathryn Jane, Robert Whitmore, and Ronald Edward Kershaw.

joined him the following year. In 1887, after a foray with his father to California, the younger Robert H. and his new wife Ellie (Taylor) bought a 240-acre ranch in the Wenas and 2,000 acres in Umptanum, two separate areas to the north of present-day Naches on the far side of Cleman Mountain. Robert and Ellie had eight children. Edward Kershaw married his wife Ora (1876–1963) on 17 December 1904 and settled on acreage in Lower Naches first established by his father. Ora Kershaw's father, the Rev. O.B. Whitmore, came to the Yakima area in 1902 to become minister of the Lower Naches Congregational Church. Edward and Ora had three children, all born in the first decade of the twentieth century: Kathryn Jane, or Kay, Ronald Edward, and Robert Whitmore.[17] When Ora died in November 1963, a perplexing headline in the *Yakima Daily Republic* declared "Mrs. Kathryn Kershaw, 86, dies," eliciting a sharp rebuke from Kay and a correction published the following day.[18]

Just prior to Kay's birth in 1907, the 1900 census counted 13,462 people in Yakima County, a number that outpaced the rest of the state; by 1917, that number had ballooned to around 62,000. The city of North Yakima swelled from 1,535 residents in 1890 to 14,082 by 1910. The burgeoning agricultural industry fueled these increases. Sensing investment opportunities in the West, eager eastern capitalists poured money into the region to acquire land and water rights in the late–nineteenth century, and the construction of major government irrigation projects in the early twentieth propelled Yakima County into one of the nation's leading economic powerhouses.[19] Due to the influx of people into Yakima County at the turn of the century, demand for irrigation water exceeded the supply available. Several privately-funded projects like the Selah Valley Ditch Company managed to transfer water directly from the creeks and watercourses feeding tributaries of the Yakima River. However, the river flow—augmented by melting snow or rain—could reach a devastating flood stage in late winter and early spring, then diminish to a mere trickle by mid-summer leaving crops parched and withered. Faced with similar scenarios all across the West, the United States government initiated the Reclamation Act in 1902 and established the United States Reclamation Service for the development of reservoirs and irrigation delivery systems. Those who used these systems had to repay any construction costs from which they received benefit. After the signing of the Act, surveys for a project on the entire Yakima River drainage from 1902 to 1905 envisioned construction of six major water delivery units and five mountain reservoirs. Three reservoirs required dams at lakes already located at the headwaters of the Yakima River in Kittitas County: Kachess, completed in 1904; Keechelus, completed in 1918; and Cle Elum, completed in 1933. On the Yakima River's main tributary in Yakima County, simple construction of a dam at Bumping Lake—completed in 1910—increased the surface area of the lake to 1,350 acres. On the Tieton River, the situation was a bit more complex. Although the Reclamation Service constructed a dam at Clear Lake (on the North Fork of the Tieton River at the west end of McAllister Meadow) in 1915, its meager capacity could not contain all the runoff flowing from the glaciers and snowpack of McCall Basin high in the Goat Rocks. After finishing the first three Yakima River projects at Kachess, Keechelus, and Bumping Lakes, the Bureau of Reclamation (renamed in 1923) set to work on the Tieton Dam at the east end of McAllister Meadow. The government purchased the entire swath of land in 1925 from the family of John Russell, a homesteader who had first settled there in 1884. After the removal of standing timber and the original cabin and outbuildings, McAllister Meadow filled with water and now forms the bottom of Rimrock Lake. Lost forever in the flooding—and uncompensated—were remnants of Miya'wax, a permanent Yakama tribal settlement at the confluence of the north and south forks of the Tieton River on the east end of the meadow.[20]

Ora (Whitmore) Kershaw and Kay Kershaw, ca. 1915 (Kershaw Family Collection).

The advent of reliable irrigation water contributed to the growth of small towns the length and breadth of Southern Yakima County, in particular: Wapato, Toppenish, Mabton, Zillah, Granger, Grandview, and Sunnyside all to the south of North Yakima; Selah to the north; Moxee to the east; and Ahtanum, Wiley City, Tampico, and Naches to the west.[21] North Yakima, "set like a diamond" at the center, was thriving at the beginning of the twentieth century, "an elegant and high-class metropolis" in the words of contemporary historian W.D. Lyman.[22] Wealthy residents supported a vibrant city center through active participation in a variety of social and religious organizations. In eastern Washington's very conservative agricultural milieu, Yakima was arguably the most liberal—or rather, the least conservative—area in southern Yakima County compared to its outlying towns and hamlets.

During this period of agricultural expansion, mineral extraction from the Cascade crest continued apace. In 1892, a group of financiers who incorporated the Yakima, Natchez and Eastern Railway Company proposed a series of tracks radiating in all directions from North Yakima including to the west along the Naches River to the Bumping River drainage, then past Bumping Lake up to Carlton Pass. The enterprise wanted to access purported coal fields in the area of Fish Lake as well as the various mining claims along the Naches River canyon.[23] In one of the more fortuitous financial failures of the late-nineteenth century, this venture collapsed in the Panic of 1893. However, the notion of such a railway to Carlton Pass was still under consideration in 1907 when the North Yakima and Valley Railroad finished a ten-mile stretch of track from North Yakima to the brand-new city of Natchez. A land development company had platted this small town in 1895. A post office operated sporadically there but only gained permanent status in July 1906, a date informally recognized as the town's initial founding. After the United States Reclamation Service set up an office and warehouse in Natchez to service the dam construction project at Bumping Lake in 1907, the town's population stood at 150, soon to increase by one with the birth of Katheryn Kershaw at home on the farm on 17 March of that year. By 1911, the dream of running steam locomotives onto the Cascade crest had faded. But, as the endpoint of the Northern Pacific's westernmost spur in the Yakima Valley, this town—renamed Naches by the post office in 1908—became the Yakima Valley's entrepot for the horse-packers and wagon trains taking supplies to government reclamation projects on the Tieton River and at Bumping Lake. W.D. Lyman reports that by 1918, Naches boasted a bank, a high school with a principal and five faculty members, a Presbyterian church, and several stores serving a community of 300.[24]

One other development affected the character of Naches: its proximity to Mt. Rainier National Park (MRNP). Established in 1899, MRNP attracted increasing numbers of visitors: in 1906, total visitors reached 1,786. By 1915, those numbers swelled to 34,814, creating a feverish demand for road building into and around the park's environs. A land survey of 1904 proposed an east-west route through the park following the star-crossed railway line running from Naches up the Naches River to Bumping Lake and over Carlton Pass: a westward extension to a point near

Ohanepecosh on the east side of Mt. Rainier would connect to a road leading to Puget Sound. Roadbuilding went from the blueprint stage to actual earth-moving when work commenced on the Bumping Lake dam in 1906 and transportation of goods from the Reclamation Service's warehouse in Natchez to the worksite became a priority. After completion of the project in 1910, further construction was put on hold, even though the Washington State Highway Commission continued to develop a roadway through MRNP to the Cascade crest from the west. However, mining operations forged ahead with private roads up the Bumping River to Copper City (around four miles east of Carlton Pass and Fish Lake), American River, and Gold Hill.[25]

With an increase in automobile ownership—in 1911, Yakima County recorded 281 vehicles, the second highest percentage, according to population, of any county in the state—Yakima County commissioners contacted their Pierce and Lewis County counterparts to plan a road linking east and west, either over Carlton Pass or via the American River. By 1913, Washington State had 22,706 registered automobiles: as these vehicles became more commonplace, pressure mounted for a trans-mountain highway. Now, interest in constructing a rail line over Carlton Pass had dissipated. In its place arose a growing demand for a roadway suitable for automobiles over the same route.[26]

Various lobbying for a road to traverse the Cascade crest near Mt. Rainier at White Pass (at the head of the Tieton River drainage), Carlton Pass (at the head of the Bumping River drainage) or Naches Pass (at the head of the Naches River drainage) lost out to the efforts of the White River Lumber Company whose directors favored a crossing at Tipsoo Lake, a site just above their holdings on the west side of Chinook Pass. In 1914, work began on the eastern portion of this new road from American River to Chinook summit, although World War I brought construction to a halt. After the war, road building on the east side made it to Chinook Pass in 1925; due to more complex rock work, west side construction took another six years to finally reach Lake Tipsoo in 1931.[27]

Nonetheless, the notion of carving some sort of roadbed through Carlton Pass died hard. An automobile route following the rail line first proposed in 1892 had proponents right up until construction began on the highway over White Pass in 1931, which took another twenty years to complete. However, in the late 1950s, the United States Forest Service—eager for handsome revenues from felling timber all the way into Blankenship Meadows—had eyes on this pathway as well. The prospect of a logging road demolishing the trail to Fish Lake and Carlton Pass from Bumping Lake raised the ire of Kay Kershaw who took on the Forest Service, as her friend Cragg D. Gilbert put it, "spitting fire."[28]

Evangelicalism

Like the topography, the cultural and social milieu of Yakima County exerted a profound influence during Kay Kershaw's life. The mountain environment along with the wholesome agricultural surroundings of her youth centered on rodeo grounds, grange halls, and the State Fair leading to her life-long passion for horses and wide-open spaces. Endemic to the region, however, was a throttling conservatism that fostered adherence to strict interpretations of fundamentalist Christianity. At times, the evangelical church even gravitated toward the toxic dogma of the Ku Klux Klan. While Kay was still a high school student in Naches, the Klan enjoyed a surge of popularity in the Pacific Northwest. Klan activity received extensive coverage in the local paper: in addition to the sensational horrors of the deep South, troubling incidents took place just across the state line in Oregon. It was only a matter of time before Klan ideology seeped over the border into the mainstream of Yakima County as well.

In W.D. Lyman's description of Naches, it is worth noting that one Presbyterian church met the needs of 300 residents in 1918. Three and a half decades later, four additional churches had opened their doors to worshippers—the Full Gospel Assembly, the Christian Science Society, the Pentecostal, and the Primitive Baptist—although the town's population had only grown to 633.[29] In other words, Naches now had one church for every 126 residents, a significant increase. The rise in small family farms and orchards in the rural areas surrounding Naches may account for this surge, but surely a corresponding acceptance of evangelical Christianity in alignment with ultra-conservative values played a part as well.

Always a potent force in the United States, evangelical Christianity gained increased traction after World War I through a new fundamentalist iteration shaped by social circumstances in America. The post-war fundamentalist movement was a loose, diverse, and mutable federation of like-minded denominations united by fierce opposition to modernist attempts to bring Christianity into line with contemporary theological thought. This fiery brand of conservative evangelicalism appealed to Protestants alarmed by the profound spiritual and cultural crises of the twentieth century. The menace of both Darwinism's anti-creationist view and Bolshevism's elimination of religion in the 1920s threatened the bedrock principles of the Christian church: that is, complete confidence in the infallibility of the Bible and acceptance of the Gospel message for a virtuous existence on earth and eternal life in heaven.[30]

Motivated by the perception that the nation's moral foundations were crumbling, evangelicals became overtly concerned with slowing or even halting the degeneration of American society. Prohibition, a constitutional ban which made the sale and consumption of alcohol illegal in the United States from 1920 to 1933, is perhaps the most familiar manifestation of evangelical activism. This success emboldened further attempts to regulate behavior anathema to the church through legislation. As in other parts of the United States, clergy throughout the Yakima Valley took this moral crusade to heart. For example, in 1923, a group of Yakima church leaders promoted a petition to the legislature to change the marriage laws of Washington State in order to make it more difficult for couples to be married "in haste" or "in secrecy." The proposed law would require a ten-day waiting period between filing for a marriage license and the wedding ceremony. During the interim, all licenses would be posted in a public place in the county auditor's office. Even this would not suffice, however: despite such potential deterrents on hasty marriage, one local Bishop proclaimed "lawful free love is near," because of Washington State's "liberal system of divorce."[31]

The clergy also raised concerns about attractions along the midway at Yakima County's Washington State Fair. This yearly event held tremendous significance in the early twentieth century when nearly half of the state's population lived in rural areas and engaged in all aspects of agriculture, animal husbandry, and the farming life.[32] A bill to ban carnivals from operating in Washington State originated in Yakima after a downtown church question-and-answer session in February 1923. By March, a barrage of telegrams from all across Yakima County arrived at the state capital in Olympia demanding that carnivals be made illegal statewide, and letters of support appeared in the local Yakima paper asserting that Jesus would never attend the State Fair if carnival concessions were present. The State Fair director succumbed to intense pressure from Yakima Valley residents by stating that he would exclude all carnival concessions from the upcoming 1923 event. In Olympia, however, the legislature did not perceive the threat as worthy of a state-wide ban and put an end to any further debate over Yakima's "Carnival Bill" after the city's short-lived petition drive.[33]

Absent from the 1922 Washington State Fair was Yakima resident and future Supreme Court Justice William O. Douglas. In his 1974 autobiography, Justice Douglas recalls leaving Yakima in September 1922—just as the Fair was in full swing—to attend Columbia Law School in New York City. Railing against Yakima's smug "high churchmen" and "hypocrites in church clothing," he makes it clear that he found the city's fundamentalist fervor appalling: "Ideas were not congenial to Yakima. The pulpits ... were filled with Billy Grahams."[34] Yet even Billy Graham, that quintessential conservative evangelical preacher of the twentieth century, would look back with nostalgia decades later on controversies such as those that roiled Yakima's congregations in the 1920s. In his scathing denunciation of homosexuality from his 1965 book *World Aflame*, in which he calls all gay and lesbian relationships a "sinister form of perversion," Graham notes, "the old-fashioned sins look almost wholesome by contrast."[35]

The Ku Klux Klan

Having reorganized in 1915, the new Ku Klux Klan—the self-proclaimed "Invisible Empire"—was in the midst of a nationwide revival all across America by the early 1920s: in 1923, total membership in the forty-eight states peaked somewhere between three and four million. Since Jim Crow laws in the South had institutionalized discrimination against African Americans, this second iteration of the Klan expanded into other regions while focusing on the intimidation of additional groups such as Jews, Catholics, "miscreants," bootleggers, "homosexuals," and immigrants. Posturing as a benevolent fraternal organization—by its own accounting no different than the Elks or the International Order of Odd Fellows—the Klan operated in the open by participating in local parades and sponsoring food distributions to the poor. Although not part of any church specifically, the Klan claimed that it embraced Protestant values, including prohibition laws. Across the country, the group adopted Christian hymns, symbols, and ideology, and, notably, many members of the clergy unabashedly promoted Klan doctrine: the bankers, lawyers, dentists, doctors, businessmen, and teachers who filled the Klan's ranks were rooted in mainline Protestantism and the evangelical movement.[36]

During this period of growth, the Ku Klux Klan found a receptive home in Oregon. In June 1921, active recruitment began in Medford, a town of 5,756 located in the southern part of the state. Within a few months, the Oregon Klan expanded efforts to Portland, Oregon's largest city, with resounding success. In two years, Portland's chapter mushroomed to 15,000 members, around 6 percent of the city's total population. That same year, more than fifty separate chapters sprang up statewide with a total membership of over 35,000, making Oregon's the largest Ku Klux Klan organization west of the Mississippi River. In the mid-1920s, the Oregon Klan wielded significant political clout, influencing the passage of an Anti-Alien Act and a School Bill intended to outlaw all private schools in the state. The group also successfully backed Walter Pierce, the Klan's favored gubernatorial candidate of 1922.[37]

Emboldened by their fruitful campaign in Oregon, the Klan set their sights on eastern Washington in 1923. In Yakima, they found fertile ground. As William O. Douglas observed, "As I grew up in Yakima [1905 to 1916], discrimination against racial and ethnic minorities was barely under the surface."[38] Local press coverage from all around the nation, the Pacific Northwest, and the rest of the state increased awareness in the Yakima region of the Klan's activities with lurid descriptions and images. Nearly every day in 1923, the *Yakima Daily Republic* featured articles and photographs of the Klan, often on the front page.[39] In February, the paper carried extensive daily reports from the Medford Outrage trials taking place just across the border. These trials were the result of three separate near-lynchings of minority and morally-suspect victims the previous year in the Medford environs, carried out by Oregon Klan members, many of whom were prominent local leaders. Oregon State attorneys did their best to prosecute the trials but were hamstrung by witnesses willing to perjure themselves to protect the local Klansmen: before the third trial could even take place, the state's frustrated team of attorneys—up against a judge and jury clearly sympathetic to the Klan—threw in the towel.[40]

Such encouraging outcomes in Oregon motivated Klan representatives to expand recruitment efforts in the Yakima Valley. Of particular interest was agitation fomented by the American Legion against Japanese-American farmers who were leasing land on the Yakama Indian Reservation. As both the Klan and the Legion saw it, this was a violation of Washington State's 1921 Anti-Alien Land Law. The Washington State legislature expanded the scope of this law in 1923 to exclude children of immigrants—who were bona fide citizens because of their birth in the United States—from holding land in trust for their parents. As a sovereign entity, the Yakama Nation considered its members exempt from following this state mandate. White farmers were outraged at both the Japanese-Americans and the Yakamas, and the Klan saw an opportunity.

The Klan assigned the Rev. C.C. Curtis, pastor of the Christian Church in Vancouver, Washington, as its designated spokesman in eastern Washington. With an eye to recruiting membership from Yakima's urban population of 19,000, the Reverend Curtis arranged a lecture inside the city limits for 22 March. One day prior to the Yakima event, Curtis spoke before a crowd of 500 at the International Order of Odd Fellows Hall in Prosser. In Yakima, Curtis's event was originally scheduled to take place at the First Christian Church; however, complaints from some members of the congregation sent the Klan scrambling to relocate. The nearby Capitol Theatre offered to host the Reverend Curtis and Yakima-area residents from all social strata—2,000 strong—filled every seat in the house and then some for his lecture.[41] Speaking for over two hours, Curtis—decked out in his Klan regalia—spent much of the time discussing his own life and accomplishments. But at the end of his speech, he summed up by declaring that every Klan member must believe in four principles: the Protestant faith; America for Americans; the supremacy of the white race; and "woman in her place and sphere with the chastity of every women [sic] protected by every God-fearing man." Before Curtis could even finish enunciating his fourth and final tenant on women, the Capitol Theatre burst into applause and hundreds of audience members rushed the stage to scoop up Klan literature and application cards.[42]

Such enthusiasm for the Klan was not unanimous, however. To his credit, Yakima's mayor R.D. Rovig stoutly refuted Klan ideology from the stage of the Capitol Theatre that evening. And the next day, W.W. Robertson, editor of the *Yakima Daily Republic*—who, on occasion, had written pieces agreeable to the local Klan concerning issues on the Yakama Reservation—recommended in this case that citizens reject its membership: "There is not going to be any invisible empire in this country. The notion that there will be, or can be, such a thing will soon pass."[43] This "notion," however, did not pass so quickly. Curtis's wife returned to Yakima in July to organize a women's auxiliary to aid the Yakima Klan. Three hundred women crammed into tiny Weed Hall on East Yakima Avenue to hear her speak.[44] The following summer, Yakima was the site of a massive Klan recruitment rally on 9 August. Despite Mayor Rovig's protestations, the city embraced the Klan, with "Welcome K.K.K." painted in large letters on the roadways leading into town. The Klan originally planned to hold their event at the Yakima County Fairgrounds but Washington State Governor Louis Hart officially withdrew permission in late July. The infuriated Klan organizers moved the rally to the Joe B. Vance farm in Ahtanum about five and a half miles

Ku Klux Klan Rally at the Vance farm, Ahtanum, Washington, 9 August 1924. Photo by Lester Abrams (Yakima Valley Museum). In a pasture five miles southwest of Yakima, three crosses strung with electric lights illuminate a nighttime crowd gathered to witness the region's second major Klan event. Estimates for attendance ranged from 12,000 to 70,000 people. The "Vote for 49" sign refers to Initiative 49, a proposal banning parochial and private schools, on the ballot in Washington State for the upcoming election in November. Lester Abrams was a professional photographer who owned a studio on Second Street in downtown Yakima: "Every Picture a Work of Art." *Polk's Yakima City and County Directory 1924* (Seattle: R.L. Polk and Company, 1924), 47.

southwest of Yakima. The city of Yakima's official streetcar operator, the Yakima Valley Transportation Company, provided special service out to Wiley City on the day of the festivities.[45]

The 9 August Klan rally at the Vance farm was a tremendous draw. Crowd estimates from Yakima's two daily newspapers varied from 12,000 to 70,000 people. Handbills distributed around Yakima clearly stated the event was "limited to law-abiding Protestant men, women, and their children." Guards were posted at close intervals around the farm to ward off "invasion or prying." By evening, parked cars at the entrance to Vance's farm stretched for half a mile in either direction and covered thirty-five acres in the pasture as people swarmed to the event. In the afternoon, a full battery of Klan speakers addressed the picnicking crowds about a variety of issues, especially Initiative 49, a bill to eliminate parochial schools proposed to the Washington State legislature based on Oregon's legislation of 1922. In the evening, hooded Klan members marched in procession around three large crosses strung with electric lights to the strains of "Onward, Christian Soldiers" played by the Klan's own Seattle band. Some 700 new members swore an oath of allegiance and knelt before the crosses to be knighted. After the initiation ceremonies, the crowd enjoyed a fireworks display.[46]

No matter the exact count of the crowd and initiates, this event was perhaps the largest ever seen in the Yakima Valley. However, some were skeptical. Referring to a headline in the *Yakima Morning Herald* published on 10 August, Wiley City orchardist Horace (H.M.) Gilbert—with 400 acres of young apple trees in the vicinity of Vance's place at risk from fireworks, careless Klansmen, and the possibility the crosses might actually burn—wrote to his mother and sister the day after the rally:

> The "Ku-Klux-Klan" [sic] had a big initiation of 800 new members last night. They held the meeting in a 40 acre salt grass pasture on the Ahtanum. They had fireworks, and 3 crosses in [sic] fire. They seem to be anti–Catholic, anti–Jew and anti–Jap chiefly. The paper said there were 40,000 in attendance. People came from a long distance, but probably 4,000 would be nearer.[47]

Gilbert argued against passage of the Klan-backed Initiative 49 in a downtown Yakima voter's forum just prior to the general election of 1924, stating the chief aim of the bill was to stir up discontent.[48]

Despite the success of the Klan's August recruitment drive in Yakima, voters statewide defeated Initiative 49 three months later during the November election. The Klan still had high hopes for Yakima, however. Twelve days after the general ballot, Klan Imperial Wizard Dr. Hiram Wesley Evans came to town with six of his staff and a host of national Klan luminaries.[49] Traveling by private railcar from Atlanta, Georgia, Evans and his entourage were on a tour of the Pacific Northwest with stops in Spokane, Yakima, Seattle, Tacoma, and Portland. Holding forth for two hours before a crowd of 1,500 at Yakima's First Christian Church, Evans took credit on behalf of the Ku Klux Klan for the election of Calvin Coolidge, the passage of recent immigration legislation, and the recruitment of many members of congress to the organization. He demanded the deportation of all aliens convicted of violating Prohibition laws and the enactment of legislation like Initiative 49 all across the nation. He closed by claiming that when the country was founded 93 percent of the population was "white, gentile and Protestant," dropping by 1924 to 58 percent.[50] The Imperial Wizard's statistics and oratory notwithstanding, the demise of the Ku Klux Klan in Washington State had begun by the time of its 1928 state convention held in Yakima before 1,500 people.[51] Yet, the Klan's legacy lingered on as discrimination and virulent anti-immigrant sentiment festered throughout Yakima County.[52] Never dormant in towns up and down the Yakima Valley, the shadow of the Klan rebounded with vigor in the post–World War II era in the guise of the John Birch Society. Whether or not teenaged Kay appreciated the underlying threat of Yakima County's conservative milieu, as an adult, she gradually came to realize those caustic forces, still at play, would infringe on the wide-open spaces she cherished.

2

Kay Kershaw and "Homosexuality" in the Early 20th Century

In his 1965 memoir, Jack Nelson had trouble categorizing his friend, Kay Kershaw:

> all of us who know her are agreed she should have been a boy. At no time, until late [sic] years at least, did she have any interest in household activities. Home was just a place to eat and sleep.[1]

Jack Nelson lived a good part of his life before the term "homosexuality" appeared with regularity in print. Kay Kershaw lived nearly all of hers at a time when the received wisdom held that gender was strictly binary. Nelson's assessment of Kershaw speaks volumes: to articulate the consensus of his neighbors he could have used the widely accepted term "tomboy," a girl who—according to the *Oxford English Dictionary*—behaves like a spirited, boisterous boy. But his word choice suggests something altogether different: with his description of Kay's ranch work and equestrian skills, Nelson portrays a girl who eschews superficial behavior and actually performs and presents herself on an equal footing with any boy. To what extent Kay Kershaw identified differently from her biological sex is difficult to assess: "gender" as we know it in the twenty-first century is an environmental and cultural construct, accommodating any number of possibilities of lifestyle choices.[2] Kershaw transcended the common twentieth-century notion of "tomboyism" and rejected mid-century cultural norms while enjoying the mountains in accordance with her own perception of life's purpose. As clinical psychologist Lisa Damour points out (quoting "Tomboy" author Lisa Selin Davis), "girls' latitude in the performance of girlhood is a rare example in which the gender deck is stacked in their favor."[3]

Acknowledging the influence of turn-of-the-century sexologists Richard Krafft-Ebbing, Havelock Ellis, and Sigmund Freud is essential to understanding how the twentieth-century concept of homosexuality developed. Social scientists of this era, many of whom were proponents of eugenics, developed methods of categorizing human behavior by dividing people into types—normal and abnormal—all with distinct personalities and physical characteristics. Through their pioneering studies in psychology, Krafft-Ebbing, Ellis, and Freud were instrumental in the study of human sexual behavior—sexology—and the twentieth-century definition of "the homosexual." Of course, homosexual activity itself existed long before the end of the nineteenth century. But the concept of the homosexual was a new proposition, stemming from the sexologists' attempts to define what was normal sexual behavior and what was abnormal. The notion of normality was related to distinct definitions of masculinity and femininity and the nexus that brings them together: heterosexuality. The effort to define the homosexual was an attempt to shoehorn a certain group of people into a strictly bifurcated schema of male and female, and the only way to accomplish this was to categorize certain people as a group falling somewhere between the rigid definitions of "real" men and "real" women. Within this subcategory were inverts (those who were inherently homosexual) and perverts (those who were born heterosexual but were somehow "corrupted" into homosexuality). This "perversion" in an individual might be the result of inadequate parenting, any number of corrupting influences as a youth, or associating with bad company as an adult. The true homosexual elicited pity while the potentially corruptible required protection.[4] Although these nascent notions of sexuality and gender played out in academic circles during the early twentieth century, they could only be seen by the general public through a glass darkly.

As Jack Nelson suggests, Kay Kershaw was the quintessential turn-of-the-century farmgirl. Given her rural Naches surroundings, the instruction and facilities associated with a formal education were rudimentary. In his 1919 account of Naches, W.D. Lyman exaggerated the status of the Naches school system. The town of Naches did not even have a school district or building until 1908. It was a makeshift affair, offering only a handful of classes run out of a six-room multi-grade schoolhouse: the graduating class of 1917 consisted of one student. However, the Kershaw farm was a good six miles southeast of Naches, so Kay and her brothers attended the older Lower Naches high school built in 1910 near Gleed, a small village located closer to home.[5] Kay was a student there from 1922 to 1925. Her picture appears in the high school's first yearbook, the 1924 *Lo-Na-Hi*, with the fifteen-member junior class standing in front of the grey sandstone entrance of the school. Kay was involved in school athletics, although options were extremely limited: she played on the girls' basketball team for three years—the only venue available for women—and wrote the sports section for the 1925 yearbook. More possibilities arose as a Camp Fire girl: in a summer session at Camp Roganunda—just a few miles up the Naches canyon from her home—Kay received Wohelo honors and appointment as an "assistant guardian" for the other girls on a three-day, fifty-mile "Vagabond" hike.[6] In the jocular comments typical for high school yearbooks, the 1924 and 1925 *Lo-Na-Hi* provide the first indications of Kay's personality and predilections. The junior class "want ads" of 1924, for example, list "Wanted—a safe method for riding a horse at breakneck speed. K. Kershaw." A couplet accompanying her senior picture in 1925 bolsters Kay's local reputation as an equestrian: "Her ambition as we know/to ride bucking broncs in a rodeo." In "The Junior Rogues' Gallery," Kershaw's major offense is cited as "the gift of gab." Her penalty: "a gag." And, in "The Brain of the School," her

The Lower Naches High School Girls Basketball Team, 1924 (Kershaw Family Collection). Kay is seated on the far right of the middle row on the main stairs of the high school.

characteristics are listed as "obstinacy" and "unadulterated nerve."[7] To be sure, Kay Kershaw's garrulous nature entertained many future guests of her mountain lodge enterprise with tall tales around the campfire. And, with her single-minded focus, she was to become a forthright and earnest advocate for Washington State wilderness issues.

As Kay came of age in the mid–1920s, print media provided the sole window for viewing the world outside of a small town like Naches. The *Yakima Daily Republic* was a regular feature in the Ed Kershaw household: numerous blurbs in the paper's "Valley People and Their Guests" and "Valley Personals" sections during the 1920s and 1930s indicate the family's communication with and interest in reading the daily paper.[8] Although the incessant thrum of evangelicalism and the Klan might drown out other articles, the received notions of lady-like comportment and elegance as well as home economics dominated news and features aimed specifically at women. Occasionally, an article that offered a glimpse into alternative lifestyles popped up. For example, an exciting story about Lydia Hutchinson, a professional dog-musher from Idaho, details her search for and rescue of a male competitor in a race that traversed Targhee National Forest in 1922: "Out in the country where the game of life is played close to the vest, they say the women of the great out of doors always help a fellow when he's down—but look out for them when he's up and going strong, for they can compete with him in anything."[9] Similarly, another article describes the career and avocation of Alma Wagen, a Tacoma school teacher who served during the summer as the only officially-sanctioned female guide in the United States at Mt. Rainier National Park: "She knows no fear in the mountains, she says, and is as much at home on the edge of a 3000' precipice as any of her sister teachers are in their classrooms." In contrast to images illustrating women's high fashion, Wagen poses with alpenstock in hand and climbing rope over the shoulder, dressed in her mountaineering garb: a khaki shirt, rugged pants, and stout knee boots. A broad-brimmed hat and natty four-in-hand necktie complete the ensemble.[10] In 1924, a photograph of Mary V. King, candidate for mayor of Boston, appeared twice in the *Yakima Daily Republic*, highlighting in particular her bobbed gray hair style and cigarette. The accompanying text describes her choice of clothing: "she feels thoroughly at home when her hands are thrust deep into the pockets of her riding trousers." King states that a woman has the "right to smoke cigarettes if she wants" and outlines her campaign platform: elimination of slums, equal pay for equal work, municipal jobs for women, and "make divorce easier and marriage harder."[11] Closer to home, articles about the local Cascadians Outdoor Club showcased Bessie Simmons, who made many club climbs of Mt. Stuart, led club-sponsored hikes, and presented talks at club meetings about her exploits, such as "how it feels to be a girl mountain climber."[12] At times, a sporadic article would appear describing career opportunities for women as an alternative to marriage, domestic life, new frocks, and card parties: "Social service … requires a high school education, hospital training if possible, a winning personality, and the ability to understand human nature. Executive ability, to some extent, is a requirement."[13] Mountaineering, outdoor adventure, social work—and even cigarettes—would all factor into Kay's adult persona.

Lesbianism

To a young woman who was expert on horseback, inured to hard work on the farm, and accustomed to mountain travel from her family's cabin at Cliffdell—a small community on the Naches River some fifteen miles by road from Goose Prairie—the idea of entering into a conventional matrimonial relationship prevalent in the 1920s must have seemed stultifying. However, economic and societal changes in motion at the end of the nineteenth century were becoming commonplace for women of the modern, post–World War I period. As a general rule in the Victorian era, educational and professional avenues excluded middle-class women, compelling many into marriages in which they were dependent on their husbands for finances and social protection. However, this began to change with the establishment of several women's colleges on the east coast of the United States starting with Mount Holyoke in 1837, soon followed by Vassar in 1865, Smith in 1872, Wellesley in 1875, and Bryn Mawr in 1886. As opportunities to attend college opened up, more women realized that they might not need marriage to survive: one could get an education, train for a profession, and earn a living while engaged in a rewarding career, all while living a life that offered freedom and independence. The prospect that a woman could now support herself within a professional arena offered a plausible excuse for resisting societal pressure to get married: pursuing a career precluded pigeon-holing as a stay-at-home wife. Post-graduation, women could find gainful and productive employment while creating all-female societies around their professions. Most important, for the first time in American history, women had the option to select whom they loved and with whom they chose to engage in a domestic relationship.[14]

The higher education system in the United States helped foster a burgeoning lesbian culture among middle-class professional women that paralleled a pre-existing working-class lesbian subculture in big cities after World War I. This global conflict marked a clear break from the societal norms and perceptions of the Victorian era. In contrast to the fundamentalist evangelicals of the post-war years, many young intellectuals and non-conformists were keen to eliminate all vestiges of a world they saw as corrupt and responsible for the war's devastation. This manifested itself in a number of ways: adoption of unorthodox clothing and hairstyles, blatant disregard for laws such as Prohibition, and the flouting of previously sacrosanct views about sexuality just coming into the public conscience as a result of the controversial work of the sexologists. Experimentation with homosexuality increased during the 1920s among college-educated youth. Established communities of women who identified as lesbians developed sporadically in metropolitan locations such as San Francisco, Salt Lake City, and New York City. However, these enclaves were few and far between.[15]

Whether Kay Kershaw considered herself a lesbian while still in high school is difficult to ascertain: as a distinct self-conceptualization, lesbianism was still in its infancy. And homosexuality in general, if acknowledged at all in rural eastern Washington, was at best considered a "disorder" or, across the state line in Oregon, couched in oblique terms: when anarchist Emma Goldman delivered a series of lectures in Portland in August 1915, the title of her "Discussion of Homosexuality" was listed only as "The Intermediate Sex."[16] For the most part, newspapers in the United States avoided the subject altogether. The term "homosexuality" only began to appear in American mainstream publications with any regularity in the mid–1920s. Between 1916 and 1946, papers in the entire state of Oregon only referred to homosexuality on two occasions. The earliest use in *The New York Times* was in May 1926, referencing a criminal psychosis that required eradication.[17]

Lesbians were far less visible to the general public than gay men during this period, although women who blatantly preferred women to men would have raised suspicion. Women who lived together were commonly considered "spinsters," unmarried and past their prime, pairing up out of economic and safety concerns. And, perhaps, some of these women may have been willfully unaware of their own predilections or, in some cases, were actually offended at being labeled lesbians.[18] In the words of historian Lillian Faderman, "One had to *see* [sic] oneself as a lesbian to be a lesbian … to admit to an aberrant sexual identity must not yet have been easy for any but the most brave, unconventional, committed, or desperate."[19]

In her varied interests, Kershaw was certainly unconventional. Yet her appearance in the Lower Naches High School junior and senior group pictures as well as in her individual portraits for the girls' basketball team from 1924 and 1925 was nothing out of the ordinary or, rather, no different than her other female classmates. In her senior portrait from 1925, Kay wears a dark V-neck dress and has a haircut typical for a young woman of the 1920s.[20] However, the transformation during her freshman year at the University of Oregon in Eugene is quite remarkable. In her portrait, found among those of the fifty female residents of Hendricks Hall, Kershaw's hairstyle—parted and cut short on the sides with swooping bangs to the eyebrows—and a man's lapel jacket, high collared shirt, and necktie contrast sharply with those of her hall-mates. Almost to a person, the other forty-nine women are coiffed in pin-curls and wear some version of a traditional feminine collar.[21]

A nurturing and hospitable environment on the Eugene campus may have cultivated explorations into alternative lifestyles for women like Kay Kershaw. In the decade between 1920 and 1930, women accounted for a record proportion of college and university undergraduate populations, doctoral recipients, and faculty members: by the end of the decade, 32.5 percent of college presidents, professors, and instructors were female. As a rewarding employment sector for women, higher education far outpaced other opportunities during this period: between 1870 and 1930, the percentage of women in all professional categories only grew from 5 to 14 percent.[22] These high numbers in the field of education emerged at the University of Oregon as well. In June 1926, the University of Oregon listed 200 faculty members at the main campus, forty-nine of whom were women. Of these, sixteen had graduated from Oregon and nine had attended either Wellesley, Radcliffe, Smith, Vassar, Cornell, or University of Michigan.[23] These eastern institutions had been at the forefront of women's education in the latter half of the nineteenth century. The women's colleges comprising the Seven Sisters in particular—Wellesley, Radcliffe, Smith, Vassar, Mount Holyoke, Bryn Mawr, and Barnard—advanced the proposition that women could live independently outside the confines of traditional matrimony. Between 1880 and 1900, only 10 percent of all American women remained single, but 50 percent of American college women stayed single during this same time period.[24] Many of these women established relationships and households with other like-minded female college graduates, setting a precedent for lesbian couples in the twentieth century. Although it is impossible to draw any conclusions about sexual orientation from faculty lists, it is not hard to imagine that some of these University of Oregon women—pioneering independent careers in an atmosphere conducive to choosing freely how to live—proved inspirational to students like Kay Kershaw.

However accepting of alternative lifestyles the University of Oregon may have been, as the state's main university it was far more urbane and cosmopolitan than Naches, even though Eugene's population was almost half that of Yakima's. This may account for Kershaw's exodus from Oregon after her freshman year to attend the State College of Washington (SCW) in Pullman: both of Kay's parents had attended SCW and her younger brother was about to enter his freshman year there. The wide-open spaces of eastern Washington's Palouse may have better suited a ranch-raised horsewoman majoring in physical education. The SCW campus featured the Department of Agriculture's 573-acre farm and, in the PE Department, women could participate in horse-riding and hiking as part of the curriculum.[25] The cultural atmosphere at rural SCW was a marked contrast to that of Oregon's. As a point of comparison, consider two similar photographs from each university's contemporary yearbook. In the 1926 *Oregana*, an image captioned "Oregon Horsewomen" tacked onto the women's athletics portion shows four smartly-outfitted equestrians riding English-style down a manicured bridle path. In SCW's 1927 *Chinook*, a photo titled "Riding" in the PE Department's section presents a group of five people on horseback—three men and two women—traversing a forested meadow riding Western-style, some wearing cowboy hats, all casually dressed.[26]

As a sophomore at SCW, Kay took up residence in fall 1926 at McCroskey Hall with sixty-eight other women.[27] At the end of the academic year in May 1927, Kay helped in the food preparation division for Women's Campus Day, serving in the Laundry Room—with her requisite apron and knife—for an hour of "shifting pie." Her younger brother, Ronald, was on campus as well that week, working with a men's crew on an unspecified task for Campus Day.[28] But perhaps, serving up a slice of pie to fraternity boys during Campus Day was not the college experience Kay had in mind, nor were the required classes she had just completed as a sophomore at SCW. As a female PE major that year, Kay would have enrolled in Normal Gymnastics 26 and 27 ("field ball," marching, gymnastics, apparatus, and clog dancing); Sports Technique 22 and 23 (rules and principles of coaching and managing tennis, archery, swimming, field ball, hockey, volleyball, baseball, and basketball); Physical Education 13 (sports [sic], marching, light and heavy apparatus, folk dances and games); plus Electives, in addition to English, Psychology, Sociology, Education, and Physiology. As a junior, she faced a full year of required interpretive dance classes.[29] For Kay, more interesting options were available back home in Naches.

Feminism and Women's Athletics

With the adoption of the Nineteenth Amendment in August 1920, women achieved two important milestones. For the first time, of course, women nation-wide were able to vote and enter politics.[30] But, female participation in mainstream athletics carried equal importance, a notion many contemporary women stated explicitly. As the decade progressed, the women's suffrage movement—a formidable force at the turn of the century—began to fracture into myriad parts. Rather than the solid voting bloc many predicted would bring about social reform, women tended to vote according to a wide variety of reasons and interests, just like men. Similarly, the anticipated take-over of politics and elected positions feared by opponents of the women's voting franchise never materialized. By mid-decade, with few women holding public office, a general decline in political reform, and scant advancement of legislative or judicial movement in relation to women's rights, many contemporary Americans looked to women's athletics for traces of the transformation in women's lives so highly touted by the suffragists.[31]

In American politics of the 1920s, two dominant viewpoints on feminism approached the basic nature of bifurcated gender from quite different perspectives. One found that women and men were different on many levels and supported legal and societal recognition of these inherent differences: The League of Women Voters and labor unions, for example, wanted labor laws and recognition that women represented a special class of citizen. The other asserted that men and women required absolute legal and social equality and promoted the passage of an additional amendment to the Constitution guaranteeing equal opportunities regardless of gender. American sports mirrored this dichotomy as well. One group, made up of top-level female athletes and their supporters, demanded that women gain admission on an equal footing into the world of sports. An opposing faction, comprised mainly of female physical education instructors—such as those leading clogging and interpretive dance classes at SCW—favored an alternative model of women's sport that recognized the inherent differences between male and female athletes. These college-level instructors believed that intense physical and mental exertion in the world of sports was simply too dangerous for women.[32]

This notion of female fragility was a holdover from the previous century. Victorian-era society exalted young women with the expectation that they would exemplify "true" femininity: moral rectitude combined with frail mind and body. From this point of view, a woman's proper place was inside the home as a wife and mother with passivity her expected demeanor. By the turn of the century, attitudes in medicine—a male-dominated profession—were slowly evolving: belief in the frailty of women was on the decline, bolstered by the emerging women's rights movement whose ideas exerted a substantial influence on popular thought. Incrementally, women gained access to physical education and organized sports, endeavors long considered an important aspect of training for young upper-class men. Until the late nineteenth century, women were discouraged from even the mildest exercise regimens as a prudent means to safeguard women's health and, principally, reproductive functions. The consensus was that too much physical activity taxed a woman's delicate constitution, putting a strain on the nervous system. This dangerous exertion would then jeopardize the uterus leading to weak and degenerate children.[33] By the turn of century, women possessed of an independent spirit and athletic enthusiasm were already challenging the concept of Victorian womanly virtues and frailty in venues on the periphery of activities normally considered "feminine." This was especially the case in skiing and mountaineering, and in the mid–1920s, Kay Kershaw threw herself into pursuing both activities with gusto.[34]

Even if Kay Kershaw had no knowledge of the leading female mountaineers of her era—pioneers of the sport such as Annie Smith Peck, Fanny Bullock Workman, or Miriam O'Brien Underhill—she nonetheless shared their spirit, energy, and zest for outdoor adventure. In the winter, Kay was an avid skier[35] and, in the summer, she did not have to venture far afield to take advantage of first-class mountaineering terrain in the Cascade Range. In September 1928, she and two other women made a successful climb of Mt. Hood in Oregon ("manless," in the style of Miriam O'Brien), proving—as the *Yakima Daily Republic* put it—that they were "real mountain climbers."[36] With the Cascadians, Kay also summited Mt. Stuart in 1929 and 1931, as well as Mt. Shuksan, Mt. Baker, and Mt. Rainier via the Emmons Glacier. In addition, she made a horse packing trip riding from Yakima to Mt. Adams in 1929 and a nine-day backpacking trip around Mt. Rainier.[37] Other early horse-packing trips include one following the Pacific Crest Trail from Mt. Adams to Cowlitz Pass in 1938; around Glacier Peak in 1939 with stops at Buck Creek Pass and Lyman Lake; and to the Olympics in 1940. Dogsledding, sailing, and snowshoeing also factored into her sport portfolio.[38]

Fishing and hunting in particular remained two of Kay's life-long passions. In the fall, she angled for steelhead, hunted ducks, and tracked elk.[39] On one elk-hunting trip in 1928, accompanied by her cousin, Ted Cleman, and a friend of his from Ellensburg, she rode a wide loop from Naches north into Kittitas County past Manashtash Lake, then west down Milk Creek, and returned home via Cliffdell. Although she did not bag an elk, she did manage to kill a wounded and enraged bear who charged her as she rode into a draw, a thrilling story perhaps embellished for the local newspaper. She had already taken a shot at an elk with her single-shot Sharps rifle: "When she drew down on the bear she discovered that her rifle had jammed and failed to throw out the empty shell. By the time she got it extricated the bear was fairly on top of her but she took aim and put a bullet between its eyes." With the help of some other hunters, Kay and her cousin skinned the bear and rode home without an elk, although she vowed to go back out and not return until she had shot one. A few weeks later, while filing for a permit at the county courthouse to ship her bear trophy, Kay indicated she would start running a trap line in the Upper Naches canyon, "an interesting and profitable occupation for the winter months."[40] A subsequent ursine encounter cemented her renown as a hunter in a story that made the Associated Press (AP) newswire when she shot a bear caught prowling through Goose Prairie in 1956. Her photograph appeared on the front page of the *Seattle Times* and an AP photograph of her posing with the seven-foot black bear made newspapers all across the country.[41]

Around the end of 1927, Kershaw began working hard to burnish her athletic reputation both locally and regionally.[42] According to the Yakima press, she was "one of the leading sportswomen of Yakima," "an ardent sportswoman," and "somewhat of a mountaineer and hunter."[43] Even during periods when Kay was not residing in Yakima, the local press kept tabs on her activities.[44] One of Washington State's premier newspapers, the *Seattle Post-Intelligencer*, remarked, "Life for Miss Kershaw

2. Kay Kershaw and "Homosexuality" in the Early 20th Century

is quite largely one athletic thing after another. For years she has been known as a fearless horse woman, a bronco buster of outstanding ability, an expert swimmer in summer and an equally expert ski artist in the winter."[45] After leaving Pullman in 1927, Kay taught swimming in Portland at Jantzen Beach, returning to Naches to help with apple harvest in the fall.[46] As chance would have it, Kershaw's return to the Yakima Valley happened to coincide with an aviation frenzy that was sweeping America. Her quest to become licensed as the first female pilot in Yakima County bolstered her meteoric rise in the public's eye. The catalyst for this infatuation was Charles Lindbergh's solo flight from New York to Paris in 1927 and Amelia Earhart's transatlantic crossing as a passenger in 1928.[47]

3

Kay Kershaw and Women's Aeronautics

Aviation developed rapidly in the aftermath of World War I, evolving into a significant cultural presence in the American consciousness by the early 1920s. Barnstorming, air shows, and the setting of speed, altitude, and distance records captured public attention; newspapers and other media hastened to capitalize on the phenomenon. This coverage presented flying as an exciting and dangerous form of entertainment. And it was dangerous indeed. Because minimal weight was crucial to getting airborne, manufacturers of the era constructed airplanes from wooden frames covered in fabric and a coat of lacquer. These flimsy aircraft were rife with problems: engines that could stop unpredictably or wings that might fall off in mid-flight compounded by irregular maintenance and inadequate instrumentation. Therefore, crashes occurred frequently, often resulting in injuries and death to the pilot as well as any passengers on board or spectators on the ground. Despite—or perhaps even because of—these dangers, Charles Lindbergh's successful flight from New York to Paris in May 1927 propelled the country's obsession with flying to new heights.[1]

Yakima embraced the excitement. The *Yakima Daily Republic* featured articles, photographs, drawings, and cartoons about airplanes and pilots nearly every day throughout the spring, summer, and fall months of 1927 and all of 1928. Yakima boasted two flight schools, one run by Charlie McAllister, the other by H.B. Fairbanks. The latter's outfit, Western Air Lines, offered a "learn to fly" program for two hundred dollars in early 1928.[2] With relish, Kay seized this opportunity to start flying, telling the paper she was "not going to school this year. Going [sic] to stay here and go right ahead with my flying until I get my pilot's license. It's all right going to school, with your parents putting up the money and all that. Easy enough. But what thrill is there in that?"[3]

The thrills began as soon as Kay started her lessons with Maurice McMechan, an airplane racer and Western Air Lines' most experienced instructor.[4] At the very beginning of May, she and McMechan made a cross-country flight from Yakima to Ellensburg. On the way back, they decided to make an unusual maneuver, flying low to the ground over the Kershaw family farm in Naches so she could wave at her parents before returning to the Yakima airfield.[5] Now a regular at the airport, Kay scored a first when she practiced airplane touch-downs on two new runways even before their 2 June dedication. She didn't taxi back to park the plane until she had satisfied herself after a half-dozen or so practice landings.[6]

As Kershaw progressed with her studies, headlines about airplane crashes and fatalities continued to mount in the local press. Around the time Kay would have begun actual flying (rather than ground school), a cartoon appeared in the *Yakima Daily Republic* with the title "The Pied Piper of Spring," showing Death playing a flute while airplanes fly overhead. During the week that she was preparing for her first solo flight in May 1928, one front page article featured three sections about fatal accidents in Sacramento, San Francisco, and Tacoma with the headline "Marine Aviators Burned to Death in Plane Crash." A piece about repatriating the body of a Mexican pilot who crashed and died in the United States followed immediately on the next page.[7] The dangers threatening airborne passengers and pilots were such a part of the national conversation that the syndicated comic strip "Major Hoople" featured a fanciful "rubber aviator's safety suit" in a series running throughout April 1928.[8] Well into the 1930s, articles about aeronautical crashes and deaths filled the pages of the Yakima daily papers.

Undaunted, Kershaw passed her private pilot's licensing exam with aplomb—another and even more exceptional first for a Yakima woman. This included three satisfactory solo landings to a full stop and maneuvering around two pylons set 1,500 feet apart in a series of five figure-eight turns at the new Yakima Airport.[9] The *Seattle Post-Intelligencer* deemed her "one of the most devoted and promising students of the art." A photo accompanying this piece shows Kay leaning against the wing of McMechan's biplane dressed like a professional pilot wearing jodhpurs, high boots, and vest, the sleeves of her white blouse rolled to the biceps, helmet pushed slightly back, goggles perched high on her forehead. Precise garb aside, the overall feel is one of nonchalance, and her broad smile speaks volumes.[10] "I got an awful kick out of it!" she enthused to the press that afternoon, asserting she "wasn't at all frightened." She continued, giving a blow-by-blow account of the experience: "I played around up there in the air—that's easy. It's the landing. If I thought I wasn't going to make a good landing all I had to do was give it more gas and get up again. I was just doing the same thing alone that I had been doing when someone else was along."[11]

Now considered a local aviation pioneer, Kay told the *Yakima Daily Republic* that she intended to continue her training in order to pilot an airplane "as her own man." The next step was to qualify for a bona fide commercial pilot's license. However, the commercial license required more solo flight time: the press said twenty hours although Kay correctly indicated that an additional fifty hours were necessary.[12] Whatever the requirement, the process was expensive, and she needed to earn money to continue. Adding to the outlay was the notion that top pilots owned their own aircraft, a situation perhaps beyond the realm of possibility for a twenty-one-year-old neophyte. "I have to make my own expenses for my flying course," she told the paper, "for to tell the truth, the folks weren't so strong for my taking it up—thought it was just one more pastime I was trying out. But it isn't. It's what I'm going to do and keep on doing."[13] Kay taught swimming throughout the summer and "helped" at the State Fair's aircraft exhibition in the fall. Beneath a photo of Kay in her aviator's outfit posing with her hand on the prop of a biplane, the *Yakima Daily Republic* reported she would be "on the job" as a "hostess" at the show. Kay shared duties at the display with Maud (Lillie) Bolin, a Yakama Nation pilot trainee at McMechan's flight school though it is not clear if they were paid. "Kathryn Kershaw and I explaining airplane motors and selling student courses in flying for Western Airlines," Bolin wrote on a black and white glossy photograph showing the two women seated at the aviation booth.[14] By the end of the year, Kershaw had acquired the reputation as "Yakima's air debutante," her moniker and name included in the caption below a photo montage of the three most prominent female pilots in the world: Mary, Lady Heath of Great Britain; Thea Rasche of Germany; and Amelia Earhart of the United States.[15] It is hard to imagine a higher accolade in the realm of contemporary women's aeronautics.

In theory, of course, the received notion of a male-female dichotomy should have had no bearing at all on aviation. An airplane is a machine that simply requires a human pilot, regardless of that person's gendered self-perception. However, aviation offers a case study of sexism in the workplace no matter which decade is examined, and it was particularly egregious during Kay's era. After women established themselves in the role of pilot by the mid-1920s, critics emerged who pushed back against the idea of a female at the controls of an airplane, arguing that they lacked "the discipline and concentration necessary to operate a complex machine."[16] Although the American press eagerly featured portraits of female aviators—as in all aspects of women's sport, the comelier the better—the accompanying articles often hinted that they were interlopers on a distinctly male preserve. Additionally, women who were learning to fly had to repel the notion that they were motivated simply by vanity and a vapid desire for publicity. In a speech before the women's Advertising Club of Baltimore, Mary Alexander, one of the first licensed pilots in Virginia, asserted that "when a woman decides to take up flying, even the people of her hometown jump to the conclusion that she is out for publicity. Men fortunately do not have to combat this stigma."[17] This attitude prevailed all across America as women struggled to find opportunities in the field of aviation.

As Kay Kershaw worked to fulfill the hours of flight necessary to obtain her commercial pilot's license, the most visible woman in aviation was Amelia Earhart. Earhart first became interested in flying at the end of World War I, absorbing all she could from military pilots training near Toronto where she was volunteering as a nurse. Earhart started flying lessons in Los Angeles, California, in early 1921 with Nelia Snook, one of the first female flight instructors in the state. It took her almost a year to log enough hours to take her first solo flight. Always aware that she trod upon a virulently gendered avocation, Earhart consciously chose to balance her interest in aviation with those pursuits more traditionally associated with feminine

Yakima Airport, 1928 (Kershaw Family Collection). Kay Kershaw stands center photograph wearing white coveralls. In the cockpit of Charlie McAllister's Alexander Eaglerock biplane: Maurice McMechan (left) and McAllister. Kneeling (from left): Del K. Sanford; [unknown]; Charlie Ryan; George Yost; Charlie O'Conner.

behavior. She never considered a career in flying until a publicist (and friend of her future husband, George Palmer Putnam) approached her with the offer to accompany pilot Wilmer Schultz and mechanic Lou Gordon on their transatlantic flight in 1928, ostensibly as keeper of the flight log. Gender was a motivating factor: her participation allowed billing the flight as the first female crossing of the Atlantic by air—in a role akin to that of an office secretary. It is no surprise that she received none of the monetary compensation awarded to Schultz and Wilmer.[18] Nonetheless, Earhart became an instant celebrity after the flight as an American aviation icon. Her confident style, unfussy dress, and authoritative manner of speaking encouraged the fantasies of clandestine lesbians in the 1930s. One small-town South Dakota woman who had the opportunity to spend a weekend with Earhart remembered sharing a kiss: "I had a feeling of intimacy, but I couldn't, I didn't dare go beyond it. She was still Amelia Earhart. She was personal yet she was impersonal."[19]

Earhart's aeronautical star continued to rise even though scores of other more accomplished female flyers vied for recognition all across the country. But even for those women with the highest profile, the economics of their chosen profession were dire. "This Trio Has Won World Renown but Unable to Pay Bills by Flying," blared the headline over a photo montage of three prominent pilots—Elinor Smith, Ruth Eider, and Amelia Earhart—in the *Yakima Daily Republic* on 5 July 1929. In the nearby columns, under the banner "Yakima Girl Flier Believes Women Can Make Air Pay," Kay Kershaw, still with only twenty additional hours of solo flight time under her belt, offered an optimistic take: "The day is coming when it will pay women to take to the air as well as men." If being a pilot offered scant prospects, Kay suggested a more financially lucrative route in "the sales game," predicting that in the next decade "airplane salesmen will be as thick as car salesmen."[20] This was clearly a notion she picked up in the months just prior to her interview. From the first of the year, *Popular Aviation and Aeronautics*, one of the country's leading magazines about flying, had promoted the idea that airplane dealerships were about to displace automobile dealerships as the new path to prosperity. Even so, the pitch strictly targeted men.[21] Jesse W. Lankford, chief of licensing at the United States Department of Commerce, told the Yakima paper that women faced dim prospects. Only seven women held transport pilot licenses, he said, compared to 4,500 men, and out of the nation's sixty-five licensed female pilots not one was engaged in commercial flying. In order to advance, Lankford went on, women "must learn a rigidly set formula, 'a man's way.'" He also pointed out that no women held any flight records—distance, altitude, or speed. But he ignored the fact that men could win far more prize money than women, and, perhaps more important, many of the record holders were military pilots who were paid to fly. He did suggest that women could find opportunities when the aviation industry needed pilots in jobs offering salaries lower than the current rate.[22]

Kershaw's obsession with flying continued throughout the summer of 1929. She flew with local pilot John Seawell up to Wenatchee from Yakima for the State Apple Blossom Festival, returning the next day with Maurice McMechan. At least twice, she leaped from an airplane to parachute down "somewhere in the Lower Valley without pay" or apparent concern for her safety. On her last descent "she landed in some brush and rather wrecked her trousers," recalled her friend Jack Nelson, amazed that she "simply volunteered" to make the jump. Kay even joined a barnstorming tour from Seattle that had stopped in Yakima on the way to Walla Walla. With Seawell, Kay flew to Grandview then on to Walla Walla. On a whim, she decided to make a parachute jump from 2,000 feet at the Walla Walla airport. Her friends from Yakima were not surprised: "she does spectacular things without the least warning," one of them said.[23]

In August, the Yakima Airport served as the end point of two air races, one from Spokane, the other from Portland. The festivities included a grand airshow on Saturday, 16 August, with 2,000 spectators in attendance who could take in a variety of events: a model airplane contest for boys, a balloon-bursting race for pilots, two fifteen-mile speed events (one for military, one for civilian planes), a relay race, and the marquee event of the day, a stunts contest for prizes and trophies.[24] Though no women participated in any of these activities, the Yakima paper, which provided extensive coverage of the air show, made space for an article in the women's section with the title "Aviator's Wives Approve the Job." The story featured a lengthy section quoting Kay Kershaw though with the intriguing caveat that she, "although not an aviator's wife and only dimly suspected of being an aviator's sweetheart, is herself a flier of first rank." Kay's extensive comments not only illuminate the barriers to women in aviation but also the challenge of quietly defying current sexual norms as a clandestine lesbian in eastern Washington during the late 1920s. Kay pretended that she was considering marriage even though the paper intimated this notion somehow did not ring true:

> Should a girl marry an aviator? It depends on how much she likes the aviator. I should prefer my future husband to be an aviator because I am so enthusiastic about flying. It would make life more congenial. Then, too, I think flying tends to produce a clean-cut type of manhood. A person who goes in for aviation has to maintain physical perfection. A flier gets a broadened view of life by seeing things in their true proportion.

Even though organizers had excluded women from the events, Kay could scarcely contain her enthusiasm for flying:

> There is a future for women in flying and once a person has been up, the thrill of it sort of gets him [sic] and he can't give it up. It also sharpens one's perceptions. About stunt flying, if one takes proper precautions about servicing one's plane and then gains sufficient altitude before attempting stunts, I think it is all right. Of course there is an element of danger but that is where the thrill comes in and it is better to get your thrills that way than at some jazz party, at least one feels much better afterward. Stunt flying is a good way to give vent to your feelings and is up to each individual flier as long as he doesn't endanger anyone else. There is something about flying that makes you feel as if the world is yours and you'd like to do something mighty and spectacular to fulfill that feeling.

Kay had bigger plans in mind for herself, too. "I'd like to make a long flight. If I could get sufficient backing and training I should like to attempt a transpacific flight for this field is newer," she said. "And I should fly in the City of Yakima.[25] I don't think the world will ever get tired of hearing about Lindy and Anne [Charles and Anne Lindbergh] but I suppose they get tired of so much publicity." But Kay surely knew that if she were to seek sponsorship from the ultra-conservative Yakima community for an airplane named *City of Yakima* to fly across the Pacific, her sexual preferences would have to remain concealed—evident in the very careful line she toed in her newspaper interview. When Kay returned to the topic of women's aviation and job prospects, she predicted that the future would require piloting skills simply to negotiate life in the modern world. "Should girls take up flying? I think everyone should learn to fly whether he intends to make a career out of it or not," she said. "It will soon be the common means of transportation and everyone should at least know how just as everyone now drives a car."[26]

This early infatuation with flying and her three parachuting incidents provided grist for the Kershaw legend mill in subsequent years, often embellished by Kay herself. One version made it to print thanks to an enthusiastic east coast biographer of William O. Douglas, Bruce Allen Murphy, who failed to realize Kay was feeding him a line while sitting around the dinner table at the Double K Mountain Ranch in 1989: "[Kay] flew the old biplanes that were used to deliver mail and had even been a wing walker in local air shows. She quit, however, on a windy day when her partner ignored her warning to wear a parachute and fell off the plane to his death." Murphy should have known better or at least done a bit of background research: as he meticulously explains about Justice Douglas earlier in his book, a good storyteller hones and shapes his or her tale, trying out one version after another as the yarn gets spun further and further from the truth. Quite similar, in fact, to Murphy's own approach as he regaled a rapt audience at the Cato Institute in 2003 with tales of his derring-do following the elderly Isabelle Lynn and Kay Kershaw on the wide, well-worn pony paths above Bumping Lake—ever so treacherous in the telling: "Wait until you go up some of those hills in the Cascades where you got a trail that's only about this wide [hands held approximately one foot apart to indicate width] and you make a mistake and you're at the bottom of a cliff. I *did* that! You're wandering along and you look down and you say 'kitty tracks: big kitty tracks. *Not good!*'" The story played well before his east coast audience in Washington, D.C.; catcalls would have driven him from the podium in Washington State. Narrow cliffside trails do exist on some class-four scrambling routes in the high Cascades, but they are far removed from the rolling forested slopes surrounding Goose Prairie. And such precipitous, treeless terrain only occasionally conforms to favorable cougar ("big kitty") habitat in Washington State.[27]

Although Kay's wing-walking story was pure fabrication, there may be more to the tale than meets the eye. A number of factors in late 1929 and early 1930 coalesced to put a damper on her dreams of a career in aeronautics and aviation sales. First and foremost, the stock market crash of October 1929 signaled that airplanes were not about to displace cars during an era of unemployment and soup kitchens. In addition, Maud Bolin, whose husband had the means to finance her flight training and purchase an airplane, eclipsed Kershaw in the region's aviation world: Bolin obtained her private license in August 1929 and took possession of a racing biplane the following month. In less than a year, she would apply for her commercial pilot's license.[28] No longer Yakima's air debutante, Kershaw warranted no mention in a late November newspaper article detailing the membership of an exclusive aeronautical club recently established in Yakima, only the second chapter of its kind in the state. Maud Bolin was the lone female in the group.[29] Even though aviation news filled the pages of the local paper every day, Kay's name did not turn up again until two articles appeared in late January 1930. Separated by exactly one week, the juxtaposition could not have been more achingly tragic.

The second article involved Kay's eighteen-year-old younger brother, Robert Whitmore Kershaw. Always close to her brothers—the three siblings were separated by less than five years—Kay enjoyed pursuing outdoor activities with them both. A photograph from around 1928 illustrates this relationship. The image shows Ron, Kay, and Robert after a day spent bird hunting. Kay, smiling broadly, stands with arms crossed between her two brothers; Ron holds up a ring-neck pheasant for the camera; and Robert, lanky with wavy hair, stands a head taller than Kay, arms akimbo. This snapshot of Robert, along with photos and his portrait from the 1928 and 1930 Lower Naches High School yearbooks, document an athletic, handsome youth. Entries in both yearbooks attest to his affable personality and affinity to sports: as a sophomore, he was a member of the basketball and baseball teams, and during his senior year, he served as vice-president of the school's Boys Club and started at center with the basketball team.[30] In September 1929, Robert entered Yakima's St. Elizabeth Hospital for an unspecified operation. He recuperated well enough to rejoin the Lower Naches basketball team as league play began in mid–December.[31]

Coinciding with the resumption of basketball season after Christmas break, the *Yakima Daily Republic* introduced a series of articles under the banner "Yakima Aviators Recall Greatest Thrill in Air" that ran from mid–January to mid–February, meant to satisfy the appetite of local readers for all things aeronautical.[32] In these vignettes, dime-store novel prose from the pen of feature writer Leonard Lerwill highlighted the near-disasters and mishaps of local pilots headquartered at the Yakima Airport. One of the first stories featured Kay Kershaw and her Walla Walla parachute jump of April 1929. In an attempt to spice up the narrative, Kay added a few details missing from other reports about the event. In her interview with Lerwill, she stretched the truth somewhat—just as she had with her bear-hunting story in October

Pheasant hunting, ca. 1929 (Kershaw Family Collection). From left: Ron Kershaw, Kay Kershaw and Robert W. Kershaw.

1928—describing how the parachute failed to open as she hurtled through the air: "But something was wrong," wrote Lerwill. "And the ground was coming up straight at her. A few seconds and she would be dashed to pieces, unless the parachute was released." According to this account, Kershaw had tugged the release ring the wrong way. Once she figured out the proper way to pull it, the parachute opened "before she had fallen many more feet" resulting in a perfect landing. With Kay as the only woman featured in the series, Lerwill felt compelled to add, "Getting the ring is a wonderful experience in the life of any girl, but with Kathryn Kershaw, local feminine pilot, it has a different significance from what it frequently has."[33]

Kay's parachute story ran on 22 January 1930, arriving in the paper on the very afternoon of Robert's eighteenth birthday. Perhaps this placement was just a happy coincidence. Alternatively, Kay may have requested that the paper print it that day as a special surprise for Robert, a dramatic tale to add to the collection of Kershaw family lore and good for a few laughs with her baby brother. However, Robert's festive birthday celebration suddenly grew serious: within hours of turning eighteen, he was struck with an acute attack of appendicitis that sent him back into St. Elizabeth Hospital. Doctors operated on the appendix immediately. Robert was recovering nicely as the week progressed until infection with sepsis brought on hemorrhaging and pneumonia. As his condition worsened, he received blood transfusions on 27 January, but to no avail. Robert passed away in the hospital early in the morning of 28 January.[34] At his funeral the following day, members of the Lower Naches High School basketball team served as pall bearers. The funeral notice published in the *Yakima Daily Republic* on 29 January listed Kay as "Miss Kathryn Kershaw, the aviatrix." This was the last time her name appeared in the paper in association with flying.[35]

On 10 January, less than two weeks prior to his birthday, Robert led his Lower Naches team as top scorer against Moxee High School; his final appearance on the court came against Tieton a week later. At the time of his death, Robert had been eighteen for just six days. His sudden demise provided a stark reminder of life's fragility and the random nature of the world. The shock of losing the family's youngest member in such a short span must have had a tremendous impact on the Kershaws, especially Ed and Ora. Jack Nelson writes that "parental objection" put an end to Kay's parachute jumping and barnstorming, reinforced, no doubt, by the barrage of aviation disaster reports that continued to fill the daily papers in early 1930.[36] Perhaps Kay needed no admonitions from her family. She resurfaced in the *Yakima Daily Republic* on 12 February in connection with the upcoming Cle Elum Ski Tournament, garnering praise for the 200 miles she had logged on skis and snowshoes and her ability to spend the winter in a drafty cabin at twenty below zero.[37] By summer, Kay had completely disengaged from aviation. As her former colleagues Maud Bolin and John Seawell joined the Pacific Northwest Air Tour of 1930 in late July through early August, Kay avoided all association with the event, leaving town on a two-week horse-packing trip above Bumping Lake on the same day the airshow arrived at the Yakima Airport.[38]

It is possible that Kay fashioned her wing-walking story as a coping mechanism for the devastating loss of her brother. Others besides Murphy—including Kershaw family members—remember hearing versions of this tale as well.[39] Although several accounts detailed wing walkers and stunt personnel throughout the United States who fell to their deaths with or without parachutes in the late 1920s and early 1930s, none of them involved Kay, even tangentially.[40] To be sure, such a story involving a Yakima personality would have provided sensational material for one of Lerwill's aviation columns. As Kay grew older, it may have been easier to conflate Robert's death with her own enhanced account of the Walla Walla jump and the fatal plunge of a fictional stunt man rather than recount for others her part in the horrible sequence of events that occurred between 22 and 29 January 1930.

4

The Great Depression and World War II

Work on the Kershaw farm provided Kay with a diversion from dwelling on Robert's 1930 death as well as a means to earn money as the nation's economy soured. While the financial debacle on Wall Street morphed into the Great Depression, Washington State remained dependent on extractive industries, especially forestry. Products from logging, fishing, agriculture, and mining enterprises represented the bulk of the state's exports and accounted for many jobs at the beginning of 1930. For apple growers in the Yakima Valley, a robust market for produce tempered the looming disaster somewhat: "We have sold most of our apples from last year—there is good demand," H.M. Gilbert wrote to his mother and sister in April 1930. Referencing some property in town he had recently sold, Gilbert continued: "there is a lot of building [construction] in Yakima this year."[1] But poor policy decisions in Washington, D.C., accelerated the national economic slump and global collapse of financial markets. In 1931, the Washington State legislature passed a bill to aid the unemployed and create public works projects to stimulate the economy. It also proposed a state income tax. Governor Roland Hartley vetoed both measures and started to slash spending which exacerbated bank failures and job losses statewide.

By the end of 1931, the produce market was faltering, affecting the economy of the Yakima Valley: "The banks here are serving us exceedingly well," H.M. Gilbert wrote to Senator Wesley L. Jones in December. "But our apple customers in various sections are hedging and delaying.... It seems too bad our domestic markets with our country's great wealth and resources cannot be reasonably financed." Gilbert expressed hope that Herbert Hoover's Reconstruction Finance Corporation—intended to allocate half a billion dollars of loans to corporations, banks, and governments—would gain traction in the Capital: "I am very fearful serious calamity is in sight unless the banks are assisted in many localities. Our usual apple customers and all business men are hesitating because bank credit or currency is way below usual."[2] Unfortunately, Hoover's program did not benefit individual Americans who were out of work and growing desperate. In Washington State, unemployment rates exceeded the national average: by late 1932, building and construction payrolls were about 10 percent of what they had been four years earlier, and those of logging and sawmills dropped by 50 percent. Total income payments in the state had dropped by 45 percent as of 1933, around average for the nation as a whole.

Hoover lost the presidential election of 1932. In the first 100 days of Franklin D. Roosevelt's administration, congress passed a series of measures to stabilize the banking system, provide emergency aid to the states, and employ the millions of out-of-work Americans. In addition, the Agriculture Adjustment Act provided help to farmers contending with a precipitous drop in commodity prices with a series of marketing agreements. A special session of the Washington State legislature passed the Washington Agricultural Adjustment Act in 1933 to set floors under the prices of many items grown in the Yakima Valley, including row crops and tree fruits. Nonetheless, times turned hard for orchardists in Yakima, forcing many families running small farms into foreclosure and into the nation-wide ranks of the unemployed. In March of 1933, President Roosevelt and his government established the Federal Emergency Relief Administration to give grants to the states to operate relief programs.

Early on, Washington State established its own similar program, the Washington Emergency Relief Administration (WERA). Throughout the state from 1933 to 1935, WERA created work programs and provided aid. To distribute federal and state welfare funds, the state legislature established in each county a public welfare office with three divisions: Relief, Child Welfare, and Social Security. By 1 April 1933, the Yakima County office was up and running, with several women working as full-time administrators and inspectors. WERA was phased out and replaced by the Washington State Department of Public Welfare (WSDPW) two years later. From her office in downtown Yakima, Gertrude Thomas served as assistant local administrator of this state agency for Yakima County.[3] Her example—along with numerous others—may have triggered Kay's departure from agriculture to pursue a career in social work, for it was evident around this time that the very nature of the American farm was undergoing a fundamental shift.[4]

Kay never stated how she felt about working on the Kershaw farm. She did, however, consistently express her love for and appreciation of horses. Family lore suggests that she enjoyed her agricultural labor as long as it involved managing horse teams in the fields, but her interest waned with the advent of tractors.[5] Many of her generation felt a certain sadness at the passing of the horse-drawn era. A contemporary of Kay's who also grew up working with farm horses reminisced, "Someone once wrote that, 'God must have smiled and opened a generous hand when he gave to man a horse' … there was a very close bond between a man's horse and himself, and the family."[6] Perhaps compounding Kay's disenchantment with farming was the male-dominated character of agriculture in the Yakima Valley: it was apparent that her father intended to hand the reins of the Kershaw operation to her brother Ron.[7] Thus, in the mid–1930s, Kay looked for an alternative career in the burgeoning field of social services.

Kay was not alone: by 1930, women represented four out of every five people in

Kay Kershaw planting fruit trees near Gleed, Washington, ca. 1930 (Kershaw Family Collection). The barn in the background is still visible from Kershaw Drive and remains in use on Kershaw Fruit Co.'s orchard there.

the fields of education and social work. Particularly for women who had no interest in marriage, the professional standing that resulted from a career in social work meant status and autonomy in the workforce. This was especially crucial for lesbians as the benevolent 1920s—an era full of hope, potential, and prosperity—segued into the more austere 1930s. Lesbians who had found welcoming enclaves in larger cities around the country now faced a nation-wide economic malaise complicating all aspects of pursuing an alternative lifestyle. As Lillian Faderman suggests, "to live as a lesbian in the 1930s was not for the fainthearted." The Depression made it difficult for all Americans to support themselves, certainly: but hostility toward independent women intensified as the notion of lesbianism as a medical abnormality gained traction. As lesbian subcultural communities shrank, a degree of self-sufficiency became crucial.[8] During this period, female social workers created a variant of the male professional: one who adopted the "male" ethos of the dispassionate expert while continuing to defer to male colleagues and bosses, perhaps providing the perfect cover for lesbians to hide in plain sight.[9]

It may be fortunate that no WERA opportunities turned up for Kay when the Yakima office first opened. She had a very busy schedule that year that would have allowed little time for full employment. Working on the Kershaw farm guaranteed ample latitude to pursue other interests. In March 1933, Kay skied with her companion Mildred Bridgeford at American River and, on at least one occasion, joined Kitty Nelson on a ski tour from Yakima to the Nelsons' home at Bumping Lake. The following month, she and her father accompanied the Cascadians on a visit to Grand Coulee. In June, Kay and Mildred headed out for a week of golf and a visit to the recently-refurbished USS *Constitution* during a stop in Seattle on its west coast tour. Over the Fourth of July, the two companions spent the long holiday at the Kershaw cabin in Cliffdell. Later in the month, Kay was gone to Portland to compete in a swim meet. She topped off the summer with a two-week horse-packing trip with Mildred from Bumping Lake to Goat Rocks, driving a buggy back to Cliffdell. Kay finished out 1933 with a final harrowing incident when she and her friend Julia Marsh were marooned by December floods at the family's Cliffdell cabin. After three days, the intrepid pair drove through two feet of water to safety in Naches.[10]

Kay's new career in social work would just have to wait until that definitive moment when tractors arrived at the family farm and her beloved draft horses were put to pasture. This may have occurred at some point in late 1934 or early 1935: she was still living in Lower Naches on the Kershaw farm when she had an operation and remained hospitalized at St. Elizabeth Hospital for three weeks throughout August 1934. From 1935 on, her name no longer appears in Yakima County directories. Nonetheless, she was employed as a home visitor by the WSDPW as of 1935. In late October, the *Yakima Daily Republic* reported that Kay bagged a deer on the Little Naches River, packing the animal out on her saddle horse. This coincided with a disastrous temperature drop all across the county that destroyed one-sixth of the apple crop. In the Gleed area near the Kershaw farm, temperatures plummeted to 4 degrees Fahrenheit, freezing picked fruit still sitting in open boxes out in the orchards. Apple harvest leading up to and including this debacle would have required all-hands-on-deck to salvage the crop. Because she was still living with her parents at home, Kay may also have helped on the farm: her successful hunt took place on a Sunday, typically a day off in the 1930s even in the middle of picking season. The *Yakima Daily Republic* kept tabs from December 1935 through early March 1936 as Kay joined groups of weekend skiers (along with her cousin, W.E.) at American River, Gold Hill, and Chinook Pass. Her name disappears from the paper after WSDPW transferred her from Yakima to Chelan in March 1936.[11]

Pat Kane

WSDPW transferred Kay from Chelan to Walla Walla in November 1936. Here she met the administrator of the Walla Walla County Welfare Department, Mary Patricia (Pat) Kane (1909–1992). Pat Kane was devoted to her chosen profession, having studied social work in college and as a graduate student at the University of Chicago.[12] In October 1934, she moved from Seattle to Walla Walla to supervise WERA in eastern Washington. When WSDPW went through another reorganization in

April 1937, state agencies in Olympia took over all welfare and social security work previously handled by the counties. As a result, Pat served as supervisor for Social Security in Walla Walla, visiting Yakima to consult with the county administrator that September. By 1938, she had become field supervisor of welfare work for nine southeastern counties in Washington State.[13] At some point in 1938, however, Pat decided to leave her position with the state and move to Seattle to work for Catholic Charities. The state reassigned Kay from Walla Walla to Kennewick after 10 October of that year.[14] Kay's identification card issued by the Washington State Department of Social Security indicates that she moved to Seattle at some point as well, probably in 1941, to work as an investigator for the King County Welfare Department.[15] Pat Kane remained with Catholic Charities until the fall of 1945, at which point she left Seattle to live full-time with Kay at Goose Prairie.[16]

Experienced in outdoor activities as a youth, Pat's opportunities blossomed after she met Kay in November 1936. A few months later, Pat confided to her siblings that she and Kay had been skiing together nearly every weekend. The two women had developed a bond, Pat effused, "beyond which I hardly believe there is one stronger between two people." Pat was totally captivated by her new friend: "she's about my age, blond curly hair, fresh lovely skin that nary a bit of rouge or powder has defiled, strong physically and mentally, my height and a few pounds extra ... [with] a grand sense of humor." Enumerating Kay's many interests—flying, parachuting, horseback riding—Pat exclaimed emphatically, "[she] is *not* the mannish type," covering her tracks by mentioning "Kay's boyfriend in Yakima" and her own wistfulness for a suitable husband. In a handwritten postscript to her sister, Isabel, Pat foresees that she and Kay remain "the good friends we will always be—that I know."[17] By spring, Pat and Kay were sharing an apartment. Swayed by Kay's enthusiasm, Pat soon acquired her own horse and tack for ninety dollars. The two began pasturing their horses together on the outskirts of Walla Walla ("two dollars per horse per month"), enjoying sunset rides out into the Palouse foothills, and trailering their steads up dirt roads to mountain trailheads on the weekends. Over the three-day July Fourth holiday, Kay and Pat made their first long-distance horse-packing trip together into the Wallowa Mountains and the Minam River basin.[18] Pat's family, her father especially, realized that the two women were bound together by more than friendship alone. Their relationship, based on a love of the outdoors, deepened over the years: a pocket-sized *Victory Picture Album*—which Kay carried with her during deployment overseas as a volunteer for the Red Cross during World War II—contains twenty photographs of their travels together, beginning with their trip into the Wallowas in 1937, followed by ski excursions to Sun Valley, Idaho, and Oregon's Blue Mountains and horse packing trips in the Cascades and Olympics.[19]

With Kay as her guide, Pat made her first visit to Goose Prairie from 11 to 14 February 1937. Driving together in Kay's "very swell 1936 Dodge deluxe coupe"—complete with heater and radio—from Walla Walla to the Kershaw cabin at Cliffdell, they set out on Friday morning to ski from the American River junction with

4. The Great Depression and World War II 45

Pat Kane, ca. 1947 (Kershaw Family Collection). Patricia (Pat) Kane (1909–1992) honed her skills as a backcountry rider after she met Kay Kershaw in Walla Walla, Washington, in 1936.

Highway 410 to Jack and Kitty Nelson's house at Bumping Lake. They spent a couple of days frolicking in the snow, playing poker by the fire with Jack, and enjoying Kitty's hearty fare. Pat was entranced by Goose Prairie's peaceful ambiance and bucolic splendor: "How I could go for that kind of life," she told Isabel. "How soon do you suppose one could retire to such a place? Maybe, about 35?? [sic] I fear it sort of got into me...."[20]

Pat was not far off the mark concerning her longed-for retirement date. A 1956 article in the *Yakima Sunday Herald* reports that Kay and Pat purchased the site for the Double K Ranch at Goose Prairie in 1945 and started work on their venture that year. A warranty deed filed in Yakima indicates the transfer of ownership of six home tracts at Goose Prairie from A.C. and Claudine A. Botsford to Kathryn Kershaw and Pat Kane on 18 May 1945.[21] So, Pat—whose birthday was on 6 March—had just turned thirty-six years old when this transaction went through. However, a photograph from Kershaw's *Victory Picture Album* shows Kay measuring a piece of lumber for a barn door (or perhaps a horse stall) as Pat looks into the camera: the photo's inscription reads "Double K—1942." The first Double K Ranch guest book has a handwritten dedication inside the wooden front cover: "June 1942—To the Double K's, Best wishes, Ellen Berndt." In addition, Kay wrote to Pat on a postcard from India featuring a photograph of an ox-drawn cart, dated 5 June 1943, "This is what we need on the Double K." Pat's father composed a 1943 letter to Pat using as

Early work on the Double K, 1942. Inscribed: "Double K—1942" (Kershaw Family Collection). Pat Kane (seated) watches as Kay Kershaw (kneeling) squares up a piece of lumber. The other two women are unknown.

the recipient heading "Double K Ranch" and the street address she shared with Kay in Seattle.[22] Thus, it may be that Kay and Pat were developing the Double K project prior to the purchase of the Goose Prairie property in 1945. Although they were able to work on their joint endeavor over weekends, rationing of lumber during the war years limited the stock available for civilian use: the government rationing board had to review all construction before every purchase of material and only the most immediate civilian needs gained approval.[23]

The June 1943 postcard to Pat resulted from Kershaw's decision to join the war effort. While Pat remained in Seattle, Kay left for special training as a personal service director to the armed forces overseas unit of the American Red Cross. From December 1942 to early May 1943, Kay received instruction in Washington, D.C., and New York. "I know my assignment and wish I could tell you but it is a military secret," she wrote to her brother, Ron. "We move with the troops and big things are going to happen … my varied background and rugged health got me this special assignment."[24] Kershaw's destination was North Africa: she went through commando training at Fort Belvoir in Alexandria, Virginia, with the understanding that she would visit battlefields to establish contacts with wounded men. "She was appointed," wrote Yakima columnist S.I. Anthon, "on the basis of her highly varied past experience, her smiling confidence even among the seriously wounded, and her known ability to handle any kind of transportation, from shank's pony to airplane."[25] Her journey to North Africa started in May, with stops in Wellington, New Zealand, Perth, Australia, and India before arriving in Alexandria, Egypt, in July 1943. She made a short trip to Tripoli in August, a tour through Syria, Lebanon, and Palestine in September, and a trip to Sicily and Italy in October.[26] At this point, or possibly in November, Kershaw suffered a debilitating injury that put an end to her Red Cross work. There has never been a convincing explanation about the exact nature of this injury or what caused it. Jack Nelson writes that Kay was "escorting a group of flyers on a horseback trip" outside of Alexandria when "her horse stumbled. She was not thrown off but the jar caused painful disc trouble in her back." Another report states that a fall from a horse caused her injury, a story repeated by Pat Kane to her sister's hometown newspaper in 1953. A third simply states that Kay broke her back in Egypt in World War II. In a conversation with the *Yakima Daily Republic*, Ora Kershaw gave no details about the accident, only that it occurred while her daughter was "helping conduct a riding club which the Red Cross had established for the service men."[27] Kay herself told the *Yakima Daily Republic* that "her injury was nothing dramatic." In this version, she was taking one of her daily rides with the soldiers when "her horse stumbled and fell on her. She was not thrown but the fall wrenched her back and caused the rupture."[28] Kershaw family lore places blame on a polo match mishap in Cairo: Kay repeated this story to the *Seattle Times* in 1973.[29] In whatever manner the injury occurred, it was anything but undramatic: after back surgery, her leg remained paralyzed requiring yet another

Kay Kershaw, 1943 (Kershaw Family Collection). Kay poses in her Red Cross uniform prior to deployment to North Africa during World War II.

round of operations. From November 1943 to around the end of May 1944, Kay spent nearly half a year at government hospitals in Cairo, then Miami, and finally at Walter Reed Hospital in Washington, D.C., before returning home to recuperate with her parents in Naches.

The most likely scenario is that Kay took a bad fall in a cross-country steeplechase, racing a braggart soldier who had the temerity to question her skill as an equestrian.[30] Despite her insouciance, the subsequent injury was quite serious: according to Jack Nelson, one of Kay's doctors at Walter Reed advised "never do any more than pet a horse for as long as you live."[31] The trauma to her spine and leg tormented Kay for the rest of her life. Along with the mythology surrounding this accident grew the notion that Kay's innate gumption and determination would never allow a broken back to interfere with her active lifestyle, and that the long period of recovery at Walter Reed had prompted some soul-searching and a fictive flash of inspiration: "Kay made the happy discovery that people should lead the kind of lives they want to, if it's possible, and she's convinced anything is possible. The next question was how to support living in the mountains? … The answer seemed obvious enough to have been preordained: a guest ranch."[32]

5

The Double K Mountain Ranch

Even though Kay may have abandoned her previous ambition to work in aviation, press coverage on the subject remained ever present, triggered by Amelia Earhart, the first woman to fly solo across the Atlantic in 1932. Newspapers hounded Earhart and her husband, George Palmer Putnam, wherever they went, rendering privacy their most valued possession. As detailed everywhere in the national press, Earhart and Putnam found refuge in 1934 for their first vacation as a married couple at a remote location in Kirwin, Wyoming, about fifty-two miles south of Cody. A friend of Putnam's, Carl Dunrud, owned the 3,500-acre Double D Dude Ranch in this former mining town. Earhart and Putnam stayed for two weeks, enjoying in particular a ten-day horse-packing trip through rugged terrain east of Yellowstone National Park. They immediately made plans to build a retreat at the Double D to use for future vacations.[1] Dunrud and his crew poured a foundation and built a preliminary base for the Putnam cabin by early 1936, with the expectation they would finish construction in 1937. One report suggested that Earhart and Putnam were planning to spend from one to three months each year at the Double D Ranch and "they even hope sometime to get snowed in for the whole season."[2] The notion of owning a dude ranch in a remote location and leading horse packing trips into the mountains while catering to the rich and famous obviously struck a chord with Kay Kershaw.

As much as Kay may have admired the aeronautical prowess of Amelia Earhart, with Wyoming's Carl Dunrud (1891–1976) she shared the same cut of cloth. A 1933 *New York Herald Tribune* article quoted George Palmer Putnam praising Dunrud as "a barber, cowboy, cook, marksman, skillful worker in leather and silver, mechanic. If you live in remote places and you wish to live prosperously and comfortably you learn to be handy."[3] Dunrud had been a horse packer in Yellowstone when he first met Putnam in 1916. The following year, Dunrud took a position at Yellowstone Park as a park ranger but Putnam persuaded the government to release him from duty to work for him while on vacation there. The two went on trips together in the West over successive years. In 1926, Dunrud traveled to New York City at Putnam's behest to assist with a hunting trip slated for Northern Canada. At the last moment, Putnam changed his Canadian plans to sail for Greenland with a group from the American Museum of National History charged with gathering animal specimens.

Because of his abilities with machinery, Dunrud signed on as second engineer with the Danish crew of the expedition's vessel. The interpreter that Putnam hoped to hire had to back out at the last minute: but Dunrud, who understood Danish and spoke Norwegian, stepped into that assignment as well. After the four-month journey in Greenland, during which photographers took pictures of him lassoing polar bears and walruses, Dunrud returned to Wyoming to start construction on the Double D Guest Ranch. In the early 1940s, perhaps with Dunrud as her model, Kay Kershaw commenced the process of replicating the Double D Dude Ranch at Goose Prairie, Washington.

A Business Opportunity at Goose Prairie, Washington

In retrospect, the post–World War II economic boom in the United States appears almost predestined, although in the war's immediate aftermath it was anything but. Servicemen returned home to uncertain job prospects while the threat of continued conflict with a belligerent Soviet Union loomed on the horizon. Nonetheless, relief that war with Japan and Germany had ended created a sense of optimism, and a burgeoning can-do spirit infused the country with dreams of prosperity and business opportunity. In late 1946, the back page spread of the *Spokesman-Review Magazine* summarized the hopes for the dawning of a new era: "another new venture born during the hectic years of war, when it would seem no one had any opportunity to plan for anything but his or her own welfare, will become reality."[4] The author was alluding to the Double K Mountain Ranch, open for business and ready to receive guests for the first months of the 1947 winter season.

After recovering from her back surgeries at home through the summer of 1944, Kay Kershaw began working on a piece of property at Goose Prairie that she would soon own. She took up residence in a tent house near a small creek that ran across the plot and began clearing, leveling, and excavating a site for a cabin. On the weekends, Pat Kane commuted from Seattle to help with the work. They hand-dug a four-foot square by seventeen-foot deep well fed by the creek and covered it with an insulated pumphouse. The two women also began hand-splitting wooden shakes—between 9,000 and 15,000 according to various reports. In the spring of 1945, a Seattle friend of Kay's, A. "Tino" Porreca, delivered plans for a three-story ranch house. They poured foundations for the lodge that spring, and by fall, Pat left her job with Catholic Charities to live full-time with Kay in the new Goose Prairie cabin over the winter. They billed this as a test to see how viable a year-round operation in the proposed lodge might be.[5]

In the spring of 1946, Kane and Kershaw began framing and constructing their Double K mountain lodge—one "K" for each of the "Double K girls."[6] The *Yakima Morning Herald* reported that the building cost forty thousand dollars—around 675,000 in 2024 dollars. Kershaw and Kane worked with a crew supervised by R.A.

Construction of the main lodge, Double K Mountain Ranch, Goose Prairie, Washington, 1946 (Kershaw Family Collection).

"Chuck" Hammond to raise a structure based on Porreca's design: a ranch house measuring 80 by 26 feet sided with fir and roofed with pine-shakes. The first floor contained a 35-by-26-foot living room finished in knotty Ponderosa pine with a native stone fireplace, dining room, kitchen, and owners' quarters. The second floor included nine guest bedrooms accommodating two persons each and two complete bathrooms with showers. With the guest cottage, 28 by 14 feet, featuring its own stone fireplace and private bath with room for two to four guests, the entire Double K facility had accommodations for twenty-two people. A decade later, Kay's construction story had changed somewhat, with Kershaw telling the Yakima paper that she and Kane had operated as contractors on the job with the help of workers hired on a day-to-day basis. "There's been some cheering-on during these labors," the *Seattle Post-Intelligencer* reported, "by the 'Dads,' Ed Kershaw, pioneer and orchardist … encouraging the dream of the Double 'K' and right with has been [*sic*] Dr. J.P. Kane, retired Tacoma physician." No doubt the two parents also delivered some funds along with the sis boom bah.[7] In his will, Ed stipulated that Ron, Kay's surviving brother, would inherit the entire Kershaw ranch operation. Support for Kay in her mountain retreat became the family's unwritten *modus operandi*.[8]

Evidently, the Double K was functioning as a dude ranch in 1946 prior to the completion of the lodge. From the beginning of the summer, Kay and Pat had a full-time wrangler, Lionel Claude "Joe" Blackburn, as part of their operation. The two partners allowed Joe to stable his fourteen horses in their barn and rent out the

West side of the main lodge, Double K Mountain Ranch, ca. 1949 (Kershaw Family Collection).

animals as his own business. In exchange, he built corrals and pole fences on the Double K property and provided horse-packing support for the occasional trip. As the summer progressed, Blackburn proposed that he work full-time for the Double K the following year. At the end of October, Blackburn went elk hunting with a friend along American Ridge. The two became separated; the friend did not return that evening. The following day, Blackburn consulted with Kay and Pat then headed back up American Ridge to search for his missing companion, who, meanwhile, had returned to Goose Prairie. Kay and Pat waited for two days before alerting the Forest Service that Blackburn himself was now lost. For an entire week, Pat and Kay scoured the area searching for Blackburn along with a party of eighty-seven volunteers. Blackburn's horse made it back to Goose Prairie minus its saddle and bridle. The following day, searchers found his saddle, blanket, chaps, and three thermoses piled neatly on a log, but no trace of Blackburn himself. A snowstorm at the end of the week brought all search efforts to a halt (although another unsuccessful attempt was made the following spring). Blackburn's wife and infant son went home with his father, a partner in the horse-rental operation retrieved the fourteen horses while the fate of Joe Blackburn remained a mystery: "Thus ends our first experience as

Kershaw family and friends at the Double K Corral, ca. 1949 (Kershaw Family Collection). From left: Pat Kane, Bob Kershaw, Betty Kershaw, Ron Kershaw, [unknown], Ed Kershaw, Eileen Ryan, Kay Kershaw. Lucky sits in the foreground.

dude ranch operators," Pat wrote to her sister.[9] Knowing his skill at tracking and woodcraft, Kay and Pat convinced themselves that Blackburn had not become lost; rather, they believed that he had abandoned his family, responsibilities, and meager job prospects in Goose Prairie.[10] Nineteen years later, a serendipitous search for another lost hunter on American Ridge found remnants of Joe Blackburn, only three-quarters of a mile northwest of Camp Fife at Goose Prairie, "a decaying skull and rotting remains of his cowboy boots" according to the *Yakima Daily Republic*'s first-hand account. With such meager evidence, the Yakima County Coroner could not determine the cause of death.[11]

Despite the inauspicious Blackburn affair, the Yakima Chamber of Commerce approved membership of the Double K Ranch in December 1946 and Kay and Pat were ready to start lodge operations on 1 January 1947. They told the *Yakima Morning Herald* they planned to operate as a dude ranch in the summer and cater to skiers in the winter. If dude ranching offered a viable summer business model in the late 1940s, offering ski service through the winter might provide additional income through snow season based on the sport's popularity in the state. To Kay, this looked like a lucrative venture for Goose Prairie.

Skiing at American Ridge[12]

Kay Kershaw was in the vanguard of skiing throughout the 1930s and 1940s, a skill that would later inform business decisions at the Double K Ranch. As a teenager, she had been an early devotee of the sport. Several 1920 photographs show her barreling downhill near Bumping Lake on a pair of skis clad in calf-high logger-style boots while leaning on a long, single pole. She often skied with her brother and friends, but was perfectly happy to head into the backcountry on her own, often for long stretches.[13] One of her solo outings, allegedly "across the Cascade range," upset her family who feared her lost, the *Seattle Post-Intelligencer* reported, "until she emerged safely."[14] One of her bolder ski tours occurred during a cold spell through deep snow in January 1928. Such difficult conditions hampered the State Game Warden who took fourteen hours to ski from the elk station at the Y through thirty-eight inches of snow to Rimrock Lake, and a Tacoma man celebrating his sixty-sixth birthday died from over-exertion walking through six feet of snow from Narada Falls to Paradise at Mt. Rainier. In addition, the weather remained sub-zero Fahrenheit for most of the month. These conditions proved irresistible to Kay who made a solo ski from Cliffdell to Bumping Lake then skied back home with her brother and his two friends toward the end of January.[15]

Kay had the good fortune to live in the Pacific Northwest, a region at the forefront of skiing's modern development in the United States. She found enclaves of like-minded outdoors enthusiasts on either side of Washington's Cascade Range. In Cle Elum, a small mining community sixty miles west of Yakima, members of the local ski club built a jump hill outside of town in the early 1920s. The group sponsored its Northwest Ski Tournament for the first time in 1923 attracting immediate interest from Yakima's Cascadians. In 1928, the club arranged two special Northern Pacific railway coaches to run from Yakima to Cle Elum and back on the day of the tournament. The following year, the Cascadians required three coaches to accommodate two hundred spectators, including Kay. What she saw that day drew her back to the Cle Elum tournament over the next four years.[16]

To bolster interest in their third annual ski tourney in 1926, the Cle Elum Ski Club added downhill races to the competition card. Expert men competed on one of the club's four dedicated ski courses, the Devil's Dive. The sole event for women—since tournament directors only allowed men to jump—was a gliding contest, probably a mundane schuss down the jump landing area: competitors had to navigate a "true course to the finish line" using "proper form and technique." In 1928, organizers moved the men's downhill to a different run, Hell's Dive, and allowed women to compete on Devil's Dive. Both were probably mass start events incorporating hairpin turns on steep, challenging terrain. Competitors raced to the finish line at the base of the jump hill, with additional points for style and technique awarded by the jumping judges. As a spectator in 1929, Kay would have seen men competing in downhill on Hell's Dive, Camel's Hump, and Rocky Run and expert women

Kay Kershaw (center) and Pat Kane (far right) with friends at the trailhead on Highway 410 before a ski-tour into Gold Hill, 1939 (Kershaw Family Collection).

negotiating Devil's Dive as well as a "ladies' gliding contest." Kay returned to Cle Elum to compete in the Devil's Dive race three times, finishing third in 1930 (collecting a box of candy in the process), first in 1931 (taking home the Cle Elum Ski Club Cup for her win), and fifth in 1933, the ski festival's' final year. She placed fifth in the women's gliding contest in 1932 when club organizers cancelled all downhill events.[17]

Closer to home, the Cascadians organized regular outings devoted specifically to skiing at various locations along the Naches River canyon in the 1920s.[18] The group also maintained a "clubhouse" structure at Gold Hill, superseded in the mid–1930s when Clarence Truitt, in his capacity as a local Boy Scout leader, converted his old mining cabin into a winterized ski hut. In spring of 1933, Lex Maxwell and Garrett Anderson, founding members of the newly-formed Yakima Winter Sports Club (later the Yakima Ski Club), began scouting terrain along American Ridge for a suitable location for ski area development, just eleven miles east of Gold Hill.[19] With a membership of 300 by early 1935, the Winter Sports Club completed construction of a ski run at the junction of Bumping and American Rivers, known variously as the American Ridge, American River Run, or American River Ski Bowl. By year's end, the local Civilian Conservation Corps (CCC) completed a brand-new public ski lodge that replaced the open-sided log lean-to used as a warming spot at the base of the ski run.[20] The Yakima club kept operating the ski area throughout the decade and into the immediate post-war years. So, by the time Kay and Pat opened the Double K Mountain Ranch on 1 January 1947, the American Ridge-Gold Hill-Chinook Pass area was already a bustling center for the state's ski aficionados.

Throughout the 1930s, Kay Kershaw continued to ski tour—with updated equipment and increasingly more stylish clothes—in the Blue Mountains of Oregon and in her home territory along the Naches River at American Ridge and the Gold Hill Ski Cabin.[21] However, advances in boot and ski technology allowed skiers like Kay to negotiate steeper slopes: by the mid-1930s, her focus had clearly shifted to downhill skiing. Just like her contemporaries all across the northern tier of the United States, Kay gravitated to ski areas that offered rope tows and chairlifts allowing more time to enjoy the descents without the tedium of climbing up a run. Nearby Sun Valley, Idaho, provided all these amenities and a splendid opportunity for regional skiers. Two photographs from Kershaw's scrapbook show Kay and her partner Pat Kane with their skis at Sun Valley resort in 1941. Another photograph labeled "Sun Valley—1939–40–41" provides a panoramic view from the top of the resort's new Bald Mountain chairlift.[22] These photographs would prove to be sadly ironic. Kay could not have foreseen that Sun Valley would be the template for ski resorts all across the West, destined to scuttle her plans for the Double K Mountain Ranch.

Kay Kershaw skiing at Stowe, Vermont, 1943 (Kershaw Family Collection). While training on the east coast with the Red Cross for deployment to North Africa, Kay took time to enjoy some downhill skiing in Vermont.

As the Double K opened in the winter of 1947, Washington State offered few options for downhill skiing. As an experienced skier who had glimpsed the sport's future in Idaho, Kay may have believed American Ridge had potential to become a downhill ski destination: the Yakima Ski Club

Base area at the American River Ski Bowl, Washington, ca. 1947 (Yakima Valley Museum). The Civilian Conservation Corps ski lodge built in 1935 stands in the background. Along with the Double K buildings and William O. Douglas's mountain retreat at Goose Prairie, the CCC lodge remains in operation and functional today.

had installed a dedicated rope tow there in late 1938. So, a cozy lodge in a peaceful valley with a practice slope just out the front door and close to ski runs on near-by Nelson Ridge or at the American River Ski Bowl would, theoretically, offer a unique business opportunity. In 1956, Kay was contemplating the installation of a portable skier's rope tow just out the front door at the Double K.[23] However, during Kay and Pat's first winter of operation only five weeks were even close to full (including an inaugural 1947 New Year's group).

A number of factors hampered the winter trade at Goose Prairie. From the state highway and entrance to the American Ridge Ski Bowl, guests had to traverse a nine-mile-long primitive county road, neither maintained nor plowed in the winter. Winters at Goose Prairie could be severe with three to nine feet of snow on the ground through March. In 1947 and 1948, Kershaw and Kane had to hire a bulldozer from Naches to plow the road at a bottom-line-busting five hundred dollars per pass while charging guests seven and a half dollars per day for room and board, including transportation. To haul in skiers and their equipment, the Double K operation finally purchased a four-wheel-drive army command car, equipped with an axe, two shovels, a cross-cut saw, two 2-by-12-inch planks, tire chains, and a blow torch (in case the motor needed thawing). By 1958, they had replaced this four-wheel drive vehicle with a tank-tracked military surplus Weasel.[24]

Far more significant, however, was the demise of skiing at American Ridge Ski Bowl. The CCC day lodge and the ski area's primitive facilities fell into disuse when the Yakima Ski Club decamped for White Pass after completion of a twenty-year highway construction project there in 1952 and the opening of a new ski area in January 1953. By comparison to American Ridge, White Pass had an additional 1,700' base elevation and was just slightly closer to Yakima via this new road. The final death knell sounded at American River when Crystal Mountain Ski Resort opened just over the ridge from Gold Hill in December 1962. Both White Pass and Crystal Mountain boasted dedicated mechanical ski lifts, higher elevations, deeper snow packs, longer runs, and more challenging terrain, rendering the American Ridge Ski Bowl at Goose Prairie obsolete.

Justice Douglas Comes to the Double K Mountain Ranch

The Double K operation fared better in the summer months, although providing feed for the horses also compromised finances. Hay and grain had to be trucked in from down the valley for the winter and getting a grazing permit from the Forest Service proved problematic in the spring of 1947. Kershaw and Kane resolved the problem eventually and received their permit, but their difficulties set the tone for encounters with the local Forest Service office over the next two decades. During the summer, visitors were, for the most part, from Seattle and the west side of the state, and a smattering trickled in from the Midwest. But locals were unwilling to pay to stay so close to home for access to regions they could easily drive to on their own. Finding clientele from outside the Pacific Northwest to fill the 1948 season thus became the Double K's number one concern.[25]

The star-power of celebrity guests such as Amelia Earhart and George Putnam had helped Carl Dunrud's business at the Double D Dude Ranch in Wyoming. Ranches in California and Nevada understood this concept as well: to attract new clientele, they offered free room and board to Hollywood luminaries like Clark Gable.[26] Perhaps these examples inspired Kay and Pat for their second season. One high-profile visitor who frequented the region was Yakima's now-famous Justice William O. Douglas, nine years into his lifetime appointment to the United States Supreme Court. After finishing law school at Columbia University in 1925, Douglas had bounced from New York to Yakima and back again, finally landing a position teaching law at Columbia. In 1929, he transferred to the law school faculty at Yale University where he honed his expertise in commercial litigation and bankruptcy law. Taking a leave of absence from Yale, Douglas joined the staff of the Securities and Exchange Commission (SEC) in 1934 and gained formal appointment by President Roosevelt in 1936. He became chairman of the SEC the following year. The relationship between Roosevelt and Douglas strengthened over the years and the president nominated him for a position on the United States Supreme Court in 1939. Douglas was only forty years old. He ultimately served on the Supreme Court for thirty-six years, the longest term of any Justice.[27]

William O. Douglas had a relentless intellect coupled with a restless soul.

During his tenure on the court, he wrote numerous articles and books on myriad topics, traveled the world, lectured extensively on the law, and wed four times. He relished his status in the nation's corridors of power but yearned for the solitude of the Cascade mountains. He despised the capital's cocktail chatter yet chafed at the small-town attitudes woven into Yakima's social fabric. He wanted marriage but his roving eye was never satisfied. One item, however, remained immutable: from the time they met, he shared with the proprietors of the Double K an affinity for the outdoors. Over the decades they remained his amiable companions whenever he wanted to escape his hectic schedule in Washington, D.C.

How Kershaw, Kane, and William O. Douglas first met is unclear. In 1996, Harvey Manning suggested that Kay was William O. Douglas's "school-days chum," although this is unlikely: Kay had attended Lower Naches High School from 1922 to 1925; Douglas graduated from Yakima High School in 1916.[28] It is possible that Kershaw and Kane met Douglas and his first wife, Mildred, in the Wallowa Mountains near the family's cabin in the early 1940s: the Douglases maintained a cabin near Lostine, Oregon, where they spent their summers during that period.[29] Local lore—bolstered by Kay Kershaw and Isabelle Lynn's own embellishments filtered through Bruce Allen Murphy's predilection for salacious details—provides an alternative account. According to Murphy, Kay got wind that Douglas was frequenting "a dude ranch run by a local doctor in Nile, farther down State Highway 410, toward Yakima. Seeking to create good word of mouth for the ranch, Kershaw offered her rival's most famous client free room and board at her place for him and all of his guests for as long as he wanted to stay."[30] This is conceivable: the owner of the Flying H Ranch on the Nile Valley Road was an osteopathic doctor, W. Douglas Holt, whose uncle and father arrived in the Yakima Valley in 1923. The Flying H opened as a dude ranch in the early 1940s, then transformed into the Flying H Supper Club after just a few years. It had a rather sordid reputation, operating as a quasi-brothel in the 1950s.[31] However, no record attests to Douglas's stay there.

During this period, Justice Douglas gained national celebrity as a contender for the vice-presidency—even as candidate for president in some circles—so the local press covered his every move: had he and his entourage stayed in the Nile, the two Yakima daily papers would have splashed the news across the front page. For example, when the story broke in July 1947 that Douglas was coming to Yakima after Labor Day to dedicate the site for the city's new hospital, the announcement made the front page with his photograph alongside. The press and citizenry were primed for his visit from 6 to 7 September, leaving little opportunity for any foray to Holt's establishment in the Nile. Douglas arrived in Yakima on Saturday afternoon to address sixty-five attorneys of the Yakima County Bar Association, then joined them for a celebratory evening dinner. He stayed overnight at Elon J. Gilbert's Snow Mountain Ranch in Cowiche Canyon just west of Yakima, then gave the keynote speech (broadcast over KIT Radio) at the hospital dedication ceremony, and was the guest of honor at a special reception at a nearby residence before returning to

Lostine that evening. All of his activities over the weekend prompted articles, photographs, and opinion pieces in both local newspapers. Even a banal letter Douglas sent to the *Yakima Daily Republic* a month later for "National Carrier Boy Day" was a frontpage feature. Stating the obvious to her readers that autumn, daily columnist S.I. Anton rhapsodized that residents of the city were always interested in the doings of Justice Douglas.[32]

During his short three-day sojourn the following year, from 19 to 21 June 1948, Justice Douglas enjoyed the company of three members of the Gilbert family: his life-long local friend Elon J., his brother, Horace N., and his niece, Jennith, both from Pasadena, California. A fourth member of the party was Mary Bradley Watkins (1911–1993), an acquaintance of Douglas's from Maryland, or in Murphy's arch manner, simply "his Washington girlfriend."[33] Watkins was the recent widow of Charles Law Watkins, a coal magnate turned painter, writer, and art educator whom she had married in 1942. In addition to inheriting her husband's fortune, Mary was also heiress—from her mother, Anna Bradley—to the vast acreage of Rosemont Farms in Rockville, Maryland. Only seventeen miles separated the farm's stables from downtown Washington, D.C. Justice Douglas met Watkins there, and the two remained friends for decades.[34] Since Douglas boarded his horses in Yakima, he would drive to Maryland on the weekends when court was in session to hire out horse and tack to spend the day riding across Maryland's open countryside. By doing so, he kept himself in saddle-shape for his strenuous summer horse-packing trips.[35]

In an interview with the *Yakima Daily Republic* as he left town after his stay at the Double K, Douglas referred to the trip as a reunion with his boyhood pal, Elon J., and as an opportunity to gather information for a proposed book on his early years in Yakima.[36] Douglas made no mention of his companion from Maryland nor of Elon's relatives from California. It was just a brief stop in Yakima for the Justice before continuing on his way to join wife and family at the Douglas summer home in Oregon. Nonetheless, Douglas liked what he saw at the Double K, writing in the guestbook, "here's to Double K—wonderfully hospitable and not too damn respectable."[37] Because eight feet of mushy snow limited trail exploration at Goose Prairie, Douglas spent a good deal of his time in conversation with Jack and Kitty Nelson—the long-time resident operators of the Bumping Lake dam—discussing mountain history for his proposed book: "I've known the Nelsons for thirty years," Douglas told a reporter who asked about his stay at the Double K. "It's a great experience to spend an evening with [them]." He indicated that he intended to return to Yakima in September to continue researching his book.[38]

Between this initial visit and the completion of his home next door in the mid-1960s, Douglas lodged at the Double K on at least twelve separate occasions, as did his first wife, Mildred (on her own with their daughter Millie) and brother Arthur in 1950. During construction of his Goose Prairie abode (which he designated "Prairie House") in 1964, Douglas and his third wife Joan took room and board with Kay and Isabelle for over three months.[39] Of course, Douglas had alternative accommodations when he returned to Washington State. With his second wife Mercedes he maintained a summer retreat north of Glenwood, Washington, near the base of Mt. Adams from the late 1950s to the early 1960s. He often stayed as a houseguest with Elon J. Gilbert and his wife, Joan, until Douglas's divorce from Mercedes in 1963. At that point, Joan Gilbert—who adored Mercedes and found Douglas's drinking and womanizing despicable—refused to allow the Justice into their Cowiche Canyon home anymore. She did concede to Elon's wishes by letting him sleep in the barn.[40]

There is no question that Douglas cultivated a devil-may-care attitude in his casual view of wedding vows and sobriety, details meticulously chronicled throughout Bruce Allen Murphy's *Wild Bill*. But the author misconstrues entirely Douglas's first trip to the Double K Ranch: it had little to do with any purported "girlfriend." For quite a while, Justice Douglas had contemplated a party to show appreciation for Kitty and Jack Nelson. He felt particularly grateful to them for accommodating him in their home as a youth and intended to devote an entire chapter to the Nelsons in his forthcoming book. Jack had just retired from his supervisor's job in 1946 and was living with Kitty in Goose Prairie near the Double K Ranch.[41] Knowing that a surprise party could only be successful if it took place near their home, Douglas enlisted Elon J. to find a suitable location for the festivities: perhaps at one point he was even considering the Flying H Supper Club in the Nile. This explains why Douglas made a quick three-day visit to the Double K Ranch in June 1948 and engaged in purposeful visits with Jack and Kitty while he was there. Everyone involved kept plans for the big event secret. Douglas went back and forth from Lostine to Seattle for various meetings that August: on one, the press caught up to him mysteriously "sauntering unrecognized about the streets of Yakima" after arriving from Bickleton. He told reporters that he and Elon J. planned to head off to Montana for a fishing trip the following week. On 1 September, the Associated Press (AP) writers found him in Seattle, coming "out of the mountains" to attend a federal judges' conference. He explained that research for his new book required retracing his steps near his boyhood home in Yakima. On the same day, Horace N. Gilbert, with his children, Jennith and Elon H., arrived in Yakima from Pasadena to visit his mother and other relatives. On 10 September, Douglas made the AP wire in Seattle again because he did not have the proper change to pay for downtown parking, complaining with jocularity that he would now be late for a fishing trip in Yakima.[42]

All the secretive to-and-fro culminated on 15 September with a surprise dinner honoring Jack and Kitty Nelson hosted by Justice Douglas at the Double K Ranch. With dishes cleared, Douglas gave opening remarks informing the honorees about the chapter he was dedicating to them in his new book. He also presented them with a copy of the chronicles of the Lewis and Clark Expedition. Horace N. Gilbert spoke next, commenting how he relished taking his children to visit the Nelsons when he had come to Goose Prairie earlier in the summer. Finally, Elon J. gave the Nelsons a portfolio of photographs he had taken of Justice Douglas on their June trip with

Kay into the Goat Rocks. *Yakima Daily Republic* columnist S.I. Anthon—one of the guests that evening—emphasized the "hours of never to be forgotten fellowship and hospitality."[43] That, in a nutshell, was the Double K way.

Whether Justice Douglas specifically considered the "one-room, tin-roofed outbuilding" at the Double K Ranch his own personal love shack from the moment he laid eyes on it in 1948, as Murphy suggests, is certainly open to interpretation.[44] Just as in the case of Amelia Earhart and George Putnam at the Double D in Wyoming, privacy—with space and time to think, reflect, read, and write—may have been at a premium for Douglas too. Justice Douglas did not return to stay at the Double K until the summer of 1952 when his first marriage to Mildred foundered and he lost access to their family cabin in Lostine. He constructed Prairie House on property adjacent to the Double K twelve years later. The obvious pleasure Douglas gained from Kershaw's company is indisputable. He admired and respected Kay with whom he shared Yakima Valley roots. "They liked to bounce ideas off each other," noted Elon H. Gilbert recently. Certainly, Douglas appreciated her down-to-earth conversation and opinions, so far removed from the polished political badinage current in the nation's capital: "They spoke the same language."[45] For her part, Kershaw must have seen something in Douglas's multi-faceted persona other than the dissolute boozehound—aided and abetted by a pandering Elon J. Gilbert—portrayed by Murphy: she certainly had little patience or need to tolerate appalling male behavior on the premises of the Double K without just cause. Legend has it that on more than one occasion, Kershaw would turn the station wagon back around after picking up Double K guests at the Yakima Airport if she did not approve of their conversation and demeanor on the way to the ranch. "I don't cotton to fools," said Kay on a regular basis.[46] In consideration of Murphy's depiction of Douglas and Elon J.'s relationship, Elon H. Gilbert opined that his uncle might have thought: "whatever makes Bill [Douglas] more productive—vodka, women, whatever—was worth it because of his great contributions. His virtues outweighed his vices."[47] Perhaps this notion influenced Kershaw's opinion as well.

Book Release Party—April 1950

At the beginning of 1950, the *Yakima Daily Republic* announced that Justice Douglas would return to town for a gala dinner sponsored by the local Chamber of Commerce in April to celebrate the release of *Of Men and Mountains*. The paper listed local guests of honor who would be on the dais with Douglas, including Dr. Douglas Corpron (an old high school chum and hiking partner), Elon J. Gilbert, Jack and Kitty Nelson, Kay Kershaw, and Pat Kane.[48] On 11 April, Douglas arrived to a rousing welcome: at the time, many considered him a serious candidate for president in 1952. "'Peanuts' is home," exclaimed one headline alluding to Douglas's alleged "schoolboy" nickname. Corpron and Gilbert met Douglas at the airport that evening, the trio's striking image featured on the front page of the *Yakima Daily Republic* the following day. In the morning, a local troop of press and photographers followed along as the three companions visited Douglas's boyhood home on North Fifth Avenue, Yakima High School, Broad's Stationery (a downtown bookstore), and his parents' graves. For some reason, Douglas cancelled his previously-scheduled lunch-time appearance at Yakima Rotary. Perhaps he ducked out for the afternoon to take a tour on the outskirts of town with Elon J., a 1923 graduate of Harvard Business School, whose latest enterprise was The Uplands: a suburban development boasting a magnificent view of Mt. Adams, carved out of a 160-acre block of Richey-Gilbert orchards some three miles west of Yakima's central district. This neighborhood's broad, winding streets still bear the names Elon selected, a testimony to his friendship with Douglas and their mutual love of the mountains: Avalanche Avenue, Glacier Way, Bitterroot Way, Snowmountain [*sic*] Road, and Douglas Drive.[49]

The festivities on the evening of 12 April at the Commercial Hotel in downtown Yakima included Douglas's introduction of his honored guests before the standing-room-only crowd. Kay received a rousing salute as Douglas entertained the audience with his signature drawl, wry banter, and dramatic pauses:

> I want Kay Kershaw to stand up. [Applause]. Now Kay needs no introduction. Kay has a lot of attributes and achievements, qualities that perhaps some of you don't know about. [Pause]. Kay can roll a cigarette in one hand and I betcha that they're not one-tenth of one percent of the members of the Chamber of Commerce of Yakima can do that! [Laughter]. And Kay can throw a diamond hitch and she's taken Elon and me back on some wonderful trips; and I'd like to take this as an opportunity to say that I think it's mighty fine that the country has a place like the Double K Ranch where people from all parts of the country can come and sleep and get good lodgin', wonderful entertainment, horses, and the scenic views that they get from the American Ridge. And I hope that, as some wag said today, that when he saw the map in the front of the book showing Double K Ranch, I did have a little bit, a little share in putting Double K on the map! Thank you, Kay, for coming [applause].

Douglas introduced Pat Kane next along with one of his hunting and fishing companions from Oregon, both of whom received accolades for their backcountry culinary skills: "Now Pat Kane as you know is the other part of the Double K.... And Pat can turn out a huckleberry pie the like of which you've never tasted." Douglas's double-entendre as he compared the kitchen talents of the two elicited guffaws, hoots, and applause from the majority male crowd: "I'll let you in on a little secret.... If I had to choose one to take into the woods, I'd take Pat!"[50] The following day, a front-page photograph in the *Yakima Daily Republic* documents the close relationship between Douglas and Kershaw—dressed for the occasion in her finest western garb—as he introduced her to the Yakima Chamber of Commerce.[51] The party continued in La Grande, Oregon, at a gala "chuck-wagon dinner" on 13 April with honored guests from Yakima in tow—including Kay, Pat, Dr. Corpron, and Elon J.—to mingle with those from Douglas's summer residence near Lostine.[52]

William O. Douglas introduces Kay Kershaw at the book release party for *Of Men and Mountains*, 12 April 1950. Commercial Hotel, Yakima, Washington (Kershaw Family Collection). Inscribed: "For Kay Kershaw with warm regard Wm. O. Douglas." Justice Douglas stands at the dais facing left; Kay Kershaw stands facing right toward Douglas. Seated to Douglas's immediate right: Jack and Kitty Nelson. Seated to Douglas's immediate left: Doug Corpron [facing Douglas]; [obscured by microphones: possibly Bradley Emery, W.A. McGuffie, or Gene Marsh]; Elon J. Gilbert [facing Kershaw]; Pat Kane [partially obscured behind Kershaw]. The next day, this photograph appeared on the front page of the *Yakima Daily Republic* with the caption "Special Friends of Supreme Court Justice William O. Douglas sat with him at the speaker's table last night at the world premiere of his autobiography 'Of Men and Mountains.' Douglas is shown introducing Kay Kershaw of the Double K mountain ranch [sic], one of the persons mentioned in his book."

During this short visit to the Pacific Northwest, Douglas made a statement that resounded all across the United States. While signing copies at Broad's Stationary, he denied rumors that his new book was a "trial balloon of his policies" for a possible bid as presidential candidate. Rather, he stated that he intended to beat the record set by Justice John Marshall for longevity on the Supreme Court. He told the press that he would stay on the bench until he was at least seventy-three in order to outpace his predecessor: "I've got a little advantage on Marshall. He was appointed when he was 45 and I started when I was 40. But then Marshall had an advantage over me: He never had a horse fall on him."[53]

The Goat Rocks Wilderness and the Double K Persona

The year prior to Douglas's book release party and his comments to the press, Jennith and Horace N. Gilbert, along with Justice Douglas, came to Yakima to celebrate the dedication of Gilbert Peak, the highest point in the Goat Rocks. Curtiss, the older brother of Douglas's friend Elon J., had died suddenly in 1947 and Douglas became the motivating force to re-name the mountain—formerly known simply as Goat Peak—in his honor. The *Yakima Daily Republic* covered the event with several columns and a half-dozen photographs from 19 to 24 August. Friends and family joined Douglas on a trek to the summit where the group placed a bronze canister in a cairn commemorating the dedication.[54]

This grand occasion lost its luster five weeks later on 2 October 1949. Before returning for the opening session of the Supreme Court, Douglas wanted to retrace a trail he planned to describe in his forthcoming book. He recruited Elon J. to accompany him on a reconnaissance mission from Lake Tipsoo on Chinook Pass to Crystal Mountain. On the ascent of Crystal Peak's west side, Douglas's horse threw him (perhaps stung by a hornet) then tumbled over him twice as he cartwheeled down the hillside. With Douglas immobilized by thirteen broken ribs and a punctured lung, Elon bushwhacked on foot to Highway 410 to flag down a motorist. Elon asked him to alert a group of his friends picnicking at Lake Tipsoo to help with an evacuation. One went in search of a state patrolman, the others went up the Pacific Crest Trail to meet Elon at the accident site and help move Douglas to a patrol car, then into an ambulance dispatched from Yakima to American River. The calamity kept Douglas in the hospital for several weeks followed by months of recuperation. Unable to attend to judicial duties, Douglas used his time to put the finishing touches on *Of Men and Mountains*.[55]

A well-worn copy of the *Yakima Daily Republic*'s front-page coverage of Douglas's accident, preserved in Kay's clipping file, documents her concern. She kept it because she had been absent from the Gilbert Peak dedication festivities as well as the Chinook Pass trauma. That year, both events coincided with high season at the Double K. Although Elon J. and Justice Douglas were planning to ride from Tipsoo to Crystal Mountain on 29 September, they had to postpone because of fog. They took a trip to Seattle to see the University of Washington–Notre Dame football game and a flight back to Yakima: all the while, Pat and Kay were hosting a group of wilderness devotees from the east coast (including Mary Watkins and her son) on a trip along the Pacific Crest Trail.[56]

This excursion followed close on the heels of the Double K's magnum opus—guiding twenty-five guests over a figure-8 loop starting and finishing at Goose Prairie for the two weeks coinciding with the Gilbert Peak dedication of 1949.[57] A year earlier, faced with too many empty weeks in the summer, Kay and Pat contracted with the Trail Riders of the West to offer their services. Sponsored by the American

Forestry Association (AFA), this organization of backcountry equestrians had sponsored a variety of horse packing trips into various national forests since 1933. The cover of the July 1948 edition of AFA's magazine, *American Forests*, featured one of Kay's promotional photographs taken to publicize the upcoming trail ride. It shows Pat enjoying a cup of coffee sitting around the campfire with four Double K clients. To prepare for this AFA trip, Kay, Elon J., and Justice Douglas made a "pilot jaunt" from 5–11 August 1948 over a route Kay had been doing since the early 1930s.[58] Douglas made this trip famous in Chapter 16 in *Of Men and Mountains*. The AFA event a week later attracted twenty-two participants from all parts of the United States, with a physician and blacksmith riding along on emergency stand-by. The *Yakima Daily Republic* reported that the AFA trip ran point-to-point from Bumping Lake over White Pass into the Goat Rocks and finished at Rimrock Lake. This would have been an interesting itinerary but a logistical nightmare, requiring trailer transport of twenty-five horses from one end of the Triangle to the other. It made far more sense to follow a variation of the pilot loop Kay tested with Justice Douglas and Elon J., a notion confirmed in a journal of the 1948 trip kept by one of the participating trail riders.[59] From 1948 to 1952, these AFA events along Kay's loop drew participants from all across the United States, Canada, and Europe. The publicity surrounding the AFA trips proved a boon to the Double K's business and the yearly figure-8 pack trip into the Goat Rocks gained the reputation as "the classic of its kind" in the United States.[60]

This initial decade of operations at the ranch—crowned each year by the two-week tour through the Goat Rocks—gave rise to a persona deliberately cultivated by the Double K women. Kay, Pat, and, subsequently, Isabelle Lynn carried out ranch work and the care of their guests with

Map 3: Kay Kershaw's loop from Goose Prairie to Goat Rocks—1949. *Yakima Sunday Herald* 11 September 1949 (Yakima Valley Museum: Sketch by Kay Kershaw).

a combination of western grit and sophisticated, east-coast aplomb. Along with a hard day in the saddle, witty and urbane conversations around the dinner table became hallmarks of a stay at the Double K: "Their bright hostessing over the affairs of the ranch," wrote the *Spokesman-Review* in an early piece about Kershaw and Kane, "is punctuated by their crisp intelligence and untiring zeal."[61] "The dude ranch," according to Cathy Douglas Stone, Justice Douglas's fourth wife and neighbor to the Double K Mountain Ranch nearly three decades later, "catered to anyone who was smart enough to love *The New Yorker* and who could take Isabelle's tart tongue."[62] Yet Kay reveled in her rough-and-tumble, cowgirl lifestyle, an attitude she shared with Justice Douglas: "I certainly didn't expect a Justice of the Supreme Court to be outfitted in dirty old jeans, torn and beat-up looking cowboy hat, and worn-out boots," Cragg D. Gilbert recalled of their first meeting in July 1946. "But that's how he and his son greeted us."[63] In an era when dungarees had become a political statement symbolizing freedom from the norms of society (and trousers in general the favored apparel of post-war lesbians), Kay, Pat, and Isabelle seldom wore anything else, along with cowboy hats, boots, Army-surplus shirts, Levi denim jackets, and bandannas. These items composed the signature look of the Double K for over four decades.[64] Brad Patterson, who lived next door to Kay and Isabelle in the late 1980s, remembered that Isabelle's suitcases containing her east coast wardrobe remained in the closet at the Double K, unpacked and intact until the day she moved out in 1990.[65] As Justice Douglas suggested in his comments about Kay before the Yakima Chamber of Commerce in 1950, hand-rolled cigarettes were de rigueur. The ingredients—"a pipe mixture wrapped in brown paper"—and proper mountain protocol created part of the allure. "To prevent forest fires," one trail rider dutifully reported, "spit on a rock. Then mash out your lighted cigarette on the wet spot. Isabelle extinguishes hers that way."[66] And Kershaw's ability to do one up in the saddle was legendary. According to a variety of sources, a wry aside circulating around Goose Prairie held that "Kay could roll a cigarette one-handed, riding at a gallop downhill in a hard wind."[67]

As much as word-of-mouth among the AFA trail riders and coverage by the local press bolstered business, the wide public attention generated by the publication in 1950 of Douglas's *Of Men and Mountains* brought national and international renown to the Double K Ranch. Stories about Pat Kane, Kay Kershaw, and the idiosyncratic characters of Goose Prairie who gathered around their hearth lent a folksy charm to Douglas's style, composed specifically for an east coast readership.[68] Whether his tales were completely truthful is open to debate. For example, in "Chapter 16: Goat Rocks," Douglas provides a rather overblown and florid account of climbs in 1948 on Old Snowy and the soon-to-be-named Gilbert Peak. He writes that in early August, Kay Kershaw and Johnny Glenn of Naches led a string of pack horses for him and Elon J. Gilbert into the Goat Rocks area; that they started from Bumping Lake, camping at Fryingpan Lake, "Slipper Lake," and West Camp; that he and Elon climbed Old Snowy on 8 August 1948; and that their climb on Gilbert

Peak occurred later that year.[69] Certainly, this refers to the 1948 test run for the AFA riders during which Kay allowed Elon and Justice Douglas to tag along. However, Douglas provides a different description, suggesting that Kershaw and Glenn had served as nothing more than porters transporting gear and provisions for Douglas and Elon's exploits. In fact, Kay—"the party leader" on this trip according to the *Yakima Daily Republic*—had personally guided Douglas into the Goat Rocks from Bumping Lake over terrain that she knew far better than he.[70] Nor is there a record of any subsequent climb on the high point of the Goat Rocks destined to become Gilbert Peak by the two friends later in the year. Still, they could have perhaps squeezed in a trip while planning the Nelsons' fête in late August or early September. But Justice Douglas scarcely allowed facts to interfere with the fabrication of a good story. As Fred Beckey observes in reference to Douglas's dramatic account of his 1915 first ascent on Kloochman Rock in chapter 22 of *Of Men and Mountains*, "the climb is described with the overstatement of an impressionable youth."[71]

Pat Kane Bows Out

Pat Kane's tenure as one of the original two Ks in the Double K moniker lasted just over ten years. Why she left remains a mystery. Although some accounts made public during Pat's lifetime state that, in 1955, she decided unilaterally to return full-time to her former profession in social work, one of Kershaw's friends suggested that the split was not mutual. Ruby Montana believes Kay intentionally ended the relationship with Pat: "She broke Pat's heart, but she had found her soulmate when she met Isabelle Lynn."[72] Collections of slides only hint at an intriguing story: from a Kodak processing box dated May 1954, one slide shows Kay, Pat, and Isabelle posing together at the Yakima airport: Pat's image is neatly snipped off in an undated print from this same slide. Another box, dated February 1955, contains several images of Kay, Pat, and Isabelle together at Goose Prairie: the shipping label from Kodak directs the slides to Isabelle at a post office box in Yakima. The last reference to Pat in the guest books is on 20 June 1955, and a quit claim deed signed by Pat Kane in October transferred her entire interest in the Double K property to Kay Kershaw.[73] Through the voluminous letters Pat left behind, her family offers this insight: "[although] there is no concrete evidence that Pat and Kay had a sexual relationship, we do know it was a caring and loving relationship—until it wasn't."[74]

In November, Pat informed her father that she was leaving Kay and the Double K Ranch for good. Writing to his daughter Isabel (and Pat's closest confidante), Dr. Kane lamented, "we heard that when she left for Arizona she *was not coming back* [sic]. We were shocked. It seemed unbelievable. We briefly were told about the ride to the city [Yakima] and the dissolution of the partnership." Perhaps the elder Kane's intuition that Kay and Pat were more than just business partners seeped into his thoughts: "We were sad to think their ten years had come to this. It seemed

On American Ridge, ca. 1958 (Kershaw Family Collection). Kay rides at the front of a group of Double K guests on American Ridge with Mt. Rainier in the background.

like a divorce—the unhappy ending of a marriage."[75] Dr. Kane was heartsick for his daughter: "when you left … that dark, cold rainy day to take your long drive over Snoqualmie Pass I felt sad and lonesome to think of all that lay ahead of you…. I wondered where you were staying and if you had shaken yourself free from the [?] of leaving behind your tall trees and the mountains you love so much…. God Bless You, your loving old Dad."[76]

With Pat's departure in late 1955, the Double K name and brand based on Kane and Kershaw no longer fit: but as Maurice Helland observed in his 1956 *Yakima Sunday Herald* article, "the owner's initials still make the name appropriate."[77] Jack Nelson, who received postal updates from Pat until the early 1960s, writes that she spent several months in Arizona after leaving Goose Prairie, then moved to Geneva, Switzerland to work in the European division of Catholic Relief Services. According to letters in the Kane Family collection, Pat lived and worked at a dude ranch—Rancho de Los Caballeros—in Wickenburg, Arizona, until April 1956, then moved to Minnesota to help her brother and his family until the end of the year. Perhaps in this remote corner of Arizona she distanced herself from her family's prying questions while she worked through a period of emotional distress.[78] During this

Yakima Airport, 1954 [Kodak Kodachrome transparency] (Kershaw Family Collection). From left: Pat Kane, Isabelle Lynn, and Kay Kershaw. Inset: an undated Pavelle Color Print on Ansco Printon paper. Pat Kane's image has been removed from the small print processed from the original Kodachrome slide, neatly trimmed to 2½" × 2¼".

time, she was applying for work overseas. She received a commission to Geneva in January 1957 and left for Europe the following month. Her work entailed extensive travel to assist people displaced by World War II. After the Hungarian Revolution in late October to early November 1956, many sought asylum in Brazil. After receiving complaints from some of these refugees, the United Nations recruited Pat to investigate the situation and provide a report of her recommendations. After three months in South America, she returned to the United States, then spent an additional three months in Europe. Nelson's last mention of Pat's whereabouts suggests correctly that she had returned from Europe to live somewhere in California. She left Europe at the end of 1959, arriving in Palo Alto, California, in 1960.[79]

Oddly, Pat cropped up in a black and white spread about the Double K in a 1961 issue of the *Cincinnati Pictorial Inquirer* that included four images provided by Sunday Group Photos: "Kay takes guiding and wrangling chores," the short prefatory blurb explains, "while Pat rustles grub and tends to housekeeping." The two photos of Kay show her saddling a horse for a guest and making saddle repairs while the two of Pat show her shucking corn and serving guests.[80] In 1965, Pat's name appeared in a column by S.I. Anthon who listed her as a hostess during a book release party for Jack Nelson at the Double K Ranch: perhaps Anthon had confused her with Isabelle Lynn.[81] After moving to Palo Alto—her father and three sisters with extended families already lived there—Pat worked as a North County supervisor of Social Services for Santa Clara County until she retired in 1973. She also served as a member of Chaplaincy Services at Stanford University for sixteen years. Pat lived in Palo Alto for over three decades.[82] A poignant postscript to a 1989 letter Kay received from a Bay Area friend concludes, "Saw Pat for dinner in Palo Alto a couple of months ago. She's getting aged and has a problem with her eyesight failing but can still drive in day time. As always, she is engulfed with the family, but has, I think, more of her own spirit." Pat Kane passed away at Stanford Hospital on 21 September 1992 at the age of eighty-eight. After a memorial service three days later at Palo Alto's landmark St. Thomas Aquinas Church, her survivors transferred the remains to Tacoma, Washington, for burial in the Kane family plot.[83]

Although Pat confided with her immediate family (principally her sister Isabel and father), about her relationship with and affection for Kay Kershaw, the true nature of the nineteen years the two spent together remains an enigma for her nieces and nephews. A story has circulated among them—half-remembered, perhaps apocryphal—that Pat maintained she and William O. Douglas had been in love and that he had even proposed to her, but because the Catholic church banned re-marriage after divorce, Pat was compelled to refuse.[84] Clearly, Pat's relationship with her extended family was a priority and—as was the case for so many gays and lesbians during this era—required a plausible fiction to maintain this close connection. In a late 1987 letter to her niece, Pat wrote, "As for me and the Double K—sometime when we can touch base, I will tell you bits and pieces of it." Unfortunately, that conversation never took place.[85]

Time to Change Partners

With the exception of a summer abroad studying in Heidelberg, Germany, Isabelle Lynn (1916–1996) had lived her entire life on the east coast before she read *Of Men and Mountains* in 1950. Justice Douglas's eloquent prose about his adventures in the Cascades and the wild terrain she imagined exploring there put into stark contrast her quotidian life in Washington, D.C. Isabelle was born in Williamsport, Pennsylvania, on 4 December 1916. Her family had pre–Revolutionary War genealogies on both of her parents' sides, the kind of white, Anglo-Saxon Protestant pedigree coveted by blue-bloods in the northeastern United States, particularly during the first half of the twentieth century.[86] After graduating from Williamsport High School in 1934, she attended "a large eastern university" and lived in Silver Spring, Maryland, for ten years serving as the director of publications at Red Cross National Headquarters in Washington, D.C.[87] A sailor as well as an accomplished equestrian, Lynn maintained membership in the Maryland Hunt Club, reflecting her status as a bona fide east coast elite. Her resulting innate grace and sophistication belied the cowgirl exterior she would adopt later. A rarefied aura permeated Isabelle's bearing throughout her entire life. "Blue jeans and flannel shirts could never cover up [Isabelle's] patrician demeanor," Brad Patterson recalled. "I think Kay admired that in her."[88]

Intrigued by Douglas's writing, Isabelle and her companion, Frances Rummell, booked a week at the Double K Ranch from 29 September to 10 October 1952. "I was so overwhelmed by the Cascades," Lynn wrote in 1961, "that I could hardly imagine returning East.... I came back again the next year, and in December resigned my job … and came West to live."[89] Rather than breaking completely with the Red Cross, however, Lynn worked as a field representative for the organization in eastern Washington and Oregon from 1953 to 1955. Although no record documents a second trip in 1953, both Frances and Isabelle signed into the guest book at the Double K on 23 May 1954 with a shared address in Olympia, Washington. Along with her signature, Isabelle adds "But sooner."[90] And soon enough indeed, Isabelle left Frances to move into an apartment near Yakima's Roosevelt Elementary School later that year. She continued her work with Red Cross as a field director until relocating to Goose Prairie to help Kay run the Double K after Pat Kane's departure in October 1955.[91]

Romantic connections emerge for many—and sometimes unknowable—reasons. Did opposites attract or was there recognition by both Kay and Isabelle that an essential common bond and way in the world existed despite Kay's proud western sensibility and Isabelle's upper-crust eastern patina? If Valentine cards between the two are any gauge, Isabelle was smitten. The cover of one of them shows a maze with tiny footprints following the labyrinth to a heart, the message inside concise and clear: "at last I've found you" with Isabelle's handwritten message underneath: "I love you, darling."[92] Another asks, "Do you know who's sending you this great big Valentine kiss? You'd better!" inscribed "My love Isabelle."[93] Once Isabelle moved to Goose Prairie, she and Kay remained devoted partners until their deaths within months of each other four decades later.

Besides her expertise as an equestrian and an uncanny knack for cooking—"a hobby," in her words, "the best carrot cake I ever tasted," according to others—Isabelle contributed formidable writing skills to augment those of Justice Douglas in promoting the Double K.[94] Although Kay claimed in 1956 that her own avocations included writing for magazines, no examples of her work survive.[95] The arrival of Isabelle that summer, however, heralded an increase in the quantity and quality of Double K-focused material in print, and a decades-long mutual admiration for one another's approach to writing evolved between Lynn and Douglas. Whereas Justice Douglas adopted a more stentorian style befitting a Supreme Court Justice in his magazine pieces for the checkout-rack trade—"The mountains of the Pacific Northwest are wild, remote, and high. They have the roar of torrents and avalanches in their throats," he bellows in *Mademoiselle*—Isabelle embraced a breezier tone: "There always has to be one day when the pack string doesn't catch up and dinner gets served at midnight. We thought this was the day, for surely the trail we had taken would be a dilly to lead a pack string over." In reaction to this 1958 article for

The Dude Rancher, Justice Douglas told Kay, "It is beautifully written and a very entertaining and descriptive piece." Emulating Douglas's own style, Isabelle occasionally shaded the facts a bit: "It was over for the year, but what a trip to look back on! ... A pack trip for the dude who thinks he's seen everything! As one of our trippers put it in our guest book: 'Double K gets A for this one.'" This "tripper" was Eileen Ryan who also happened to work as an assistant wrangler for the Double K.[96] By 1959, Lynn had adopted Douglas's literary persona as a seasoned mountaineer in another spirited piece for *The Dude Rancher,* the rugged writer ready to test her mettle against the natural elements: "Optimism being characteristic of mountain people, ourselves no less, the next morning we packed up our camp and took off back to the trail junction. That day we spent riding down impossible pitches—only to have to come up again—and crawling brush."[97] These trivial pieces benefited business at the Double K by keeping the ranch's name in the public eye throughout the 1950s. But with a new decade, more important matters loomed for both the Justice and the freshly-minted mountain woman to tackle. The United States Forest Service and a changing society would present challenges far more worthy of their combined efforts.

6

Interlude: Shifting Perceptions During the Cold War

The McCarthy Era and Homosexuality

The Soviet Union's aggression in Europe after the end of World War II resulted in a stand-off on either side of the Iron Curtain and near-mass hysteria in the United States, epitomized by the rabid anti-communist miasma of Senator Joseph R. McCarthy. As the most strident member sitting on the Subcommittee on the Investigation of Loyalty of State Department Employees, McCarthy was dogged in ferreting out all subversive elements, real or imagined, from the government's rolls. In February 1950, Undersecretary of State John Peurifoy announced that he had recently fired a number of "homosexuals" from his department, setting off a furor over the security risks posed by "sexual perverts" in the government. Congressional Republicans leveraged these concerns into an attack on the Truman administration. They vilified homosexuals as emotionally unstable, morally corrupt, vulnerable to blackmail, and considered them as a threat to the moral health and security of the United States.[1] Guy George Gabrielson, National Republican Party chairman, sounded a full-throated endorsement of McCarthy and a Cold War clarion call in his first letter of 1950 to members of the Republican Party: "Perhaps as dangerous as the actual communists are the sexual perverts who have infiltrated our Government in recent years." At the end of April 1950, Republicans classified ninety-one individuals accused of "homosexual activity" as security risks and had them removed from the State Department. The Truman administration accused McCarthy and his allies of shifting from a witch-hunt for communists to one targeting gays and lesbians because their efforts were losing steam: "There is a great desire [among Republicans]," the Democratic chairman of the Senate subcommittee, Millard Tydings, told the press, "to shift from Communists to homos." An AP story a month later quoted Senate Republican leader Kenneth S. Wherry, who warned that 3,750 "sex perverts" worked for the government in Washington, D.C. They were subject to a sinister plot: "A Red fifth column is using sex degenerates for subversive purposes."[2]

Yakima's local paper was not quite so strident with its reports on the hearings, though they still read as alarmist. Robert W. Lucas, executive editor of the *Yakima Daily Republic*, addressed the Yakima Chamber of Commerce—whose membership included Kershaw and Kane—about Senator McCarthy at the end of April after attending a meeting of the American Society of Newspaper Editors in Washington, D.C. He told local business leaders, "Mr. McCarthy's whole crusade is confusing, period. His charges are reckless and thinly supported with evidence. Mr. McCarthy has found material for his crusade in the fact that homosexuals were found in the State Department and discharged. The stand against homosexuals was taken because homosexuals are a dangerous factor in the State Department."[3] Although Lucas may have found McCarthy's charges confusing, to him, the discovery of homosexuals at State provoked grave concern. In an editorial a few days later, Lucas emphasized the need to "dismiss individuals who may not be disloyal but who also may be security risks just the same. These would include homosexuals who may be blackmailed into disclosing confidential information."[4]

This editorial piece combined with the terse and brutish discourse in the *New York Times* and AP's national wire speaks volumes about the perception of homosexuality all across post-war America: that gays and lesbians engaged in a perverse and nefarious lifestyle subject to exploitation by Communist agents. Their activities therefore constituted a threat to the security of the United States, equivalent to any Soviet aggression, a viewpoint that illustrates how attitudes falling within the realm of acceptable social conduct in one period can morph into the perception of sickness and dangerous anti-social behavior in another. This oscillation in regard to emotional desires, creation of sexual categories, and the definition of mental illness was especially profound between the end of the Depression and the start of the Cold War era. Gays and lesbians faced a formidable bank of enemies simultaneously during this period in social, scientific, religious, and legal realms.[5]

Men made up the lion's share of those reporting on national issues in the middle decades of the twentieth century with a male-oriented, patriarchal perspective permeating the way society in the United States received a common body of accepted facts. Not surprisingly, a masculine bias toward homosexuality colors any discussion of gay and lesbian issues during this period. For these newsmen, the observation of how gay men present differently from straight men and the conceptualization about how they would interact sexually was comprehensible from their point of view: aspects of lesbianism, on the other hand, were not. They had barely a clue about lesbian groups within their community or even the ways in which lesbians associated with one another. From a heteronormative viewpoint, gay men appeared more socially and sexually deviant than lesbian women and thus became portrayed that way in the general culture. For this reason, gay men received the brunt of societal condemnation and discrimination from law enforcement, jurists, and legislators alike. Once discovered, lesbians seemed no less pernicious, but with the need for women in the workforce during World War II, as a whole a more accommodating view prevailed. In the military, female applicants who displayed masculine characteristics could pass the psychological exam prior to induction because the armed services needed women who wanted to perform work traditionally associated with men. Conversely, the examiners would have disqualified an effeminate male enlistee.[6]

Whether lesbian or straight, women could experience adventure and find a place in the workforce during the war years that otherwise would have excluded them. Female independence from the strictures of a patriarchal society was, in short, one positive aspect of the tragedy of war. A 1943 cartoon that ran nationally in newspapers illustrates this notion. A woman of Amazonian proportions, clad in coveralls and grasping a lunch-pail and ball-peen hammer, strides off to work with "her own man's-size pay envelope" stuck in her tool pouch. Standing at the front door, her tiny, apron-clad husband holds a broom and frying pan in one hand and gesticulates with the other, shouting, "but remember, you gotta come right back as soon as the war is over!" Grinning over her shoulder, his wife replies, "Oh yeah?"[7] The female worker in this image is a metaphorical genie, finally released from the imprisonment of her societal bottle. Getting her back inside that bottle as GIs returned home proved to be a post-war conundrum.

The immediate post-war era, however, brought a significant societal change for women. The social freedom and economic independence enjoyed by the women who had served in the military or in the workforce now clashed with the mores of a previous era, many considering their wartime behavior threatening to the traditional, pre-war social order. The lenient policies of the military toward homosexuals during the war years went through a significant transformation as the war wound down. The armed forces delivered dishonorable discharges to thousands of gays and lesbians, loaded them onto transport ships, and dropped them at the nearest United States port. Many of these now-besmirched individuals felt that a return home would be impossible. Some simply decided to remain where they landed bolstering gay and lesbian enclaves in New York City, San Francisco, Los Angeles, and Boston. This led to the establishment of a larger gay and lesbian subculture in the United States. Creating nurturing enclaves in urban centers, the gay and lesbian communities offered comfort and support while individuals navigated the oppressive American conformist culture that arose during the Cold War era.[8]

As men mustered out of the military and returned to civilian jobs and home life, women, in particular those who now preferred to operate independently, impeded expectations of a return to "normalcy." The pre-war idealization of a traditional hearth and home became the symbol of American values and the very manifestation of nationalism and anti-communist identity. The transmogrification of lesbianism's anti-establishment independence into a psychosis or sickness proved to be a useful method for isolating such women from a society preoccupied with conformity. The post-war school of Freudian psychoanalysis found that homosexuality, or "disturbed sexuality," could always be traced to a mild mental illness, or neurosis. If untreated, or if it became severe, these psychiatrists believed it could develop into a full-blown psychosis, impairing a patient's connection to reality. Therefore, some felt justified in managing homosexuality as if it were a symptom of an illness, treatable and curable. In Freudian psychology, neurosis could take the form of an incapacity for achieving any kind of personal happiness or satisfaction from life. Thus, any psychological problems a gay or lesbian patient might express in treatment could be categorized as manifestations of their homosexual perversity rather than of the garden-variety difficulties found among members of the general population. The American Psychiatric Association continued to include homosexuality on its list of mental disorders up until 1973.[9]

The return to a pre–World War II status quo became the lodestone for American society in the 1950s. In this milieu, psychoanalysts willingly promoted heterosexuality by curing those afflicted with the neurosis of homosexuality. Popular magazines reported on the scientific approach to curing gays and lesbians through psychoanalysis, often adopting the very language and attitudes of the psychiatrists and printing the medical literature's own tales of murder, suicide, and seduction of the innocent. These salacious notions proved intriguing and soon found their way into trade magazines and pulp novels.[10] The steady barrage of negative press coverage reinforced the notion that homosexuals were unreliable and damaged.

For rural lesbians such as Kay Kershaw, Pat Kane, and Isabelle Lynn, who lacked the community support found in large urban centers, the post-war public perception of homosexuality as a mental illness and a national security issue—now the received wisdom throughout American society—demanded an even greater level of secrecy. This required a clandestine existence and a place to hide in privacy in order to camouflage an important part of one's life at all times.[11] Fortunately for Kay, Pat, and Isabelle, they managed to conjure the perfect cover: "spinster" cowgirls operating a dude ranch in the small hamlet of Goose Prairie, Washington, population ten.[12] No direct evidence links the proprietors of the Double K Ranch to lesbian communities regionally or nationally: the three of them were quite circumspect in what they confided and to whom. But such lack of documentation does not mean they were cut off and isolated. Guest books and photo albums spanning almost half a century indicate that the "Double K girls" offered a nurturing community in this quiet oasis for women across a wide spectrum of gender orientations. As one guest at an all-female weekend exclaimed, "Hurray for womanhood!!"[13]

William O. Douglas and the Supreme Court

From the outset of his career on the bench, William O. Douglas advocated for the individual rights of the disadvantaged and dispossessed. His opinion in the case of *Skinner v. Oklahoma* (1942), in which the state of Oklahoma mandated sterilization for habitual criminals, formed the genesis of his legal philosophy. Focusing his insight on the due process and equal protection clauses of the Fourteenth Amendment, Justice Douglas wrote that the Oklahoma law did not apply equally to all felons because it allowed an exception for embezzlers. He identified the right to procreate as fundamental, and argued that any legislation restricting that right would be subject to strict legal scrutiny. This strict judicial scrutiny test set the standard for due process and equal protection analysis from that point forward, a potent tool in advocating for the rights of the disenfranchised and disempowered.[14] These issues were of particular interest to Douglas who grew up poor and had a great deal of empathy for those who suffered discrimination based on their economic and social status. From early on, he sympathized with gays and lesbians who were commonly marginalized within general society. Douglas first encountered a gay man as a student at Whitman College in Walla Walla, Washington, an individual who "expressed his sexual interest in an unmistakable way. I pushed him away and left, and I avoided him thereafter. I was not angry, I was only sad."[15] As an adult pursuing his career in Washington, D.C., at the SEC and subsequently on the Supreme Court, he encountered other gay men and realized the extent to which homosexuals as a class faced harassment by governmental institutions. Noting that the District of Columbia hired a staff to patrol parks and men's rooms in an effort to induce solicitation, Douglas used Washington, D.C., police tactics to illustrate his dissent in *Osborn v. United States* (1966): "Peepholes in men's rooms are there to catch homosexuals."[16] A similar situation involved Walter Jenkins, an aide to President Lyndon Johnson, whom the authorities caught having sexual contact with another man at a YMCA near the White House. Johnson summarily forced him out of government service. This had a profound impact on Justice Douglas who often mentioned the incident. Douglas's fourth wife, Cathy Douglas Stone, recalled the Justice saying on many occasions, "Can you imagine someone on the police force actually hanging out in public toilets? What do they say to their children when they say 'Daddy, what did you do today?'"[17]

Douglas considered homosexuality a part of the "tapestry of life," in Douglas Stone's words, since "he had many friends over the years" who were gay.[18] He was equally at ease with lesbians as with gay men before he ever met Kay Kershaw and Pat Kane. In his autobiography, Douglas lists a few of the New Deal Democrats whom he particularly admired, among them Frances Perkins (1880–1965), Franklin Roosevelt's Secretary of Labor from 1933 to 1945. Perkins was part of the circle of lesbian friends—couples such as suffragists Nancy Cook and Marion Dickerson; Elizabeth Fisher Read and Esther Lape; and activist friends Molly Dewson and Mary Dreier and their respective partners—with whom Eleanor Roosevelt socialized in the capital. As First Lady, she had pressed President Roosevelt to appoint Perkins to the Labor post. Perkins, who was married to an invalid husband, also maintained a romantic relationship—and subsequently lived together in Washington, D.C.—with Mary Harriman Rumsey, founder of The Junior League. Eleanor herself was involved romantically with Lorena "Hick" Hickok, an American journalist.[19] As a confidante and friend to both Eleanor and Franklin, Justice Douglas would have been acquainted with some—if not all—of these women as well.[20]

At the time, sodomy laws rendered particular sexual activities—usually defined as oral and anal sex—between same-sex couples illegal in all forty-eight states. In theory, these "crimes against nature" statutes applied to everyone although they were rarely enforced against heterosexuals. The Supreme Court was reluctant to determine the constitutionality of any case that dealt with aspects of sexuality whether they were sodomy laws, or laws relating to gender equality or interracial marriage. The first case involving questions of homosexuality did not reach the court until 1958 in *ONE, Inc. v. Olesen*. The plaintiff, *ONE*, was a magazine written for a homosexual readership and, as with many other publications, delivered via the United States Post Office. The government held that the content of this magazine was obscene and therefore constituted a violation of federal law against the distribution of such material through the mail. By accepting this case, the Supreme Court started on the path to clarifying the definition of homosexuality. Is it behavioral? Is it an illness? Does it define a national menace, a criminal activity, or does it simply designate another minority group? The court's ruling in *ONE, Inc.* hinged on determining whether homosexual content in and of itself renders a publication obscene. In deciding for the plaintiff, the Court ruled that a homosexual magazine did not automatically equate to obscenity even as the federal government virulently persecuted gays and lesbians in the civil service and the military.[21]

ONE, Inc. represented a landmark decision in jurisprudence affirming the right to free speech for the gay and lesbian community. Justice Douglas played a key role in this case as a result of his dissent in an earlier decision, *Roth v. United States* (1957). In determining First Amendment protection of previously unprotected obscene material, the Court defined "obscene" as material that appealed to the "prurient interests" of the average person applying contemporary community standards: the majority opinion defined "prurient" as eliciting "lascivious desire or thought." In his dissent, Douglas wrote that the government had no standing to determine whether a given piece of literature provoked lustful thoughts: "the arousing of sexual thoughts and desires happens every day in normal life in dozens of ways."[22] In other words, these "lustful thoughts" were individual, internal, and thus a matter of privacy. Another case before the Supreme Court, *MANual Enterprises, Inc. v. Day* (1962), reaffirmed the prior decision in *One, Inc.* that magazines aimed at a gay readership were not in and of themselves obscene. Crucial in this decision was the notion that obscenity standards should be no different for magazines targeting a gay and lesbian audience than for those aimed at heterosexuals.[23]

A third case, *Rosenberg v. Fleuti* (1963), brought significant questions before the court concerning government policies that labeled homosexuality as a mental illness and a psychosis and categorized homosexuals as sexual perverts with psychopathic personalities.[24] Three years later, Douglas questioned the constitutionality of the government's use of the vague phrase "psychopathic personality" in defining homosexuality in his dissent in *Boutilier v. Immigration and Naturalization Service* (1967). In their thorough research for *Courting Justice,* Joyce Murdoch and Deb Price unearthed the original version of Douglas's dissent, in which one particular line alludes to his close relationship of nearly two decades with Kay Kershaw. "The homosexual is one," he wrote, "who but for the grace of God, might be almost anyone," before changing the phrasing to define the homosexual as one "who, by some freak, is the product of arrested development." This "freak-of-nature" notion was more in keeping with prevailing attitudes. However, Douglas cites throughout his decision the precedent-breaking research of Alfred Kinsey. In his 1948 bestseller, *Sexual Behavior in the Human Male*, Kinsey upended the common view in the United States that homosexuality was an anomaly. He also cites David Abrahamsen's book on criminality in which the author describes the duality of sexual identity: "One may within certain limits say that the homosexual is an individual who really belongs to the opposite sex. All people have originally bisexual tendencies which are more or less developed." It is interesting to note that on the page following the one cited by Douglas here, Abrahamsen writes that homosexuality was more common among women than among men. As Murdoch and Price point out, Douglas's dissent in *Boutilier*, although lacking in many respects, still expressed the rights of gays and lesbians more cogently than any other Supreme Court document written prior to 1985.[25]

These four cases played a crucial role in getting the issue of equal rights for gays and lesbians before the Court. However, the pivotal concept for future LGBTQ+ legislation evolved from Justice Douglas's opinion in *Griswold v. Connecticut* (1965). Although this was just one item out of his vast body of work—according to Bruce Allen Murphy, Douglas authored 1,164 legal opinions, 486 dissents, thirty-two books, 200 articles, and over 900 speeches, more than any other member of the Supreme Court—none has had greater impact on American jurisprudence.[26] *Griswold* challenged the constitutionality under the Fourteenth Amendment (due process and equal protection) of an 1879 Connecticut state law banning "any drug, medicinal article or instrument for the purpose of preventing conception." In 1961, a Yale gynecologist, C. Lee Buxton, opened a family-planning clinic in New Haven with Estelle Griswold, head of Planned Parenthood in Connecticut in direct violation of this statute. The police raided the clinic on 10 November 1961, arresting Buxton and Griswold. They were charged, convicted, and fined for aiding and abetting a crime: the state's higher courts upheld their convictions. The Supreme Court determined that the state of Connecticut's ban on the use of contraceptives—or even counseling about their use—contravened the right to privacy of married couples in violation of the Constitution. Writing for the majority, Douglas argued that the Bill of Rights—specifically the First Amendment (free speech), the Third Amendment (prohibition on the forced quartering of troops), the Fourth Amendment (freedom from search and seizure), the Fifth Amendment (freedom from self-incrimination), and the Ninth Amendment (the people retain rights even though not specifically enumerated) when viewed through the Fourteenth Amendment creates a right to privacy upon which the government must not intrude. He maintained that the specific guarantees found in the Bill of Rights have "penumbras" or shadows emanating from them that "help give them life and substance."²⁷ Although the concept of penumbral law as applied to the Constitution existed before Douglas's tenure on the Supreme Court, he was its most articulate interpreter. Prior to *Griswold v. Connecticut*, Douglas incorporated the notion of penumbra into his written decisions and dissents eight times.²⁸ In 1965, Douglas employed this evocative conflation of Plato's allegory of the cave with the image of Mt. Adams looming over the Yakima Valley to conceptualize the magisterial might of the Bill of Rights casting its aura over people all across the country, from a small family-planning clinic in Connecticut to a dude ranch in Goose Prairie.²⁹

Douglas's opinion in *Griswold* produced a long shadow. Almost immediately, gay and lesbian communities seized on its implications. In San Francisco, the Daughters of Bilitis (DOB)—established in 1955 and the nation's first lesbian rights group—connected the *Griswold* decision with their own advocacy for an individual's right to sexual privacy in early 1966. In their newsletter report on a speaker who argued that state laws prohibiting homosexual activity were unconstitutional, the editors cited specifically the Supreme Court's recent ruling on anti-contraceptive laws in *Griswold*. As predicted—DOB estimated it would take twenty to thirty years of legal challenges—this theory advanced by increments.³⁰ In *Eisenstadt v. Baird* (1972), the Court extended the right to privacy afforded married couples to unmarried persons under the equal protection clause of the Fourteenth Amendment. The combined arguments in *Griswold* and *Eisenstadt* provided precedents in *Roe v. Wade* (1973), affirming the right of women to seek an abortion through the first trimester based on the due process clause of the Fourteenth Amendment.³¹ Douglas's writing in *Griswold* finally had its greatest impact with Justice Anthony Kennedy's opinion in *Lawrence v. Texas* (2003). The Court affirmed the notion promoted by DOB four decades prior, that a Texas law criminalizing sexual relations between two members of the same sex was unconstitutional under the equal protection clause of the Fourteenth

By the campfire, ca. 1960 (Kershaw Family Collection). Standing: William O. Douglas (left) and Kay Kershaw; seated: unknown.

Amendment. Citing *Griswold* as "the most pertinent beginning point" for scrutinizing an individual's right to privacy, Kennedy incorporates Douglas's imagining of the Bill of Rights: "*Eisenstadt* contains well known dictum relating to the 'right to privacy,' but this referred to the right recognized in *Griswold*—a right penumbral to the *specific* [sic] guarantees in the Bill of Rights, and not a 'substantive due process' right."[32] Justice Kennedy once again cited *Griswold* in his opinion in *Obergefell v. Hodges* (2015), ruling that the fundamental right to marriage is guaranteed for couples of the same sex under the due process and the equal protection clauses of the Fourteenth Amendment.[33]

The *Yakima Herald-Republic* concluded its extensive coverage of Justice Douglas's death in January 1980 with a begrudging assessment of his legacy: "His legal output was vast, but few of his many opinions had achieved the status of landmarks."[34] That assessment is hard to square with the significance of *Griswold v. Connecticut* in the intervening four and a half decades. Few would have predicted that Douglas's opinion in *Griswold* would have instigated such a monumental sea-change in LGBTQ+ rights in 2015, and, after lying unchallenged for over half a century, become a stalking horse for an ultra-right-wing faction of the Republican party as well as the Supreme Court itself in 2022. As of this writing, conservative justices now form a super-majority on the bench, adhering to a strict reading of the original language of the Constitution. In October 2022, newly-appointed Justice Ketanji Brown Jackson formulated a liberal riposte to the originalism espoused by this group, foreshadowing renewed debate over *Obergefell v. Hodges* and, ultimately, the foundational precepts of *Griswold*.[35]

Writing in 2001—two years prior to *Lawrence* and fourteen prior to *Obergefell*—Murdoch and Price acknowledged that the "well-adjusted" relationship between Kay Kershaw and Isabelle Lynn may have influenced Douglas's attitude toward homosexuality,[36] even more so given his own fractured marriages. But in retrospect, it is now clear that the two of them offered much more than a tangential example coloring Douglas's view on gays and lesbians: they represented a paradigm that precipitated a fundamental shift from 1965 to 2022 in the nation's understanding and interpretation of the Bill of Rights, the very cornerstone of American democracy.

7

Cougar Lakes Wilderness—
The First Decade (1958–1968)

Prologue

Kay Kershaw and Isabelle Lynn passed away within just a few months of each other in 1996, Kay at the age of eighty-nine, Isabelle at seventy-nine. For nearly half of their adult lives, each of them focused on preserving the environs around Bumping Lake in the form of a Cougar Lakes wilderness. Throughout the era described in the previous chapter, fraught as it was with overt conservatism and anti–LGBTQ+ sentiment—especially virulent in eastern Washington—Kay and Isabelle forfeited all claim to privacy in their very open and public passion for the land. They understood they were living through an inflection point: old-growth forests and wilderness areas were imperiled, potentially forever, by the USFS's unbridled policies and hubris which threatened everything the Double K Ranch owners held dear.

In contrast to Carl Dunrud's Double D Ranch in Wyoming, where riders could roam free across 3,500 privately-owned acres as well as bordering access to nearly 2.25 million additional acres in Yellowstone National Park, the Double K Mountain Ranch sat on a comparatively meager 10-acre parcel inside a Goose Prairie subdivision. Fortunately, the Snoqualmie National Forest and access to the Pacific Crest Trail, the Goat Rocks, Mt. Rainier National Park, and Mt. Adams surrounded the Double K [see maps 1 and 2]. In the early years of its operation, the setting seemed remote, vast, and inviolable with almost unlimited capacity for pack trips through untrammeled natural settings. However, the situation devolved rapidly. "Five years ago," Isabelle Lynn wrote in 1961, "our eyes were opened to the fact that this area is *not* [sic] sacrosanct. The Forest Service, with no word to anyone, made a large timber sale six miles down the Bumping River from us. They took a beautiful stand of Ponderosa pine, built a road almost to the top of American Ridge, ruining a beautiful summer trail up Fife Creek, and left behind an unbelievable shambles of down trees and half-burned slash, side-hills deeply rutted and eroded by bulldozers, and thousands of damaged young trees."[1] This wake-up call galvanized Kershaw, Lynn, and William O. Douglas into action for the protection of the Goose Prairie environs. The three of them became vehement environmental activists in the 1960s.

The trio's joint advocacy for wilderness has been well-documented and justly praised. Indeed, it is now conventional wisdom that Justice Douglas roused the environmental movement in Washington State from the mid-1950s to the 1970s, organizing activists on all levels locally, regionally, and nationally.[2] Douglas knew how to "speak Eastern" (along with Lynn) to well-placed individuals in the bastions of power, and his stature as a Supreme Court Justice lent tremendous weight to his advocacy.[3] But this championing for the cause did not happen of its own accord. He and his two Bumping Lake neighbors stood on the shoulders of other Yakima area residents whose efforts preceded—and subsequently bolstered—theirs as part of a much wider coalition of like-minded advocates. These local predecessors paved the way for the Goose Prairie cohort, working just as hard as they did for the preservation of the Cascade mountains.

Whipsawed by the fits and starts of establishing a wilderness area at Bumping Lake, Kay and Isabelle devoted over a quarter of a century to the environmental movement in Washington State. To understand the complexities of this project and why it consumed their energy for so long requires an appreciation of environmentalism's history in the Pacific Northwest and the effect it had on the effort during the latter half of the twentieth century to shepherd a seemingly straight-forward piece of legislation through thirteen sessions of Congress and seven Presidential administrations. Lamenting the contentious and protracted fight that had consumed the better part of her time and energy for twenty-eight years, Kay told the *Seattle Post-Intelligencer* in 1989, "We fought for decades to save [the wilderness]. Sometimes that didn't make us too popular around here."[4]

Birth of Environmentalism

In the United States at the turn of the last century, a split between those promoting preservation of wilderness and those favoring conservation—in the now-outmoded sense of conserving resources for sustainable exploitation—created a philosophical dispute over the use of public lands where stores of timber and minerals, once considered inexhaustible, were shrinking. The establishment of a series of National Parks—Yellowstone in 1872, Yosemite in 1890, and Mt. Rainier in 1899—blurred this late-nineteenth-century schism. The new parks were economically worthless for resource extraction, but perhaps valuable as tourist destinations with potential for future economic growth. The revolutionary concept of economic value inherent in a tract of land, protected for its own sake, proved a boon to preservationists. Advocates for saving scenic lands could justify the establishment of wilderness areas based on the very arguments made by conservation proponents on the other side of the issue. However, this notion remained a hard sell in the early twentieth century. Most communities considered mining and logging more tangible economic drivers than a nebulous faith in the nation's nascent tourist industry.

With Yosemite and Yellowstone parks established, President Benjamin Harrison signed the Forest Reserve Act of 1891, setting aside 13 million acres of forest land all across the American West to deter an increase in illegal resource extraction and rampant land speculation. The Act also allowed a president to increase protected acreage unilaterally, thereby encouraging Harrison to create the Pacific Forest Reserve in 1893. This reserve centered on the crest of the Washington Cascades in an area forty-two miles long and thirty-six miles wide embracing the bulk of Mt. Rainier and most of the Triangle. In 1899, President William McKinley authorized Mt. Rainier National Park and the Rainier National Forest on contiguous lands beyond the park's borders. A McKinley appointee, professional forester Gifford Pinchot, assumed responsibility for this new tract as the head of the nation's Division of Forestry. Under Theodore Roosevelt's administration, Pinchot lobbied to have forest reserves such as the Rainier transferred from the Department of the Interior to the newly-created United States Forest Service (USFS) within the Department of Agriculture in 1905. Roosevelt and Pinchot shared a common belief in the policy of conservation premised on the judicious use of the nation's natural resources through government management. Individuals like John Muir opposed this concept: he advocated for the preservation of America's remaining undeveloped lands as a bulwark against an increasingly urbanized and industrialized society.[5]

Pinchot's policies emphasized multiple use of USFS land and a sustained yield from its forest products. By the early part of the twentieth century, an expanded USFS administered some 150 million acres of unclaimed timberland, withdrawn from the public domain ostensibly to protect watersheds and prevent indiscriminate mining and logging. Although touted as stewards of the land, USFS promoted grazing rights for sheep and cattle, logging, construction of water-power facilities, mining, and developing recreational sites. Pinchot's directives concerning these activities prioritized the needs of local industries.[6]

In 1916, Congress created the National Park Service (NPS) to administer the national parks with a mandate to preserve their scenic beauty. NPS assumed stewardship of any new parks or wildlands transferred from land under USFS jurisdiction thus creating conflict with Pinchot's utilitarian Forest Service. And USFS administrators worked hard to defend "their" territory. As tourism grew in the 1920s and more people visited the national parks, NPS gained the reputation as the government agency best-suited to administer not only scenic areas but also sites of historic and archaeological significance. Late to the game, USFS argued that it could match NPS in providing recreational facilities—roads, camping areas, picnic spots—in addition to regulating resource extraction on public lands. USFS proposed designating primitive areas, a classification setting aside scenic lands under its jurisdiction, and managing them for their wilderness values. The 1929 regulation for creating such primitive areas, however, did not prohibit USFS from allowing grazing, logging, and road construction within them. Nebulous directives and minimal support from regional USFS employees led to more precise and restrictive regulations in the 1930s.[7] During this period, two significant sections of USFS land in Washington

State received primitive area status: the Goat Rocks in 1931, with 44,500 acres in the Triangle (expanded to 77,440 acres in 1935), and the North Cascades, encompassing 801,000 acres. The latter combined and enlarged the Glacier Peak and Whatcom Primitive Areas into one region extending north from the Stehekin River drainage to the Canadian border just east of Mt. Baker.[8]

These changes coincided with a national upheaval caused by the Great Depression. In response, Congress passed President Franklin Roosevelt's Economy Act of 1933. The legislation slashed government spending and granted Roosevelt limited powers to reorganize executive branch agencies into a more cohesive and efficient entity. This was of timely benefit for NPS. Between 1933 and 1935, the agency more than doubled in size with the transfer of battlefields, historical sites, cemeteries, and national monuments to its purview from other federal departments. NPS also gained responsibility for emergency relief, public works projects, and the development of national recreational planning.[9] The exigencies of the Depression forced USFS to consolidate as well. As part of this process, the agency dissolved the Rainier National Forest District in 1933, transferring jurisdiction of the areas within the Triangle to management by the Snoqualmie National Forest District.[10]

The passage of the Park, Parkway, and Recreational Area Study Act of 1936 expanded the role of NPS in drafting policy for the use of public lands and facilities all across the United States. The agency focused to a large extent on the Pacific Northwest, recommending in late 1937 the creation of a single magnificent national park comprising nearly the entire Cascade range in Washington State—an area of some 5,000 square miles including Mt. Adams, Mt. St. Helens, Mt. Rainier, Glacier Peak, and Mt. Baker. Immediate and vehement opposition to this high Cascades national park poured forth from logging and mining companies as well as local businesses and concerned citizens. They argued that such a park would lock up the state's natural resources and destroy local economies in the depths of the Depression. USFS joined forces with the opposition because the creation of this park would mean the transfer of enormous parcels of land out of the agency's jurisdiction.[11]

In 1939, a group of business leaders, alarmed by this proposed park, formed an advisory panel as an adjunct of the Washington State Planning Council to study the NPS proposal. It is no surprise that the advisory panel's recommendation to the governor categorically disapproved of the creation of more national parks out of USFS lands along the Cascade crest. The group emphasized the importance of the USFS multiple-use principles already in place, thus assuring the continued practice of industrial resource extraction. For proponents of wilderness, the report outlined a stark scenario: no further lands in the Cascades converted into national parks; timber on public lands managed to provide an uninterrupted supply of forest products; prospecting and mining continued and encouraged; government agencies and private industry cooperating in the construction of roads throughout the Cascades; and grazing areas left open for the use of domestic animals.[12] By 1941, suffering from a lack of widespread public support in Washington State, the high

Cascades national park proposal collapsed. World War II curtailed further discussion about national parks as more pressing issues consumed the nation. Logging on public lands increased due to demand from the government during the early years of the war. The Sustained Yield Management Act of 1944 allowed USFS to sign agreements with the logging industry and local communities to ensure a continuous flow of lumber.[13] This cooperation continued after the war as well.

Growth of Environmentalism After World War II

The United States experienced an unprecedented population surge in the postwar years coupled with renewed economic growth. A resulting nation-wide housing boom in the early 1950s increased the demand for timber cut from USFS lands. At the same time, sweeping cultural changes were afoot in America with the rise of a new generation who valued wilderness as a benefit to outdoor lifestyles rather than as a storehouse for commercial exploitation. As a result, memberships swelled at the Sierra Club, the Wilderness Society, the Mountaineers, the Cascadians, and other similar organizations. A growing number of wilderness advocates began to question the USFS multiple-use policy which implied managing resources such as timber, rangelands, recreation, minerals, and wildlife equally, but in fact clearly favored logging over the preservation of wild and primitive areas. The aggressive management style of Richard McArdle, USFS Chief Forester from 1952 to 1962, epitomized this notion. Hoping to run his agency at a profit, McArdle relegated wilderness concerns to the backburner while increasing logging and road construction in conjunction with private industry.[14] His tenure led to increased friction between USFS and NPS as well as scrutiny and criticism in the press. McArdle's administration refused to transfer land to the Park Service, denied access to NPS personnel who were analyzing public land under USFS jurisdiction for potential wilderness, and ignored correspondence between the two agencies on the subject.[15]

A series of decisions by McArdle's USFS in the mid–1950s alarmed those who valued wilderness in the Pacific Northwest. In 1954, the agency proposed constructing a road around Clear Lake at the western end of Rimrock Lake with an extension up the North Fork of the Tieton River toward the eastern edge of the Goat Rocks Wild Area.[16] The following year, USFS redrew the boundaries of Oregon's Three Sisters Primitive Area to allow more logging access with only the very highest sections of ice and rock left as wilderness. In 1956, the agency proposed a similar plan for Washington's Glacier Peak Primitive Area. This proposal involved logging roads and timber cutting in untouched regions of the Stehekin Valley, the Agnes Creek drainage, and Cascade Pass. Sandwiched between Three Sisters to the south and Glacier Peak to the north, wilderness advocates living near Yakima County's side of Goat Rocks galvanized to push back before the region's wilderness disappeared forever.

During this period, the Cascadians organized opposition to USFS policies in association with the Mountaineers, Mazamas, the Wilderness Society, and the Sierra Club. In the 1930s, the Yakima group had already made common cause with these other environmental organizations. At the request of Mazamas, the Cascadians joined the Federation of Western Outdoor Clubs (FWOC), a consortium focused primarily on preservation of wilderness areas in the American West. Early Cascadian newsletters featured articles touting the ethics of these associated groups and the Cascadian masthead proudly proclaimed its FWOC membership.[17] Having disbanded during World War II, the Cascadians reorganized in 1948 under the guidance of Curtiss Gilbert's sons, Cragg and Bruce, along with local climbers Lex Maxwell and Louis Ulrich. As experienced pioneers of mountaineering and skiing in the Cascades before the war, these Yakima residents reacted with alarm to the encroachment of logging further into the Cascades under the USFS mandate during and immediately after the war years.[18] Many Cascadians were also early members of the Seattle-based North Cascades Conservation Council (NCCC). Among them was Chuck Hessey, a long-time Naches resident and groundbreaking ski mountaineer. For nearly two decades, he was eastern Washington's prime mover in the fight to preserve wilderness in the Cascades.

Chuck Hessey, Jr.

Charles D. (Chuck or, to his close friends, Chas) Hessey, Jr. (1908–1989), was born in Yakima and began skiing as a youngster. In the 1920s, he started visiting Clarence Truitt's Gold Hill cabin to reconnoiter ski terrain near Chinook Pass. This sport became his life-long infatuation. Chuck attended SCW from 1926 to 1928 then worked for his father at Roslyn Fuel Company in Yakima and as a surveyor for Cascade Lumber Company for some twelve years. He spent four winters living at Truitt's cabin in the late 1930s where he met Marion Monter. The two became legendary companions in the development of skiing in Washington State, eventually marrying in 1954. Chuck served with the United States Army during World War II distributing medical supplies in India and Burma. Returning to Naches after the war, Chuck resumed his forays to the Gold Hill cabin and ski explorations of Washington State's backcountry. Around 1947, Truitt's health began to deteriorate and he could no longer handle the cabin's maintenance. He transferred ownership to a group of fifteen people among whom were Chuck Hessey, Marion Monter, Elon J. Gilbert, and Curtiss Gilbert's sons Mark, Bruce, and Cragg. Truitt died soon after, and responsibility for the cabin's upkeep and operation passed to Chuck and Marion.[19]

Earlier than most other residents of Washington State, Chuck and Marion realized the existential threat USFS policies posed to the Cascade wilderness. Chuck had backpacked and ski toured extensively throughout the Cascades both winter and summer from his youth. He pioneered skiing in the Goat Rocks, making one five-day trip up the North Fork of the Tieton River to McCall Basin in 1945; he and Bruce

7. Cougar Lakes Wilderness—The First Decade (1958–1968)

Gilbert made the first ski descent down the eventual site of White Pass Ski Area in 1952. He enjoyed in particular the Lyman Lake region, part of the Glacier Peak Primitive Area near Stehekin. In 1946, Chuck spent five weeks skiing in the upper Stehekin Valley, then three more weeks exploring the environs around Lyman Lake. The following two years, he made successive three-week trips into Lyman Lake in the spring. Marion accompanied him on another ski trip there in 1956.[20]

As USFS piled one devastation onto the next from 1954 through 1956—especially the logging road up the North Fork of the Tieton River and the proposed timber cutting operations at Three Sisters and Glacier Peak—Chuck resolved to advocate for the region's vulnerable wilderness, excoriating the Forest Service at every turn.

Spurred into action by his dogged opposition to USFS policies, he served as president of the Cascadians in 1956. In block text on the frontispiece of the club's first full-length annual, Chuck excerpted the Club's By-Laws espousing the promotion of the Pacific Northwest and Washington State and the preservation of its forests and wilderness. In addition, he affirmed the club's affiliation with other like-minded organizations.[21] Hessey served as the Cascadians' Conservation Committee chairman from 1958 to 1969 as well as on the NCCC board of directors and in various other capacities for the group from its inception in 1957 to 1974.[22]

Chuck was also an avid photographer and filmmaker. He carried his bulky 16-mm movie camera and film cannisters into the backcountry to document trips he made as an assistant leader with Truitt's Yakima Boy Scout troop, on his ski excursions, and in various other outdoor activities in

Charles (Chuck) Hessey, Jr., ca. 1960 (Yakima Valley Museum). Charles Hessey (1908–1989) was a pioneering ski mountaineer in the Cascades and a dedicated environmentalist active with the Cascadians and NCCC from the mid-1950s to the mid-1970s. He was also a professional photographer and filmmaker.

the mountains from the mid-1930s through 1971. He filmed many of his pioneering ski tours into Lyman Lake and the Goat Rocks, now considered important primary sources for the history of Pacific Northwest ski mountaineering. In the 1950s, Chuck shifted the focus of his documentary skills to saving Washington State's threatened wilderness areas. With Marion as co-producer—as well as porter for camping gear and extra film—Chuck shot footage showcasing the beauty of Glacier Peak, the Pasayten, and the North Cascades, often with his own narration calling for preservation of Washington's wild and scenic lands. He and Marion traveled throughout the Pacific Northwest to lecture and screen the films. In 1958, he collaborated with David Brower of the Sierra Club to produce "Wilderness Alps of the Stehekin," a successful publicity piece instrumental in the establishment of the North Cascades National Park.[23]

Hessey was curmudgeonly, parochial, infuriatingly opinionated, and, unfortunately, prone to writing racially biased and anti-Semitic screeds to the local newspaper as he got older. He penned a vicious rebuttal to the Rev. Jesse Boyd's 1968 guest editorial on the Black Power movement and the legacy of slavery, upbraiding the Reverend Boyd for his "un-Christian" attitude.[24] In the 1980s, he had a running feud in the letters to the editor section with local educators (and others) over the Holocaust.[25] Apparently, this was part of his worldview from early on. In a disconcerting comment from a report about a Cascadians ski trip to Gold Hill in 1940, Bill Hassell facetiously refers to "the president of the Gold Hill Chamber of Commerce Chas. Hessey (Alias Gold Hill Goebels [sic])."[26] By April 1940 (and year-end publication of this Cascadians pamphlet), the entire world knew about Goebbels' hatred of the Jews through his prominent and well-documented role in the *Kristallnacht* pogrom throughout Germany on 9 to 10 November 1938. So, Hassell's cavalier use of Goebbels' name in connection with Hessey cannot be dismissed easily. In Europe, anti-Semitism was rife in skiing: Nordic, Germanic, and Slavic people considered the sport their domain from the turn of the nineteenth century.[27] Chuck's own Bible studies reinforced his anti-Semitic notions. He wrote a fourteen-page manifesto, "Food for Wondering Minds," in which he argues that a worldwide Jewish plot based in the Soviet Union—a variation on the infamous *Protocols of the Elders of Zion*—intended to eliminate Christianity: the new Zion would arise in North America led by white Christians of Anglo-Saxon ancestry.[28] Chuck refused to accept any criticism of his viewpoint, whether from his friend, Cragg D. Gilbert ("Dear Cragg: A Nazi is a member of the National Socialist party—and that I ain't. You must learn to be more exact in your defamatory pigeon-holing") or from the nationally-known broadcast evangelist Garner Ted Armstrong who wrote:

> Your anti-Jewish prejudice is very obvious.... For you to allege that you see a "growing Jewish influence" in our organization [The Worldwide Church of God] is laughable! ... I utterly and totally disagree with you, Charles ... and if I have in any sense hurt your feelings, please forgive me—but after all, you invited me to 'set you straight' if I wished. In this case, I wished.[29]

At least Garner Ted Armstrong wrote back. As Chuck himself observed in response to a letter received from H.M.S. Richards at the Voice of Prophecy radio ministry, "Thank you for taking the time from a busy life to drop me a line. Perhaps the fault lies in my communication, but few ministers acknowledge my letters."[30]

The John Birch Society in Yakima County

The John Birch Society (JBS) grew into a virulent force in Yakima County during its heyday during the 1960s and 70s, and clearly influenced Chuck Hessey's thinking. He acknowledged reading Robert Welch's *Blue Book* and other Birch material but came into open conflict with the local Yakima JBS chapter over his support of environmental causes. From that point forward, Hessey returned their vilification in kind.[31]

JBS flourished across the United States but found quite fertile ground in the Pacific Northwest: ten months after its foundation, a two-day seminar took place at the Olympic Hotel in Seattle in September 1959, enlisting some of its first and most powerful members. In Yakima, JBS received substantial support from Floyd Paxton (1918–1975), inventor of Kwik-Loc bag closing devices. Paxton served on the national JBS council and lavishly funded the organization's messaging in regional media as far away as Lewiston, Idaho, published an ultra-conservative newspaper, the *Yakima Eagle*, and made four unsuccessful bids for Congress from 1966 to 1974 under the aegis of his own political organization, the Conservative Party. Even after Paxton's death in 1975, the county's JBS chapters and their American Opinion bookstore in Yakima proved particularly adept at stirring local political passions about alleged subversives, support of law enforcement, unfettered access to guns, opposition to the United Nations, taxes, fluoride in the water, sex education in public schools, homosexuality, and nuclear disarmament.[32]

Although Kay and Isabelle lived in a remote location, the JBS undercurrent throughout Yakima County was a constant menace. Initially, JBS members believed Communists controlled Dwight D. Eisenhower's Republican Party. This notion had its roots in Senator Joseph McCarthy's hearings concerning communist influence and homosexuality in the military and government during the early 1950s. The election of John F. Kennedy over Richard Nixon in 1960 realigned JBS affiliation with the Republican Party: Birchers transformed into staunch Republicans supporting arch-conservative Barry Goldwater in the 1964 presidential election. In his enthusiasm, Floyd Paxton offered employees at his Yakima manufacturing plant a "Bonus for Barry Plan" of an additional month's pay if Goldwater won. Between Gleed and Naches near the Kershaw family orchards, a billboard-sized "Goldwater 64" sign painted on the concrete wall of a fruit warehouse faced Highway 12 for years.[33]

In 1968, the message of white supremacist presidential candidate George Wallace paralleled that of JBS: local chapters provided many Wallace campaign aides and staffers. These JBS acolytes adhered to strict conservative ideologies current in the Republican Party, including opposition to women's issues such as abortion, the Equal Rights Amendment (ERA), feminism, and lesbianism. The head of Selah's JBS chapter cautioned readers of the local paper that "women who fall for the ERA are victims of the biggest con game since Barnum."[34] Pushing back against such ultra-conservative cultural forces, the redoubtable Bella Abzug expressed the affinity between the John Birch Society and the Ku Klux Klan: "they obviously want women to keep washing their sheets."[35] But JBS went even one step beyond the Klan, conjuring a meta-framework out of a number of conspiracy theories based on seemingly isolated events. The group envisioned a cabal of "internationalists, greedy bankers, and corrupt politicians" who controlled both the United States and the Soviet Union: "If left unexposed, the traitors inside the U.S. government would betray the country's sovereignty to the United Nations for a collectivist New World Order, managed by a 'one-world socialist government.'"[36]

The dog-whistles in the JBS worldview—a precursor to Q-Anon's in the twenty-first century—meshed with those stated explicitly in Chuck Hessey's manifesto: that communism was a Jewish plot to rule the world. JBS inveighed against perceived liberals in the government such as Washington State's Senator Henry M. Jackson and Justice William O. Douglas, who had forcefully condemned the McCarthy hearings in his dissent to *Dennis v. United States* (1951). This drew the ire of JBS by the end of the decade: "The John Birch Society in the state of Washington," Douglas wrote, "had long advertised that I was the only 'known Communist' in Yakima County."[37]

Charles Hessey and Justice Douglas crossed paths at Gold Hill over the years and, at least once, during an overnight confab hosted at the Double K Ranch.[38] Even though JBS kept both in the cross-hairs, the pair inevitably would have been at loggerheads on nearly every issue: one can only imagine a discussion between them with Douglas's liberal views on one side, Chuck's arch-conservative conspiratorial ravings on the other.[39] Nonetheless, Chuck was an early and full-throated advocate for the wilderness areas of the Cascades and on this point, he and Justice Douglas concurred: Chuck could be disarmingly rational if his Holocaust denials and white supremacist rants remained out of the conversation. As abhorrent as some of Chuck's beliefs were, anyone who currently enjoys the mountains of Washington State is indebted to his efforts on behalf of the environment.[40] From early on, Chuck and Marion's wilderness advocacy provided a template for Kay Kershaw, Isabelle Lynn, and Justice Douglas. They were all pulling together to establish a Cougar Lakes Primitive Area near Bumping Lake in the early 1960s. Subsequently, the Goose Prairie contingent joined the Hesseys in the crusade to establish the North Cascades National Park.

The Battle Over Cougar Lakes Begins

In the early 1940s, USFS designated around 90,000 acres near Bumping Lake as the Cougar Lakes Limited Area, a classification which temporarily protected the region pending further study for wilderness classification. After World War II, however, USFS reassessed such areas as demand for timber skyrocketed and the conflict over the classification of the Pacific Northwest's old-growth forests grew virulent between preservationists and the logging industry.[41] Business leaders such as George C. Wall, president of the Chelan Box and Manufacturing Co., and the Rev. Robert Riley Johnson, president of the Lake Chelan Chamber of Commerce, prognosticated an impending economic disaster if tracts of wilderness remained off-limits to logging. The two addressed a gathering in 1957 about a proposed Glacier Peak wilderness area at the head of Lake Chelan, warning that its establishment would shut down sawmills and destroy the timber industry throughout the region. They reported that 2,000 out of the 2,300 residents of Chelan had signed a letter in opposition. The Spokane Chamber of Commerce concurred, voting to reject the proposal in its entirety.[42]

The brouhaha over Glacier Peak galvanized environmental activists in the Pacific Northwest. In the 1950s, no organized group interested in wilderness existed. The establishment of the Glacier Peak Wilderness—with its "starfish boundaries" protecting only the ice and rock above the 4,000-foot level—left out the surrounding valleys targeted by USFS for future multiple-use: that is, for industrial-scale logging. "It was then we realized we would have to fight," recalled Sierra Club's Brock Evans, "if we ever wanted to have anything left at all, especially in the north [part of Washington State] where so many ancient forests were threatened."[43]

This agitation by private industry to gain more and more logging access roiled the Pacific Northwest. At Bumping Lake, USFS's mid-1950s timber sale on American Ridge caught Kershaw and Lynn off-guard. The two were not even aware that USFS had designated a Limited Area at Cougar Lakes until they read an article by Karl Onthank, founder of Oregon's Friends of the Three Sisters Wilderness (FTSW), listing it as such. Kay and Isabelle contacted him for advice: he suggested reaching out to Charles Hessey, chairman of FWOC's committee studying all of the limited areas in Washington and Oregon and thus one of the region's most knowledgeable resources. Expressing surprise to Onthank that their neighbor was so involved with environmental issues, Kay wrote to Charles's affable partner, Marion Hessey, immediately.[44]

Charles Hessey had been proselytizing for wilderness long before Kay and Isabelle wrote to Onthank in 1958. Expanding his activism from solo efforts earlier in the decade, Charles held sway in the Cascadians as acting president in 1956 and head of its conservation committee in 1958. He was also on the board of the Seattle-based NCCC from its inception in 1957. As a result, he had established connections with co-board members David Brower, the first executive director of the Sierra Club; Phillip Hyde, the Sierra Club's foremost photographer; and David Simon, a member of FTSW. Since the mid-1950s, the Hesseys had lived full-time in the Naches River canyon just down the road from Goose Prairie. While Marion worked for Gilbert Orchards during the week, Chuck spent most of his time as caretaker of the Truitt cabin at Gold Hill, less than seven miles away as the crow flies from the Double K Ranch. As members of the small community residing year-round along the Highway 410 corridor, the Hesseys and the proprietors of the Double K knew each other well. Therefore, Kay's purported ignorance of Charles's involvement with environmental issues in her letter to Onthank is curious, although a clash of personalities probably accounts for her reluctance to acknowledge it.

In particular, Charles did not mince words over his disapproval of horses in the wilderness due to the damage they caused to trails and campsites. He pointed to the huge, hundred-hoof Trail Riders of the West trips—such as the ones run by Kershaw from 1948 to 1952—as the most egregious example. He wrote several letters to USFS demanding restrictions on horse packers, eventually convincing the Cascadians and NCCC to back his point of view. As a result of Hessey's input, the Forest Service instituted tentative horse and group limits as well as stock grazing restrictions in the Glacier Peak Wilderness Area in 1966. These developments reached Goose Prairie in 1967, causing Kay and Isabelle to protest the yearly twenty-five dollar USFS land-use fee for their commercial operation which also capped at eleven the number of horses they could employ. By the late 1970s, USFS regulations mandated a limit of a combined "12 heartbeats" for groups in all wilderness areas whether human, equine, or canine.[45] It would take several years before the chilly reserve between the Double K duo and Hessey—all three irascible, all three unwilling to suffer fools lightly—began to thaw, allowing them to join forces under the aegis of NCCC. In this regard, Justice Douglas appeared to be the motivating factor.[46]

Clearly the interests of Kershaw and Lynn coincided with the like-minded NCCC at the Western Hearings on the Senate Wilderness Bill on 7 November 1958, in Bend, Oregon. Kay and Isabelle were there to state, "The national forests are our livelihood and people come from all over the world to see the wonders of the unspoiled country of the western United States. We take nothing from the forest, but we give something of the forest to all who come our way."[47] However, Charles Hessey stole the show with his impassioned critique of USFS and its timber policies: "The decision to destroy wilderness is a *final* [sic] choice," he told Senator Richard Neuberger of Oregon. "Any legal protection we give to wilderness now, Congress can revoke if the national welfare demands it. *We want this power only in the hands of Congress* [sic; emphasis added by NCCC newsletter editors]."[48]

The National Wilderness Protection Act prompted the subcommittee on interior and insular affairs to hold these 1958 hearings attended by Kershaw, Lynn, and Hessey. Since 1939, the whims of regional foresters either determined or influenced "wilderness" and "wild" designations on tracts of Forest Service land.[49] This proposed bill aimed to codify uniform designation and protection of wilderness all across the United States with the sanction of Congress. As Lynn explained in a 1960 opinion piece for the *Yakima Daily Republic*, paraphrasing Hessey's statement two years prior, "[The Bill] would put control of our wilderness areas where it belongs: in the hands of all the people, speaking through their representatives in the Congress

7. Cougar Lakes Wilderness—The First Decade (1958-1968)

of the United States."⁵⁰ The Wilderness Bill, as it came to be known, was the brainchild of Howard Zahniser (1906-1964), for two decades the head of the Wilderness Society in Washington, D.C. He drafted the first version of the bill in 1956 which was introduced in the Eighty-Fourth Congress. It was reintroduced in the Eighty-Fifth Congress in 1958 going through sixty-six revisions and three more congressional sessions before President Lyndon Johnson signed the bill into law on 3 September 1964 as the Wilderness Act of 1964. These revisions entailed numerous fact-finding commissions and hearings conducted by both Senate and House Subcommittees on Interior and Insular Affairs. Conservationists viewed the Wilderness Bill as the fundamental building block for the preservation of scenic areas throughout the United States. It provided the impetus for groups such as the Cascadians, the Mountaineers, Mazamas, and NCCC to advocate for wilderness areas in Washington State at Glacier Peak, North Cascades, Alpine Lakes, and Cougar Lakes. Zahniser's proposal recognized that without congressional legislation, wilderness areas faced degradation while acknowledging that they could

USFS group photograph on the Mather Memorial Parkway near Mt. Rainier National Park, ca. 1957 (Forest History Society, Durham, NC). From left: USFS Chief Forester Richard McArdle; Pacific Northwest Regional Forester J. Herbert Stone; and Snoqualmie National Forest Supervisor Laurence Barrett. The Mather Memorial Parkway, established in 1931 along a 75-mile section of Highway 410, stretches from east of Enumclaw, Washington, over Chinook Pass through the Naches River canyon to the Chinook Pass Work Center (approximately eleven miles southeast of the highway's junction with the road to Goose Prairie).

also serve multiple purposes and still maintain a wild character. He suggested continued administration of the lands under their current jurisdiction—whether NPS or USFS—but with a mandate for preservation. Zahniser also sought to establish a council of federal administrators and citizens to focus on wilderness preservation issues.[51]

These parameters did not sit well with Chief Forester McArdle. He decried wilderness areas because they excluded "the majority of people," made it impossible to control for insects and fire, and adversely affected multiple-use regions. In addition, he believed that Douglas fir would not reproduce itself unless managed by humans. Had there been any doubt, he publicly sided with business over conservation, stating, "Eastern Washington will choose bread and butter over aesthetics."[52] Regional adherents to McArdle's point of view were legion. Bert Cole, Washington State's Public Lands Commissioner, argued that the Wilderness Bill represented a grave danger to Washington's economy. All around the state, newspaper editorials roundly condemned the proposed legislation. To be sure, wilderness advocates in the Pacific Northwest had an uphill battle ahead.[53]

The Copper City Timber Sale: Justice Douglas Joins the Fray

As NCCC wrangled with the Forest Service over a Glacier Peaks Wilderness Area in the late 1950s, Kershaw and Lynn watched in horror as loggers, at the behest of USFS, continued to saw down trees in areas along the Bumping River. Particularly disconcerting was a proposed timber sale west of Copper City. USFS intended to excavate a road extending one and a half miles in the direction of the Cascade crest and Blankenship Meadows to access downed timber in 1960. This situation caught the attention of Justice Douglas who brought his formidable personality into the mix alongside Kay and Isabelle.

By this time, Douglas had committed himself unabashedly to the side of conservationists. He had alluded to environmental issues in *Of Men and Mountains* a decade earlier, and over the ensuing ten years, his stance aligned increasingly with the more urgent views of the Sierra Club, Wilderness Society, and other similar wilderness proponents. In early January 1954, he had sent a letter to *The Washington Post* opposing a highway along the old towpath of the Chesapeake & Ohio Canal and challenged the editors to accompany him on a March hike along its length from Washington, D.C., to Cumberland, Maryland. The idea caught fire with bags of mail arriving at both the paper and Douglas's office. The publicity generated by the hike propelled the Justice into the limelight as an environmental activist. Two years later in 1956, capitalizing on his stature, Olaus Murie, director of the Wilderness Society and his wife, Mardy, recruited Douglas to accompany them on a trek through the Sheenjek River Valley in Alaska's Brooks Range. Douglas's charisma drew more and more attention as he continued to promote conservation in the United States. A gaggle of reporters tagged along as he hiked a stretch of beach destined for highway construction on the western edge of Washington State's Olympic National Park in 1958. The media attention broadcast the conflict between conservation and development to audiences both regionally and nationwide.[54]

Douglas began to wield tremendous influence on environmental issues. And the national consensus was shifting with him. Justice Douglas had served on the board of the Sierra Club in 1960 until potential litigation by the club against the government compelled him to resign in 1962.[55] Other groups with the Sierra Club's national reach, such as the Wilderness Society and the Audubon Society, attracted more members while gaining significant political clout. The publication of Rachael Carson's *Silent Spring* in 1962 raised national awareness about the dangers of pesticide use and the importance of environmental protection. The next year, Secretary of the Interior Stewart Udall brought environmentalism into the mainstream with his book *The Quiet Crisis*, a treatise on the conservation movement in the United States and the crucial relationship between humans and the natural world. Riding the wave of the conservation movement's burgeoning ranks, both authors motivated an awakening in American perceptions about the environment and wilderness. In the same vein, a popular series of coffee-table folios published by the Sierra Club in their Exhibit Format Series—featuring the photography of Ansel Adams, Philip Hyde, and Eliot Porter—exulted in the beauty of the nation's wild areas. These handsome volumes proved particularly effective in promoting an environmentalist agenda.[56]

USFS timber-cutting policies prompted Douglas's philosophical shift. The agency's depredations on the home turf he remembered so fondly from boyhood rankled most. He stated his position in concrete terms with a 1954 letter to Snoqualmie National Forest Supervisor Laurence O. Barrett opposing the road up the North Fork of the Tieton River to the southern border of Goat Rocks.[57] When USFS ignored his tempered and considered opinion, Douglas adopted a more forceful stance in conjunction with Kershaw and Lynn objecting to the road proposed from Copper City to Blankenship Meadows. In reaction, the agency bristled. Many USFS administrators considered Douglas's activism unwarranted meddling in Forest Service business: "I have met several forest service [sic] district timber sales staff men who are trying to undermine your effectiveness by saying you really don't know what it is you are criticizing in the Forest Service," NCCC President Patrick Goldsworthy wrote to Douglas in 1962. "I believe this is just more character assasination [sic] as being attempted by the Forest Service...."[58]

Concurrently, years of contentious interaction with USFS from the Justice's colleagues at the Double K led to hardened acrimony: "We are viewed with such suspicion by the Forest Service," wrote Isabelle in 1966: at the local Naches District Headquarters, staffers referred to Kershaw and Lynn as "the blister sisters."[59] The bitterness extended to the regional office as well. Writing to Don Campbell, Forest Supervisor for the Snoqualmie National Forest, for example, Isabelle fumed, "Yes, I would like to hear something further on your rationale for keeping quiet on your management philosophy—the one you do not want discussed, that is. To refresh your memory, your letter of December 13 asking me not to quote you is what I'm referring to." To her credit, Isabelle thought better of her two-page harangue a month later with a follow-up apology.[60]

Douglas initiated his own aggressive assault on USFS with a series of letters in autumn 1960. He alerted Sierra Club's David Brower about the situation between Bumping Lake and Blankenship Meadows, citing "friends of mine" (no doubt, Kershaw and Lynn) who had heard local loggers say "'the timber involved is worthless but of course there is the road-building job.'"[61] A similar letter went out the same day to Pauline Dyer, president of FWOC.[62] With Kershaw and Lynn again the obvious unnamed source, Douglas wrote to his friend, Washington State Senator Scoop Jackson, warning that a timber sale and road construction between Copper City and Blankenship Meadows "will put jeeps right on top of the Cascades." Douglas pleaded for assistance in delaying the timber sale until a public hearing could be arranged.[63] A letter from Supervisor Barrett about the impending sale sent to both Justice Douglas and Senator Jackson did little to quell alarm over the consequences. Writing again to Jackson, Douglas called Barrett's rationalizing of the sale "very, very specious." Douglas contended that USFS was intending to build roads right up to the edge of a wilderness area just as it had done in the Goat Rocks.[64] In a consequential letter written in November 1960, Douglas implored David Brower to rally Sierra Club's membership in support of local activists fighting back against the Forest Service. He provided the names and contact information for two individuals on the ground in the Bumping Lake area. First and foremost was Kay Kershaw in Goose Prairie, the second, Charles Hessey in Naches.[65] By proposing both Kershaw and Hessey to Brower, Douglas began joining politically and philosophically opposed individuals—even those with whom he himself may have had differences of opinion—into a unified front all under the aegis of the nation's most influential conservation group. This was one of Douglas's greatest contributions to the environmental agenda in Washington State.[66]

Despite Douglas's letter writing campaign, Barrett paid scant attention to protestations about the Copper City timber sale. USFS Forest Supervisors by custom ran their districts as fiefdoms and Barrett clung to that tradition in "his" Snoqualmie.[67] Barrett's imperious attitude propelled Charles Hessey into a frenzy of activity. He realized the Wilderness Bill would get the decision-making power out of the hands of USFS supervisors like Barrett and provide the salvation of all local preservation efforts in Washington State. The Hesseys attacked the alignment of USFS, business, and eastside press boosterism with vehemence.[68] After initial attempts at bonhomie with Barrett proved fruitless, Kershaw and Lynn followed suit sending letters and editorial pieces to the local newspaper on a wide variety of environmental issues and statements to regional congressional hearings gathering citizen input for the Wilderness Bill. Many never saw print.[69]

Although both of their names appeared in these missives, Isabelle's mordant wit and acerbic tongue are unmistakable. In reply to an opponent of the Wilderness Bill who invoked the name of Theodore Roosevelt in the *Yakima Daily Republic*, she suggests, "Theodore Roosevelt's remarks on multiple use are subject to interpretation in 1960, but it must be apparent to anyone who can spell 'Theodore' that TR would have been in the forefront of the battle for the passage of the Wilderness Bill, laying about him with his big stick."[70] In another letter to the paper during the height of the Cold War, she states, "We all worry, and rightly, about the future and the bomb ... let's worry a bit about our drive to conquer and destroy Nature, i.e., ourselves, along with worrying about Russia's drive to destroy us. Nature can be a considerably more effective opponent than Russia."[71] She was a bit more circumspect in a submission to the House Subcommittee on Public Lands of the Committee on Interior and Insular Affairs in 1962, ending with a sardonic aside: "While those who oppose the [Wilderness] bill at the hearings [held in Washington, D.C.] have outnumbered its proponents, the important fact is that the number of pro-wilderness witnesses who have written letters and statements and sent telegrams for the record considerably outnumber the bill's opponents. This is understandable: Those who are against the bill are opposed for commercial reasons. (We shall hazard a guess here that their witnesses and lobbies are tax-deductible expenses)."[72] Despite such wry digressions, Lynn's prose is not quite as glib as when she was writing for *The Dude Rancher* magazine: now, the stakes were far higher.

Kershaw and Lynn Propose a Cougar Lakes Wilderness Area

In addition to their letters, editorials, and statements to Congress on the Wilderness Bill, Kershaw and Lynn pursued a parallel campaign with USFS: changing the designation of the Cougar Lakes Limited Area to a permanent Wilderness Area. With the help of Howard Zahniser of the Wilderness Society—the three of them met when Zahniser came to Yakima for a speaking engagement in January 1961—Kay and Isabelle drafted a Cougar Lakes wilderness proposal, which they submitted to USFS on 12 February 1961. The proposal included modifications to the Cougar Lakes Limited Area by dropping land north of the Naches Highway and extending the borders east to include Nelson Ridge and Mt. Aix. The changes increased the total area to 125,000 acres all within a single contiguous roadless area.[73] From the outset, the Cougar Lakes proposal belonged to Kay and Isabelle: this fact soon got lost as other more powerful regional and national organizations subsumed their campaign.[74]

In the spring, the Cougar Lakes coalition sought support among the conservation community. NCCC—with Charles Hessey serving as an officer for the period 1961–62—agreed to co-sponsor the proposal and published Kay and Isabelle's draft in their July 1961 newsletter.[75] For his part, Justice Douglas wrote a memorandum to Orville Freeman, President Kennedy's newly-appointed Secretary of Agriculture, recommending that all activity concerning the Copper

City timber sale—located on land now proposed by Kay and Isabelle for wilderness protection—come to a halt until the Secretary had a chance to review the situation.[76]

In mid-August 1961, three distinguished guests arrived at the Double K Mountain Ranch to spend a week inspecting the proposed Cougar Lakes area: Supervisor Barrett of the Snoqualmie National Forest; Harvey Broome, president of the Wilderness Society and a Sierra Club board member; and George Marshall, both a member of the Wilderness Society's governing council and the managing editor of the Society's *The Living Wilderness* magazine (he also served as a Sierra Club board member). On 14 August, Kay Kershaw accompanied them—along with F.H. "Spike" Armstrong, supervisor of the Naches Ranger District and a few other Double K guests—to Nelson Ridge and Mt. Aix. During this ride, Armstrong and Barrett let slip that the Copper City timber sale was a *fait accompli*.[77] As a result of this trip and the comments from the two USFS representatives, Broome and Marshall pledged that the Wilderness Society would join NCCC in co-sponsoring Kershaw and Lynn's Cougar Lakes proposal.[78]

A few weeks later, Justice Douglas and his wife Mercedes arrived in Goose Prairie for a week-long stay. On one of the days, he arranged a loop trip from the Double K around Copper City, Twin Sisters Lakes, and Blankenship Meadows.[79] Kay, Mercedes, Supervisor Barrett, District Ranger Armstrong, and a few other Double K guests rode along with him. The jaunt focused on a visit to view Copper City and the new road and to discuss the timber sale there. Assuming full responsibility for promoting the sale, Barrett argued with Kershaw and Justice Douglas that the road and tree-cutting had not affected the aesthetic value of the area. He further maintained that only the highest reaches of a potential wilderness area should be protected because the timbered valleys held "great economic value." Of the total amount of lumber in the Copper City

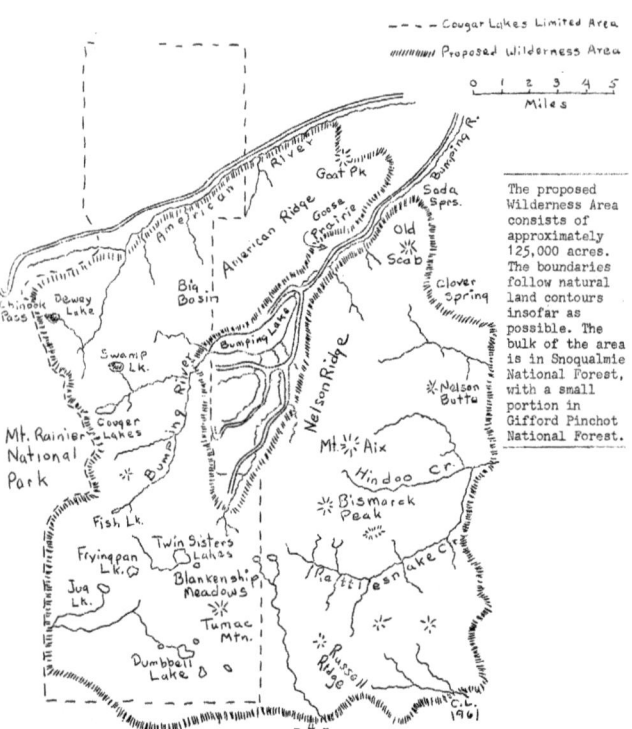

Map 4: Kershaw and Lynn's Cougar Lakes Wilderness Proposal—1961. *NCCC Newsletter* July 1961: 4 (North Cascades Conservation Council: Carmelita Lowry, cartographer).

project, over 70 percent came from three-year-old blown-down trees. Barrett maintained that this was a salvage operation to avoid economic loss and to prevent insect infestation and fire hazards. But the project's greatest value lay in the road extension allowing access to future "harvestable" stands of trees. As Barrett pointed out to Kershaw and Douglas, the status of a Limited Area under USFS parameters only meant that the supervisor "thinks twice" before logging.[80]

But Barrett was blowing smoke as well. He told a staff member of the Senate Interior and Insular Affairs Committee that he appreciated the attention of Senator Jackson and Justice Douglas because it forced him to recognize "the value and necessity of keeping some of our land in its natural setting."[81] At Douglas's behest, Jackson demanded an explanation from USFS concerning plans for extending the road past Copper City up to Fish Lake. The agency justified the logging operation as an effort to curtail insect infestations in the region's downed timber. Douglas responded that downed timber was everywhere: Barrett only used infestation as a pretext for continued logging around Bumping Lake.[82] Writing on behalf of the Cascadians in 1962, Charles Hessey expanded on Douglas's argument. Relying on his fieldwork experience with the Cascade Lumber Company, Hessey countered that areas of blown-down trees were a natural part of the landscape and quite common in the forest: "if the dangerous condition attributed to this one had any basis in fact our forests would long ago have been wiped out by infestation."[83]

Appalled by what he had seen on his ride to Copper City, Justice Douglas described the situation to David Brower as "a destructive Forest Service project." He was dismayed as well by Barrett's duplicity and cavalier attitude toward wilderness. Douglas reported that Barrett had promised Kay and Isabelle there would be no other timber sales at Cougar Lakes pending a comprehensive study. But Douglas understood that Barrett had plans to build a five-mile road above Bumping Lake toward Fish Lake to access more blown-down timber and to remove one and a half million board feet just below it. "The man is a saw-logger—first and last," Douglas continued, portraying a forest supervisor bent on producing revenue from his domain and "keeping loggers happy." He urged the Sierra Club to press for changes in the law so that public hearings had to occur prior to any tree-cutting or road building commenced and that such hearings should take place before a panel independent of USFS.[84] As Kershaw, Lynn, and Hessey had argued previously, curtailing the ability of a handful of USFS administrators—cozy with the timber industry—to determine the fate of wilderness was of paramount importance. Douglas's proposed legislation would provide the means to accomplish this.

The notion of holding USFS accountable through such public hearings had its genesis in the resolutions adopted by the NCCC board of directors at its very first meeting in 1957.[85] The utility of public hearings gained traction in the eyes of NCCC in 1958 during Congress's simultaneous investigations concerning the Wilderness Bill and Glacier Peak Wilderness Area. By early 1959, NCCC's board realized that public hearings were quite an effective tool for broadcasting concerns about regional environmental issues.[86] Even opponents of wilderness had to acknowledge how the hearings had damaged their position. In 1960, W.D. Hagenstein, executive vice-president of the Industrial Forestry Association, advised his membership that going forward, they had to employ "the same mob psychology" as NCCC in USFS public hearings.[87] As congressional deliberations over the Wilderness Bill ebbed and flowed in 1961, NCCC urged members to write their representatives and demand even more hearings. NCCC republished Justice Douglas's letter to David Brower in October and continued to stress the importance of public hearings until passage of the Wilderness Bill in September 1964.[88] Section 3 of this Bill states specifically that local public hearings must precede any proposed action or change in boundaries on land or water under NPS or USFS jurisdiction.[89] Historian Adam Sowards asserts that the public hearings format included in the 1964 Wilderness Bill proved to be "one of the wilderness movements crowning achievements and a significant contribution to American democracy."[90]

After the ride with Justice Douglas, Supervisor Barrett was definitely into full "saw-logger" mode by autumn 1961: "The road to Blankenship Meadows is progressing despite your efforts to stop it," Cragg D. Gilbert wrote to Douglas in September. "The local Forest Service officials assume that they have complete authority over that limited area's destiny and their ideas are anything but of a conservation nature ... the value of the timber in that particular sale will come nowhere close to paying for the cost of the road to get it out. This in my opinion is pure folly. Anything that you can do to slow down this move to open up Blankenship Meadows, Twin Sisters, etc. will be greatly appreciated."[91] Prompted by Gilbert's letter, Douglas contacted Senator Jackson, suggesting that removal of Barrett and his immediate supervisor from USFS might be the only recourse for saving the Cascades: "[Barrett] is quite an unreliable person," Douglas fumed. "Unless we get rid of men like Barrett and [Region 6 Regional Forester J. Herbert] Stone, that whole Snoqualmie that you and I love so much is going to be completely chewed up, commercialized, civilized, motorized, and paved perhaps. In any event, the end of the wilderness under that regime is pretty close."[92] In a follow-up letter to Jackson a month later, Douglas unleashed another scathing denunciation of Barrett, referring to him as "an intellectually dishonest person."[93]

Along with Kershaw and Justice Douglas on the 1961 daytrip with Barrett rode a biochemist from St. Louis, Missouri, Carmelita Lowry (1927–1974). This was Lowry's third visit to the Double K after her initial visit in September 1957, and Barrett's comments and attitude toward the area were so disconcerting that she flung herself headlong into the environmental maelstrom: "Natch I'll be in there with you," she wrote to Kay and Isabelle, "to help activate people and raise general hell."[94] Already a member of NCCC, in October 1961, she joined forces with her friend Eileen Ryan (who had originally introduced Carmelita to the Double K Ranch) to keep fellow members apprised of developments in the Cougar Lakes region. She applied her artistic skills to cartography, providing the original maps of the proposed Cougar

Lakes wilderness published in the NCCC newsletters of the early 1960s (see map 4).[95] She began advocating in 1958 for passage of the Wilderness Bill, paying her own way to Washington, D.C., to testify before the House Interior Committee in 1962. Committee chairman John Saylor praised her statement, expressing his appreciation that she had come to the Capitol simply on her own behalf rather than as a representative of an organization.[96] Right from the very beginning, few, other than Justice Douglas, Kershaw, and Lynn, did more than she in the battle to gain wilderness designation for Cougar Lakes. In fact, following the ride with Barrett, Lowry pledged her allegiance to the "C.L.W.A."—an acronym either for the Cougar Lakes Wilderness Area, or perhaps for a group organized spontaneously under the rubric Cougar Lakes Wilderness Alliance—writing in the guest book, "Here's to the fight!! [sic]."[97] Justice Douglas even had enough trust and respect for her opinion that he forwarded a confidential 1971 letter about Cougar Lakes from Senator Jackson.[98] Ever the wilderness booster, Lowry's last entry in the guestbook reads, "And here's to CLWA, and all our other great plans."[99] After her untimely death in 1974, Isabelle and Kay waged a contentious campaign with the government to have a region near Bumping Lake named in Lowry's honor in gratitude for her devotion to the Cougar Lakes project. USFS vehemently opposed the proposal, basing one of its four specious objections on "the appropriateness of a Spanish surname" in relation to other features in the area. Ultimately, the Double K women succeeded in their bid: the Washington State legislature designated a remote spot due east of Copper City "Carmelita Basin" in October 1975.[100]

In early spring of 1962, Kershaw and Lynn received written assurances from Region 6 Regional Forester Stone that USFS was "carefully considering" their proposal for Cougar Lakes and that he would assign additional field study to determine its suitability for wilderness.[101] Nonetheless, three timber-cutting operations were either currently running or in the planning stages there. Searching for clarification on USFS timber policy, Kershaw contacted Justice Douglas for guidance. He did not sugar-coat his reply: "I am afraid there is nothing on the horizon that can be greeted with cheers and enthusiasm ... if you happen ten years from now to see a few trees standing, you will have cause for rejoicing. But if you think that all is well, or that policies have changed, or that somehow or other we are going to save the sanctuaries I think you are going to be greatly disappointed."[102] A 28 May letter from Supervisor Barrett reinforced Douglas's gloom and doom. It detailed how Copper City timber salvage was in full swing, the road complete, lumber trucked away, and another sale in the North Fork of Rattlesnake Creek (on the east slope of Nelson Ridge) planned for 1963. Barrett wrote that crews were already marking timber selectively in an effort to camouflage the project. The Fish Lake timber salvage operation remained on the table: pushing a road four or five miles southwest to Fish Lake along the Bumping River would provide access to downed trees as well as encourage the demand for established campgrounds and picnic areas around the lake's rim. This contradicted both Barrett's assurances to Kay in September 1961 that USFS had no intention to build a road to Fish Lake as well as his statement to the Wilderness Society in March 1962 denying plans to salvage blowdown or extend roads above Bumping Lake.[103] Justice Douglas was having none of it: "Region 6," he wrote to Senator Jackson in late February, "is the most reactionary lumber-minded Forest Service office in the country. I think they are quite irresponsible, and I have come to the reluctant conclusion that they never mean what they say."[104]

As logging continued at Copper City through the summer of 1963, Kay and Isabelle kept up a steady campaign to halt it.[105] However, Secretary of Agriculture Freeman had taken an interest in the Cougar Lakes area earlier in May. In a letter to Senator Jackson, Freeman stated that the timber sale in the Rattlesnake Creek area had been put on hold until summer of 1963 pending a new resource management plan for high mountain areas in USFS regions of the Pacific Northwest. The Secretary also indicated that Kershaw and Lynn's wilderness proposal for Cougar Lakes merited attention and that he would press USFS for early completion of its study of the area.[106] Yet timber sales were developing apace throughout the rest of the state, much to the consternation and alarm of NCCC. Writing to Senator Jackson in July 1962, NCCC President Goldsworthy pleaded for help in stopping timber sales adjacent to areas slated for wilderness consideration, citing in particular the Alpine Lakes and Cougar Lakes Limited Areas and the North Cascades Primitive Area.[107]

This whole Copper City episode took on a life of its own by the early 1970s. Writing in 1971 for the readership of a magazine devoted to environmental concerns, Isabelle claimed that a powerful storm on 12 October 1962 had devastated the west coast from California to Vancouver and blown down the trees at Copper City as well. Her timeline thus places the Copper City sale in 1964 and timber cutting operations in 1965:

> We were fighting rearguard actions against the Forest Service—over the Copper City timber sale, for one example. This involved a blowdown, largely of hemlock, resulting from the famous 1962 Columbus Day storm that leveled trees all over the Pacific Northwest. No one would buy on the first offering. Who wants hemlock down two years under Cascade winters? Despite strenuous efforts by Justice Douglas, Senator Jackson, and [Oregon] Senator [Wayne] Morse, who took the request right up to then–Secretary of Agriculture Orville Freeman, the sale was finally made, sweetened by half a million board feet of standing white pine, not to mention a contract for the road extension to within a mile and a half of the crest of the Cascades. And there was a sale planned (indeed, the trees to be cut still bear slashes of blue paint) on the North Fork of the Rattlesnake River that conservationists, with formidable help from Justice Douglas and Senator Jackson, opposed. We won that one.[108]

In another version from a NCCC newsletter of the same period, Lynn hews a little closer to the facts. Without specifying a date, she writes that the Copper City sale was "a salvage of a blowdown, sweetened with standing timber. It was a hard-fought lost battle that resulted in the extension of the Copper City road a mile and a half closer to the crest of the Cascades…. The blowdown was the excuse; the road the prize."[109]

North Cascades National Park Takes Priority

After decades of friction between USFS and NPS, Agriculture Secretary Freeman and Interior Secretary Udall brokered a truce in January 1963—the so-called "Treaty of the Potomac." The moratorium aimed to bring order to national wilderness issues by eliminating inter-agency animosities, rivalries, and competing claims. Both departments agreed that formulating policy for the North Cascades of Washington State should take precedence from the outset. To gather information, a five-member interdepartmental study team set up hearings and public comment sessions in 1963. From 15 to 24 July, the North Cascades Study Team made a preliminary visit to tour the periphery of the Washington Cascades from White Pass to the Canadian border focusing on Mt. Baker, Lake Chelan and the Stehekin valley, as well as Mt. Rainier. Sub-study teams spent the summer doing field work in the Snoqualmie, Wenatchee, Okanogan, and Mt. Baker National Forests. With their initial groundwork completed, the Study Team scheduled public hearings over a five-day period from 7 to 11 October in Wenatchee, Mt. Vernon, and Seattle.[110]

In anticipation of these sessions, Justice Douglas adopted a concept from the American Revolution to the ensuing struggle to establish wilderness in Washington State. To monitor British activities, American colonists across the continent had organized Committees of Correspondence to keep fellow revolutionaries apprised of noteworthy regional events. In a similar fashion, Douglas envisioned a centralized committee to coordinate communication among the diverse groups of conservationists around the United States and provide local groups with national assistance.[111] "[Douglas] seemed to have a rather different—but very effective way—to rouse us," recalled Brock Evans.[112] To facilitate this idea, the Double K Ranch hosted the "Committee on Correspondence on the North(ern) [sic] Cascades" on 21 to 22 September 1963. Eighteen people besides Kay and Isabelle attended, including Justice Douglas and his third wife, Joanie; NCCC President Patrick Goldsworthy; NCCC Vice-President Charles Hessey; his activist wife, Marion Hessey; a selection of NCCC officers and board members; J. Michael McCloskey, FWOC's Northwest Conservation Representative; and David Brower, Chief Executive of the Sierra Club.[113] Although no records exist, the agenda surely included how to deliver testimony and written statements before the Study Team's hearings in October. Because the establishment of a North Cascades National Park remained NCCC's immediate priority, the organization put other proposals for Alpine Lakes, Cougar Lakes, and North Cascades Wilderness Areas on the backburner.[114] But these areas were not completely forgotten and hope remained that all would eventually gain wilderness status. "The wilderness of the North Cascades is a national resource of the future," William O. Douglas wrote in his introduction to the Sierra Club's *The Wild Cascades*. "We need a number of protected wildernesses along the Cascade range—the Cougar Lakes Wilderness to take care of the overflow from the Rainier Park, the Alpine Lakes Wilderness, the North Cascades Wilderness. But we also need—and most of all—a North Cascades National Park."[115]

With testimony received and field work completed, the North Cascades Study Team made its recommendations in October 1965. In a triumph for NCCC, these included the establishment of a 698,000-acre North Cascades National Park and four new Wilderness Areas (Alpine Lakes, Enchantment, Okanogan, and Mt. Aix, totaling 720,000 acres) and enlargement of Glacier Peak Wilderness and Mt. Rainier National Park. But no one involved in the process had even submitted Kay and Isabelle's Cougar Lakes proposal to the Study Team for consideration and evaluation. Rather, the Study Team proposal outlined a much-reduced Mt. Aix Wilderness Area of 45,000 acres with undefined boundaries and the redesignation of Cougar Lakes (along with two other regions at Alpine Lakes and Monte Cristo) from Limited Area status to USFS multiple-use management.[116] According to USFS guidelines on multiple-use, it was now within the agency's purview to determine the most judicious use of this 228,000-acre transfer. Decision-making power concerning Cougar Lakes would return to local USFS officials.[117]

Not everyone on the Study Team concurred with the final recommendations, however. One team member, Owen Stratton, wrote a letter of dissent in which he decried the omission of any description of the Cougar Lakes Limited Area's aesthetics. He surmised that USFS's eagerness to return the region to multiple-use elevated economic interests over the intrinsic value of wilderness. Stratton questioned the rationale behind the USFS decision concerning the proposed Mt. Aix Wilderness Area: "the Forest Service seems to me to be saying, in effect, that it is alright to put Mt. Aix and its immediately surrounding area in wilderness status since it is the kind of country that only some eccentric in superb physical condition would go into. It is good for nothing else, the Forest Service seems to say, so let's put it in wilderness."[118]

NCCC rejoiced, of course, that the decades-long dream of a North Cascades National Park was one step closer to reality. However, the board of directors understood that the recommendations were a mishmash of compromises worked out between the Departments of Agriculture and Interior and expressed disappointment that the other proposed wilderness areas received short shrift from the Study Team. To NCCC, it appeared the study group considered commercial timber cutting in wilderness a trade-off for the establishment of national parks. The group vehemently disagreed with the truncated Mt. Aix Wilderness Area, insisting rather that the designation should include the entire area lying to its west right up to the border with Mt. Rainier National Park.[119]

Industry backers in Washington State, on the other hand, found much to like in the multiple-use re-classification under the Study Team's recommendations. Commissioner of Public Lands Bert Cole resolutely backed this new status for Cougar Lakes. Cole, who ran a sawmill in the logging town of Forks on the Olympic Peninsula before taking office in 1956, favored the USFS recreation designation which allowed for "sanitation" cutting in multiple-use regions. He also believed that USFS did a better job of providing "mass recreational needs" than NPS.[120] For his part,

Supervisor Barrett was enthusiastic about the Study Team's conclusion and tried to explain USFS policy concerning Cougar Lakes going forward in his remarks to the Yakima Chamber of Commerce in February 1966. Pushing back against Stratton's critique as a "misunderstanding," Barrett stated, "We have no intention of harvesting the area beyond removal of dead and diseased trees." The areas outside of the 45,000-acre Mt. Aix wilderness would be divided into three sections with different management policies allowing timber removal, additional campground and picnic area construction, and trail and road building. "It's not in the best interests of the general public," he concluded, "that it be made a wilderness area."[121]

Stratton's dissent notwithstanding, it is no surprise that Kay and Isabelle boiled with rage over the Study Team's report, now compounded by Supervisor Barrett's comments. "The fact is there is no misunderstanding," Isabelle countered, "for beneath all these splendid reassurances emerges the same old master plan that Barrett and Region 6 have been promoting for years ... ream everything except the top of Mt. Aix. Well, come to think of it that's pretty useless country: no trees to speak of—make it a wilderness—give 'em a couple of hundred acres of grass to go with it. That should shut them up. If it doesn't, claim 'foul'—misunderstood." Isabelle did not mince words in reaction to Barrett's opinion about the general public's best interests: "What are these 'best interests'? Who determined them? On what basis? Which general public—Yakima? Ohio? Florida? The public that wants to keep this area intact? The road builders? The loggers? Fishermen? Hunters? Hikers? Riders? Campers? THE OWNERS [sic]? *That* general public? Come, come, Mr. Barrett, we aren't all *that* stupid."[122]

Kay and Isabelle begged Justice Douglas to intercede somehow.[123] And they were not alone. Letters and telephone calls swamped his office from people concerned about Supervisor Barrett's comments as reported in the *Yakima Morning Herald*. In an exchange with Secretary of Agriculture Freeman, Douglas wrote to thank him for allowing proponents of preserving Cougar Lakes to express an opinion before he made any decisions, his letter formulated from "dozens and dozens of letters and telephone calls from people who have been panicked by the kind of thing Larry Barrett is telling the Yakima people."[124] Significantly, one letter Freeman sent offered a glimmer of hope and, perhaps, some good news to pass along to Kershaw and Lynn: "We have lots of problems in the North Cascades," he wrote. "The Cougar Lakes Area is one that we have no reason to push now. Let us get some of the other problems worked out and then we can get together on the Cougar Lakes Area."[125]

Supervisor Barrett did not share Secretary Freeman's geniality. In a vindictive move aimed at local opponents of USFS policies, the regional office of the Snoqualmie National Forest decided to oust the Gold Hill ski club from their cabin in 1966. Barrett determined that the group—led by the Hesseys, Tom Lyon, and Cragg D. Gilbert, all vocal critics—were violating an "occupancy trespass" on the old Truitt mining claims. The Snoqualmie regional office therefore terminated their lease effective immediately. Barrett understood how devastating this would be for the

Gold Hill ski club and the Hesseys, a situation apparent as well to Justice Douglas: he featured Elon J. and Cragg D. Gilbert, Charles Hessey, the old Truitt cabin, and Gold Hill's terrain in Chapter 20 of *Of Men and Mountains*.[126] Douglas intervened on behalf of the ski club with a letter to Edward Cliff, USFS Chief Forester in June. Through Douglas's effort, the Washington, D.C., office extended the lease for the Gold Hill ski club with a special permit to allow operation through 1971.[127]

After two and a half years of hearings, field work, and recommendations, the U.S. Bureau of the Budget started drafting legislation based on the North Cascades Study Team's report, testimony before the Senate Interior Committee, and Washington State Governor Dan Evans' Area Report and Recommendations. Planning for the Introduction of a bill to create the North Cascades National Park and Okanogan, Alpine Lakes, Enchantment, and Mt. Aix Wilderness Areas began in January 1967.[128] In Yakima meanwhile, a familiar wilderness foe, the Rev. Robert Riley Johnson, organized opposition to the North Cascades proposal. A decade earlier in Chelan, Johnson had rallied businesses against Glacier Peak Wilderness. In the interim, Riley relocated to Yakima to become rector of St. Michael's Episcopal Church. In September 1966, Johnson gathered a group of cattlemen, sheepherders, "sportsmen," and four-wheel drive enthusiasts into Outdoors Unlimited, an organization whose express purpose was to defeat any proposal for wilderness in the North Cascades and to promote timber industry interests at Bumping Lake. Charles Hessey soon discovered that prior to studying for the ministry, Johnson had pursued a law degree and lobbied in Washington, D.C., for timber companies such as Boise-Cascade, one of the largest employers in Yakima County at the time.[129] The Reverend Johnson argued that an overwhelming majority of Yakima County residents opposed wilderness. To refute this claim, Justice Douglas compiled a report on hearings sponsored by the Yakima Chamber of Commerce about the proposed Cougar Lakes Wilderness held in Yakima in January 1966. He concluded that those supporting wilderness far outnumbered those against.[130]

After a year of deliberation by the Johnson administration, Washington Senators Jackson and Warren G. Magnuson filed a North Cascades National Park bill on 20 March 1967. The bill included a 10,000-acre enlargement of Glacier Peak Wilderness, the establishment of a 100,000-acre Ross Lake National Recreation Area, and a 500,000-acre Pasayten Wilderness Area east of the lake. However, the bill lacked wilderness proposals for Alpine Lakes and Cougar Lakes. Jackson and Magnuson may have considered that the two southern wilderness areas would suffer in comparison to the much more scenic North Cascades.[131] In April, two days of Senate hearings in Washington, D.C., brought representatives of Federal and State agencies as well as groups from industry, Chambers of Commerce, and conservation organizations to testify. Outdoors Unlimited president the Reverend Johnson traveled all the way from Yakima to the nation's capital to testify. Such a trip was expensive: but Johnson had sent out an appeal letter for additional funds printed on St. Michael's Episcopal Church stationary to fight "aggressive, articulate, misguided-groups [sic] such as the Sierra Club and the North Cascades Conservation Council representing a tiny portion of the population."[132] The Reverend was less than forthright before the Senate hearings when he stated that Outdoors Unlimited was ambivalent about the North Cascades bill. He requested more study on behalf of the organization's purported membership of over 18,000 in Washington, Oregon, Idaho, and Montana.[133] Senator Jackson returned to Washington State for subsequent hearings throughout May in Seattle, Mt. Vernon, and Wenatchee. Charles Hessey, representing NCCC as its First Vice President, testified before Jackson in Wenatchee. "A national park is the only answer," he pleaded. "There is no alternative."[134]

In the wrangling over the Senate bill, the Cougar Lakes proposal appeared to slip away, fading from the consciousness of the conservation community: "It's a miracle that Cougar Lakes even survived the decade," wrote Carmelita Lowry in 1971.[135] However, a dedicated coterie led by Kershaw and Lynn kept the faith that wilderness designation would come eventually. Their efforts did not go unnoticed. Edward C. Crafts, chairman of the Study Team, speaking on 23 April 1966 at the Sixth Biennial Northwest Wilderness Conference in Seattle, admitted surprise that they had received hundreds of letters and petitions from all over the United States protesting the re-classification of the Cougar Lakes Limited Area. In late 1967, Brock Evans, Northwest representative of the Sierra Club and FWOC, praised the "dedicated watchdogs in the Yakima River valley" whose advocacy for Cougar Lakes never waned.[136]

While NCCC was consumed with the North Cascades Park legislation, Isabelle and Kay had a new issue to contend with at Goose Prairie. In a 1966 letter to Justice Douglas, Secretary of Agriculture Freeman affirmed that the Bureau of Reclamation had plans to enlarge the reservoir capacity at Bumping Lake.[137] Yakima's main newspaper promoted the project, arousing Kay and Isabelle's wrath: "Your editorial demonstrates not so much a wide familiarity with the proposed project as an overpowering desire to have all this federal money in Yakima County. Large federal expenditures of this kind usually carry the odor of tainted meat to you, but this one smells pretty much like roses, hmmm?"[138] Two years later, Democratic Senators Jackson and Magnuson joined Republican Congressional Representative Catherine May to advocate for a 30-million-dollar bi-partisan expansion of the lake. Through Justice Douglas's efforts, the Bureau held a hearing on the Bumping proposal in Yakima in January 1968. Representative May appeared alongside a number of dignitaries and the Yakima Chamber of Commerce to promote the expansion citing benefits such as jobs, flood control, supplemental irrigation storage, and expanded recreational development. Isabelle and Kay found the latter singularly disconcerting: "It is the plan for 'development' that makes one cringe; million-dollar campgrounds, roads, and a honky-tonk lake with greatly increased facilities for boat launching and the concomitant speedboats and waterskiers … they certainly do not have to be in wilderness-quality country, particularly in areas where weather for water sports, exclusive of simply helling around in a speedboat, is no more than 2–3 [*sic*] months." Their irritation with Yakima's primary media continued unabated. In covering the hearings, "the Yakima newspapers chose to behave as if they were a government-controlled press." In her wrath, Isabelle took a potshot at Outdoors Unlimited for good measure: "We *were* spared a sermon by the Reverend Riley Johnson, but it is interesting to speculate on the nature of the politicking he was indulging in the night before the hearing in his favorite corner of the Chinook Hotel." Tying the Bureau of Reclamation's proposal to the NCCC's decade-long push for a North Cascades National Park and a national wilderness system, Lynn wrote, "The enlargement of Bumping Lake will by no means preclude the establishment of the Cougar Lakes Wilderness Area, but it will cut it down in size, and worse, the additional roads and campgrounds, plus the enlarged lake, will make the area far more accessible and will attract far more people...."[139] Melding into one newsletter the transcript of a speech by Cragg D. Gilbert favoring wilderness legislation, Isabelle's Bumping Lake report, and Justice Douglas's 1966 survey refuting the Reverend Johnson's claims of local support, NCCC president Goldsworthy exhorted his membership to provide a flood of testimony in person before yet another congressional hearing on the North Cascades scheduled for 19 and 20 April 1968 in Seattle. In conjunction with Goldsworthy, Brock Evans took a more direct approach. For three months starting in January 1968, he drove the length and breadth of the state to convince sympathizers to organize and provide testimony in April.[140]

Evans's dogged person-to-person crusade along with Goldsworthy's appeal to NCCC members worked splendidly. An overflow crowd of nearly 800 witnesses crammed into two hearing rooms and adjacent hallways of Seattle's Benjamin Franklin Hotel. Chairman of the House Interior Committee Wayne Aspinall of Colorado—a tenacious opponent of wilderness—was not amused as he elbowed his way through the lobby: "I don't know who these people are ... this whole thing has been ballooned all out of proportion here."[141] According to Goldsworthy, supporters of the park proposal far outnumbered those in opposition led by Outdoors Unlimited. The group had threatened to overwhelm the proceedings. Instead, only a handful of witnesses appeared. Even the Reverend Johnson, Outdoor Unlimited's "explosive spokesman," failed to show up.[142] After two days of hearings, Aspinall promised that he would "do his darndest" to get the bill out of committee before August. After more than sixty years, the bill establishing a North Cascades National Park finally came to fruition in September 1968. As Brock Evans recalled recently, "We had to establish ourselves as a political force opposed to USFS and its allies ... if we had lost or compromised too much on the North Cascades campaign, I doubt that our political power would have ever been respected again and protecting anything else would have been so much more difficult."[143]

8

Interlude: Isabelle Lynn and Justice Douglas Help Kay at Goose Prairie

While Kay and Isabelle prioritized battling the Forest Service over logging and the Bureau of Reclamation over expanding Bumping Lake, they still had a business to run. On the face of it, the Double K Mountain Ranch was a thriving concern, viewed by many as an example of successful private outdoor enterprise. In a presentation to a North Cascades Outdoor Recreation Conference in 1974, one consultant cited Kay and Isabelle's marketing savvy in narrowing the focus of their operation to a specific clientele: "Kay Kershaw and Isabelle Lynn … have defined their market very well…. Their advertising specifies they are looking for serious horseback riders. Their ranch is not the kind of ranch that you would take a family to. There is no swimming pool, no television, no tennis courts. In fact, after 10 o'clock at night there are no lights because they have their own generator…. They don't want children at the ranch and in their advertising they have specified 'No small children.'"[1] From Kay's sardonic point of view, children needed to receive the same training as Lucky, the Double K's resident spaniel.[2] The Double K brochure made this ban on children explicit, as did sporadic advertisements in regional newspapers. In one incongruous placement in the *Spokesman Review*, an ad for the Double K Ranch blares "Adults only" under the text of an article promoting the dude ranch vacation in the Pacific Northwest as a wholesome family activity: "Particularly folks from the east hanker to sample, or continue life's other side, an unhindered, carefree, back-to-nature vacation on a western ranch. Mothers know it is a healthy life for the kids where they are out of harm's way, and she can have a complete rest."[3]

This 1961 puff piece painted a rosy picture, but in reality, the Double K's restrictions on guests limited cash flow in a recreation sector whose business model was in decline. The dude ranch industry had expanded rapidly in the 1920s and early 1930s, reaching its peak around 1938. Another burst of growth occurred during the late 1940s and early 1950s. But consumer interest in this type of vacation began to fall off from that point forward. Statistics from Montana—home to perhaps the largest guest ranch network in the United States—indicate that in 1944, sixty dude ranches were operating; in 1969, that number had dropped to forty-six. The corresponding guest visits declined from approximately 10,500 in 1944 to 6,800 in 1969.[4] The trend was the same, if not worse, in eastern Washington. After the establishment of White Pass Ski Area and Crystal Mountain Resort within a decade of each other between 1953 and 1962, it no longer made sense to run the Double K Ranch as a winter recreation center. These year-round economic factors meant that the Double K enterprise continually operated at a loss. Explaining her dude ranch business to the *Yakima Sunday Herald* in 1956, Kay lamented, "Even now, it's not so much a living as a way of life."[5]

The lifestyle—not the income—kept Kershaw and Lynn working at their ranch in Goose Prairie right up to 1990. The placement in the *Spokesman Review* notwithstanding, Kay and Isabelle hardly advertised in the Pacific Northwest after the late 1950s, preferring to cater to visitors from the east coast through word of mouth. The Double K connection to Justice Douglas proved beneficial in that regard. Return clientele made up the bulk of their guests by the mid–1970s. To fill the guest ranch in autumn, Kay had guided hunting trips during elk season through 1964. But she felt that both the number of elk and quality of hunters had deteriorated: "Slobs, nearly all of them," she told *Yakima Herald-Republic* columnist Jim Gosney in 1978. "The same as with a lot of other interest groups."[6] These "interest groups" Kershaw and Lynn encountered during the complex and protracted battle to preserve Cougar Lakes certainly affected their attitude toward the business. With each passing year, they watched as more hikers, horseback riders, off-road vehicle operators, and snowmobilers ran roughshod over the Bumping Lake region. By the mid–1970s, they themselves had cut back on both the number and size of their trips into Cougar Lakes and environs. Kershaw and Lynn came to the realization that Charles Hessey had been right all along: the Double K's own horses were muddying and gouging many of the trails and meadows in their beloved wilderness.[7] By the 1980s, Kay had eliminated the string of pack horses and was hosting only six or seven guests at a time: gone were the days of week-long stays at the lodge. Most of the clientele only wanted to come for a weekend of walking, hiking, or birdwatching.[8]

Kershaw and Lynn devoted almost as much time to screening their guests as they did to ranch chores: "There's a lot of correspondence with our guests," Isabelle told Gosney in 1978. "We want to know about them, what they like to do while they're here, what they like to talk about. Then we try to match them up with other guests. Most of the time it works, but a few times we've had to ask someone to leave."[9] They did manage to attract an interesting clientele over the years. As their advocacy for wilderness grew alongside that of Justice Douglas, the Double K Ranch hosted several individuals connected to the environmental movement such as David Brower of the Sierra Club, Harvey Broome and Susan Alexander of the Wilderness Society, and Harvey Manning of The Seattle Mountaineers.[10] Justice Douglas proved to be an adept recruiter, notably prompting Charles Reich (1928–2019), author of *The Greening of America*, to vacation at the Double K. Reich graduated from Yale Law School in 1952 and clerked for Associate Supreme Court Justice Hugo Black for the 1953–54 session in Washington, D.C. Reich met Justice Douglas during this period and the two became life-long friends with a shared love for the wilderness. Through Douglas, Reich began visiting the Double K Ranch and immediately fell under the spell of Kay and Isabelle. He booked numerous trips to Goose Prairie over the decades and maintained a cordial relationship with the two proprietors, especially Isabelle: along with Justice Douglas, her name appears in the acknowledgements of his blockbuster book, a result perhaps of their mutual interest in the craft of writing.[11] Reich made his first trip to the Double K in 1956 while he was working for two law firms in New York and Washington, D.C. He went back to Yale to teach law in 1960, leaving and returning periodically over the decades.

Although the Hollywood movie star set never materialized as Kershaw and Lynn had hoped, CBS sent a television crew to Goose Prairie for a 1972 documentary on Justice Douglas. The renowned news correspondent Eric Sevareid along with Burton Benjamin, executive producer of news and documentaries and a CBS vice-president, stayed at the Double K in August of that summer. They, too, were captivated by the affable owners.[12] And Justice Douglas, sometimes accompanied by the occasional houseguest, would pop over every now and again to the delight of Kay and Isabelle's clients: "Thanks very much for the *memorable* cocktail party with Justice Douglas [and Justice William] Renquist [sic] [and] wives. Thanks!"[13] Isabelle's nephew, Seth Lynn, Jr., reminisced about one particular visit to the Double K in 1965: "[Douglas and his third wife, Joanie] breezed in, unannounced … for dinner…. My father [Seth Lynn, Sr.], a country lawyer from Pennsylvania, sat transfixed at the table. Had never seen him so cowed before or after!"[14]

A smattering of individuals with international connections made for some intriguing entries in the guest registers, sparking speculation and questions from clients. Kershaw and Lynn were only too happy to conjure wild yarns inspired, no doubt, by *au courant* spy novels and James Bond movies. Perhaps Justice Douglas had a hand in encouraging this aura of intrigue, based on remarks alongside his signature during the height of the Cold War: "en route to India and Russia," on one occasion, and "en route to Karachi, Kabul, Tehran, Baghdad, and Istanbul" on another.[15] A few other far-flung entries include Charles de Selincourt, Eton College, England; Mary Anne Smith of the American Embassy in Addis Ababa, Ethiopia; Myron Bemont Smith, Secretary of the American Institute for Persian Art and Archaeology in New York City; Gabriel Daniel Etukudo of Enugu, Nigeria; Kerstin Kuhlman of Mariehamn, Åland Islands (Finland); K. Kiyomiya and M. Kojima of Tokyo and Yokohama, Japan; and Samir Deeb, American University of Beirut, Lebanon.[16] These exotic names and locales spawned some extravagant tales. In 1968, one imaginative and enthusiastic journalist, Mort Cathro, arrived to write a piece about Kay and Isabelle for the *Oakland Tribune*. Charmed by his hosts during his twenty-four-hour stay, Cathro wrote in the guest book, "Two good girls plus one good time equals one good story." He did indeed come up with some tantalizing yarns within a very short period.

Apparently, while signing into the guestbook, Cathro had thumbed through the pages and asked Kay and Isabelle about a few of the entries. In his piece that ran a few weeks later, Cathro reported, "Among their guests have been Supreme Court Justice William O. Douglas (who has a home adjoining the Double K property), a prime minister of Norway, a shah of Iran, and other assorted dignitaries."[17] Cathro had the story about Justice Douglas right, but his "prime minister of Norway" was in reality Paul Gruda Koht, Norway's Ambassador to the United States from 1958 to 1962: Elon J. Gilbert accompanied Koht during his stay in 1962, no doubt at the request of Justice Douglas. The "shah of Iran" was actually Manoutchehr Kazemi, whose beautiful Persian calligraphy is the most eye-catching of all the entries in the Double K logs. Hardly a "shah," Kazemi was an Eisenhower Fellowship recipient from Tehran with expertise in industrial engineering, row crop farming, and economics. At the time he signed the guestbook, he was visiting the western United States to view Hoover Dam and a variety of irrigation projects. Kazemi had served as a translator in Iran for Douglas—appointed by the Shah—on his 1950 trip through the Middle East with his son and Elon J. He stayed at the Double K with Justice Douglas in 1963 after touring agricultural locations in Yakima.[18]

As amusing as it may have been for Kershaw and Lynn to read Cathro's flights of fancy, they found even more to appreciate in his journalistic rendition of the two proprietors: "[The Double K] is, I feel pretty safe in saying, the only [dude ranch] anywhere operated solely by two independent and outspoken middle-aged spinsters." The article ran with a cartoon of Kay and Isabelle wearing cowboy clothing and exaggerated ten-gallon hats, next to a gangly horse under the headline "Spinsters Run Isolated Dude Ranch." Kay and Isabelle considered this so ironic that they copied the cartoon and headline verbatim for their annual Double K Christmas and New Year greeting card for 1969.[19]

Despite the press coverage, enamored guests, and international clientele, bills still needed payment as revenue dwindled and expenses rose. By the late 1960s, Lynn was investigating whether she could tap into her Social Security account to keep the business afloat. After her fifty-first birthday, she sent a Request for Statement of Earnings query to the Social Security Administration. She received a form letter read-out of her account showing that she had earned $19,922.19 from 1937 through June 1967 and that she only had twenty-two hours of coverage out of the necessary twenty-seven to be insured for at least the minimum retirement benefits at age 65. The numbers and required hours had not changed when she made the same request seven years later in 1974.[20]

Apparently, Isabelle's straitened circumstances had been a point of discussion with her brother, Seth McCormick Lynn, prior to an exchange of letters in 1975. At issue were thirty-two acres of Pennsylvania land in the vicinity of Duboistown and Armstrong Township inherited by the descendants of Isabelle's grandfather, Seth T. McCormick. The rights of ownership had become rather complex, and Isabelle's brother was handling the details for a quit-claim deed. Isabelle's consideration for the transfer of her interest in the property amounted to 500 dollars, the equivalent

8. Interlude: Isabelle Lynn and Justice Douglas Help Kay

Double K Mountain Ranch Christmas Card, 1969 (Kershaw Family Collection). On the cover is a drawing of a Christmas bell with the Double K logo. The text reads (in script font): "Greetings from the two…" and opens to the interior seen in this image, featuring the art work and title of Mort Cathro's *Oakland Tribune* article.

of nearly 3,000 dollars in 2024. Writing to Isabelle, Seth suggests how they would have to proceed in communicating with the local bank: "The only thing I need from you is a letter directed to Northern Central Bank … making out a case of your need of funds beyond your income (e.g., medical expenses, food for the horses, declining business, soaring taxes, etc., etc.) … in amelioration of your 'tight money' situation."[21] Isabelle followed up with a letter to the Trust Department, stating that her brother's arrangements would enable her to clear up "some long-standing debts."[22] The back and forth between the two siblings from October through December 1975 over the quit-claim deed is a remarkable mix of passive-aggressive acrimony and familial good wishes. In her final letter to Seth on the subject—accompanying the one addressed to the Trust Department at Northern Central Bank—Isabelle writes, "I hope the enclosed suffices. It really shattered my nerves, not to mention my morning to write it. You would have to be (a) female, and (b) me, to understand that one perhaps…. We are having, as a long-standing custom, the Kershaw tribe and affiliates for the day on Thanksgiving. That usually ends in a grand rousing argument too. Love to you and Jane."[23]

Although Isabelle downplayed her role as instigator during the traditional Kershaw Thanksgivings at the Double K, argumentation was part and parcel of every yearly event. "Thanksgiving was contentious—always," Ed Kershaw recalled. "Isabelle would argue with you just to find out what you believed." And Kay followed suit as she sparred with her more politically conservative relatives. Ed made a point of studying current events and preparing himself mentally before arrival to be ready for Kay and Isabelle's "test." At times, Kay's brother Ron had heated exchanges with Isabelle: "she knew how to push Dad's buttons." The relationship Ron had with Pat Kane, in Ed's opinion, had been much smoother. "[She was] brilliant and articulate, certainly," Isabelle's nephew Seth remembered within the context of familial relationships, "but often caustic to the point of being savage."[24]

Sonic Booms, Jeeps, and ATVs

Kershaw and Lynn tried to recapture the character of the late 1940s to mid-1950s when dude ranches flourished and the Bumping Lake environs were primitive, beautiful, and unsullied by modern life. But the mechanized excesses of the latter half of the twentieth century continued to impinge on the idyllic setting at Goose Prairie. In addition to modernized methods of logging on the ground—using heavy equipment and chainsaws—disturbances overhead disrupted the Double K's peace and quiet as well. With ramped-up United States involvement in the Vietnam War, the Air Force Aerospace Defense Command operated supersonic SR-71s over the Cascade mountains, many flying north over the west coast from Beale Air Force Base in California. The resulting sonic booms were disconcerting with potentially dangerous ramifications. Kay, Isabelle, and Justice Douglas complained to officials at McChord Air Force Base—located just south of Tacoma—but their entreaties went unheeded in 1967. Douglas had written from Goose Prairie on their behalf to Robert McNamara, President Lyndon Johnson's hawkish Secretary of Defense: "The sonic boom is having disastrous consequences in the valley. We are now accustomed to having pictures knocked off our walls. Our neighbor lost many rocks from his chimney.... I write you because local objections go unnoticed. Your Air Force people out this way are very callous." McNamara answered with several paragraphs detailing the necessity of flights from Beale and expressed dismay over Douglas's charge that Air Force personnel were "callous." He requested more specific details.[25] McNamara's response prompted one of Douglas's most blistering letters to a public official. He equated McNamara and the Johnson Administration's bloodthirsty savagery in Vietnam with an attack on the local residents of Goose Prairie, implying two in particular:

> Your letter of July 15 relative to disastrous effects of your sonic boom in the wilderness area of the Pacific Northwest has been received. The victims of this callous federal program for which you claim responsibility are so helpless that I am arranging to put your letter in a public file so that their attorneys will have the benefit of your confession of responsibility. I assure you, Mr. Secretary, that your "villagers" here [in Goose Prairie] are not as voiceless and impotent as your "villagers" in Viet Nam.[26]

Undeterred by McNamara's brushoff, Justice Douglas wrote to both Senator Magnuson and President Johnson in August to present his case: "The sonic boom is doing us in at Goose Prairie.... McNamara writes polite letters that tell us to go to hell.... People here are up in arms; and many lawsuits will follow." Those potential Goose Prairie litigants probably inhabited the Double K. In reply, President Johnson indicated that restricting flights by the Air Force would be "impractical" and "perilous."[27] Douglas's complaints prompted further explication from Air Force Secretary Harold Brown: "While I wish it were possible for us to accommodate your personal desires as well as those of thousands of other American citizens experiencing the same disturbances, I can only reiterate the previous position of President

Johnson and Secretary McNamara. To provide unequivocal advance notification of supersonic flight would be both impractical and perilous.... To tie these [aircraft defense] forces to a timetable of any sort is to ignore the unpredictability of the enemy threat."[28]

This should have sufficed for Justice Douglas, had it not provided yet another example of the Johnson Administration's duplicity. Douglas caught wind from press reports in early 1968 that Senator Frank Church of Idaho had convinced the Air Force to curtail supersonic flights over Idaho's Sun Valley resort during the winter, ostensibly to avoid destabilizing the snow and causing avalanches. This was blatantly spurious reasoning: in the late 1960s, the Sun Valley ski patrol was at the forefront of avalanche control work on the area's groomed slopes. A far more likely scenario was that Sun Valley's wealthy clientele found the sonic booms distracting, and the vacation trade was one of Idaho's main economic drivers. This surely outraged Douglas, who would have found this class distinction galling. "I wonder why we can't get the Pentagon to keep the sonic boom away from the eastern slopes of the Cascades … from July 1st to October 1st, when those slopes are so heavily occupied by people on horseback," Douglas wrote to Scoop Jackson in February.[29] Senator Jackson concurred. He wrote to Secretary Brown on behalf of Justice Douglas asking for an explanation of this discrepancy and contacted other officials in the Pentagon. They confirmed the Sun Valley flyover policy but also informed Jackson that the Air Force planned to cut back testing operations of strategic reconnaissance during the summer of 1968, reducing the number of sonic booms over the Cascades. In the meantime, Jackson asked Douglas for a list of trails that posed the gravest danger to horse and rider in the Cascades to forward to the Air Force in hopes they might avoid them. Douglas provided the names of nine paths used by the Double K Ranch in the vicinity of his home at Goose Prairie.[30] But it was all to no avail. The reply to Jackson from Secretary Brown allowed for scant solace. The Secretary offered contradictory and disingenuous reasoning for his obviously biased policy in Idaho. Brown admitted that tests conducted by the Federal Aviation Administration in 1965 had revealed sonic booms could not cause an avalanche, even in high-hazard areas. Nonetheless, the Air Force suspended supersonic flights over Sun Valley "in consideration of the expressed public concern." Secretary Brown distinguished between skiing at a resort and horseback riding by arguing that the former represented a seasonal activity undertaken in just a few specific areas in the mountains whereas horseback riding occurred throughout the year all across the nation. Therefore, limiting supersonic flights to accommodate equestrians would mean a total ban on supersonic flights everywhere in the United States. These factors, Brown concluded, "make it impracticable to do what [Douglas] suggests."[31]

Although national defense issues may have curtailed further discourse on the sonic boom problem, Kershaw and Lynn did not remain silent and ineffectual on other matters. Mindful of and nostalgic for their previously unsullied paradise, they bemoaned the demise of an area that had become "desecrated by the profligate waste of the 'modern' vacationer."³² This was not due to sonic booms and timber cutting alone: motorized trail vehicles were encroaching on the Double K ambiance as well. The prevalence of jeeps on logging roads already presented a point of concern in the late 1950s. Ex-GIs who had experience with the four-wheel drive vehicles from both the Pacific and European theaters realized the jeep's potential during hunting season.³³ During his 1960 letter-writing campaign against the Copper City timber sale, Justice Douglas emphasized the threat of jeeps gaining access to the Cascade Crest and Blankenship Meadow.³⁴ But the introduction of the low-priced Tote Goat—a gasoline-powered trail bike in mass-production by 1960—changed the dynamic of vehicles in the wilderness. "Perhaps jeeps do have a legitimate use on mountain roads," Isabelle wrote in reference to the Tote Goat, "but mountain roads have an end, and where the road ends trouble begins—for the country."³⁵ These tiny scooters could travel on narrow mountain trails previously inaccessible to motorized vehicles such as the larger, four-wheeled jeeps. Tote Goat use proliferated in eastern Washington to such an extent that in less than a year, Justice Douglas included their vilification along with that of jeeps in his 1961 correspondence on environmental issues.³⁶ Charles Hessey ridiculed them as a cheater's way into the wilderness in his guise as the sarcastic Les Braynes in the NCCC newsletter. Each year, the use of newer, more powerful motorcycles increased in the mountains, prompting Cragg D. Gilbert to denounce them publicly in 1967. The USFS appeared not to be concerned about this new mode of trail use: "The word from on high in Washington," Isabelle Lynn wrote indignantly, "was that 'trail bikes do less damage than horses to a mountain trail.'" As motorcycling proliferated, the USFS struggled to maintain order in the areas under its jurisdiction. In 1969, the agency issued a special map and trail log—*Trail Bike Trips, Wenatchee National Forest*—showing sixty trails covering more than 460 miles open to motorcycles. "The motorized outdoorsman has become an important member of our family of forest users," the brochure states hopefully.³⁷

With the advent of snowmobiles in the winter, the Bumping Lake area became a mecca for year-round motorized off-road recreation by the early 1970s. Kay and Isabelle were infuriated. A Double K campaign against the use of off-road vehicles (ORVs), all-terrain vehicles (ATVs), and snowmobiles ensued. Their first point of contact was, of course, Justice Douglas. "I was talking with a man from the Council for Environmental Quality based at the White House," Douglas wrote to Lynn in November 1971. "[They] are now tackling the snowmobile and tote goat problem."³⁸ The "problem," as delineated by Isabelle, was that "we are in the same position now with snowmobiles that we were a few years ago with trail bikes." However, the situation had become worse during the winter of 1971–72, with snowmobiles now outnumbering motorcycles almost ten to one. Addressing Don Campbell, USFS Snoqualmie National Forest Supervisor, in January 1972, Isabelle complained:

> [At Goose Prairie] cabin camps have been taken over by snowmobilers ... The only people who would rent these places are the most undesirable element you could imagine. They *brag* about their refusal to obey the law. They have made a shambles of the area,

ignoring and tearing down (repeatedly) private property signs, leaving garbage, raising hell up here until 4 a.m. on weekends. Not one in ten has a license for his machine. They are, by law, excluded from the [Bumping Lake] road, except beyond the post office where the plowing ends.... For the first time ever we have a winter road [plowed by the county from Highway 410 to Goose Prairie] and it should be for those people who come up here seeking the quiet of the mountains in winter. Instead they get noise, smoke, rough characters, and the makings of a first-class mess.[39]

In early February, Kershaw took their fight to the Washington State Department of Ecology with an idealistic yet impractical proposal that all manufacturing of ATVs, ORVs, and snowmobiles should be prohibited in the United States, or at least their use should be banned in Washington State. In reply, Ecology's John Biggs told Kay that the state legislature would consider a bill in the next session proposing designated trails for ORVs in order to avoid future conflict with non-motorized users. Biggs also informed Kay that President Nixon had signed an executive order in February requiring government agencies to develop regulations limiting the areas and conditions under which ATVs, ORVs, and snowmobiles could operate.[40]

In order to broadcast their concerns to a wider audience, Lynn began to compose an article for *National Parks and Conservation Magazine*, the official publication of the National Parks and Conservation Association. This group—founded in 1916 as the National Parks Association—monitored commercial efforts to exploit the national parks and, by 1970, expanded its purview to include environmental issues as well. Isabelle had sold two pieces to the magazine earlier in the winter and had pitched the idea for another on the subject of motorized vehicles in the wilderness to the editor, Jan Schaeffer.[41] This was going to be a hard-hitting exposé along the lines outlined by Kay in her letter, demanding the total elimination of ATVs, ORVs, and snowmobiles from the United States. She contacted the White House Council on Environmental Policy as well as William Ruckleshaus, Administrator of the Environmental Protection Agency (EPA), to inform them she was writing this piece for the National Parks and Conservation Association. She requested an immediate response from each agency on what they proposed for "curbing, or better yet, eliminating these machines from the American scene."[42] Isabelle received a reply from the EPA which outlined the agency's funding of studies on unregulated gasoline-powered engines such as those used in motorcycles and snowmobiles. The EPA letter included a copy of President Nixon's Executive Order regarding the use and control of ORVs on public lands.[43] However, Isabelle had already completed her article for *National Parks and Conservation Magazine* by the time the EPA letter arrived. She sent her piece, titled "Do We Let the Knuckledraggers Take Over?"—along with some of her slides and additional photographs from the USFS—to Schaeffer at the end of March.[44]

The manuscript Lynn submitted pulls no punches. Her unapologetic stance is clear from the outset: "There is no halfway position on ATVs, ORVs, and snowmobiles. There is no useful compromise that can be reached on allowing them to use this piece of mountainside, that alpine meadow or those designated trails. They simply have to *go* [sic], to be outlawed in the United States." She disparages the owners and operators of these off-road vehicles as "knuckledraggers" with a nod to the term's inventor, "a skiing conservationist friend" (no doubt, Charles Hessey):

> And what would be your guess as to the numbers of opaque-eyed, slackjawed pure troublemakers right out of the cinematic *Clockwork Orange* among them? Or put another way: How many do you think would qualify as "Outstanding Young Man of the Year"? "Most likely to succeed"? "Little old lady in tennis shoes"? My guess is fifteen percent. Maybe twenty. In other words a good eighty percent of these people appear to have slipped their leash.[45]

Continuing in this vein, Lynn takes issue with foreign and domestic vehicle manufacturers, President Nixon, the Washington State Director of the Department of Ecology, USFS Regional Forester Rexford Resler, and "government at all levels wringing its hands and mouthing platitudes."[46] That is, a searing jeremiad from Isabelle's sharp pen. It proved a bit much for the editors of *National Parks and Conservation Association Magazine*. "They like the piece but feel that in its present state it's too rich for their blood." Isabelle wrote soon after. "They want me to re-write it—'dumb it down' as it were. I am not willing to do that since I'm convinced the subject has to be dealt with firmly and realistically."[47]

Disappointed that her piece had been turned down, Lynn asked Justice Douglas for advice. He suggested that she contact Jack Kessie, Managing Editor at *Playboy*, with whom he had published a series of articles from 1967 through 1970.[48] "In light of Women's Lib, I dare not write him first, of course—or do I?" quipped Douglas.[49] In a follow-up letter, Douglas reconsidered his advice: "What you really need is a person who knows the market and an agent that might help you." He recommended Robert Lantz "one of the best in New York City and [who] would give you considered treatment." Lantz specialized in movie packaging and had recently formed a partnership with the influential editor Candida Donadio. One of Donadio's first business deals was to sign Joseph Heller, author of *Catch 22*; her current stable of writers included Saul Bellow, John Cheever, and Phillip Roth. The Lantz-Donadio group was clearly a powerhouse on the New York literary scene.[50] Douglas warned, however, "the trouble with *Playboy*, *Sports Illustrated*, *Harpers*, and the rest of them is that the Advertising Department may bear down against certain types of articles. The motorcycle manufacturers, snowmobile manufacturers, etc. may have important accounts in some of those magazines."[51] In the interim, Sheldon Wax had taken over the position held by Kessie at *Playboy*. Nonetheless, Wax's assistant replied to Isabelle's query with a note rejecting the piece and confirming Douglas's caveat, explaining that *Playboy* had already run several articles on ORVs. She enclosed with the rejection notice copies of two recent articles: one on dune buggies, the other on snowmobiles. Lynn fired back: "Thanks for your note and the clips from present issues of Playboy. It's obvious I made a considerable gaffe in submitting an anti-toy piece to the magazine! I was recalling Playboy of a couple of years ago when it was rather full of just such 'anti' articles."[52]

Understandably crestfallen by two back-to-back rejections, Isabelle contacted Justice Douglas once again. He approached the Lantz-Donadio group and asked one of their agents, Hy Cohen, to get in touch with Isabelle: "I am writing you at the suggestion of Justice William Douglas who feels that your talent deserves a wider audience than is presently provided by wilderness magazines."[53] Cohen offered an open-ended invitation to submit whatever sort of material or ideas she had for consideration. Isabelle jumped at the chance, sending Cohen two articles: the one on ORVs she had pitched to *National Parks and Conservation Magazine* and *Playboy* and another on the Second Amendment, titled "Large and Small Bores in the National Lands." Cohen replied, "I've received and read—relishing your indignation—your two pieces: 'Knuckledraggers' and 'Bores.' They are presently at Redbook which has been known to take flyers for right causes."[54] But Cohen had to inform Isabelle that the editors at *Redbook*, although sympathetic to the subject matter, were reluctant to "enter into the fray with your own unrestrained, no-holds-barred commitment. I've tried to interest them in a regular feature column, but again, to no avail."[55]

Douglas must have been aware, however, that Isabelle had a separate project in the works besides the "Knuckledraggers" and "Large and Small Bores" screeds when he contacted Cohen. "If you have, or are presently working on, a book, and if you would like this agency to represent [you], we would be happy to consider your work," the New York agent wrote to the Goose Prairie author. This response provided the encouragement Isabelle had longed for: "Some time this fall, I want to try a book idea out."[56] Working on her manuscript over the next three years, Isabelle came within a hair's breadth of recognition during the early 1970s in the nascent field of feminist/lesbian fiction. Isabelle's detour into the world of letters continues in the Appendix.

9

NEPA, RARE I and II, and Cougar Lakes Legislation (1969–1980)

In just over a year, Congress received three bills addressing the stand-off over Cougar Lakes. On 14 October 1970, Representatives John Saylor of Pennsylvania and Julia Butler Hansen of Washington introduced an Omnibus Wilderness Bill in the House during the Ninety-First Session of Congress to designate eleven new wilderness areas, including 220,000 acres at Cougar Lakes. On 11 December 1971, for the Ninety-Second Session, Senator Henry M. Jackson introduced his own bill written specifically for consideration of a Cougar Lakes Wilderness Area, proposing a 152,000-acre Mt. Aix Wilderness Study Unit plus a surrounding Cougar Lakes Recreational Area of 115,000 acres. Washington's Fourth District Representative, Mike McCormack, submitted companion legislation in the House. A study of the Mt. Aix area over two years would make recommendations—after public hearings—on the feasibility of wilderness classification for the region.[1] NCCC was ecstatic over this development. The organization considered the Cougar Lakes Wilderness proposal part of the "unfinished business" left over from the North Cascades Study Report of 1965. NCCC president Goldsworthy compared both Jackson's and Saylor's proposals to the one developed by USFS and recommended by the North Cascades Study Team in 1965: "Senator Jackson's new proposal is far more acceptable as it [is] almost identical with the [NCCC]'s Cougar Lakes Wilderness proposal…."[2] This proposal claimed by Goldsworthy as NCCC's own was, of course, the original work of Kershaw and Lynn. It had been a long process spanning a decade to advance their idea to this point: it would take just as long again to finally attain their goal.

Having a proponent like Scoop Jackson (1912–1983) provided a considerable advantage in all matters legislative. Jackson served the State of Washington in the House of Representatives from 1941 to 1953 and in the Senate from 1953 to 1983. His unusual blend of politics combined hawkish support of the military and holding a hard line against the Soviet Union while backing social welfare programs, civil rights, and labor unions. These points of view aligned with those of his fellow Washingtonian William O. Douglas, with whom he maintained a cordial relationship throughout their mutual careers in government. Like Douglas before him, the Democratic Party considered Jackson a viable presidential candidate: he actually campaigned for the nomination in 1972 and 1976.[3] And again, like Justice Douglas, Senator Jackson—with more than forty years of experience in Congress—wielded considerable influence in the nation's capital. However, as the long-serving chairman of the powerful Senate Committee on Insular and Interior Affairs (Committee on Energy and Natural Resources as of 1977), Jackson could directly impact environmental legislation in ways that Douglas, as a Supreme Court Justice, could not. Jackson's introduction of his Cougar Lakes bill during the Ninety-Second Congress was a powerplay, arranged with Douglas to force the hand of USFS: "I think that probably the introduction of a bill to make the Cougar Lakes Primitive Area into a Wilderness Area," Douglas wrote to Jackson, "would have the decided effect of expediting the Forest Service hearings on the matter." Douglas's "cc" at the bottom indicates Isabelle Lynn as a recipient.[4]

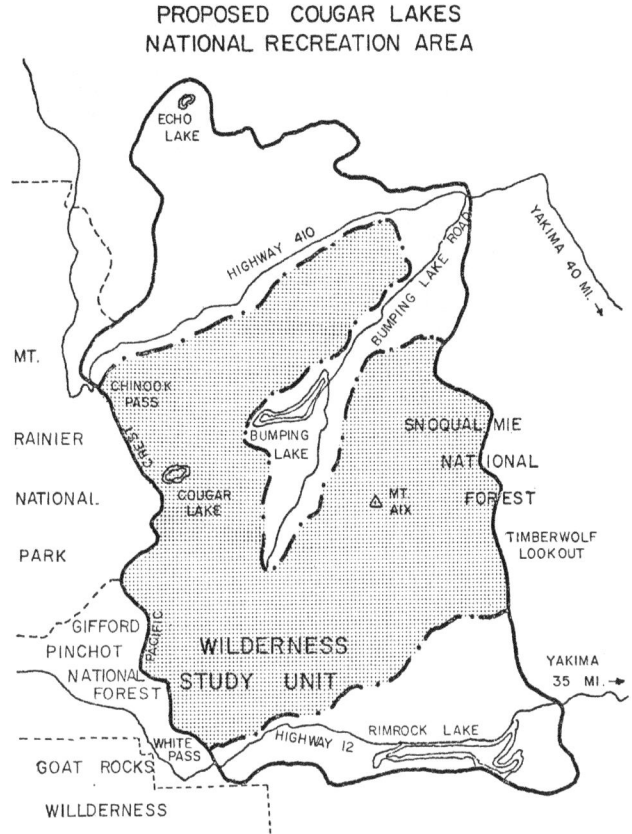

Map 5: Senator Jackson's Cougar Lakes Proposal—1971. *Wild Cascades*, October–November 1971: 21 (North Cascades Conservation Council: Noel McGary, cartographer).

But sticklers in Congress insisted on following the Wilderness Act of 1964 to a tee, now made more complex by a variety of environmental laws enacted in the late 1960s and early 1970s. Jackson himself had crafted one of the most significant changes, the National Environmental Protection Act of 1969 (NEPA). Under NEPA, participation by and input from other government agencies and the public increased. In addition, prior to any development within a roadless area, planning by government agencies required publication of an environmental impact statement (EIS). Production of an EIS depended upon the expertise of a variety of specialists—hydrologists, soil scientists, wildlife biologists—to provide the basic information undergirding the document, a time-consuming and painstaking proposition.[5]

William O. Douglas drafting his decision on *Dexter v. Schrunk*, 29 August 1970 (Kershaw Family Collection). On the reverse, in Isabelle Lynn's handwriting: "Bill Lower Lookout, August 1970 (papers in Terry v. Schrunk [sic])." [Terrance Doyle (Terry) Schrunk served as mayor of Portland, Oregon, from 1957 to 1973.] In this photograph, Kay Kershaw documents a famous William O. Douglas vignette. On 28 August, three Oregon attorneys hiked six miles from Goose Prairie into a Double K campsite at Lower Lookout to request a temporary injunction from Douglas—in his capacity as the Supreme Court's liaison to the Ninth Circuit Court of Appeals—in a lawsuit filed by the American Civil Liberties Union against Mayor Schrunk and the Portland Police Bureau (for using excessive force dispersing anti-war protesters during a student strike at Portland State University). After arguing their case, the trio left papers with Douglas, who told them he would deliberate overnight and leave a decision for them on a nearby stump in the morning. One attorney—the other two were incapacitated by the twelve-mile roundtrip the previous day—hiked back to find a handwritten note on the stump denying the request. The *Oregonian* reported the incident three days later along with a reproduction of Douglas's note. Phil Cogswell, "Decision Left On Stump: Lawyers Hike 6 Miles in Woods to Find Justice Douglas," *Oregonian* 1 September 1970. Over the course of two decades, as the Double K crowd embellished and retold the story, it took on legendary status, amplified even further in 2003 through the hyperbolic prose of Bruce Allen Murphy. See Murphy, *Wild Bill*, xiii–xvi.

NEPA combined with the Wilderness Bill required both USFS and NPS to make recommendations for wilderness areas within a ten-year period. Although Congress would have the power to create a wilderness without waiting until 1974, those odds were long. In 1972, the head of the House Interior Committee, Wayne Aspinall—still a dedicated opponent of environmental legislation—insisted on the completion of all the Wilderness Bill's mandated reports under NEPA before any further debate on wilderness designations and USFS agreed to prepare an EIS for every roadless area in the national forests. Justice Douglas believed the mining lobby—a powerful force in Colorado—had pressured Aspinall. Thus, the United States Geological Survey and Bureau of Mines were analyzing Cougar Lakes, delaying the USFS report until at least 1973.[6] Kay and Isabelle found themselves at wit's end. To Douglas, Isabelle expressed appreciation for his efforts as well as those of NCCC's Harvey Manning and Carmelita Lowry. "You are doing great things," she wrote, continuing in all caps: "BUT WHAT IN THE HELL IS ANYONE ELSE DOING?"[7]

In early 1972, Douglas encouraged Kay and Isabelle to form a committee to keep Cougar Lakes alive and present in the public—and congressional—eye.[8] But this response to Isabelle portended a gradual disengagement from environmental activism. His health was failing as he approached his seventieth birthday in 1968. On June 3, Douglas collapsed on the bench while hearing oral arguments before the Supreme Court. Staffers rushed him to Walter Reed Hospital where doctors diagnosed heart arrhythmia. Surgeons implanted a pacemaker that required additional medication to control his cardiac function from that point forward. He continued to have problems with his pacemakers, undergoing three surgeries within an eleven-day period in May 1971.[9] Writing to Isabelle from the hospital, Douglas bantered, "Those high-priced doctors did such a terrific job that the surgeons at Walter Reed told me late last night they feared they had caused an infection in the pocket in which the new pacemaker rests so I am now under a new kind of barrage and on a very restricted regime. I apparently have a very alarming allergy," adding with a handwritten asterisk and scrawl, "to doctors."[10] Despite his good humor, matters deteriorated in short order. On 31 December 1974, Douglas suffered a massive stroke that left him wheelchair-bound with impaired speech and diminished mental concentration. As his condition worsened through 1975, he realized that he would not be able to continue with his pre-stroke routine. Wracked by "incessant pain," Justice Douglas retired from the Supreme Court on 12 November 1975 at the age of seventy-seven during his thirty-sixth year on the bench.[11]

The Cougar Lakes Wilderness Alliance

Taking Douglas's 1972 committee suggestion to heart, the Double K coalition got to work. In early June 1972, Charles Hessey reported to the NCCC Board of Directors that a new group, tentatively named Keep Cougar Lakes Wilderness, would elect officers at a special meeting at the Double K Ranch that month. At the next meeting, he reported that the organization, now the Cougar Lakes Wilderness Alliance (CLWA), had the approval of Representative Mike McCormack and would categorically not concern itself with the Bumping Lake expansion project proposed by the Bureau of Reclamation.[12] A special announcement in *Wild Cascades* later that year proclaimed the establishment of CLWA with the sole objective, according to Hessey in his capacity as president, of protecting the Snoqualmie and

Gifford Pinchot National Forests, i.e., the Cougar Lakes area. A star-studded lineup of CLWA honorary members included Justice Douglas; Senator Jackson; Congressional Representatives Julia Butler Hansen, Mike McCormack, and John P. Saylor; Brock Evans (soon to be appointed the Sierra Club's Washington, D.C., representative); NCCC's Patrick Goldsworthy; and a selection of Double K stalwarts: Kay Kershaw, Eileen Ryan, and Carmelita Lowry.[13] Other local and national organizations banded together with NCCC into the nation-wide Cougar Lakes Conservation Coalition to bolster the activity of Yakima's CLWA.[14]

How long Charles Hessey remained at the helm of CLWA is difficult to determine. NCCC's Harvey Manning groused to Kay and Isabelle at the end of 1970: "Chuck, I realize, operates on a rather remote level—an attractive place to operate, but frequently not relevant to the world as is." Isabelle raised concerns with Justice Douglas that Hessey, "the obvious person to whip up the Cascadians," was losing focus on the Cougar Lakes project: "he won't whip up anything." Losing patience when faced with his dithering, Kay exploded at one point: "never mind the thinking, just do it."[15] By November 1975, Isabelle had taken over as CLWA president, and with Hessey out of the picture, she could expand the group's efforts to opposing the Bureau of Reclamation's Bumping Lake enlargement as well.[16] In May 1976, a confidential report from the Wilderness Society's Northwest representative to Brock Evans described the CLWA as "not well-organized. Needs more new bodies. Isabelle Lynn ... is dynamic leader but she has less than enthusiastic group to work with."[17]

During this transitional period, Hessey had become increasingly obsessed with disproving the Holocaust and constructing elaborate conspiracy theories based on his skewed interpretation of the Bible. In a letter to Kay and Isabelle, Carmelita Lowry asked wryly, "[Is the fourth congressional district] [b]ig enough to include someone who is a little less odd than Chuck Hessey?"[18] By 1975, Charles was using the back side of CLWA stationary as scrap paper to type out rough drafts of letters to various religious leaders expressing his ideas. Perhaps there had also been a complete break with NCCC. In the early 1970s, Hessey served with Harvey Manning, Goldsworthy, and two other NCCC members on a crucial committee to review the group's Alpine Lakes Wilderness proposal and recommend enlarged boundaries as a major NCCC policy position for 1973. In early May of that year, Hessey was re-elected to his post as First Vice-President of NCCC for a term ending 1 May 1974. Along with his duties with CLWA, these activities with NCCC boded well for his continued role as an environmental elder statesman in the Pacific Northwest. NCCC issued its last official communication with Chuck on 31 October 1974. By 1976, his name disappeared from the NCCC masthead and he was no longer listed as a member of the Board of Directors, a position he had held since 1957. This indicates a complete termination with the organization he helped establish, perhaps initiated by Hessey himself in his delusional state. Goldsworthy, with whom Hessey had maintained a cordial relationship over the course of two decades, added a handwritten note on a NCCC fund-raising letter in 1984, "We still really do need your support."[19]

Roadless Area Review and Evaluation

The Wilderness Act of 1964 designated fifty-four wilderness areas and, as noted above, required that the Secretaries of Agriculture and the Interior conduct ten-year reviews of other lands suitable for wilderness designation. Of course, wilderness areas already existed prior to passage of the Wilderness Act: for example, the Goat Rocks Primitive Area, set aside for protection by USFS in 1931. Such regions automatically transformed into "wilderness" under the 1964 legislation. For other primitive areas, the bill mandated the completion of studies, hearings, and recommendations within ten years. Out of this requirement, the USFS developed a procedure known as Roadless Area Review and Evaluation, or RARE I. Between fall 1971 and summer 1972, the USFS had inventoried and studied 1,449 roadless areas containing 55.9 million acres.[20] As a result of RARE I, USFS Chief Forester John R. McGuire designated four new Wilderness Study Areas south of the Highway 410 including Cougar Lakes.

In the meantime, environmental groups from all parts of the United States determined that RARE I was seriously flawed: it left 44 million acres of previously protected roadless areas vulnerable to development. Several of these groups and private individuals filed lawsuits against the Department of Agriculture to force more rigorous investigation of the wilderness potential for each of the roadless areas omitted under RARE I. In six straight decisions, judges ruled that USFS had not acted properly. After the Sierra Club won its case in 1973, USFS agreed that it would preserve all "non-selected roadless areas" as is, pending further evaluation of their wilderness potential. Based on a comprehensive format developed by Assistant Secretary M. Rupert Cutler, the Department of Agriculture ordered a new study of all roadless areas, known as RARE II, in 1977. The first phase of RARE II aggregated a national inventory of all roadless and undeveloped lands under the jurisdiction of USFS with the potential to become wilderness. As part of the inventory process, the agency scheduled hundreds of public workshops throughout the United States in July and August.[21] By early 1978, USFS collated data on more than 1,900 inventoried roadless areas for computer analysis in order to develop uniform RARE II land-use alternatives all across the United States. These would provide a framework for a nationwide RARE II draft environmental impact statement (DEIS) scheduled for release in June 1978. The DEIS outlined the details and data for further public involvement, leading to a final RARE II EIS with recommendations in early 1979.[22]

This reevaluation process suspended all progress on a Cougar Lakes wilderness. While the Roadless Area surveys of RARE I and RARE II were in flux, USFS continued work on a Naches-Tieton-White River Land Use Plan from 1974 through 1976 to determine how to manage land to the north and east of Mt. Rainier National Park.[23] Under a separate process, USFS also pursued a Cougar Lakes Wilderness Study. Both undertakings analyzed prime sections inside the heart of the Triangle. Just as the RARE II public workshops were gearing up in 1978, USFS released a recommendation for a 176,791-acre Cougar Lakes Wilderness. The report suggested that the region's scenic values were "exceptional" and the opportunities for solitude "outstanding."[24] NCCC's Patrick Goldsworthy expressed astonishment that the USFS now endorsed a 300-percent increase in the Cougar Lakes wilderness. Pressing the advantage gained under the nascent RARE II reevaluation, Goldsworthy suggested a counter-proposal: inclusion of a 67,000-acre parcel north of Highway 410 in addition to the portion to the south for a total of 257,000 acres. This would extend the wilderness from White Pass on Highway 12 on the south to the old Naches Pass Trail to the north and include Norse Peak, Fife's Peaks, and the Greenwater River.[25] Earlier in the decade, William O. Douglas had expressed his alarm that the Sierra Club wanted to include this section north of Highway 410 in a Cougar Lakes wilderness. Brock Evans, who unilaterally surveyed and mapped the area for the Sierra Club in 1970, "got quite a lot of flack" from Kershaw, Lynn, and Douglas over this issue. Douglas believed the additional acreage would imperil the project, writing to Kay and Isabelle:

> I believe it was the Sierra Club that made this second unit [to the north of Highway 410] an adjunct of the original Cougar Lakes. Actually, if it is to be a wilderness area, I think our primary task is to get disassociated from it because we do not know that area and it should stand or fall on its own.... I think, if you all agree, I will have a talk with Scoop [Jackson] within the next few weeks and ask him to introduce a bill that restricts Cougar Lakes to the original Cougar Lakes and not to the north side.[26]

By the end of 1978, however, Evans, Douglas, Lynn, and Kershaw all faced the same disconcerting prospect: both sections on either side of Chinook Pass teetered perilously close to losing any wilderness protection at all.

Cougar Lakes Wilderness Encounters RARE II—1978

USFS slated public hearings in Yakima and Tacoma for February 1978 concerning five proposed EIS alternatives for Cougar Lakes.[27] Any hopes that the Yakima session would be orderly and well-mannered were dashed immediately. "We're tax-paying citizens who feel our recreational areas are being closed off," a local booster of the 20,000-member Pacific Northwest Four-Wheel Drive Association told the *Yakima Herald-Republic* a month before the meeting. The group demanded a postponement until other public events could be scheduled for Seattle and the Tri-Cities.[28] Parroting Boise-Cascade's dire warnings about wilderness in the press, some local critics expressed concerns about the local economy. Ken Wilcox, executive director of Backcountry Horsemen of Washington, speculated, "The amount of timberland removed from production will probably affect some horsemen's jobs." To address these economic concerns and work out a compromise on the USFS proposals prior to the hearing, the Yakima County Commissioners appointed a working group representing the interests of Boise-Cascade, the Yakima Chamber of Commerce, the

State Sportsmen's Council, the Roza Irrigation District, CLWA, labor organizations, off-road vehicle users, and backcountry horsemen. Isabelle was dubious about the commissioners' motives: "No one has the statistics to show that a wilderness area will have a detrimental impact on Yakima County. The adverse economic impacts which some predict are pure fantasy."[29] It is no surprise that the committee members could not agree on any of the five proposals offered by the USFS in its EIS. The group asked for a delay until completion of the economic and land-use studies for all roadless and undeveloped areas within the Naches-Tieton-White Pass Area.[30]

The hearings went on as scheduled, however. In Yakima, twice as many advocates as opponents of the wilderness designation congregated on 4 February in the downtown Convention Center, although it appeared just the opposite to one overwrought NCCC representative who drove from Seattle to attend: "We knew we were in jeepcountry [sic], the land of wilderness haters, as the parking lot was already filled with their four-wheel drive vehicles. One look at the audience in the hearing hall confirmed our anticipation that we would be outnumbered by the wilderness opponents."[31] Sixty-five people presented oral testimony, including a spokesman for Washington State Governor Dixy Lee Ray, a vehement opponent of wilderness designation for Cougar Lakes: "Wilderness areas are for the use only by the elite, the wealthy, and the hardy," according to Ray's declaration. "less than ten percent of the public can take advantage of a wilderness area." Isabelle Lynn countered: "Wilderness is not closed to the people. It is closed to logging and mechanized travel. Everyone else is welcome—hunters, hikers, skiers, snowshoers, fishermen, and rockhounds, in short, people." Governor Ray preferred a multiple-use designation allowing timber removal and ORV use. "I don't want to hear that some middle-aged kids can't get into these areas on their own two feet," scoffed Kay Kershaw. The now-retired and wheel-chair-bound Justice Douglas reacted to the hearings with more measured circumspection: "The good Lord only provided us with so much land and it is up to public officials to make those critical decisions which will ensure that future generations will have the same opportunity as many of us have to enjoy the excitement of a wilderness experience."[32]

An even greater pro-wilderness majority showed up for the hearing in Tacoma the following week. Around 250 people filled the venue with 70 percent favoring the expanded, north-south Cougar Lakes Wilderness proposal. Nonetheless, those opposing wilderness were more outspoken than they had been in the Yakima session. Wilbur Hallauer, Director of the Department of Ecology, opened the oral testimony delivering the same anti-wilderness statement on behalf of Governor Ray as in Yakima. The mayor of Tacoma demanded that USFS stop withdrawing land for wilderness in Washington State. Steve Edmundson, a member of a rock and gem club, proclaimed, "Many of our members are elderly and want roads into Cougar Lakes so we can pursue our hobby. We have no intention of standing aside to let the younger generation use these areas as wilderness." On the other hand, Mike Ruby of Seattle had an alternative proposal concerning one particular member of Edmundson's "elderly" generation: he suggested naming the proposed wilderness after William O. Douglas. The timber industry—absent in Yakima—fielded over twelve speakers in Tacoma to testify against wilderness. Stewart "Stu" Bledsoe, representing the Washington Forest Protection Association, argued that timber "harvested" from the Cougar Lakes area could produce 32 million board feet and support 602 jobs.[33] This suggestion, and Governor Ray's unabashed support for logging, prompted Kay to scratch out a cartoon for publication in the NCCC newsletter: it depicts a clear-cut Cougar Lakes area with Tote-Goats running amok across a stump-filled landscape. Overhead, a tram carries sightseers to the summit of Mt. Aix.[34]

Bledsoe's opinion on jobs and production exemplified the influence of the logging industry over the USFS decision-making process for Cougar Lakes. Public forests had been under intense commercial pressure: board foot totals taken

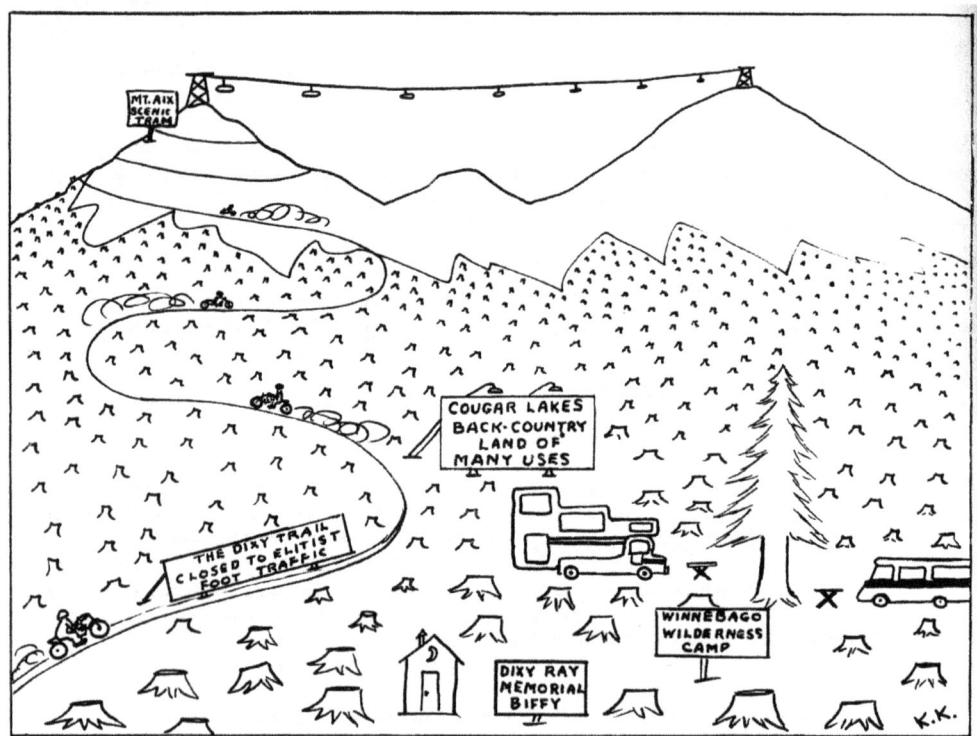

DIXY'S VERSION OF COUGAR LAKES

Kay Kershaw, "Dixy's Version of Cougar Lakes," *Wild Cascades* (Winter 1978) (North Cascades Conservation Council). In this cartoon, Kay Kershaw documents her anger and frustration with Dixy Lee Ray, Washington State's governor from 1977 to 1981. Ray was a Democrat and acclaimed marine biologist who nonetheless promoted unrestricted growth and commercial development throughout the state. During the Cougar Lakes Hearings, her official position categorically opposed wilderness designation. In Kershaw's apocalyptic rendition of Goose Prairie's future, stumps stretch to the horizon as motorcycles zoom up trails "closed to foot traffic" and a tram carries sightseers to the denuded summit of Mt. Aix. In the foreground, gigantic Winnebago campers park next to a single tree and an outhouse dedicated to "Dixy Ray."

from national forests went from 5.8 million in 1955 to 14.8 billion in 1969. The government's own projections in 1973 indicated that many regions had already been over-cut. An agency-wide Emergency Directive mandated an even flow and non-declining yield for all USFS lands in order to maintain current timber yields into the future. The 1976 National Forest Management Act included a similar provision.[35] In Washington State's federal forests, the most extensive logging occurred in the Gifford Pinchot National Forest (Gifford-Pinchot). Its jurisdiction encompassed the pre-eruption Mt. St. Helens, Mt. Adams, the Goat Rocks, and a sizeable stretch of Washington State's portion of the Pacific Crest Trail. The Gifford-Pinchot's very northeastern corner extended to Fish Lake and the Bumping River headwaters—quite literally the Double K's backyard. In contrast to the Mt. Baker-Snoqualmie National Forest, located close to Puget Sound and its dense population centers fostering a conservation-minded, outdoor recreation-oriented constituency, the Gifford-Pinchot was in the less-populated southwest section of the state. Here the gentle terrain suits felling trees and, in many communities bordering the forests, job opportunities centered on logging.

In 1974, USFS admitted in a letter to Senator Jackson that it had over-cut the Gifford-Pinchot and could not sustain the current level of logging operations without federal aid. Still, USFS allowed removal of 414 million board feet in 1976, once again exceeding totals from any other federal forest in the state. But more trees cut did not necessarily translate into more jobs created: exports of unprocessed logs from the United States to Japan—two-thirds of which came from Washington State—grew from 150 million board feet in the early 1960s to nearly three billion board feet cut annually by the end of 1978.[36] This was anathema to many in the environmental movement. Clear-cutting and wholesale liquidation of old growth timber had rendered the Gifford-Pinchot indistinguishable from privately-held, industrial tree farms. As Isabelle Lynn described it to the Seattle press in 1978, "the place looks like a moth-eaten bear rug."[37]

Cougar Lakes Wilderness Encounters RARE II—1979

The 1976 USFS recommendation for a 138,854-acre Cougar Lakes wilderness was a regional decision made separately—and prior to completion of—the national RARE II survey and evaluation process. That the two would collide at some point in 1979 was perhaps a foregone conclusion, or so it appeared to the NCCC board of directors. In its 1978 annual report to the membership, the board raised the alarming prospect that Cougar Lakes—now tantalizingly close to wilderness designation—might fall into the category of roadless areas designated for study under RARE II's byzantine procedures.[38] Their misgivings proved prescient. In June 1978, USFS mandated a delay of any decision on Cougar Lakes until completion of the national RARE II Study in early 1979. This stimulated a bit of optimism though:

the 1978 RARE II study offered 175,000 acres to be adjusted based on public input, a potential increase of some 36,000 acres over the 1976 Cougar Lakes proposal. The RARE II DEIS listed ten options for this expanded acreage with the public encouraged to make recommendations between June and 1 October about three roadless area alternatives: designation as wilderness; management as non-wilderness (and therefore multiple-use); or delay for future planning consideration. USFS devised a ten-step wilderness attribute rating system (WARS) intended to provide an objective, quasi-scientific evaluation of each of the proposed areas in terms of its own wilderness qualities. At that point, USFS would review the opinions and make a decision in January 1979 in a national EIS for the seventy-five roadless areas on 2.1 million acres in Washington State.[39]

The earlier optimism faded quickly: Cougar Lakes acreage under consideration for wilderness went from 138,854 to zero in a matter of five months. USFS determined that Washington State offered "better places for wilderness" than at Cougar Lakes. In contrast to the plaudits about scenery and solitude written into the 1976 USFS Cougar Lakes Survey, John Rogers, Supervisor of the Wenatchee National Forest, now described the region as the "area left over when God was finished making the world."[40] The public input gathered by USFS between June and October 1978 formed a crucial aspect of this decision: concerned citizens wrote more letters about Cougar Lakes than any other roadless area in the state. However, this body of "written messages" was open to interpretation. Robert Lewis, a planning officer for the Wenatchee National Forest declared that about 60 to 65 percent of the feedback favored non-wilderness alternatives.[41] At step two of WARS, Region 6 Forester Dick Worthington and his staff in Portland, Oregon, decreed that the public wanted non-wilderness designation for Cougar Lakes based on Lewis's documentation. Environmentalists took issue with this, noting that the total percentage cited by Lewis included pre-printed cards, questionnaires, form letters, and petitions circulated by anti-wilderness groups and industries. On the other hand, the total number of personal letters—which USFS had affirmed would receive greater consideration in the final decision process—painted rather a different picture: 516 personal letters filled the USFS files in favor of wilderness in contrast to sixty-nine opposed.[42] The low WARS score at step two put the region at a disadvantageous position: Cougar Lakes would have to receive an extremely high rating on wilderness attributes to get transferred from "non-wilderness" to "future planning" designation. By step five, the WARS score remained so low that multiple-use at Cougar Lakes appeared unavoidable. However, the tenth and final step of the WARS process involved a meeting in Washington, D.C., with M. Rupert Cutler, Assistant Secretary of Agriculture.[43]

In November, Secretary Cutler summoned Regional Forester Worthington and Chief Forester McGuire to a four-day meeting to discuss the RARE II decisions. Worthington arrived with "a mountain of RARE II information" on what should be wilderness: he brought nothing to the meeting that indicated support for any manner of wilderness designation at Cougar Lakes. Cutler—a former college professor who had also worked as a lobbyist for the Wilderness Society in Washington, D.C.—kept company with Doug Scott and Brock Evans, both of whom had been involved with NCCC, and by extension, with Kershaw and Lynn's Cougar Lakes wilderness proposal. In addition, Brock Evans was an honorary member of CLWA advocating on behalf of the Cougar Lakes region since his first trip there in 1966. Evans and Scott had the ear of the new assistant secretary and they were elated that he held the reins of the fate for Cougar Lakes: "[Cutler] was one of us," Evans said recently. "He understood the issues: we could just pick up the phone and call."[44]

In the meeting with Worthington and McGuire, Cutler made it clear that there would, in fact, be a Cougar Lakes wilderness. Cutler insisted on a narrow, salamander-shaped strip of land on either side of the Pacific Crest Trail from White Pass to Chinook Pass to serve as a bridge connecting Goat Rocks to Mt. Rainier National Park (MRNP). Overruling the USFS determination, Cutler designated as wilderness 23,000 acres out of the 1976 Cougar Lakes Survey: 11,200 acres in the Wenatchee National Forest and 11,795 acres in the Gifford-Pinchot.[45]

This was a crucial moment in the history of the region. Without Cutler's intervention, the notion of a Cougar Lakes wilderness would have evaporated, with restoration impossible after inevitable degradation from multiple-use logging and development. Forty-two years after this meeting, Rupert Cutler recollected, "Worthington was ... in my view a classic 'timber beast,' as the saying went, and not enthusiastic about wilderness. Chief John McGuire was a 'cards-held-close-to-the-vest' fellow who carried out my directions but clearly was uncomfortable with my 'political' direction, given that the Forest Service was unused to any direction from the [Agriculture] Secretary's office."[46]

Nonetheless, Cutler's decision—made while faced with the impossible task of analyzing every roadless area

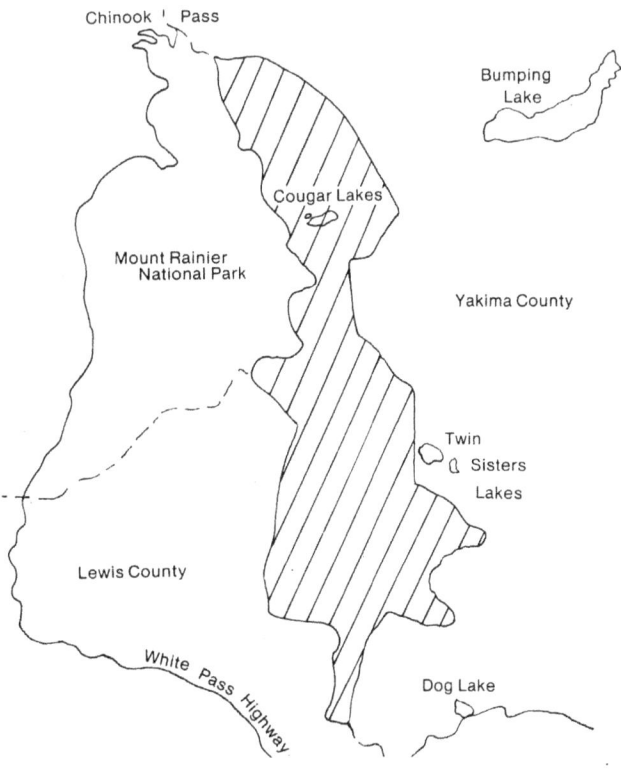

Map 6: Rupert Cutler's Cougar Lakes Proposal—1979. *Yakima Herald-Republic*, 8 April 1979 (Yakima Valley Museum).

in the United States through the RARE II lens—disappointed many wilderness advocates and opponents alike. On the one hand, nine Central Washington county commissioners had joined together to prevent any further USFS wilderness studies in the state for months prior to the final RARE II deadline in October 1978, and Boise-Cascade had been at loggerheads with CLWA over Cougar Lakes for years. On the other, proponents were horrified by a massive 80 percent reduction in wilderness at Cougar Lakes from one USFS report to the next in less than a year. Many thought that the "outrageous" elimination of Cougar Lakes wilderness acreage in 1978 was simply a ploy to boost it in the final stages of the RARE II process and "look good." For Isabelle, the increase from nothing to 23,000 acres was "preposterous ... a gratuitous insult" to those who had worked for more than a decade to establish a Cougar Lakes wilderness. As the *Yakima Herald-Republic* summed up the situation at the beginning of 1979, "[USFS] has apparently succeeded in pleasing almost no one with the results of its RARE II study."[47]

Cougar Lakes Wilderness Goes to Congress—1979

Part of the RARE II protocol required incorporating input from other government agencies into the EIS. Commenting on the Cougar Lakes RARE II decision, NPS disagreed with USFS concerning the amount of land that should be designated wilderness. Park Service director William J. Whalen considered the reductions to the Cougar Lakes proposal excessive, suggesting instead a designation of more than 160,000 acres in order to buffer the east side of MRNP. The significant difference of over 138,000 acres between the two recommendations led to an interagency fracas as each vied for the support of President Jimmy Carter. The White House Office of Management and Budget (OMB) served as referee on the issue while also considering comments by the Department of Ecology and the Environmental Protection Agency. Across the entire state of Washington, NPS recommended eight times as much land for wilderness as USFS: a total of 1.3 million acres compared to 256,000 acres of additional wilderness and 220,000 acres designated for further study earmarked in the RARE II report. The remaining 1.6 million acres of the more than 2 million acres of roadless area would be open to multiple-use logging and development.[48]

Some members of Congress grew concerned that wrangling over wilderness would lead to a protracted legal battle. Representative John Seiberling of Ohio, who chaired the House Public Lands subcommittee, believed that such litigation and further delaying tactics could jeopardize the entire RARE II process. Enlisting the aid of Mike Lowry and Joel Pritchard, two congressmen from the west side of Washington State, Seiberling made a concerted effort to increase the amount of wilderness in RARE II. The three congressmen allied with NPS, the White House OMB, the Bureau of Land Management, and the Council on Environmental Quality to boost the acreage. In March, Pritchard and Lowry wrote to USFS to suggest including all

176,000 acres of Cougar Lakes in wilderness. Mike McCormack, Washington's representative for the fourth congressional district, disagreed. Rather, he offered his own Cougar Lakes proposal more in line with his vocal anti-wilderness constituents in Yakima County. This combination of congressional pressure, fear of time-consuming lawsuits, and national publicity over the RARE II wilderness process all had an effect on President Carter. His recommendation to Congress in mid-April increased Cutler's thin 23,000-acre strip along the Pacific Crest Trail to a more robust 129,320 acres.[49]

By June 1979, Congress had three separate Cougar Lakes proposals to contend with. In addition to the one presented by President Carter in April, Lowry and Pritchard had formulated a bill encompassing 270,000 acres, adding Mt. Aix, American Ridge, Tumac Mountain, Timberwolf Mountain, and the Norse Peak areas on the north side of Highway 410 to Carter's 129,320 acres.[50] When contacted by the local paper, Boise-Cascade's spokesman replied that his reaction to the Lowry-Pritchard bill was "probably unprintable." McCormack's idea found greater acceptance with the timber industry: another 15,600 acres encircling Mt. Aix added to the 23,000-acre strip of wilderness along the Pacific Crest Trail, plus 100,200 acres classified under a new designation as "limited recreation," open to development and motorized vehicles.[51]

Over the next year, the ensuing competition over the Cougar Lakes Wilderness proposals grew increasingly contentious between Pritchard and Lowry on the one hand and McCormack on the other. An omnibus wilderness bill before the House complicated the issue: it included a release provision precluding management as wilderness for non-wilderness areas awaiting further RARE II study after 1984. Debate over the release provision language in this omnibus bill and squabbling among the Washington delegation over the size of the Cougar Lakes

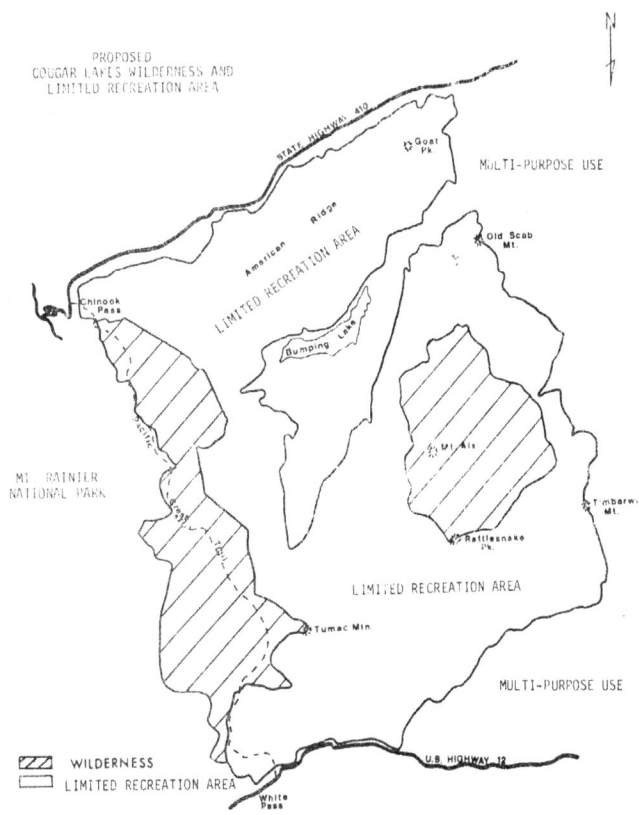

Map 7: Representative Mike McCormack's plan—1979. *Yakima Herald-Republic*, 16 April 1979 (Yakima Valley Museum).

wilderness compelled House Public Lands chairman Seiberling to postpone further consideration until Pritchard, Lowry, and McCormack had resolved their differences.[52] In the meantime, USFS stated that the southern section of the proposed Cougar Lakes wilderness would be managed as wilderness until Congress acted on one of the proposals before it. However, the agency would manage the northern section—where the quality of timber was superior to the southern—as part roadless, part multiple-use with several timber cuts scheduled. Alarmed conservationists worried that logging there would render the area non-wilderness before Congress ever made a determination on a Cougar Lakes bill. Pritchard and Lowry pleaded with regional USFS administrators to postpone these timber sales.[53]

Republicans Take Control—1980

As movement on a Cougar Lakes bill stalled, the 1980 elections swept the Democrats out of office ushering in the conservative Republican administration of Ronald Reagan. Although Democrats still held a majority in the House, for the first time since 1953—in either chamber—Republicans now controlled the Senate. This new political era significantly altered national policy-making decisions portending a sea-change in environmental legislation as well. "Well, I lived through Harding, Coolidge and Hoover so I suppose I'll make it," Isabelle wrote to Scoop Jackson's assistant just before Reagan's inauguration in 1981. "We have to have action on Cougar Lakes early this year—in the first 3 [sic] months in fact—or it will be 4 [sic] years before there would be another chance—or never. I'd guess never."[54] Isabelle had the timeline right: in April, California's Republican Senator S.I. Hayakawa sponsored a bill endorsed by the Reagan administration that would force Congress to meet strict deadlines for deciding whether areas under consideration for wilderness would be permanently set aside or opened for commercial use. Hayakawa's proposal potentially allowed mining, logging, and other industry on 51.4 million acres of national forests. The legislation would open up 36 million acres immediately. In addition, Hayakawa insisted on a "hard release" provision for lands under scrutiny: once released from set-aside, Congress could never again consider them for inclusion in the national wilderness system. Reagan's new Deputy Secretary of Agriculture, Richard E. Lyng, told the Senate subcommittee on Public Lands that after ten years of study and litigation, "we can no longer afford further delays."[55]

On 5 March, Representatives Pritchard and Lowry reintroduced their Cougar Lakes Wilderness bill in the House for the Ninety-Seventh Session of Congress. The new Washington delegation hoped to put together a wilderness package including areas across the state that all seven representatives could agree upon. "We'll hammer it out—soon, I hope," Lowry told the *Seattle Times*.[56] Republican Sid Morrison became the newest member of this Washington State group, carried into office by the Reagan tsunami to replace Mike McCormack in the fourth congressional district.

Morrison had served in the Washington State House of Representatives for eight years until his election to the State Senate in 1974. His party appointed him Republican deputy whip as a freshman congressman based on his extensive legislative experience. Wielding influence at the Capitol almost from the outset, Morrison rushed headlong into resolving the long-standing issues over wilderness and roadless areas in his region.[57] Initially, Kay and Isabelle were optimistic that he would support a Cougar Lakes wilderness, at least in the southern parcel. And even the Sierra Club considered Morrison someone they could work with, noting his eagerness to resolve the wilderness debate. But Kay and Isabelle started to have doubts, writing to the Sierra Club's Northwest representative:

> [Morrison says] we couldn't make the area to the south of Chinook Pass a wilderness because it receives too much use. If he doesn't want the south unit and is not especially interested in the north unit but would go along if some other congressman introduced it (I trust you pointed out that "some other congressmen"—Pritchard and Lowry—have already introduced it) just what *is* he interested in supporting? A place in Ohio, possibly.... Did you ask Morrison why the North Fork of the Rattlesnake is "a fire waiting to happen" any more than any other place in the Cascades?[58]

Although he never answered that particular question, Sid Morrison believed that his skill-set honed as a state-level legislator could facilitate negotiations over the creation of wilderness in his own congressional district. However, in 1984, after four years of hard-earned experience, he made his opinion crystal clear: "Don't ever put anything into wilderness that you might want to take out later because you'll face opposition from environmental groups."[59] Kay and Isabelle taught Morrison that lesson incrementally from the very start of his congressional career: "my visits with them," he said, "were challenging but delightful."[60]

At the beginning of May, Deputy Secretary of Agriculture Lyng testified before the House Subcommittee on Public Lands and National Parks. Lyng stated that the Reagan administration would support the designation of some 200,000 acres of wilderness in Washington State, although none would be allocated at Cougar Lakes. Rupert Cutler, now senior vice president of the Audubon Society, remarked that the Reagan administration's stance "flies in the face of sound professional forest practices judgement." Sid Morrison attempted to spin Lyng's words, suggesting that this point of view was not "anti-environmental." Rather, he conjectured, "it just means, let's turn Cougar Lakes back to the Forest Service, and the Forest Service will be responsible for its management. The sense I get is that the Forest Service would keep most of Cougar Lakes in a non-commercial category."[61]

Contrary to Morrison's Pollyanna prediction, USFS had a timber sale of 15.4 million board feet on the books for 1985 within the boundaries of the Cougar Lakes wilderness area in a little less than ten months' time.[62] Acting unilaterally, USFS began offering timber sales that would effectively remove lands from wilderness consideration while Congress was in the midst of reviewing a wilderness bill. With the Reagan administration's policy on the record concerning Cougar Lakes, nothing prevented USFS from doing just as it pleased. A new sale posted in May 1982 to the east and south of Bumping Lake scheduled for 1986 prompted Isabelle to state, "The proposal is a disaster. The soil is too fragile to support the kind of management suggested by the Forest Service." Representative Morrison became the pivotal player in this melee as it unfolded within the boundaries of his congressional district. His frustration was palpable. Morrison had to broker a deal between the zero-wilderness option at Cougar Lakes favored by the Reagan administration and the Pritchard-Lowry proposal for 278,000 acres while the Senate Energy and Natural Resources Subcommittee wrangled over Hayakawa's release language and USFS sold off the region's timber. Legislative logjams occurred at several levels, and Morrison wanted to avoid pushing a Washington Wilderness bill to the forefront too soon: it had the potential to become a battleground for acrimonious debate concerning national release language.[63]

In light of these divergent issues, the Washington State congressional delegation realized that they had to come to an agreement on wilderness. Morrison predicted that if the Washington delegation could compromise on boundaries for the Cougar Lakes Wilderness, the Reagan administration would consider an endorsement of the compromise. He believed that the acreage allocated for Cougar Lakes in Lowry and Pritchard's bill was untenable. Wooed by a Seattle developer with a decades-long obsession for constructing condominiums overlooking Crystal Mountain Ski Resort, the freshman congressman gave his total support to deleting the northern section of Cougar Lakes from the wilderness bill. This would allow private logging in the old-growth forests north of Highway 410 and construction of the condominiums as well as a tram line to expand Crystal Mountain ski area into the Morse Creek drainage. These proposals horrified environmentalists. Even for USFS, it was a bridge too far and Morrison's ill-conceived notion went nowhere.[64] But he had an alternative plan for sweetening the deal on Cougar Lakes involving another major ski area development within his district. He proposed carving 2,500 acres out of the Goat Rocks Wilderness along the southern border of White Pass Ski Area following Hogback ridge all the way to Shoe Lake saddle and east to encompass Miriam Creek drainage.

The notion of expanding into the Goat Rocks existed almost from the inception of White Pass Ski Area: serious deliberations between the Forest Service and White Pass Corporation stockholders concerning lifts into Miriam Basin took place in August 1957 and continued into the early 1960s.[65] By the late 1970s, White Pass Ski Company (WPSC) had formulated grandiose plans for eight new ski lifts there. Representative Morrison told the *Yakima Herald-Republic* that one of the top priorities for the Washington State congressional delegation was formulating a plan that included a White Pass ski area expansion.[66] Morrison's new scheme to remove 2,500 acres from wilderness for "a more sympathetic view of the Cougar Lakes Wilderness" incensed Kay and Isabelle—"he has been too influenced by the timber people and ORV types"—who expressed their outrage in a letter sent to Senators Slade

Gorton and Jackson: "the suggestion that 2500 acres of the Goat Rocks, including portions of the Pacific Crest Trail, be turned over to [WPSC] is out of the question."[67]

The majority of Yakima's CLWA aligned with Kay and Isabelle's opposition to Morrison's expansion proposal. Kay's nephew, Bob Kershaw along with Cragg D. Gilbert, formed a local task force in early spring of 1983—the Committee for Reasonable Wilderness—to work out a compromise with input from CLWA, WPSC, and Washington State's congressional members. As two individuals who maintained a high-profile in Yakima agriculture, Kershaw and Gilbert lobbied influential members of the farming community to support compromise wilderness legislation. By early 1984, the combined efforts of these groups reduced Morrison's 2,500-acre swath of ski expansion territory to a more reasonable 500 acres.[68] This accommodation seemed reasonable to Kay and Isabelle who wrote to John Seiberling: "Purists though we have been, we have learned that not much is accomplished without a little *quid pro quo*, and we feel this is very little."[69]

Nonetheless, larger groups such as the Sierra Club and The Wilderness Society along with regional affiliates were loath to approve a precedent-setting removal of wilderness for commercial exploitation.[70] Faced with a self-imposed deadline on the last day of February 1984, the ten-member congressional delegation presented an ultimatum to local, regional, and national environmental organizations: either they acquiesce to redrawing the Goat Rocks Wilderness boundary to accommodate expansion of the ski area in exchange for wilderness designation on either side of Chinook Pass or the Cougar Lakes area would be substantially reduced. Senator Gorton said that environmentalists had a choice of accepting one plan or the other, adding that most members of the congressional delegation preferred a larger Cougar Lakes and modifications

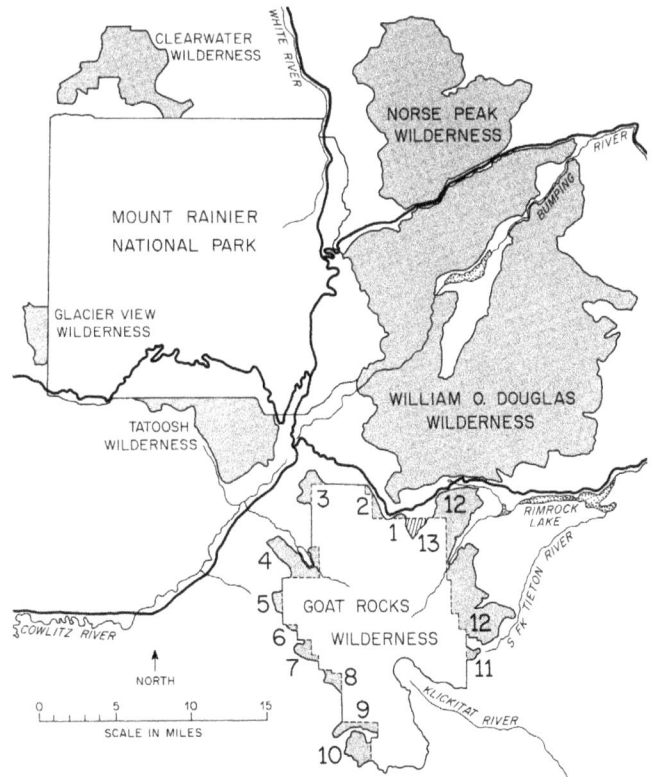

Map 8: William O. Douglas and Norse Peak Wilderness Areas—1984. *Wild Cascades*, Fall 1984: 15 (North Cascades Conservation Council: Noel McGary, cartographer). Shaded areas 1–12 signify additions made to the Goat Rocks. Number 13 indicates the area deleted from wilderness for commercial development by WPSC.

favorable to WPSC. Clearly upset that his plan to take 2,500 acres out of wilderness for the use of WPSC had been gutted the previous year—or at least feigning anger—Sid Morrison told the *Yakima Herald-Republic* that opposition by "conservation groups" threatened to scuttle the entire wilderness bill.[71]

Crafting a comprehensive Washington Wilderness Bill that included a compromise on Cougar Lakes took only a week. In exchange for the 500 (later increased to 900) acres delivered to WPSC, the package totaled 191,445 acres: a wilderness area at Cougar Lakes of 150,075 acres south of Chinook Pass and 41,370 to the north known as the Norse Peak Wilderness. Speaking to the press—both as a WPSC shareholder and the secretary-treasurer of the Committee for Reasonable Wilderness—the laconic Cragg D. Gilbert simply stated, "We are very happy about it."[72]

Unfortunately, neither Justice Douglas nor Scoop Jackson were alive to celebrate an event that had taken a quarter of a century to accomplish: Douglas had passed away in 1980 followed by Jackson, who succumbed to heart failure in 1983. However, their legacies were not forgotten. The congressional delegation determined that the Cougar Lakes area would be named the William O. Douglas Wilderness and designated a 50,000-acre addition to Glacier Peak Wilderness as the Henry M. Jackson Wilderness [see Maps 1 and 8].[73] Both embodied fitting tributes for two fierce environmental proponents in Washington State.

10

How Cougar Lakes Became the William O. Douglas Wilderness

The Last Years of Justice Douglas (1974–1980)

After William O. Douglas's death on 19 January 1980, Charlotte Mayerson, his editor at Random House, put it bluntly in a letter to Kershaw and Lynn: "Bill died so hard and took so long to do it, it was as if that indomitable spirit were working against him."[1] Douglas had been admitted to Walter Reed Army Medical Center on Christmas Eve 1979 suffering from pneumonia and kidney failure, almost five years to the day after his debilitating stroke on New Year's Eve 1974. To many, that stroke marked the beginning of the Justice's endgame: "in view of his lamentable condition you perhaps feel that you lost him many years before his actual death," a Double K friend wrote in a note of condolence.[2]

Since his collapse on the bench in June 1968, Justice Douglas's heart condition had been a matter of concern. A decidedly conservative shift in the United States during the Nixon administration compounded his ongoing health issues. Douglas was always a controversial figure, and his liberal viewpoint raised the hackles of the Republican party. Animus toward Douglas came to a head in 1970 when Republican House Minority Leader Gerald Ford instigated impeachment proceedings against him. Douglas had already convinced himself that he was under surveillance by the government; his sense of paranoia only increased while the House Judiciary Committee investigated his case. He wrote to Kay and Isabelle in May warning them to be vigilant:

> I wrote you last fall or winter that federal agents were in Yakima and Goose Prairie looking me over at Goose Prairie. I thought they were merely counting fence posts. But I learned in New York City yesterday that they were planting marijuana with the prospect of a nice big tv-covered raid in July or August. I forgot to tell you that this gang [the Nixon administration] is not in search of truth. They are a "search and destroy" people.[3]

After an eight-month study, including the examination of some half million pieces of Douglas's papers, the Judiciary Committee ruled that no grounds for impeachment existed. Nonetheless, the whole impeachment idea cropped up again briefly in 1973 when Douglas issued a stay on the Nixon administration's bombing campaign in Cambodia.[4] Perhaps two credible threats of impeachment in a span of three years put extra strain on him.

After his stroke in 1974, Justice Douglas believed that he would recover the ability to walk and insisted on continuing his regular routine with the Supreme Court even as his mental concentration took a turn for the worse. In June 1975, he attended his fiftieth reunion at Columbia University where he received special honors, then he and Cathy Douglas left the east coast for their annual summer trip to Goose Prairie. It proved quite difficult. With high hopes that a Double K wrangler might saddle up a horse so he could ride again with Kay and Isabelle, Douglas arrived in Goose Prairie only to find that he could not even traverse the driveway with his walker. Confinement in a wheelchair while surrounded by his beloved mountains at Goose Prairie was almost too much to bear. Aware that Douglas was spending the summer at Goose Prairie, Charles Reich wrote to Kershaw and Lynn in early August: "Just wanted to say Hi … hope you're having a fine summer. [Justice Douglas] looks awful on TV—I guess you can see him and tell for yourselves. If he's in bad shape, we owe it to him to tell him to retire, I feel. But let's hope he's OK."[5] He wasn't. In September, Justice Douglas made a disastrous decision to hear oral arguments in a case at the Yakima County Courthouse. His appearance attracted a crowd of journalists and photographers who documented his incapacitated state during the proceedings.[6] Clearly the time had come to broach the subject of retirement, but those close to him knew it would be a fraught exercise. Isabelle and Kay contacted Charles Reich to ask for help. They invited him to come stay at the Double K and join in a concerted effort to reason with Douglas. Reich arrived at the end of September and spent three days in contentious discussions to no avail: "A visit to remember!!! Lots of love," Reich scrawled in the Double K guestbook.[7]

Douglas returned to the Capital, but found that it was too difficult to continue his duties at the Supreme Court. A few days after announcing his retirement, he asked Lynn to gather up some government documents still in his study at Prairie House and ship them back to Washington, D.C.[8] The following week, Mayerson confessed to Kay and Isabelle that she was in a "gloomy" mood: "The situation changed from day to day, up and down, heartbreaking and, alternately, encouraging. As you know, [Justice Douglas] is now with Dr. Packer [sic] in Portland whom he feels is his only hope. Well, I suppose that being there will bring some comfort and, in that sense, it's probably OK." Douglas had decided to seek treatment at a special stroke care unit of Good Samaritan Hospital and Medical Center in Portland run by his long-time friend and personal physician, Joseph Paquet. Douglas's son, Bill Jr., accompanied him on the trip to Oregon while Cathy remained in Washington, D.C.: "The role of madame is so ambiguous that I can't hardly write about it nor even think about it clearly," Mayerson wrote. "I wish we could have a good chat."[9] Although the physical therapists at Good Samaritan sincerely hoped Douglas might regain some basic ability to write and perform functional tasks, the prognosis was not encouraging: "I don't expect recovery," Paquet told the *New York Times*.[10]

Kershaw and Lynn tried to get in touch and offer encouragement while Douglas underwent treatment: "I greatly enjoyed the telephone message which I got from you and Kay in Portland," Douglas wrote. "I wanted to return it but there was no possible way." As he recuperated in the stroke clinic, his thoughts turned to Goose Prairie: "Since I was not very far away I entertained [the idea of visiting Goose Prairie] but the weather predictions were so uncertain and the doctors looked askance to the whole idea so I finally dropped it. We had toyed with the idea of being at the Prairie for Christmas but that has not been possible to work out so we will be dancing around your tree in spirit even though we will not be there physically."[11] Even though the trip to Goose Prairie the previous summer had been difficult, Douglas still held out hopes that he could return. Before he announced his retirement, he had written Kay and Isabelle about arranging secretarial staff for the coming summer.[12]

Although his stay at the stroke clinic had not changed his immobilized status, Douglas insisted on another short foray to Goose Prairie for the summer of 1976. To accommodate him required a detailed battle plan with everyone pitching in at Prairie House. Accompanied by his law clerk, Bob Deitz, Justice Douglas would be met in Portland by his son and Dr. Paquet; he would stay overnight at the Good Samaritan stroke clinic or longer, if need be, then he and his son would fly to Yakima. His neighbor, Ira Ford, would deliver his car to the Yakima airport and, in the meantime, two RNs—Gary Schnabel and Stephanie Fennimore—would drive to Goose Prairie to take up residence, hired as "'housekeepers,' because Justice doesn't think he needs a nurse." Bill Jr. would stay with his father until 25 July; he would be on his own for a week with the two RNs and then his wife Cathy would arrive on 2 August. Kershaw and Lynn assumed responsibility for setting up a communications system—either CB or ham radio—between Prairie House and the Double K. Horses and hay would arrive on 19 July. "The key seems to be whether the Justice likes Gary and Stephanie," Justice Douglas's secretary wrote tentatively.[13] He did not: the Goose Prairie trip was cut short after Bill Jr. left and the two strangers arrived: "I think Cathy had [Stephanie] in mind as a housekeeper," Douglas wrote to Isabelle after returning to Washington, D.C., at the end of July, "but we decided against hiring her, and against hiring her boyfriend, Gary. So if you see them on the place, chase them off."[14] Acting according to his wishes, Isabelle and Kay sent the two on their way. "I'm glad Gary and Stephanie have disappeared," he fumed in a follow-up letter a week later.[15] The two RNs notwithstanding, things went well enough. "It was nice to be at Goose Prairie," Douglas wrote to Isabelle, "and I hated to leave. It was a special joy to see you and Kay. I think I'll be back, although on this trip I thought it would be the last I'd ever make. The aches and pains persist, and I am weaker than I was last summer, I think."[16] Douglas's secretary followed up a few weeks later: "The Justice is well. In fact, he seems better now than when he went West. Maybe he had to go in order to realize that as much as he loves it out there under the present circumstances he is better off here where he has a definite routine. I'll keep you posted."[17] But even Justice Douglas himself began to realize that, perhaps, he would never return. He wrote to Kay, "I miss seeing you and Isabelle. I am not sure if I will get out to Goose Praire [sic] next summer or not. I hope I do, but the catch is getting a nurse that is competent and one that I can afford."[18]

Unfortunately, Douglas's condition continued to deteriorate and a subsequent trip in 1978 was out of the question. It took nearly two years before Cathy Douglas returned to Goose Prairie in October 1979. She told the *Yakima Herald-Republic* that her husband wanted to come back, although she was less enthusiastic about arranging travel across the country to a location so far from medical assistance.[19] Douglas's frequent backcountry companion Cragg D. Gilbert knew how much he longed for the mountains: "He wanted to come out here so badly during the last few years and yet he knew that he just couldn't."[20]

With his passing just a few months after Cathy Douglas's 1979 interview, letters and requests for comment inundated Kershaw and Lynn. "He was a remarkable man," Kay told the *Everett Herald*. "Really, he was two men: the public man and the private man. Up here we knew the private man."[21] Kay and Isabelle chose to remember this private version of their friend. Robert Utter, Chief Justice of the Washington State Supreme Court, invited them to a memorial service in Olympia scheduled for 28 January. They declined, citing winter conditions at Goose Prairie which precluded an absence of twenty-four hours. "Bill's death left a great gap in our lives … our close association with him over many years has provided memories we shall cherish for the rest of our lives."[22] How to best memorialize that deep bond inspired Kershaw and Lynn to redouble their efforts to get Cougar Lakes Wilderness through Congress and have it named after William O. Douglas.

Cougar Lakes Wilderness Renamed (1980–1984)

When President Ronald Reagan signed the Washington Wilderness Bill in July 1984, Sid Morrison was ecstatic, proclaiming that this would be "the last major wilderness bill" of the twentieth century. Congress had passed legislation that year adding more than 3.6 million acres of wilderness in eight states. Such an impressive raft of wilderness bills advanced through the legislature due to a final resolution on release language: that is, details describing how roadless areas which had not received wilderness designation would be managed going forward.[23] Washington State was abuzz with the passage of the region's Wilderness Act, and the announcement that Cougar Lakes Wilderness would be named in honor of William O. Douglas prompted a euphoric Morrison to tell the *Yakima Herald-Republic*, "[It's] hard to put your finger on who actually initiated the naming of this new wilderness after Douglas." The paper reported that Morrison and Cathy Douglas had discussed the matter "some years ago" and that Kershaw and Lynn had expressed "consistent interest."[24] But the Double K duo's effort involved a bit more than Morrison and the local paper let on.

As noted earlier, Mike Ruby of Seattle proposed naming the Cougar Lakes Wilderness after Douglas in February 1978 at the Cougar Lakes public hearings in Tacoma. Ruby's inspiration may have been the dedication of the C & O Canal to Douglas in May of the previous year. Nonetheless, his proposal struck a chord with NCCC who highlighted it in their newsletter in early winter of 1978.[25] Thus, the notion had currency in environmental circles before Douglas's death on 19 January 1980, and it gained additional traction immediately after. In a handwritten letter dated 20 January, Isabelle stated, "I have written Denny [Miller, Senator Henry M. Jackson's chief of staff] this a.m. to remind him of our conversation in August about naming CLWA [Cougar Lakes Wilderness Area] for Bill—and *not* [sic] naming Baldy for him."[26] Just a few days later, she wrote to Betty Fletcher, a judge recently appointed to the Ninth Circuit Court of Appeals, that "we have been working hard on the Cougar Lakes bill—among other things to change the name of it to the W.O.D. [William O. Douglas] Wilderness—and the quashing of the enlargement of Bumping Lake."[27] Kay and Isabelle's colleague, CLWA president Philip Johnson, wrote a letter of condolence to Cathy Douglas, suggesting that the Cougar Lakes Wilderness be named for the late Justice.[28] A letter to Isabelle arrived at the beginning of February stating, "Well, we were privileged to know [Douglas]. Let's hope you win on naming the Wilderness area after him."[29]

Evidently, Kershaw and Lynn had suggested to Cathy Douglas that she contact President Carter about renaming Cougar Lakes, indicated in a letter Isabelle received from Monty Podva, Justice Douglas's last law clerk: "As you know by now I followed up Cathy's phone conversation to the White House aides with a letter to the President. I'm sure that he will be in communication with the Senator's [sic] from Washington about it, so I'll just leave that end of things to you."[30] In his letter to Carter, Podva stated that naming the wilderness after Douglas would be a most fitting tribute: "Needless to say, by quashing the enlargement of Bumping Lake and including the greatest land area possible within its boundaries, the Justice's final battle on behalf of the environment will be won. His spirit will roam that familiar territory forever."[31] In a Valentine's Day letter to Kay and Isabelle, Podva listed a few of the suggested memorials to Douglas's memory, noting that Cougar Lakes had been his top choice: "I have this straight from a now heavenly source, to wit, the horse's mouth."[32] This prompted Lynn to contact Brock Evans, now an Associate Executive Director for the Sierra Club in Washington, D.C. Evans and Doug Scott, the Sierra Club's Director of Federal Affairs based in San Francisco, had published a piece in the *Washington Post* suggesting that the Middle Snake River—where Douglas had thwarted a proposed dam (now a "non-dam," in their words, between Washington and Idaho)—would be a fitting memorial to him.[33] "Yes, this is a nice mental concept," Isabelle wrote, referring to the non-dam idea. "But, as you may know, we have something far more [tangible] in mind ... naming the Cougar Lakes Wilderness after him."[34] She followed up with a letter to the editor of The Wilderness Society's magazine: "We are working hard toward having Cougar Lakes Wilderness named for Bill. Everyone seems to like the idea enormously, including Senator Jackson. I hope you will give this a plug in the magazine."[35] Clearly, Kay and Isabelle's behind-the-scenes work was crucial to the July 1984 decision by the Washington congressional delegation to name the new wilderness after Justice Douglas. But they deflected any praise for the accomplishment. "We hold you largely responsible for getting the ponderous machinery in gear and going somewhere," Isabelle wrote to Kay's nephew Bob, who had the ear of Representative Sid Morrison. "You really went *somewhere*."[36]

On 29 September 1984, a crowd of around one hundred gathered at Bumping Lake for the official dedication of the new William O. Douglas Wilderness Area. Sid Morrison served as master of ceremonies, calling to the dais Yakima County Commissioner Jim Whiteside and congressional representatives Joel Pritchard and Mike Lowry. Burton Benjamin, executive producer for CBS, who knew Justice Douglas and the Cougar Lakes area from his work on Eric Sevareid's 1972 documentary, told the crowd, "I can't think of a more appropriate tribute to Douglas." Isabelle Lynn related how the honor was "something we had prayed for for [sic] years, but were sort of afraid to mention on account of the Justice was kind of controversial." As a representative of the original CLWA, its first president, Charles Hessey, provided a written message.[37] Among those signing the guest register during an after-party at the Double K were Benjamin, Morrison, and Whiteside with their spouses. In addition, Justice Douglas's friends and Double K regulars Cragg D. and Virginia Gilbert, former wrangler Tim Franklin, and Kay's nephews Bob and Ed with their spouses mingled with the invitees at the Double K's well-stocked bar.[38]

Reflecting on their campaign in 1987, Kay and Isabelle wrote, "it makes our original 1961 proposal of 125,000 acres seem downright obsequious. As a matter of fact, it was—we were just kind of messing around in a field new to us, and hoping."[39] Nonetheless, the establishment of the William O. Douglas Wilderness area was their crowning achievement after a struggle spanning almost a quarter-century. Perhaps the most evocative documentation illustrating this notion—among the myriad articles, letters, and testimonies that exist in local, regional, and national archives—lies in the nearly unbroken string of annual Double K Mountain Ranch Christmas cards in the Kershaw Family collection. With the exception of just a few, nearly all feature the Double K Mountain Ranch or Kay and Isabelle, sometimes with horses, often with Lucky, and sometimes just Lucky alone. However, in 1984, the Double K Christmas card highlights a blurry, out-of-focus photograph of Kay and Isabelle with Sid Morrison—their erstwhile nemesis—taken at the celebration dinner at Goose Prairie after the dedication ceremonies for the William O. Douglas Wilderness. And the following year, another photograph from the dedication ceremony is the centerpiece of the 1985 Christmas greeting. Kay and Isabelle stand with beaming smiles next to the brand-new William O. Douglas Wilderness placard carved out of rough-hewn wood marking the boundary line near Goose Prairie. Lucky, of course, sits patiently at their feet.[40]

Despite the successful outcome for Cougar Lakes, some holdover issues demanded resolution. One was the future of Prairie House, Douglas's mountain retreat. Long before his debilitating stroke curbed his trips to Goose Prairie, Justice

Douglas had pondered what to do with his summer home. In March 1974, he wrote to Kershaw that he was contemplating the transfer of his property to the National Trust for Historic Preservation. Referencing the ski area development boondoggle unleashed by Chet Huntley outside of Bozeman, Montana, in the early 1970s, Douglas states, "The last thing I want is to have Prarie [sic] House end up as one of these Big-Sky projects. It's a fear I have for the whole Prarie [sic]." He suggested that Kay consider donating the Double K Mountain Ranch lodge to the Historic Trust along with him to preserve the "wilderness character" of their properties.[41]

After Douglas's death in 1980, Cathy Douglas rented Prairie House to a series of tenants for some ten years. Among them were local restauranteurs Brad Patterson and John Gasperetti who became close friends with their neighbors, Kay and Isabelle. "They weren't so friendly at first," Patterson recalled. "Step one was when they finally said 'hello.' The second step was an invitation to come join them for a Double K Drifter."[42] In an effort to preserve the character of Prairie House and the legacy of Justice Douglas, Cathy approached USFS, the Nature Conservancy, the Wilderness Society as well as the State of Washington with a proposal to designate the property as an environmental retreat together with the

Happy Holidays, 1985 (Kershaw Family Collection). Isabelle (left) and Kay pose with Lucky next to the new William O. Douglas Wilderness placard near Goose Prairie, 1985.

Double K lodge. Kershaw and Lynn held out hope that this public space designation would morph into a wilderness learning center, publicly owned and operated by USFS. However, other Goose Prairie residents vehemently opposed this idea. Many expressed their dislike for Douglas's strong environmental stances and liberal ideas and skepticism about a greater role of USFS in the community. "Some of them don't like the idea of tour groups or seminars in their backyard," a spokeswoman for the Wenatchee National Forest told the *Seattle Times*. "And if the wilderness center went ahead it could become a national attraction."[43] The state would have had to dedicate several hundred thousand dollars to complete the project; complaints to the legislature from eastside residents put an end to any hope of such funding. Proponents dropped the idea and Cathy Douglas sold the property to a private owner in 1990.[44]

Another major unresolved issue was the enlargement of Bumping Lake. After a series of droughts in the 1970s, a diverse group of Washington State and federal water, fish, and resource agencies, the Yakama Nation, regional irrigation districts, county and city governments, and environmentalists began working on a comprehensive plan to integrate storage capacities at Keechelus, Kachess, and Cle Elum Lakes at the head of the Yakima River with those at Rimrock and Bumping Lakes on the Naches River. Because of the ramifications to their property posed by expanding Bumping Lake, Kershaw and Lynn were dedicated opponents from the outset. Both relished providing pithy one-liners to the local paper on the subject, labeling as "yahoos" and "yokels" opponents aligned against them in agriculture while backing up their arguments with specific facts and figures from the government's own studies. To the ends of their lives, Kay and Isabelle remained committed to defeating the government's proposal: "I'm 60 years old and Kay (Kershaw) is 70," Isabelle told the *Yakima Herald-Republic* in 1977. "We're not trying to save anything for ourselves—how much time have we got left?"[45] In 1985, an ill-advised *Yakima Herald-Republic* editorial suggested that with Justice Douglas dead, buried, and no longer occupying Prairie House, the time had come for the Bumping Lake enlargement to proceed. Isabelle penned a furious rebuttal: "For your information, Justice Douglas was fighting the enlargement long before he owned a square foot of Goose Prairie ... [he] always hated boondoggles."[46] Even as late as 1988, Kay served on the board of Citizens for Responsible Water Projects (CRWP) which addressed the distribution of water in the Yakima River drainage from a conservation perspective. Rather than expanding Bumping Lake, CRWP favored the construction of the Wymer dam and storage site on Lmuma Creek, a relatively low-elevation off-river area along the main stem of the Yakima River between Yakima and Ellensburg.[47] The delicate balance between supporting fish runs in the Yakima and Columbia Rivers and the needs of agriculture in the Yakima Valley remains a perplexing problem. As of this writing, the expansion of Bumping Lake is still on the table and subject to continued debate and controversy.[48]

The William O. Douglas Wilderness Campaign and Its Aftermath (1984–2010)

The editor of the *Yakima Herald-Republic* praised fulsomely the new William O. Douglas Wilderness Area as a "fitting memorial" to Yakima's most famous resident. Misconstruing the geography of the regions in question, special praise went to the congressional committee that came up with the compromise allowing WPSC to expand by "taking a 500 acre hillside out of the Cougar Lakes designation." However, certain problems arose as a result of this decision: "Environmentalists objected to the 'precedent' of altering boundaries of an existing wilderness. But if they lose 500 acres in one section of wilderness area and gain several thousand new acres in other parts of the same area, as well as an expanded Goat Rocks, then we feel that's a precedent of the most positive proportions."[49] Representative Mike Lowry stated that he understood a "trade-off of over 36 to one" certainly resulted from the Goat Rocks deletion, but never intended that his congressional committee would set a precedent for those seeking similar changes in boundaries elsewhere.[50] NCCC's Patrick Goldsworthy matched the editor of the *Yakima Herald-Republic* in his enthusiasm for the passage of the Washington Wilderness Bill. However, he considered reconfiguring the boundaries of Goat Rocks Wilderness to accommodate WPSC a dangerous paradigm: "Such deletions from our Wilderness and National Park systems must never be allowed to occur again!"[51]

As euphoria over the new additions to wilderness dissipated, environmentalists began reassessing this compromise over the deletion from the Goat Rocks.[52] Proponents of the expansion at White Pass Ski Area maintained that removal from Goat Rocks Wilderness of Hogback Mountain and its gentle basin to the north was an intentional tradeoff that resulted in new wilderness areas elsewhere in the state.[53] Kevin McCarthy, WPSC's general manager from 1985 to 2021, recalled, "The understanding from those of us involved with the ski area [was] that an additional 30,000 acres was added to the new Cougar Lakes/William O. Douglas and Norse Peak Wildernesses in exchange for the removal of 800 acres from the Goat Rocks Wilderness for the development of alpine skiing at White Pass."[54] Opponents, such as former Cougar Lakes Wilderness Alliance president Phil Johnson, argued otherwise: "It was not a swap. But the dispute [over the Goat Rocks deletion] held up the whole wilderness bill, so in an effort to show some flexibility we didn't argue against it."[55]

Eager to gain revenue from the ski expansion, USFS affirmed that Congress agreed to remove these lands from wilderness to facilitate expansion of White Pass. However, Don Rotell, Naches District Ranger, qualified this notion by adding that "the idea [must] prove environmentally sound."[56] In this statement, Rotell referred to requirements established under NEPA, mandating public input and an EIS. In other words, even though the deletion of Hogback Basin from wilderness would allow USFS to study its potential for ski development, the Wilderness Act did not specify any particular type of ski development nor did it require there be any development at all.[57] This study process proved time-consuming as environmental groups and the Yakama Nation demanded that USFS follow the letter of the law in its analysis of the ski area expansion. McCarthy points out that even though the addition to wilderness was immediate, "the 800 acre portion of the [Washington Wilderness Bill] set aside for alpine skiing required the addition of a NEPA process which ultimately took 25 years to overcome."[58]

At first eager to support compromise, Kay and Isabelle reverted to the opinion they had expressed in 1983 to Senators Gorton and Jackson on reconfiguring the boundaries of Goat Rocks: "the attempt to shatter a wilderness precedent in behalf [sic] of a commercial whim is unbelievable."[59] As 500 acres initially carved out of the Goat Rocks grew by half-again as much and the modest proposals of the 1984 compromise morphed into a full-blown reconfiguration of this enhanced parcel of former wilderness, the two women shifted their allegiance to a local grass-roots effort dedicated to addressing multiple concerns downplayed by the Forest Service and WPSC. In 1992 and 1997, an amalgamation of environmental groups and the Yakama Nation managed two successful appeals of the USFS Records of Decision on the White Pass expansion. In 2007, after retooling their proposal to conform to spotted owl provisions in the Northwest Forest Plan of 1994, USFS determined that the expansion of the ski area would proceed with the installation of two new chairlifts (later increased to three) and a 2,000 square-foot lodge (later expanded to 5,600 square feet).[60] The following year, the Western District of the United States District Court in Seattle denied a third appeal by the combined tribal and environmental alliance. WPSC opened their newly-annexed addition to its area in December 2010.[61]

Epilogue

By the late 1980s, Kershaw and Lynn knew they had to vacate Goose Prairie. Visits to the Double K Ranch were in decline: in 1988, sixty-five guests signed in to the register. In 1989, the number dwindled to fifty-nine. That year, Kay confided to the *Seattle Times* that all their horses were gone and that she and Isabelle would simply direct their clientele outside for birdwatching and hiking. Kay's health problems—including three knee repairs—had concerned her friends since the late 1970s. "We're getting on," Kay told the *Yakima Herald-Republic*. "I'm 82 and I've been patched up a lot."[1] Suffering with skin cancer from sun exposure over the years, Kay also had a modified radical mastectomy and a cancerous lymph node removed in 1987. Her doctors placed her on a regimen of estrogen blockers and chemotherapy that interfered with fulfilling daily chores around the ranch.[2] Reflecting on Kay's medical condition and continued residence at Goose Prairie, Pat Kane remarked from Palo Alto, "my fine, old partner, Kay Kershaw, is still there—eighty years old—three knee replacements (one had to be done two times) and just a few weeks ago, a mastectomy."[3]

Although the living room and upstairs bedrooms were still comfortable and cozy, the underpinnings of the Double K lodge—the basement heating, laundry, and electrical areas—were showing their age. And Kay and Isabelle still did all their cooking on a wood stove.[4] "Bob and I were enabling life and existence at the Double K," Ed Kershaw recalled, referring to his brother and business partner in agriculture. "The generator was shot, the well was dry, so we had to ask ourselves: do we want to be running a farming operation in the mountains?"[5] In 1989, Kay and Isabelle decided to move to Yakima where they could hunker down in a modest house in a quiet west-side neighborhood.[6] Acquiescing to local opposition to combining the Douglas property with the Double K to establish an environmental study center, Kay and Isabelle put their property up for sale. "We knew that a live-in manager would be required," Ed explained, "so we said 'let's sell it and find [them] a happy home.'" A variety of west-side buyers expressed interest: early on, Mike Passage, a vice-president with Kidder-Peabody in Seattle, along with his wife seemed serious about taking over the business, and Seattle entrepreneur Ruby Montana with her partner were on the cusp of purchasing the Double K until their financing fell through. With a loan from the Kershaws—no bank would lend money on a property without a bona fide electrical hookup—Tom and Kathleen Anderson took possession of the property in August 1990. The Andersons operated the Double K for five years until selling it to the current owners in 1995.[7]

Health issues dogged Kay and Isabelle in their final years with a significant decline for them both in the spring and summer of 1995. Nonetheless, they managed to attend the wedding of their grand-niece Kristin Kershaw in 1991, dressed, of course, in their signature dungarees and plaid shirts.[8] They remained involved with environmental issues from their home in west Yakima, boldly expressing their opinions on the agenda of newly-elected Vice-President Al Gore and President Bill Clinton in 1993.[9] Garrulous to the end, they enjoyed visits with their local physicians and maintained a cordial relationship with their home caretaker, Connie Langston. Ed Kershaw paraphrased Kay's outlook on her doctor's appointments: "It was nice to have a conversation with someone who has half a brain." And the local medical community reciprocated: Kay's orthopedic surgeon remembered lively discussions during office visits with the two companions about the books of William O. Douglas.[10] John Barany, internist for both Kay and Isabelle, recalled the fantastic stories that peppered many a visit and, less happily, Isabelle's penchant for questioning inconsequential medical details. Her frequent displeasure led to discord and, Barany admitted, "Isabelle fired me. Later, she wanted to come back, but I helped her find someone else. I bet you five cents she caused friction wherever she went."[11]

Isabelle passed away at the end of March 1996. She had been estranged for decades from most of her family back east. The Kershaws arranged a memorial gathering at Goose Prairie for 21 July, hoping that Kay—suffering from yet another leg injury—could attend. However, what appeared to be a broken leg turned out to be the result of a fast-moving bone cancer. On the Friday before Isabelle's service, Kay succumbed to this sudden onset at the age of eighty-nine. The following Sunday, friends, family, and neighbors gathered at the Double K lodge for a noon memorial service. Afterwards, under shadows cast by an ancient forest canopy, attendees scattered Kay and Isabelle's ashes on the grounds of the ranch, joining forever their remains with the land they had fought to protect for so long.[12]

* * *

Born in 1907—thirteen years before women nationally gained the right to vote—Kay Kershaw lived an extraordinary life. By the time of her death—just a few months after the Supreme Court's 1996 decision in *Romer v. Evans* affirming equal protection for the LGBTQ+ community—she had experienced a sea-change in American jurisprudence. In her own way, Kay, with her partners Pat Kane and Isabelle Lynn, played a part in shaping the course of these LGBTQ+ political issues as well as critical environmental decisions. Just as fascinating—and instructive—was her ability to navigate the circumscribed social milieu in conservative Yakima County. How did she manage to do it? Certainly, support from the Kershaw family as well as a generous amount of pluck and determination in a locale that was under the radar helped. The

Kershaws idolized their "Aunt Kay," and Isabelle too. "They were the most bonded couple I've ever met," Kay's great-nephew, Tripp Robinson, recalled. "You always sent a card addressed to both of them." Their independent streak was a point of pride and inspiration as well: "No one else I knew cut their own path so completely."[13] By the 1970s, Kay and Isabelle had established themselves locally as larger-than-life personalities: Kay was "a remarkable woman ... at once earthy, blunt, funny, loyal, fearless and buoyant," according to the *Yakima Herald-Republic*. "[The Double K girls] are legends, you see, and legends don't ebb away."[14]

Those individuals well-acquainted with Kay and Yakima County have offered a variety of possibilities on how she managed to thrive in this conservative corner of Washington State. Ed Kershaw emphasized that Kay's father helped finance the Double K operation initially, a devotion that he and his brother continued throughout Kay's life.[15] Many local members of the gay and lesbian community have suggested that the undeniable economic stratification existing in Yakima favored those who had wealthier acquaintances. Brad Patterson, who also lived his entire life in Yakima, proposed that Kershaw and her partners were not overt lesbians, a point reinforced by Kay's niece, Mary Ann: "there were no public displays of affection between Kay and Isabelle." More to the point, "they were good people who treated others well with politeness. Kay was very private, lived simply with no fluff: she drove an old beat-up car ... she was very smart and knew who to surround herself with: those who didn't care what side of the fence you were on."[16] The isolation of Goose Prairie enhanced her success. Ginger Hislop, a centenarian who moved to Yakima with her husband in the 1940s, recalled that "the Double K girls weren't in town. They were up at Goose Prairie, so no one paid them much attention."[17] Indeed, many local residents remained completely unaware of the Double K Ranch or that the proprietors were in a life-long lesbian relationship.[18] Ruby Montana remembered that horse-packing operators in the area considered Kershaw a wise local elder with a wealth of experience to share: many would stop by the Double K Ranch to consult about trails and weather.[19]

This contrasts with the experience of Kay's long-time friend Justice William O. Douglas, who by the nature of his very public position in government, led a much higher-profile life. Treated with deference in the nation's capital, Douglas often clashed with his conservative home town. "All those young wives," the *Yakima Herald-Republic* wrote, mocking this local love-hate relationship, "all those flaming liberal court decisions, the articles in those dirty magazines and some of those books! Revolution! My God, the man wrote about revolution!"[20] As Hislop describes the general consensus: "people in Yakima either thought he was great or despised him."[21] But as both he and the city's contemporary population aged, the majority came to appreciate at least some of Douglas's contributions and his unmistakable place in history. The naming of the Yakima federal courthouse in his honor while he was still alive and of the wilderness area surrounding Cougar Lakes after his death bear witness to this change in perspective. Kay and Justice Douglas shared important traits—iconoclasts who defied convention, played according to their own rules, and found respite in the mountains surrounding Bumping Lake. In the end, both have become venerated Yakima personalities.

* * *

The 1992 memorial service for Pat Kane at Palo Alto's St. Thomas Aquinas Church took place on 24 September, one of those beautiful Northern California autumn afternoons, the sun honey-drenched, the shadows deep.[22] The setting proved to be uniquely appropriate. Two decades prior, this same building—an architectural gem on the corner of Waverley and Homer Avenues and the city's oldest house of worship—had gained renown as the backdrop for a droll funeral scene when the two main characters meet in *Harold and Maude*, a 1971 cult classic film shot in the Bay Area. Ruth Gordon stars as Maude, a strong-willed woman on the cusp of her eightieth birthday who insists on living life—and ending it—on her own terms. The movie evokes the free-wheeling spirit of the late 1960s, and Maude's fictional life serves as an apt analogue to those of Kane, Kershaw, Lynn, and Douglas in the latter half of the twentieth century. "If you wanna be me, be me," Maude sings to her young co-star at one point. "And if you wanna be you, be you."[23] In the lands surrounding Cougar Lakes, those inimitable denizens of the Double K Mountain Ranch had managed to do exactly that.

Appendix: The Literary Odyssey of Isabelle Lynn

"I want to be a paperback writer"[1]

On Valentine's Day 1970, the release of a slim novel written by an obscure professor of Classics at Yale University upended the market for popular literature in the United States. Originally composed as a screenplay, Erich Segal's *Love Story* made publishing history in 1970: in just over two months, it rose to the top of the *New York Times* bestseller list and remained there for an entire year. It continued to top the list through mid–February 1971, at which point Harper and Row had one million hardcover copies in print. By mid–November 1970, orders for the paperback edition exceeded 4.3 million copies, with another 600,000 printed a week later. This was the largest total paperback debut in publishing history up to that time. Even a month after the paperback version hit the bookstores, 2,000 hardback copies sold each week, propelling *Love Story* into the stratosphere as 1970's top-selling work of fiction in the United States. In all, Segal's book sold more than 21 million copies and was translated into some twenty languages. The film adaptation by Paramount Pictures became a box office sensation as well. The movie opened nationwide on Christmas Day 1970 and garnered the largest opening-week receipts in American cinematic history. *Love Story* went on to become the number one box-office hit of 1971, grossing more than 48 million dollars (around 369 million dollars in 2024). The film won five awards at the Golden Globes, including Best Drama and Best Screenplay for Erich Segal. It also received nominations for seven Oscars, winning one for Best Musical Score.[2]

The *Love Story* phenomenon of 1970–71 was as unexpected as it was remarkable. The United States had endured a difficult period at the turn of the decade, with assassinations, street protests over racism and politics, increasing crime and drug use, and a seemingly endless and unpopular war in Vietnam. Contemporary popular culture—for example, *Easy Rider* (1969), *Midnight Cowboy* (1969), *Catch-22* (1970), and *M*A*S*H* (1970) in film, and *Portnoy's Complaint* (1969), *Slaughterhouse Five* (1969), and *Deliverance* (1970) in literature—reflected many of these complex issues, often with a healthy dose of sex and violence thrown in. Erich Segal's work, on the other hand, eschewed these controversial themes: by contemporary standards, his was a simple, formulaic, even banal tale, and as such came in for some harsh criticism: "cutesy dreck" in the words of one of his Yale colleagues.[3] Yet *Love Story* created an irrefutable economic juggernaut. Segal, already well-compensated for his work on the Beatles' 1968 *Yellow Submarine* screenplay, accrued even greater wealth from *Love Story* in the early 1970s. Offers for additional movies, plays, books, and appearances flooded in. This once obscure professor of comparative literature became an internationally recognized personality in the early 1970s with an A-List celebrity status that endured for many years.[4]

Segal's *Love Story* was a slightly more sophisticated rendition of the popular paperback romance novels—epitomized by the Harlequin Romance series—that filled the nation's ubiquitous bookracks from the early 1950s. Pocket Books, founded in 1939, revolutionized the publishing industry in the United States by arranging with four independent magazine and tabloid wholesalers for distribution into newsstands, drugstores, grocery stores, and variety stores all across the country, dramatically increasing outlets beyond the few thousand dedicated bookstores located in the nation's urban centers. This led to a huge jump in book sales: in 1941, after only two years in business, Pocket Books had rung up total sales of 8.5 million copies. An expansion in mass-marketing of books followed and continued to accelerate through the 1970s. "Being published in paperback," recalled British author Royston Ellis, "was then a sign of popular success."[5]

The proliferation of titles in all manner of genres created a niche market for pulp novels with explicitly lesbian themes—over 500 titles by one reckoning—between 1950 and 1965. These books often featured sensationalized covers meant to appeal to the voyeuristic tastes of a heterosexual male audience. Generally, they were cautionary tales warning women about lesbianism, chronicled as a deviant aberration leading to a lonely, desperate life, deep psychosis, or even suicide. However, for many under-the-radar lesbian readers desperate to find any kind of representation in popular culture, these pulp novels were "crucial 'survival literature.'"[6] Titles that attempted at least a modicum of character development while expressing a woman's point of view were particularly evocative. Two early novels offering these characteristics proved quite popular: *Women's Barracks* by Tereska Torrès, published in 1950, and Vin Packer's 1952 *Spring Fire*. By 1975, Torrès's tome had sold 2.5 million copies; Packer's totaled 1.5 million. Significantly, these numbers only reflect bookstores sales: at the time, no one kept records for sales at newsstands, grocery stores, and the like. "We were amazed, *floored* [sic], by the mail that poured in," the author of *Spring Fire* revealed in a 1989 interview. "That was the first time anyone was aware of the gay audience out there."[7]

These early volumes inspired Ann Weldy to write an enduring series of books under the pen-name Ann Bannon. Promotion of lesbian literature featured regularly in *The Ladder*, the magazine of San Francisco's Daughters of Bilitis (DOB) from 1956 to 1972: from early on, the publication's DOB Book Service boosted sales of Bannon's *Odd Girl Out*, *I Am a Woman*, *Women in the Shadows*, and *Journey to a*

Woman.⁸ Interest in these and subsequent books by Bannon continued within the pages of *The Ladder* until the end of the magazine's run in 1972. Her canon of work became a gold standard used by the magazine to assess all other lesbian literature.⁹ After 1965, mainstream publishers stopped printing lesbian pulp novels due to an increase in the amount of explicit lesbian-themed pornography issued by independent start-ups. A series of rulings by the Supreme Court—particularly *Memoirs v. Massachusetts* (1966) which defined pornography as "material ... utterly without redeeming social value"—opened the field to purveyors of "adults only" publications.¹⁰ With this onslaught of lewd writing—"pointless filth" in the words of *The Ladder*'s long-running literary critic, Barbara Grier (aka Gene Damon)—nostalgia grew for the old paperbacks of the genre's "good" days of the mid-1950s to early 1960s.¹¹ Perhaps in reaction to the decline in worthwhile reading material, serious authors of the late 1960s paved the way for a surge in defiant, lesbian-feminist literature released during the 1970s. Especially influential was the self-published release of *A Place for Us* by Alma Routsong in 1969 under the pen-name Isabel Miller. Routsong found a publishing house willing to print her book two years later using her own name and with a new title, *Patience and Sarah*. Concurrently, Bannon's second novel, *I Am a Woman* (1959), surfaced again as a reprint from the original publisher in 1970, delighting Barbara Grier at *The Ladder*. By this point, she deemed Bannon's books a "classic series of paperback Lesbian novels" and "collector's items these days."¹² The second publication of this archetypal lesbian novel along with the release of Routsong's—both buoyed up by Erich Segal's smash hit—helped reinvigorate the market for escapist romantic fiction aimed at gay and lesbian readers in the early 1970s.¹³

Crucifixion Land

Isabelle Lynn had literary aspirations from an early age. As a high schooler, she entered an article in the High School Reporters' Contest sponsored by Pennsylvania State College and the Pennsylvania Newspaper Publishers' Association. Although she did not receive a prize, she gained commendation from the Director of the Department of Journalism at Penn State College who ranked her piece in the top 15 percent of the two hundred contestants.¹⁴ As an undergraduate, Lynn began working on her first major literary effort, *Crucifixion Land*, a novel set in post–World War I Germany that she completed around 1937. The story follows the tribulations of a Jewish family from near the end of the war—Isabelle writes in the margin of her manuscript on page one "April 1916"—to around springtime 1937.¹⁵ Most of the story takes place in Heidelberg: Isabelle had spent a year there either as an undergraduate or teaching English after graduation. She embellishes her text with descriptions of the city and environs: the Neckar River, the Königstuhl, the Hauptstraße. And Isabelle clearly admired the great lyric German poets such as Heinrich Heine

(1797–1856) whose stanza "Neuer Frühling gibt zurück, was der Winter dir genommen" (the coming Spring gives back what Winter has taken from you) becomes a leitmotif repeated in German throughout *Crucifixion Land*.[16] But the politics and zeitgeist of Nazi Germany obscured the charms of medieval Heidelberg and the luster of German poetry during her sojourn abroad.

Lynn's Wanderjahr coincided with an ominous period in Germany. Adolf Hitler had come to power in January 1933, and the Nazification of the nation was well underway by the time she arrived in Heidelberg. In June 1936, for example, the National Socialist Party's Propaganda Ministry set up an office in town to take over the celebration of the 550th anniversary of the founding of the University of Heidelberg. Black-coated Hitler guardsmen marched through the city to present arms on the town square at a flag presentation ceremony. For the celebration, the Propaganda Ministry altered the façade of a new building given to the university in 1931 by former United States ambassador Jacob Gould Schurman and other American alumni. A new inscription "To the German Spirit" had replaced the original words "To the Eternal Spirit." In place of a statue of Athena, the Greek Goddess of Wisdom, a golden swastika and German eagle now surmounted the frieze. Hitler himself came to the festivities along with an entourage that included Heinrich Himmler, Joachim von Ribbentrop, and Joseph Goebbels who—as Minister of Propaganda— delivered the main address. Several American guests who had studied at the University or visited there before World War I told the *New York Times* that they could scarcely recognize it through the changed atmosphere: "Old Heidelberg was dead and had been replaced by a German training school for … 'political soldiers.'"[17]

Isabelle's experiences living in the midst of this troubling shift in German civil affairs permeate the storyline of *Crucifixion Land*. The narration follows the life of Max Goldstein, a violin prodigy, whose life is crushed by anti-Semitism. He falls in love with a young English girl, Anne—the sister of one of his non-Jewish classmates from the Berlin Conservatory—but is thwarted in his devotion to her by his status as a German Jew. It is she who quotes Heinrich Heine, holding out the possibility that they might be reunited at some point in a more sanguine future. However, Max gradually loses all hope and falls into despair after Nazi thugs mutilate and kill his landlord, a friendly Jewish baker. Isabelle informs the reader that "even Max in his wildest dreams could not have imagined what was in store for him and his fellow Jews in this country that had truly become a 'crucifixion land.'" This statement of the book's theme and title appears within a few paragraphs of the first mention of "Hakenkreuz" (hooked cross), perhaps Isabelle's intentional juxtaposition within a Christian context of both the persecution of Jews in Germany and Hinduism's ancient swastika symbol now debased by the Nazis.[18] Tricked by a paid Jewish collaborator into attending a meeting of refugees intent on fleeing Germany, Max is arrested and shipped to a concentration camp where he suffers countless indignities and witnesses the deaths of numerous inmates. Driven half-mad from hunger and frustration, he strikes a guard and is sentenced to death. On the day of his execution, Max kills his guard with a makeshift knife, managing to escape from the camp and travel cross-country toward the border with Switzerland. Just a day from his goal, Max's thoughts turn to his English love, now on her way to America: he plucks a wildflower whispering out loud Anne's line from Heine as a bullet from a German farmer's rifle strikes him dead: "[His] hand closed tightly on the flower, relaxed, and lay still."[19]

When Lynn was composing *Crucifixion Land*, the horrors of World War II remained years in the future: thus, her novel begins and ends with imagery from World War I, the most devastating event in world history up to that point. In the first chapter, Max's father, Oberleutnant Karl Goldstein, serves his country while tolerating blistering anti-Semitism from his comrades. Goldstein dies in the trenches without ever having seen his young son. The final scene with Max and the wildflower is an homage to the very popular 1930 film, *All Quiet on the Western Front*, adapted from Erich Maria Remarque's 1928 novel, *Im Westen nichts Neues*. In the film version, the German protagonist, Paul Bäumer, is close to returning home at the end of the war. He sees a butterfly just beyond the edge of the sandbags while at his post in the trenches: as he reaches to touch the insect, a French sniper fires his weapon: we see Bäumer's hand grasp, relax, then lay still, "one of the most poignant and memorable scenes in film history."[20]

With her manuscript completed sometime in late summer of 1937, Isabelle sent a copy off to Whit Burnett, founder and editor of *Story* magazine and the Story Press in New York City. Burnett established his bona fides when he discovered the author William Saroyan in 1933, buying close to thirty of his short stories for publication or for distribution to other outlets. Burnett obviously had a discerning eye for literary talent. In the 1940s and 50s, he published works by William Faulkner and unknown authors such as Joseph Heller, Carson McCullers, Truman Capote, and Norman Mailer.[21] So it must have been a disappointment to receive a rejection letter from Burnett in November, although he does include some encouragement:

> We have all read "Crucifixion Land" with the greatest of interest. I think that it is a well done literary job and our only thought has been whether a book like this could make its way. Our final feeling is that it might but we rather doubted it under our aegis. There have been several books on somewhat the same theme and, unfortunately, the demand has been so small they have all lost money. It is possible some other publishing house might feel differently about this and I would suggest that you send it around.[22]

In a follow-up response, Burnett recommended a few other high-profile New York City publishers such as Reynal and Hitchcock, Alfred Knopf, Covici-Friede, and William Morrow.[23] However, *Crucifixion Land* never found a home. Perhaps the similarities between the ending of *All Quiet on the Western Front* and Isabelle's adaptation may have been too glaring for acquisition editors at the major publishing houses. Or maybe it was the turbulence of the times: as Lynn was shopping her manuscript around New York City in 1938, the story line appeared dated after Nazi Germany occupied Austria in early March and Czechoslovakia's Sudetenland in September, followed by Goebbels' nation-wide Kristallnacht pogrom in November.

Nazi Germany invaded Poland in September 1939 and the world descended into military madness once again.

Structure of Grief

After the war, Lynn engaged the services of A.L. Fierst, an agent in New York City, to help boost her writing career. Fierst hustled manuscripts through advertisements in the back of literary magazines such as *Writers Digest*. He offered a mail-order course through which an aspiring writer could submit a manuscript along with a fee: Fierst would read and critique the writing, then provide a lesson plan for developing an author's craft going forward. This provided a double money-making enterprise: Fierst accrued a steady stream of income stoking the dreams of would-be writers while gleaning the rare talents who emerged from his correspondence courses and signing them to contracts. Fierst actually did manage some noteworthy deals. In 1946, for example, he simultaneously negotiated radio and screen rights for *Purgatory Street*, a mystery novel by Roman MacDougald, with NBC's Mollé Mystery Theater and International Pictures.[24] By November 1949, Isabelle had perhaps submitted a number of stories and fees to Fierst who dutifully wrote back with his critiques. She writes:

> I am enclosing another story I have done, and whatever else may be wrong with it, if it clashes with any of the taboos I hope the clash is sufficiently subtle that it will get by. I found your criticism of the other story I sent you interesting and stimulating and, of course, profitable. If the enclosed check for $3 is not enough will you please let me know and I'll supplement it. I'm looking forward to hearing from you on this one.[25]

Although the manuscript for "the other story" has been lost, the one she enclosed to Fierst in 1949 was a nine-page double-spaced manuscript, *Structure of Grief*. The "taboos" which Lynn mentions may refer to the subject matter: the hollow, insincere emotions of Helaine, the central character, who is attending the funeral of her domineering father after years of acrimonious separation. In a particularly purple passage, Isabelle describes her protagonist's detachment while trying to conjure the appearance of grief:

> she had to call up the memory of dear little Timmy, her mutt pup, who had died horribly under the wheels of a truck. *That* had forced the tears from her reluctant eyes, *that* had made her grief real, *that* had made her socially acceptable, not only to her aunt and her father and her friends, but, more important, to herself.

Helaine's cynicism is appalling as she contemplates dealing with the funeral home:

> Choosing a casket was part of the game. None was cheap; some were "less expensive" than others. All were imposingly polished, with shiny metal handles. And with a spray of pompon chrysanthemums and lemon yellow ribbons trailing across the lid, one might even think of an enormous and wonderful Christmas present inside. And oh what a surprise an unsuspecting Pandora would get if she lifted the lid!

Her thoughts on the undertaker's trade are stomach-churning:

> And the powder they used. Mortician's powder. Nothing in the world smelled like it. Why not Elizabeth Arden or even Avon? Why this special, sickening, thick concoction that was so revolting it filled years of nightmares? If the scent had not dissipated by Judgment Day, Helaine was sure the dead would all be floundering in a miasma of mortuary powder.

Yet at the end of the story, she overhears the funeral directors' whispered discussion as she peers at her father's corpse in the viewing room: "Everyone in town knew she worshipped him. [Her father] was all cut up when she got that job out of town. He was crazy about her too. Real close family. They say that's the reason she never married." As Helaine looks down at her hands, she sees that the knuckles were "livid" from gripping the edge of the casket. "And her tears were falling on her father's shirt front."[26]

The Loved One, Evelyn Waugh's 1948 short satirical novel, may have been the inspiration for Lynn's *Structure of Grief*. Waugh's book is based on a series of visits with morticians at Forest Lawn in Los Angeles: his characters include a funeral cosmetologist, Aimeé Thanatogenos and Mr. Joyboy, the head mortician. However, Waugh's wry take on the funeral industry—"thoroughly horrible and fiendishly entertaining," according to the *New York Times*—was in stark contrast to Isabelle's macabre portrayal of Helaine's inner turmoil.[27] This was perhaps too dark to appeal to the taste of New York City's literary milieu. *Structure of Grief* never appeared in print, although Isabelle tried shopping it again in New York some twenty-five years later.

The City Within

In late December 1971, just after Erich Segal's *Love Story* had crested its meteoric rise, an article in *Newsweek* caught Isabelle's eye. The piece, "Erotica for Women," detailed how—in the wake of women's liberation and the sexual revolution—a London-based publishing firm was planning to print "erotic books for women by women." This new series from Orlando Press would be an offshoot of Olympia Press, a "paperback porno empire" founded by Maurice Girodias (1919–1990).[28]

Born in France, Girodias had been in the publishing business in Europe for decades, specializing in erotica. In Paris, he made his name as the publisher of Henry Miller's *Tropic of Capricorn*, William S. Burroughs' *The Naked Lunch*, Jean Genet's *The Thief's Journal*, works of Lawrence Durrell and John Glasco, and, most famously, Vladimir Nabokov's *Lolita*. Hounded by French authorities, Girodias relocated Olympia Press to London in partnership with Britain's The New English Library in 1966. That association lasted less than two years; Girodias moved again, this time to New York where he found a wide-open market for erotica in the United States: "People will soon tire of the vulgar, exotic sex fiction of the last few years," he told the *New York Times* in 1968. "A new form of erotic literature is going to emerge from the dungheap of pornography. We are moving to a new, more refined form of fiction that's more autobiographical and tolerates a greater erotic content."[29]

In the *Newsweek* piece, Lynn read the comments of the Orlando Press spokesperson, Ann Rosenberg, "a fetching former biologist," who stated, "in recent years women have begun to come to terms with their own sexuality." Because of this, the world of publishing had been overlooking "a vast new market." But Rosenberg, echoing Girodias's 1968 comments, insisted that the Orlando books would be erotic, not pornographic: "Erotica tends to be a bit more artistic and plays on the emotions … women are more likely to be aroused by very strong emotional responses to situations." Girodias added, "the time has come when a woman can write about her sexuality, not as a degrading thing, but as something she can enjoy in a poetic and eventually aggressive manner." He went on to say that the list of new titles from Orlando would launch in late spring of 1972: at the beginning, however, he did not want to publish books on lesbian love: "We don't want to identify Orlando as a homosexual series."[30]

This article likely inspired Lynn either to embark on a new writing project or polish one she had in progress. In a matter of months, she had a completed manuscript of a novel, *The City Within*, prepped and delivered to Girodias. The story is set in 1950s Washington, D.C., the "city within" referring to a group of women who hold high-level government jobs but lead a covert lesbian lifestyle off the clock. The central characters are Julia Barrett, or Julie—only recently at ease with her lesbianism—and her partner Kate (no surprise at the choice of name here) whose guilt from an anguished adolescence influences her worldview. A web of extra-relationship liaisons creates tensions between the two, ultimately reconciled during a separation of several months. The narrative is driven by dialogue and mutual respect in the give and take of maintaining a loving, committed relationship between the two protagonists as well as in the secondary ties to their other friends and lovers.

Although very few people knew that Isabelle wrote *The City Within*, a discerning reader can find Easter eggs hidden by her throughout the text. For a book about lesbians set in Washington, D.C., a surprising number of German phrases pepper the dialogue, perhaps reflecting Isabelle's time spent in inter-war Germany: although *Kaffeeklatsch* (an informal coffee get-together) is not such an unusual term in casual American banter, *Sehnsucht* (yearning), *Weltschmerz* (melancholy) and *Lebensraum* (living space) definitely are.[31] The latter had a singularly weighted significance in the aftermath of World War II: the concept of *Lebensraum* as space for the German people to procreate in a region free of non–Aryans was a major theme of Adolf Hitler's *Mein Kampf*. Perhaps Lynn meant it to reflect a more benign iteration of the term as part of the nineteenth-century German Romantic movement (along with *Sehnsucht* and *Weltschmerz*, two of the genre's defining themes) in relation to a group of people—lesbians, for example—who needed to live in an environment that permits growth, development, and expansion.[32] Nonetheless, the appearance of

Lebensraum is jarring within the context of a sophisticated post–Holocaust tale of female relationships.

Close acquaintances of Kershaw and Lynn understood that martinis, a gin and tonic, or a scotch on the rocks anchored any happy hour. As Isabelle quipped to Justice Douglas, "a bloody Mary without vodka is a bloody Shame [sic]."[33] Thus cocktails appear frequently throughout *The City Within*, sometimes shared with friends whose names were familiar around the Double K: Bill, Kay, Isobel, Jane, and another acquaintance, Eloise, "who was from Washington, the state, not D.C."[34] In several instances, Isabelle uses her main character, Julie, to allude to William O. Douglas ("Bill, especially, with his kind brown eyes, bright and somewhat flattened behind his thick-lensed horn rims. He was my particular favorite") and his difficulties with arch-conservative foes, either accusations that he was a communist sympathizer: "Like HUAC [the House Un-American Activities Committee], I saw a conspirator under every bed"; or as the target of the John Birch Society in Yakima County: "She spent dinner haranguing us with platforms that made Robert Welch look pretty middle-of-the-road."[35] In reference to homosexuality, Julie echoes Douglas's dissent in *Osborn v. United States*: "If you're the sort of person who goes around getting himself trapped by furtive cops in public johns you aren't very responsible anyway, are you?"[36]

Through her characters, Lynn voices interesting points of view on lesbianism from her perspective in the early 1970s: the ability of gay women to blend into the scenery more easily than gay men; the difficulty of imagining gay men together; the preponderance of morose books about homosexuals.[37] Quite revealing are her descriptive scenes illustrating the class divide between Julie's sophisticated government office crowd and the butch-femme milieu at a Washington, D.C., gay nightclub. Julie and her friends are approached by two blue-collar "dykes," Gerry and Lou, dressed as men, who are aggressively and obnoxiously on the make. The disgust expressed by Isabelle's main characters to Gerry and Lou's advances is palpable. Delineating this sub-culture dichotomy current in the 1950s, Lillian Faderman writes: "wealthy lesbians seem sometimes to have found butch/femme roles and dress aesthetically repulsive."[38]

It is not clear whether Isabelle initially contacted Girodias on her own or through Hy Cohen, the New York contact brokered by Justice Douglas on her behalf. Although she refers to a book idea in her letter to Cohen in June 1972, she had already received a reply from Girodias by May: "I am enormously pleased that you want to publish *The City Within* as part of your new Orlando series. The terms you offer sound satisfactory to me, and I am returning the signed contract herewith." The terms were heady indeed: simultaneous publication in four languages in the United States, England, France, Germany, and Italy; an advance payment of 4,000 dollars—equivalent to around 30,000 dollars in 2024; royalties determined at a generous 10 percent on all copies sold up to 5,000, 12.5 percent on the next 5,000, and 15 percent on any copies sold beyond 10,000; and a 66-percent-to-the-author split with the publisher of net revenue from licensing for all rights to radio, television, and motion pictures. With a list price of $6.95 for the hardback version, the potential for an immediate and handsome remittance was enticing, and the contract included a munificent paperback option as well.[39]

As a soon-to-be international author, Lynn worried about her privacy. Writing to Girodias, she states:

> Much as I regret it, I must ask you to protect my anonymity—because of my business, my family and many friends who would be upset.... Of course, I have no objection to Olympia Press' knowing who I am and what I do, so feel free to ask whatever you want to know.... Meantime, I think the name "Jane Clark" that I picked for a pseudonym is singularly dull and I'd like the opportunity to change it sometime before publication.[40]

By early June, Isabelle had settled on a more suitable nom de plume: Elisabeth Newbold, nicknamed "Lis" (mimicking her own Double K nickname, "Iz"). She even fabricated a backstory for a press release, based loosely on her life, shaving a decade off her age:

> "*The City Within* is my first published fiction," writes Elisabeth Newbold, who signs her real name to factual articles for magazines. She enjoyed producing this novel because it allowed wide scope for a fertile imagination and an outlet for her inexhaustible store of opinion and relevant trivia. "The characters are all conglomerates," she says, adding that *The City Within* is not autobiographical in any sense except that she did spend 10 [*sic*] years with a Federal agency in Washington, D.C., which is the book's locale. Her close friends who read the manuscript do not identify Lis with Julie, though many of the conversational phrases are happily familiar. Miss Newbold was born in Ohio, grew up in Illinois and received a magna cum laude in English from Ohio State "about 30 [*sic*] years after James Thurber ... another way of saying I'm in my late forties." Her interests are legion, but for some time she has been most combustible (and knowledgeable, her friends say) on dangers to the ecosystem, including population growth. She works out in her head complete outlines and even key phrasing as she explores the ~~Arizona~~ [*sic*] Oregon countryside or gardens. Her ability to identify grasses and ferns has become neighborhood folklore. Asked to comment about *The City Within*, Miss Newbold replied: "I wrote it for women. It's about women. What more fascinating subject is there?"[41]

Flying high with the prospect of having a book in the works and representation in New York by Maurice Girodias, Lynn proposed submitting *Structure of Grief* to literary magazines under her new pseudonym: she forwarded a revamped manuscript under the name Elisabeth Newbold and informed him she was thinking about an article "on female homosexuality. As far as I know, no one has ever written anything very sensible on the subject." She planned to have it ready before *The City Within* hit the bookstores.[42] This curious statement suggests that Kay and Isabelle were unaware of *The Ladder* which, at this point, DOB had published for sixteen years and featured fiction and articles by many well-respected writers. By 1972, the mailing list exceeded 4,000 subscribers with a hand-to-hand distribution that increased the magazine's number of readers exponentially.[43] Alternatively, Isabelle may have been aware, but disdained the publication as too limited in scope, believing that her writing abilities could bring issues of lesbianism to a wider audience through a venue more within the mainstream.

The City Within was set to go to press by late spring of 1973. One of the first proofs went to Kay and Isabelle's Double K friend Charles Reich. Reich was already a well-known and much sought-after author: his book, *The Greening of America*, had been on the market for years with the distinction of achieving non-fiction bestseller status on the *New York Times* book list opposite Segal's *Love Story* in late 1970 and early 1971.[44] At the time, Reich was just coming to terms with his own homosexuality and contemplating a move to San Francisco's vibrant gay community. In April 1973, he informed Isabelle that he intended to go to San Francisco for an extended stay: "I am anxious to see the proof of the book and if you have it available now, send it to the Yale Law School."[45] He received his copy in May but had not had a chance to read it when he wrote, "Despite all the frustrations, I know you must feel great to see yourself in print. Congratulations!"[46] By June, Reich had finished reading and felt overwhelmed: "I love your book—and love you more because of it." At her request, Reich provided a review that Girodias and Olympia Press could use for publicity purposes.[47] Reich's review moved Isabelle deeply: she immediately transcribed his handwritten pages into a typewritten document and forwarded it to her publisher:

> I received Charles Reich's comments on the book. It is enclosed. What he says about *The City Within* had a terrific effect on me. The question arises what are we going to do ... with this. Mr. Reich writes me we can use it any way I like. It is my thought that it should be sold, on Mr. Reich's behalf, naturally, to a really high-class buyer: *New York Times*, *Harper's*, *Atlantic*, *World* and/or *Saturday Review*, whichever it is at the moment—or perhaps the *Sunday Washington Post*. In any case, do *something* with it. It's pure gold.[48]

Isabelle's letter to Girodias indicates that they had been corresponding over the summer about publicity and other matters. One point of discussion was compiling a list of recipients for promotional advance copies. Isabelle suggested sending them to *Redbook* magazine, New York City's *The Village Voice* and *Ms.* Magazine. Others should go to lesbian and/or feminist icons Gloria Steinem, Jill Johnston, Ti-Grace Atkinson, Kate Millett, Germaine Greer, Charlotte Wolfe, Betty and Theodore Roszak, and Diane Harris (formerly at Macmillan Publishing) as well as Norman Mailer.[49]

However, a few details troubled Lynn. It had been over a year since she had sent Girodias her revised version of *Structure of Grief*: "Are you thinking of what you might do with [it]? I think *Redbook* is worth a try on that." In addition, she had received no response about other prospects for her book: "Every time I say 'movie' you say nothing. I hope you will make every effort (for both our sakes) to sell [*The City Within*] to the movies ... And I look forward to hearing from you—and lots of luck to both of us."[50] Perhaps this alerted her that something was amiss in New York City.

Meanwhile, the printing and release of the book was progressing apace: Isabelle received proofs for the dust jacket in May featuring a statuesque woman gazing demurely downward, right hand to her neck, left breast just barely covered as her white gown drapes off her shoulders to the ground. The image is superimposed over a photograph of the United States Capitol Building.⁵¹ In the summer, an encouraging letter arrived from Girodias's new editor and in-house publicist, Susan Sueyres:

> I personally like the book and professionally (having previously worked at Bantam Books, Random House, and Harper & Row) think it has good potential to reach many different kinds of readers. I think the public is ready to consider the whole subject of homosexuality and your book bridges a gap between two worlds that are not so very different.... We think the book can do very well—and expect to sell paperback rights to a good house.⁵²

Sueyres wanted some guidance on publicity, inquiring whether Isabelle would consider doing anonymous interviews by telephone. Isabelle replied that written interviews would be her preference because of the lack of phone service at Goose Prairie and a reluctance to have her area code known if she fielded calls from Yakima: "I insist on anonymity. I rather like the book myself, you know, and I find it, frankly, tiresome as hell not to shout from the housetops *I* [sic] wrote it. But consideration for my family, my business, and friends make that impossible."⁵³

Isabelle sidestepped any troubling questions from friends and family about her publishing process by saying she had authored a cookbook.⁵⁴ But those trusted readers to whom Lynn had sent advance copies of *The City Within* were aware and enthusiastic. Her friend Charlotte Mayerson, an editor at Random House who was working with Justice Douglas on his autobiography, wrote, "The story is perceptive and compassionate and I'm really proud that you made me such a fine gift."⁵⁵ Charles Reich had passed his copy around to acquaintances during his stay in San Francisco. One of them was Jim Brogan, an English professor at San Francisco State University who had initiated perhaps the first course on homosexuality in the United States in 1969. During the fall semester of 1973, Brogan was teaching, for the second time, a

Dust-jacket proof for *The City Within* by Elisabeth Newbold, 1973 (Kershaw Family Collection).

brand-new course, "Gay and Lesbian Love in Literature," and Reich had high expectations that Brogan would incorporate *The City Within* into the syllabus. Another friend of Reich's loved the book and suggested Isabelle's publisher contact Up Haste, a women's bookstore in Berkeley.[56]

In anticipation of an August release, the publicity staff involved with Girodias's publishing house managed to get a mention for *The City Within* into the *New York Times* on 30 June 1973 with a terse recap: "Women in love with each other."[57] In September, they put together an advertisement using Reich's name, highlighting his authorship of *The Greening of America*, for the *New York Times Book Review*: it incorporated excerpts of his commentary under a pen-and-ink rendering of two women's faces:

> A novel about two worlds, the outer world of Washington, D.C. and an inner world of lesbian relationships ... the book is remarkable for its portrayal of both.... The point of the book is not the issue of lesbianism, but the ideal of a truly enriching relationship ... sexual identity doesn't matter in the end ... quality does. And this book has quality, wit and superb readability ... a pleasure to read.[58]

With rave reviews from early readers, publicity already placed with the leading source for literary reviews in North America, a potential movie contract hopefully in the works, and books in hand, Isabelle anticipated her new life as a successful author.

Maurice Girodias Associates, Inc. v. Lyle Stuart, Inc.

In his 1968 interview with the *New York Times*, Maurice Girodias made an offhand remark that spoke volumes on his business ethics: "Running an enterprise in erotic books is an outright pleasure in New York, where everyone swindles everyone else."[59] And to be sure, while Isabelle Lynn dreamt in Goose Prairie of anonymous interviews and Hollywood movie rights, Maurice Girodias was wheeling and dealing in the Big Apple. In fall of 1972, he found an equal match to his own questionable business practices when he embarked on a co-publication program with Lyle Stuart Publishers (LSP) applicable to around twenty books per year.

Lyle Stuart (1922–2006) began his career in publishing with the foundation of *Exposé* (later changed to *The Independent*), a magazine that printed controversial articles and stories other entities would not touch. He established Lyle Stuart, Inc. in 1955, taking on unconventional book projects: Fidel Castro's *History Will Absolve Me*; a six-volume "History of Eroticism"; and a book on erotic Hindu sculpture, *Kama Kala*, that was originally banned in the United States. He made a number of shrewd moves in the book business, most notably the publication of Ferdinand Lundberg's *The Rich and the Super-Rich* and the best-selling 1969 novel *Naked Came the Stranger*, an elaborate hoax perpetrated by *Newsday* columnist Mike McGrady. He was averse to giving any of his authors either advances or contracts, made his employees handle garbage collection, won and lost fortunes at the casinos, owned a ten-and-a-half-acre vacation spread in Jamaica, and reveled in being an eccentric: "a walking idiosyncrasy, and one of the most interesting characters in the business."[60]

The contract between Girodias and Stuart stipulated that LSP would finance and distribute in the United States and Canada books selected, edited, and published by Girodias under a new imprint: "A Maurice Girodias Book Distributed by Lyle Stuart Inc." LSP agreed to guarantee the cost of production including printing, typesetting, dust jacket production, and bookbinding. For this advance investment, the two parties would divide the net proceeds from sales and distribution with 25 percent to LSP, the remainder to Girodias. This arrangement removed and separated Girodias' books in North America from the translation and subsidiary rights arranged with Capito N.V., the entity which held Lynn's original contract signed in May 1972.[61]

According to the initial arrangement, both Girodias and LSP would share a listing as joint publishers. However, Bantam Books had indicated an interest in purchasing the paperback rights to one of the first Girodias titles. LSP offered to restrict the co-publication arrangement on that one particular book and sign individual distribution, financing, and profit-sharing agreements for the rest of Girodias' publications, one book at a time. In the end, this arrangement applied to four books only, rather than to the twenty titles per year originally agreed upon. These four books—including *The City Within*—carried the joint imprint shared by Girodias and LSP.

It took less than a year for the business partnership to devolve into a bitter dispute. Sometime in September of 1973, just as her book made the pages of the *New York Times*, Isabelle realized something had gone awry. She contacted the Scott Meredith Literary Agency in New York for advice:

> In May 1972, a novel I wrote was bought by Capito N/V. In the contract they guaranteed me a $4000 advance. The book was to have been published simultaneously in four languages as a paperback, the American edition by the then Olympia Press in New York, which was being run by Maurice Girodias. Various things happened over the next two years and I spent almost as much time getting *any* advance as I did writing the book. They still owe me $1500, though this should have been paid by the spring of '73. The book was finally published in August '73 with arrangements for distribution by Lyle Stuart. Meantime Capito had long since disappeared from the scene (with no explanation) and Girodias, now calling himself "Maurice Girodias Associates," is nominally the publisher. I have no contract with him, and indeed Capito broke the terms of our contract before the ink was dry. So here I am—in a ridiculous position: the book exists, but it is not available anywhere ... so apparently it is not being distributed.... Evidently the entire first edition is sitting in a warehouse in New York.[62]

Unfortunately, Meredith had little consolation or advice:

> I'm afraid there doesn't seem much we can do for you. If Capito legitimately sold rights to your book to Maurice Girodias, the fact that it's since disappeared doesn't effect [sic] the legitimacy of the contract. Further, it's almost impossible to prove that a publisher's doing nothing about promoting a book ... unless he's not distributing the novel at all,

there's not much to be done about it. You might want to go ahead and sue, but while you might win your case it would certainly be costly.[63]

By the end of 1973, the promotional sum total for *The City Within* consisted of the dual ad placement and recap that had appeared in the *New York Times* in September. Lynn had friends and acquaintances search for copies of her book in Philadelphia, Chicago, Seattle, San Francisco, New York, Washington, D.C., and elsewhere around the country to no avail: the book was not in distribution. Concerned about the status of *The City Within*, she contacted a Girodias associate in January 1974 who informed her that as of the end of the year, total sales were only 1,014 out of the 5,000 copies from the first press run.[64]

The partnership between Girodias and LSP deteriorated precipitously over the course of 1974. By late November, LSP sued Girodias for $24,526.29, claiming that he had refused to carry out the terms of their contract for the publication of the four books released under their joint imprint. Girodias declined to pay, counter-claiming that LSP had failed to market and promote the four books while withholding a full accounting of sales and expenses. Because the print run of the four books listed LSP as the distributor, Girodias could not solicit the help of a different entity for distribution, thus precluding any further sales.[65] To substantiate the claim that LSP had been negligent in its obligations to Girodias to promote and sell the books, Girodias' lawyer used *The City Within* as an illustration:

> Charles Reich's analysis of that book also shows that this was a highly promotable novel, which contained all the ingredients of a great success. *The City Within* being a roman à clé [sic] using as backdrop certain Washington circles, presented under a very unusual light, it would have been very easy to promote that particular book locally, by obtaining the help of Washington jobbers and retailers: which the Distributor neglected to do, in spite of the Publisher's insistence.[66]

At some point just prior to LSP's lawsuit (probably in late November when she was already in Washington, D.C., for a meeting of the trustees of the National Parks and Conservation Association on 20 November), Lynn went to New York to meet with Girodias and assess their situation. He explained that he had run into difficulties because of LSP's failure to fulfill its obligations under the terms of their contract creating a severe financial crisis for his company: "a large Gallic snow job," as Isabelle's inimitable wordsmithing memorialized the encounter. According to Girodias, Isabelle agreed to wait for payment until his financial situation improved.[67] In a follow-up letter to Isabelle after their meeting, Girodias acknowledges her concerns and asks forgiveness for the debacle he had created:

> I would like to thank you for your understanding, friendly attitude with respect to what happened to *The City Within*, and to my enterprise. It all derives from the colossal mistake I made in going into business with Lyle Stuart. I am sure that things would have been much better if I had starved and done these books on my own—instead of going into partnership with that man, and starving. But of course my starving is no excuse for what I did to the authors concerned, and there is no apology humble enough for the misdeed.[68]

In this letter, Girodias informs Lynn that LSP had initiated legal proceedings and suggests that she might help with his lawsuit against LSP: "It can be done in the name of Elisabeth Newbold, of course, and in writing." Girodias included two documents from the American Arbitration Association detailing the claims and counter-claims between Girodias and LSP. However, before Girodias had even composed his letter, Isabelle had contacted an acquaintance at Random House who recommended she get in touch with Jeffrey Laytin, a young New York attorney specializing in intellectual property issues.[69]

The whole affair proved quite confusing and reading the arbitration documents did not help clarify matters. Writing to Charlotte Mayerson, Isabelle details some of her frustration and laments:

> These two documents raise (for me, anyway) more questions than they answer.... I don't expect you to answer these, you understand, I'm simply speculating, and I sure as hell could use some advice.... I have no desire for a trip down the garden path with some goddam *man* [sic], for Christ's sake, so give your biased opinion: what shall I do now, Daddy? Write a deposition for Maurice? If so, saying what?—"I HATE LYLE STUART"? [sic] Who would believe life could get so complex for a simple mountain kid. Kay sends love too.[70]

By January 1975, Lynn had established a relationship with Laytin, forwarding all her letters, notes, and the arbitration documents. She had Lyle Stuart in her sights and contemplated joining with Girodias in a lawsuit against him. In her letter to Laytin she requested help gaining the balance of the advance owed to her by Girodias and to ensure that she retained the legal title to her book so that she could try to resell it to another publisher. Isabelle was taken aback when she saw that Lyle Stuart—rather than focusing on distribution of *The City Within*—had turned to hawking Good Earth soap (Magic Grass, Pink Melon, and Green Bean fragrances) on the pages of the *New York Times*.[71]

By the end of January, Laytin made contact with the frazzled Girodias—"a mess," in Lynn's words—who explained in a follow-up reply that LSP had failed to provide adequate service plunging his business into "a permanent financial crisis from which we have been unable to extricate ourselves ... [Isabelle] would have a better chance to obtain damages by directing her claim against [LSP] than against ourselves." Laytin followed up by telephone during which an agitated Gorodias argued that he was virtually bankrupt and that any litigation against him would be fruitless. Therefore, Laytin suggested going after Lyle Stuart to claim the remaining 1,500 dollars due on Isabelle's 1972 advance and to reclaim the rights to *The City Within*.[72]

Girodias appeared distraught to Isabelle and Jeffrey Laytin for a reason: his fortunes had taken a turn for the worse during this period in venues unrelated to the Lyle Stuart situation. In 1974, Girodias found himself in hot water with the United States government after publishing *President Kissinger*, a pornographic novel featuring then–Secretary of State Henry Kissinger; the State Department was not amused and initiated deportation proceedings in May of 1974. When Immigration and Naturalization Service gave him until 15 June to return to France, Girodias scrambled to get married to a U.S. citizen in an effort to remain in the United States. Meanwhile, Sir Cyril Black, a former member of the British Parliament and an ardent sponsor of the Rev. Billy Graham, sued Girodias and an associate for the publication of a pornographic paperback, *Sir Cyril Black*. Lawyers for the two parties eventually settled the one-million-dollar libel suit for 100,000 dollars in early June 1975.[73] It was quite apparent that trying to recover money from Girodias for *The City Within* would be a fool's errand.

On 25 March 1975, Laytin wrote to Lyle Stuart requesting the money due Lynn and outlining how he, Girodias, and Capito N.V. were now jointly responsible for any damages sustained resulting from the publication of Isabelle's book. Laytin requested payment plus a full accounting to date of book sales: otherwise, legal proceedings would commence against all three entities for copyright infringement, conspiracy, and breach of contract along with all attorney's fees and interest.[74] At this point, the legal documentation ends: whether Isabelle recovered the rights to her book or ever received the final installment on her advance from 1972 is unknown. However, the entire process had consumed three years, the unsold books were gathering dust somewhere in New York, and the market for lesbian erotica had moved on. From the perspective of the freewheeling 1970s, Isabelle's cocktail-swilling protagonists appear oddly out of synch with the times; within the novel's historical setting, these federal employees working in 1950s Washington, D.C., are scarcely aware of the anti-gay witch-hunts roiling the nation's capital during the red scare. Any potential *The City Within* may have possessed as a lesbian blockbuster had dissipated, eclipsed by more recent and relevant releases such as Rita Mae Brown's 1973 coming-of-age tale, *Rubyfruit Jungle*, and June Arnold's *Sister Gin*, a gritty novel set at the opposite end of the age spectrum, published in 1975.[75] Even though Lynn kept her brief foray at the vanguard of lesbian literature a closely-guarded secret her entire life, she remained inwardly quite pleased with her accomplishment, and justifiably so. Those close to her knew about it though: Ruby Montana recalled that Isabelle proudly pulled a copy of *The City Within* from the Double K bookshelf to show her when she visited in the late 1980s.[76]

Chapter Notes

Sources and Abbreviations

Brock Evans Papers: *Brock Evans Papers, Access Number 1776-17 Box 84 of 86, File: Cougar Lakes and Clearwater 1973-76*. University of Washington Libraries, Special Collections

Double K Papers: *Double K Mountain Ranch Records, 1958-1972, Access Number 2133-001*. University of Washington Libraries, Special Collections

GFC: Gilbert Family collection, held privately

KaFC: Kane Family collection, held privately

KFC: Kershaw Family collection, held privately

LOC: Library of Congress

NCCC records: *North Cascades Conservation Council Records, Access Number 1732-001, -011, -015*. University of Washington Libraries, Special Collections

NYT: *New York Times*

WOD: William O. Douglas

YDR: *Yakima Daily Republic*

YH-R: *Yakima Herald-Republic*

YMH: *Yakima Morning Herald*

YSH: *Yakima Sunday Herald*

YVM: Yakima Valley Museum

YVMCDH papers: Yakima Valley Museum, Charles D. Hessey, Jr., papers

YVMGF: Yakima Valley Museum, Gilbert Family collection

YVMWOD: Yakima Valley Museum, William O. Douglas collection

Introduction

1. Isabelle Lynn, letter to Harvey Manning, 4 March 1966 (NCCC records, 1732-011, Box 6).

2. William O. Douglas, *Of Men and Mountains* (New York: Harper, 1950), 7.

3. Douglas, *Of Men and Mountains*, 7.

4. *Griswold v. Connecticut*: 381 U.S. 479 (1965), 483-85. Douglas uses the term "penumbra" six times in his summation.

5. Chris Geidner, "The Court Cases That Changed L.G.B.T.Q. Rights," *NYT*, 19 June 2019.

6. See Justice Clarence Thomas's concurring opinion in *Dobbs v. Jackson Women's Health Organization*: 597 U.S. 215 (2022): "in future cases, we should reconsider all of this Court's substantive due process precedents, including Griswold, Lawrence, and Obergefell ... we have a duty to 'correct the error' established in those precedents."

7. On wildflowers see William O. Douglas, letter to Kay Kershaw, 23 February 1959; Kay Kershaw, letter to William O. Douglas, 28 September 1959 (William O. Douglas Papers, Box 1011, file: Kay Kershaw) (LOC); William O. Douglas, letter to Isabelle Lynn, 8 April 1976 (KFC); William O. Douglas, *My Wilderness: The Pacific West* (Garden City, NY: Doubleday, 1960), 126, 129-30; desk top in William O. Douglas office display, YVMWOD. On martinis see William O. Douglas, letter to Kay Kershaw, 14 April 1966 and 12 December 1970 (Double K Papers, file 1-1); Douglas, letter to Isabelle Lynn, 25 February 1971 (Binder no. 2, LOC Manuscripts Environmental articles, Supreme Court cases, YVMWOD); "The Return of the Irate Birdwatcher," *Wild Cascades* (Fall 1984): 26; office photos, Box 44, file 44-1 YVMWOD; Double K Ranch lodge interior photos in "Double K Holiday 74 75 76" and "Photo Album: To Kay and Isabel [sic] a few records of the great 1976 September! From Lil & Shirl" (KFC); Isabelle Lynn, letter to Harvey Manning, 16 May 1967 (NCCC records, 1732-011 Box 6). On recipes see "scalloped eggplant"; "macaroon pêche ('make your own goddam macaroons')"; and "Steak Barbecue Sauce (Justice William O. Douglas)" [recipe cards] Seth McCormick Lynn, Jr., collection; "Dinner 'Fir' Douglas," [Double K Mountain Ranch dinner menu], 8 July 1950, YVM archives, Document Box 222.

Chapter 1

1. Jack Nelson, *We Never Got Away* (Yakima: Franklin Press, 1965), 177.

2. William D. Lyman, *History of the Yakima Valley, Washington: Comprising Yakima, Kittitas, and Benton Counties*, vol. 1 (Chicago: S.J. Clark, 1919), 84.

3. Lyman gives the date as 18 October; Fred Beckey suggests 19 September. Lyman, *History of the Yakima Valley*, vol. 1, 128; Fred Beckey, *Cascade Alpine Guide: Climbing and High Routes, Columbia River to Stevens Pass* (Seattle: The Mountaineers, 1973), 55.

4. In addition to Maps 1 and 2, an online

version of the NCCC newsletter, *Wild Cascades* (Fall 1985–Spring 1987), contains maps showing many of these geographical features [http://npshistory.com/newsletters/the-wild-cascades/fall-1985-spring-1987.pdf]: 15, 16–17. Note the second map is oriented so that north is on the right side of the page.

5. William O. Douglas, "339: Houston, Texas, State Bar of Texas, 6 July 1972": 1 (WOD Speeches Binder #11, nos. 332-365-D, 2/9/1972–1979, YVM-WOD); Bob Wazeka, "The Crusade for Cougar Lakes," *The Living Wilderness* 42, no. 143 (October/December 1978): 27. Douglas conflates "vsiak kulik svoe boloto khvalit [every sandpiper praises its own marsh]" with "vsiakii chert v svoem bolote vorochai [let every devil rule over his own marsh]."

6. Douglas, *Of Men and Mountains*, 279–80; "Marathon of the Mountains, 1927 Cascadian Annual," *Cascadian Annual—Then and Now— 60th Anniversary 1920-1980*, 6–7 (YVM archives, Cascadians Box 3a 1937-1964 and 3b 1965-1985).

7. "Cascadians Plan Summer's Outing," *YDR*, 14 February 1923. The trip included visits to Yakima Park, Summerland, Paradise Valley, and Indian Henry's Hunting Ground.

8. William D. Lyman, *History of the Yakima Valley, Comprising Yakima, Kittitas, and Benton Counties*, vol. 2 (Chicago: S.J. Clark, 1919), 1021–22; "Newspaper Writer Succeeds By Taking Own Advice," *YDR*, 2 May 1930. Although Gilbert's given name is commonly spelled "Curtis," the correct spelling is "Curtiss," as found on both his birth and death certificates. Cragg M. Gilbert, email correspondence, 23 August 2020.

9. According to family lore, *Krag the Kootenay Ram* was the inspiration for the name of Curtiss's son, Cragg D. Gilbert, inherited by his grandson, Cragg M. Gilbert, as well. Cragg M. Gilbert, email correspondence, 23 August 2020.

10. Curtiss Gilbert, Scrapbook (1898–1912), ninety-one pages (GFC). For more details on Gilbert's excursions, see William D. Frank, "Early Climbing History in Washington State," in *Let's Take the Sporting Route: Mountaineering in Central Washington 1949-1970*, ed. William D. Frank (Yakima: Yakima Valley Museum, 2022), 5–9.

11. Cragg M. Gilbert, "Yakima's Boy Scout Troop 9," in *Let's Take the Sporting Route*, 23–27; "It Happened Here: Curtiss Gilbert teaches boys how to survive in the outdoors, life," *YH-R*, 13 January 2020; "Remembering 'The Big Trip': Event, award will honor Yakima Valley family for contributions to Scouting," *YH-R*, 19 April 2016; Lloyd Phillip Johnson, *Where's Frank? An Intrepid Leader, 18 Boy Scouts, 10,000 Miles in an Open Truck* (Virginia Beach: Koehler Books, 2016); "Boy Scouts Back From Their Trip," *YDR*, 30 August 1935; "Area Leader Dies Suddenly," 3 October 1947. Many Troop 9 Scouts served in World War II and credited Curtiss with helping them survive the rigors of war. See S.I. Anthon, "Daily Mirror of Life in Yakima," *YDR*, 20 December 1943. One Troop 9 alumnus wrote from his post: "We are at a decided advantage, because we did go thru Scouting under the leader's eye of a swell guy who taught us things that are invaluable now. I hope we all do what you expect of us." Lieutenant Webb Hayes, letter to Curtiss Gilbert, 27 January 1943 [four handwritten pages] (GFC).

12. William O. Douglas, letter to Cragg D. Gilbert, 28 March 1949. YVMGF, Box 3.

13. Henry A. McCormick, *An X-Ray on the Naches Valley: A Typical Illustration of Rural Life in the Valleys of Yakima with Naches Avenue of North Yakima, Washington, Supplementary* (North Yakima: Republic, 1911), 62, 80–91. Currently, Rim Rock Drive is named Kershaw Drive. See "North Yakima RFD 6," *Polk & Company Directory Yakima 1918* (Seattle: R.L. Polk and Company, 1918), 314. A photograph of Kay Kershaw ca. 1930 shows her planting trees on the west side of the road with the Kershaw barn in the background (KFC). See photo on page 42.

14. The Yakima War was the result of broken treaties between the Confederated Tribes and Bands of the Yakama Nation and the United States government as well as outrages suffered by tribal members at the hands of white settlers. See A.J. Splawn, *Ka-Mi-Akin: The Last Hero of the Yakimas*, 3rd ed. (Caldwell, ID: Caxton, 1958), 38–63; Lyman, *History of the Yakima Valley*, vol. 1, 222–65; Kent D. Richards, *Isaac Stevens: Young Man in a Hurry* (Provo: Brigham Young University Press, 1979), 235–72.

15. C.M. Barton, "North Yakima," *The Northwest Magazine*, May 1889: 18–22.

16. R.N. Baskin, *Reminiscences of Early Utah* (Salt Lake City: [Baskin?], 1914), 108, 130; "David Evans Company (1850)," *Pioneer Data Base 1847-1868 The Church of Jesus Christ of Latter-Day Saints* [https://history.churchofjesuschrist.org/overlandtravel/companies/114/david-evans-company]; Cragg M. Gilbert, interview with Robert C. Kershaw, 11 May 2019 (YVM Archives); George W. Woodhouse, letter [recipient unknown], 22 February 1930. "Descendants of Samuel Kershaw," ancestry.com (KFC).

17. Robert Kershaw, "Will of Robert Kershaw" [handwritten document, four pages, dated 20 June 1896] (KFC); "Open House Today Honors Pioneers' Golden Wedding," *YMH*, 17 December 1954; Lyman, *History of the Yakima Valley*, vol. 2, 982–83; Gretta Petersen Gossett, typewritten notes, [no date] (YVM archives, Naches file); Augustina Eastland, interview with Robert H. Kershaw, 17 March 1936 [two pages typed] ("Kershaw, Robert H. and Family" in Biography Files, YVM archives).

18. Mary Ann (Kershaw) Robinson, interview, 28 April 2021; "Mrs. Kathryn Kershaw, 86, dies," *YDR*, 27 November 1963; "Mrs. Ora Kershaw," 28 November 1963. The paper also mistakenly reports Ora's birth year as 1881.

19. Olin D. Wheeler, "The Yakima Valley," *The Northwest Magazine*, February 1894: 22–26; E.V. Smalley, "Winter Sunbeams in the Yakima Valley," March 1894: 22–28; Victor H. Smalley, "A Visit to

North Yakima, Wash.," July 1897: 11–12; *An Illustrated History of Klickitat, Yakima and Kittitas Counties: With an outline of the early history of the State of Washington*, eds. William S. Schiach and Harrison D. Averell (Chicago: Interstate, 1904), 194; Lyman, *History of the Yakima Valley*, vol. 1, 328; Gossett, *Beyond the Bend*, 335–41; Gretta Petersen Gossett, "Naches All Because of Water," [typewritten manuscript, 9 July 1963, twenty-six pages] (YVM archives, Naches file).

20. Lyman, *History of the Yakima Valley*, vol. 1, 365–76; "John Russell Homestead (Circa 1885)" [http://www.cowichecalls.com/stories.asp?storyID=7]; Verne F. Ray, "Native Villages and Groupings of the Columbia Basin," *Pacific Northwest Quarterly* 27, no. 2 (April 1936): 146.

21. Lyman, *History of the Yakima Valley*, vol. 1, 785–810.

22. Lyman, *History of the Yakima Valley*, vol. 1, 403, 786.

23. Barton, "North Yakima," 19.

24. Schiach and Averell, *Illustrated History*, 186; Lyman, *History of the Yakima Valley*, vol. 1, 459, 470, 786; *Yakima Herald*, 13 May 1907; 3 December 1907; 25 October 1911; "Naches," *YMH*, 1 March 1953; Gossett, *Beyond the Bend*, 78, 261, 280, 354. The name of the town, river, and mountain pass—variously spelled Natchez, Natcheez, Nachess, and Naches over the years—derives from Native American language. Although many sources speculate that this translates to "rough" or "turbulent water," the exact meaning is unknown. See "Valley Names of Indian Origin Poetically Descriptive of Sites," *YMH*, 24 June 1956. Naches officially incorporated in 1921.

25. David Louter, *Windshield Wilderness: Cars, Roads, and Nature in Washington's National Parks* (Seattle: University of Washington Press, 2006), 11–13, 17, 33–34; "Mount Rainier History," National Park Service [https://www.nps.gov/mora/learn/historyculture/mount-rainier-history.htm]; Gossett, *Beyond the Bend*, 279.

26. W.W. Robertson, Editorial, *YDR*, 13 October 1924; Gossett, *Beyond the Bend*, 273–80; Louter, *Windshield Wilderness*, 19–20.

27. Louter, *Windshield Wilderness*, 63–67; Gossett, *Beyond the Bend*, 281, 283, 287, 289.

28. Cragg D. Gilbert, letter to William O. Douglas, 15 September 1961 (GFC).

29. "Naches," *YMH*, 1 March 1953.

30. George M. Marsden, *Fundamentalism and American Culture*, 2nd ed. (New York: Oxford University Press, 2006), 3–4, 153; Marsden, *Understanding Fundamentalism and Evangelicalism* (Grand Rapids: William B. Eerdmans, 1991), 1–4.

31. "Yakima Ministers Seek Change in Marriage Laws," *YDR*, 15 January 1923; "Lawful Free Love is Near," 17 March 1923. This waiting period is known as publishing the banns in the Catholic Church and other Christian denominations.

32. Lyman, *History of the Yakima Valley*, vol. 1, 487–95; "Growth by State or Territory," chart in "Lesson Thirteen: Cities and Hinterlands: The Modern Northwest," in John Findlay, "History of Washington State and the Pacific Northwest," Center for the Study of the Pacific Northwest, University of Washington [https://www.washington.edu/uwired/outreach/cspn/Website/Classroom%20Materials/Pacific%20Northwest%20History/Lessons/Lesson%2013/13.html].

33. "Would Boost Carnival Bill," *YDR*, 1 March 1923; "Letters From the People," 3 March 1923; "Carnival to Be Banned from 1923 State Exhibit," 5 March 1923; "Carnival Bill is Killed," 8 March 1923.

34. William O. Douglas, *Go East, Young Man the Early Years. The Autobiography of William O. Douglas* (New York: Random House, 1974), 16, 60, 62, 127. See also William O. Douglas, "261: The Guidance Center New Rochelle, NY 23 May 1964": 2 (WOD Speeches Binder #8 nos. 224–264, 10/14/62–7/26/64 YVMWOD): "In the town where I grew up, the Establishment was a combination of church and monied interests ... heavy on the side of the status quo."

35. Billy Graham, *World Aflame* (Garden City, NY: Doubleday, 1965), 22. Graham's attitude had not changed one iota as of 1975. Addressing a question about lesbianism, Graham states: "But let me say this loud and clear! We traffic in homosexuality at the peril of our spiritual welfare." See Billy Graham, *Blow, Wind of God! Selected Writings of Billy Graham*, ed. Donald E. Demaray (New York: Signet, 1977; reprint of Baker Book House, 1975), 17–18. His stance softened somewhat in the following decades. See Michael G. Long, *Martin Luther King, Jr., Homosexuality, and the Early Gay Rights Movement: Keeping the Dream Straight?* (New York: Palgrave Macmillan, 2012), 57–59, 140–42.

36. Marsden, *Understanding*, 54–55; Ben Bruce, "The Rise and Fall of the Ku Klux Klan in Oregon in the 1920s," *Voces Novae* 11 (2019): article 2; Kelly J. Baker, *Gospel According to the Klan: The KKK's Appeal to Protestant America, 1915–1930* (Lawrence: University Press of Kansas, 2011), 8–10; David Chalmers, *Notes on Writing the History of the Ku Klux Klan* (Gainesville: University Press of Florida, 2015), 37, 54.

37. Bruce, "The Rise and Fall," 1, 4–8.

38. Douglas, *Go East*, 69.

39. Just a sampling from the *Yakima Daily Republic* front page in January 1923: "Ku Klux Klan sign of the fiery cross," 5 January [photo]; "Ku Klux Give Judge Bouquet," 16 January; "Klan Cyclops with hooded kidnapers [sic]" and "Court in Kansas Rejects Plea of Night Rider Klan," 20 January; "Black Mask Mob Lynched Worker" and "Cyclops Told Phone Girl to Ban Mer Rouge Calls," 23 January; "Governor Warns Klan to Keep Hands Off Kidnaping [sic] Inquiry Morehouse Parish," 24 January; "Probe Into Black Hood Crime Now Closed," 25 January; "Test Case Made of KKK," 27 January; "Trials for Klan Killings Started," 29 January.

40. "Night Rider Trials Begin," *YDR*, 27 February 1923; "Jurors in Medford Trial Quizzed as to

Prejudice," 28 February 1923; "Terrorism in Medford Case," 1 March 1923; "Hale Carried to Tell Tale," 5 March 1923; "County Judge Named as One Masked Rider" and "Second Trial Sensational," 14 March 1923; "Oregon Rider Prosecutions End in Fizzle," 15 March 1923.

41. Upon opening in 1920, the brand-new Mercy Theatre (re-named the Capitol Theatre a year later) listed 1,916 seats, with "more numerous and larger" fire exits than required by state building codes. "Beautiful Mercy Theatre Opens Here This Evening," *YDR*, 5 April 1920; "Seating Arrangement of Lower Floor" and "Seating Arrangement of Balcony" in *Mercy Theatre Souvenir Opening Program, April Fifth and Sixth*, 10, 12 (YVM Box DBX 257, file "Mercy Theater Opening—1920").

42. "Public Meeting on Klan to Take Place Thursday," *YDR*, 19 March 1923; "Church Board Withdraws Offer of Pulpit to Klan" and "Imperial Klan Lecturer is Now Looking for Hall," 21 March 1923; "Klan Lecturer to Speak," 22 March 1923; "Rovig Replies to Klan Talk," 23 March 1923; "Klan Lecturer Draws Crowds," *YMH*, 23 March 1923; "Klan Lecturer Speaks," 24 March 1923.

43. "Rovig Replies to Klan Talk," W.W. Robertson, Editorial, *YDR*, 23 March 1923. An editorial by Robertson just six days later demands resolution of the Yakima Valley's "Japanese question ... the sooner they go the sooner the reservation will come into its own." *YDR*, 29 March 1923. The following year, Robertson took issue with Native Americans receiving the right to vote: "The act of conferring citizenship and the privilege of voting at elections on Indians is an idiotic piece of legislation.... We have long had too many people in this country who are incapable of intelligently performing the duties of citizenship, and it was not necessary for congress to provide us with more." *YDR*, 15 August 1924. However, Robertson denounced Klan lynchings in the South unequivocally. Robertson, "Heroes in Alabama" [editorial], 12 June 1947.

44. "3 Hundred [sic] Women Hear About Plans to Organize Unit to Work With K.K.K.," *YDR*, 18 July 1923.

45. "Klan Denied Use of Fair Grounds," *YMH*, 26 July 1924; "Program Ready for Klan Meet," 6 August 1924; "Klan Plans for Its Ceremonial," *YDR*, 9 August 1924; T.A. Rogers, letter to Governor Louis F. Hart, 15 August 1924 (YVM).

46. "Klan Ceremonial Comes Tomorrow," *YDR*, 8 August 1924; "Klan Plans Its Ceremonial," 9 August 1924; "Klan Ceremonial Holds Big Crowd," 11 August 1924; "40,000 See Klan Give Obligation to Large Class," *YMH*, 10 August 1924; Lester Abrams, "Yakima, Washington August 9, 1924" [photo] (YVM). See photo on page 18.

47. Horace M. Gilbert, letter to Francelia Amsden Gilbert and May Gilbert, 10 August 1924 (GFC).

48. "School Bill is Talked by Pastors at Meeting," *YDR*, 20 October 1924. Initiative 49 was a contentious issue during the campaign season. See "Initiative 49 is Criticized," *YDR*, 20 October 1924; "That School Bill," 24 October 1924; W.W. Robertson, Editorial, 28 October 1924; "Crowd Forces Orator to Quit," 29 October 1924; "Initiative 49," 1 November 1924.

49. The "Imperial Wizard" was the commander-in-chief and head of the Ku Klux Klan. Hiram Wesley Evans (1881–1966) was a dentist from Texas who served as Imperial Wizard from 1922 to 1939. At the time of his trip to the Pacific Northwest, Atlanta was home to Klan national headquarters.

50. "Klan Imperial Wizard Dated," *YDR*, 13 November 1924; "Klan Imperial Wizard Speaks," 17 November 1924.

51. "Klan Closes Its State Meeting," *YDR*, 18 June 1928.

52. Thomas H. Heuterman, "Bifurcation: How the Wapato, Washington *Independent* Covered Japanese in the Yakima Valley, 1920–1942," Paper presented at the Annual Meeting of the Association for Education in Journalism and Mass Communication (San Antonio, Texas, 3 August 1987) [45 pages]: 30–33; "Negro with White Woman Is Given Fine In Court," *YDR*, 8 July 1929; "Legion Contests Are Started Today: Ban On Filipino Influx Wanted By Convention," 16 August 1929; "Local news items: Klanswomen to meet," 18 September 1929; "Negroes Routed by Wapato Mob," *YMH*, 10 July 1938.

Chapter 2

1. Nelson, *We Never Got Away*, 177.

2. Julian Gill-Peterson, *Histories of the Transgender Child* (Minneapolis: University of Minnesota Press, 2018), 59–61. Current literature expresses this dichotomy with the terms cisgender (a person whose personal identity and gender corresponds to their birth sex) and transgender (a person whose personal identity and gender does not correspond to their birth sex).

3. Lisa Damour, "'Tomboy' Looks At Gender Roles, and Role-Playing Through the Ages," *NYT*, 7 October 2020.

4. Jeffrey Weeks, interview on "London Weekend Television, Gay Life," London Minorities Unit, 1981 ["Being Gay in the Thirties (Gay Life)"] 34:46 [https://www.youtube.com/watch?v=FzPzb3exfVc]: 13:58–17:12, 33:25–34:07; C.A. Tripp, "Who Is a Homosexual?" *The Ladder* 10, no. 3 (December 1965): 15–23.

5. Rose Palmquist, "History of the Naches School District," *Yakima Valley News* 8, no. 28 (21 December 1961): 9–12; Jean E. Wade, *Schools of Yakima County* (unpublished manuscript, 2006–07): 583–93 (YVM archives); Gossett, *Beyond the Bend*, 167; Lyman, *History of the Yakima Valley*, vol. 1, 365, 470. Gleed is an unincorporated community located halfway between Naches and Yakima, named after homesteader James Gleed (1835–1904). The barn he built in 1885 is still standing just outside

of town on Old Naches Highway. "Supplementary Listing Record: James Gleed Barn," United States Department of the Interior, National Register of Historic Places [https://npgallery.nps.gov/GetAsset/4f490584-08fd-4082-809a-2828dce6bbd9]. In the early decades of the twentieth century, poor roads made travel extremely difficult throughout Yakima County. In 1917, for example, in order to play a basketball game in nearby Selah (a twelve-mile trip by road today), the Naches High School team took the train to Yakima, then a trolley to Selah. The return by trolley required an overnight hotel stay in Yakima before boarding the train back to Naches the next day. Palmquist, 9.

6. "100 Happy Girls Frolic at Camp Fire Headquarters," *YDR*, 12 August 1924.

7. *Lo-Na-Hi 1924* [Lower Naches High School yearbook, 1924]; *Lo-Na-Hi 1925* [Lower Naches High School yearbook 1925] (YVM archives); two black and white loose photographs of Lower Naches High School 1924 girls' basketball team (KFC).

8. "Valley People and Their Guests," *YDR*, 3 February 1923; "Valley Personals," 26 October 1928; 9 July 1930; 7 July 1931; 11 July 1931; 13 July 1934; 6 August 1934; 5 July 1935; 14 October 1935; 11 July 1936; 7 August 1936; 18 August 1936; 8 September 1937.

9. "Girl Heroine of United States Dog Derby Hopes to Win in Great Contest to Be Run from Ashton," *YDR*, 2 February 1923.

10. "Girl Serves As Mountain Guide," *YDR*, 12 September 1922.

11. "Preaches Freedom for Women and Is Candidate for Mayor of Boston," *YDR*, 21 August 1924; "Woman Candidate for Mayor of Boston Offers Platform with Unusual Planks," 31 October 1924.

12. "Cascadians Plan Annual Meeting," *YDR*, 1 January 1923; "Cascadians Plan Summer Outings," 14 February 1923.

13. "High School Girls Hear Talk on Social Service," *YDR*, 6 March 1923.

14. Lillian Faderman, *Odd Girls and Twilight Lovers: A History of Lesbian Life in Twentieth-Century America* (New York: Columbia University Press, 1991), 12-13; Faderman, *To Believe in Women: What Lesbians Have Done for America—A History* (Boston: Houghton Mifflin, 1999), 5-9; Colin R. Johnson, *Just Queer Folk: Gender and Sexuality in Rural America* (Philadelphia: Temple University Press, 2013), 4-5, 110-11.

15. Faderman, *Odd Girls*, 62-65, 79-81.

16. "'Billy' Sunday Berated," *The Morning Oregonian*, 2 August 1915. This article lists the full title of Goldman's lecture as it appeared on handbills printed on 1 August in Portland: "The Intermediate Sex, a Discussion of Homosexuality." See handbill, "Emma Goldman lectures in Portland, Oregon, August 1, 1915," Jewish Women's Archive [https://jwa.org/media/handbill-advertising-group-of-lectures-by-goldman-in-portland-oregon]. Subsequent newspaper editions cut the reference to homosexuality from the title: "In the Passing Show," *Oregon Daily Journal*, 3 August 1915; "Emma Goldman" [advertisement], *The Morning Oregonian*, 6 August 1915.

17. Lillian Faderman, *The Gay Revolution: The Story of the Struggle* (New York: Simon & Schuster, 2015), xix-xx; "Criminologist Thatcher Goes Back of 'Hosing' to Causes," *The Morning Oregonian*, 21 November 1916; "Heads Will Roll," *The Oregon Statesman*, 3 July 1934; "Current Magazines," *NYT*, 30 May 1926. George Bernard Shaw refers to "homosexual brothels of Berlin" in "Common Sense About the War," *NYT*, 22 November 1914.

18. Elizabeth Lapovsky Kennedy, "'But we would never talk about it': The Structures of Lesbian Discretion in South Dakota, 1928-1933," in *Inventing Lesbian Cultures in America*, ed. Ellen Lewin (Boston: Beacon Press, 1996), 18-19.

19. Faderman, *Odd Girls*, 67; Allan Bérubé, *Coming Out Under Fire: The History of Gay Men and Women in World War Two* (New York: The Free Press, 1990), 28; Margot Canaday, *The Straight State: Sexuality and Citizenship in Twentieth-Century America* (Princeton: Princeton University Press, 2009), 174-75.

20. *Lo-Na-Hi 1924*; *Lo-Na-Hi 1925*. It is interesting to note that activist Eve Adams, author of *Lesbian Love*, traveled around "the apple country" of Yakima County on a hitchhiking trip to Seattle sometime during Kay's time in high school. Jonathan Ned Katz, *The Daring Life and Dangerous Times of Eve Adams* (Chicago: Chicago Review Press, 2021), 126.

21. "Hendricks Hall," *Oregana* 1926 [University of Oregon Yearbook 1926], 269; "University of Oregon Faculty and Student Directory 1925-1926" [Associated Students University of Oregon Graduate Manager's Office], 37. Five black and white photographs in *My Memory Book* ("U of Oregon 1920") document Kershaw's new hairstyle.

22. Patricia Albjerg Graham, "Expansion and Exclusion: A History of Women in American Higher Education," *Signs* 3, no. 4 (Summer 1978): 764-65; Patsy Parker, "The Historical Role of Women in Higher Education," *Administrative Issues Journal* 5, no. 1 (Spring 2015): 4.

23. "Catalogue 1925-1926: Announcements 1926-1927," University of Oregon Bulletin 23, no. 7 (June 1926): 8-20. The University of Oregon's School of Medicine and its Extension Center operated out of Portland. The School of Social Work lists six additional female associate faculty members, all registered nurses.

24. Faderman, *Odd Girls*, 14; *To Believe in Women*, 175-96.

25. *Chinook* 1927 [State College of Washington Yearbook 1927], 88-89, 152.

26. *Oregana* 1926, 216; *Chinook* 1927, 152. A letter from Pat Kane to her sister suggests that Kay may have taught riding classes at University of Oregon. Pat Kane, letter to Isabel Kane, 19 July 1937 (KaFC).

27. *Chinook* 1927, 303.

28. *Washington State Evergreen* [State College

of Washington student newspaper], 16 and 18 May 1927.

29. *Thirty-fifth Annual Catalogue of the State College of Washington for 1926 Pullman, Washington June, 1926* (Olympia: Jay Thomas, Public Printer, 1926), 329, 332, 337. Field ball is similar to contemporary field handball, played with a ball whose circumference is around 28 inches. Each team has eleven players. See "Rules for Field Ball," *American Physical Education Review* 24 no. 35 (1929): 304-7.

30. The Washington State legislature amended the state constitution in 1910—joining Wyoming (1869), Colorado (1893), and Utah and Idaho (1896)—to guarantee some women full voting rights.

31. Mark Dyreson, "Icons of Liberty or Objects of Desire? American Women Olympians and the Politics of Consumption," *Journal of Contemporary History* 38, no. 3 (July 2003): 436-37.

32. Dyerson, "Icons of Liberty," 444-46.

33. Rebecca A. Brown, *Women on High: Pioneers of Mountaineering* (Boston: Appalachian Mountain Club Books, 2002), 7.

34. In Norway, women had been active on skis since the latter half of the nineteenth century. The notion of ice-skating—a "ladylike" activity performed within the urbanized and artificial confines of an ice rink—was in stark contrast to women's skiing which represented unfettered freedom to roam wide-open spaces. This sense of adventure associated with breaking away from societal norms imbued skiing with an aura of late-nineteenth century bohemianism. Similarly, mountaineering offered women another way to enjoy physical activity with a freedom long denied in contemporary societal venues. See William D. Frank, *Everyone to Skis! Skiing in Russia and the Rise of Soviet Biathlon* (DeKalb: Northern Illinois University Press, 2013), 32-33.

35. See Chapter 5, "Skiing at American Ridge."

36. "Three Yakima Woman [sic] Prove They Are Real Mountain Climbers as They Ascend Mount Hood Easily," *YDR*, 6 September 1928; eight black and white photographs ("Mt. Hood Cimb [sic]"), *My Memory Book* (KFC).

37. "Cascadians Scale Lofty Stuart Peak," *Seattle Post-Intelligencer*, 3 June 1929; "Grease Paint to Aid Cascadians on Mt. Stuart Hike," *YDR*, 22 May 1931; "Many Living Creatures Found Upon Summit of Mt. Stuart By Climbers," 1 June 1931; "Mountains Attract Many Cascadian Club Members," 31 July 1931. On trips to Mt. Stuart and into Goat Rocks, Kay also furnished a pack train for the Cascadians to carry loads into base camp. Thirteen black and white photographs ("Around Mt. Rainier in nine days—back packing 1920"); ten black and white photographs ("Mt. Stuart Climb"); seven black and white photographs ("Mt. Adams horse-back trip 1929 Sept."); ten black and white photographs ("Mt. Shuksan climb" and "Mt. Shuksan Summit"); twelve black and white photographs ("Mt. Baker climb," "summit," "Mt. Baker Lodge,"

and "Ice Wall"); nine black and white photographs ("Emmons Glacier climb" and "Mt. Rainier Summit"). *My Memory Book* (KFC); Six black and white photographs (KFC).

38. Ten black and white photographs ("Mt. Adams 1938," "Surprise Lake—Rusty, Dandy—Ranger," "Cowlitz Pass—1938," "Glacier Peak—1939," "Buck Creek Pass," "Olympics—1940"), *Victory Picture Album* (KFC). The 1938 trip along the Pacific Crest Trail probably ended at Bumping Lake after crossing Cowlitz Pass. One loose photograph ("K and Marcella") ca. 1925 shows Kay on snowshoes with a companion. In another loose photograph ("Aunt Kay by her sailboat"), Kay adjusts a line from the dock, ca. 1940. Two additional black and white photographs (one loose, the other labeled "Sailing—Puget Sound" in *Victory Picture Album*) from the same day show a party of four, including Kay, sailing on the water. A black and white photograph dated July 1955 shows a sailboat on the water (unidentified). In *My Memory Book*, a photograph ("Paradise") shows a dogsled team resting in the snow at Paradise, Mt. Rainier, ca. 1929.

39. "Many Yakima Women Make Good Records As Both Hunters and Anglers," *YDR*, 16 September 1937.

40. "Fishing Rules for Next Season Drawn by Yakima County Game Commission," *YDR*, 12 December 1928 [clipping in KFC]; black and white photograph ("Hunting—Yakima"), *Victory Picture Album* and black and white photograph (loose in KFC). In the loose photograph, Kay displays a brace of ducks on the back hood of a car with Pat Kane, ca. 1942. In the other, Kay poses with her father; "Girl Aviator Is Off to Hunt Elk With Cousin," *YDR*, 19 October 1928; "Valley Personals," 26 October 1928; "Yakima Girl Hunter Gets Bear As Wounded Animal Charges At Her During Her Trip After Elk," 27 October 1928 [clipping in KFC]; "Girl Plans to be Trapper," 11 December 1928 [clipping in KFC]; "Girl Flyer Kills Charging Bear; She's Going Back To Get An Elk," *Seattle Post-Intelligencer*, 28 October 1928. Kay's cousin, Edward Ambrose (Ted) Cleman (1885-1937), was the son of Mary Elizabeth Kershaw (daughter of Robert H. and Mary Harrison Kershaw) and John Cleman whose name graces the distinctive feature looming over Naches—Cleman Mountain.

41. Maurice Helland, "Introduction to West: Guest Ranches Lure Visitors from Afar To Cascade Slopes," *YSH*, 27 May 1956; "Woman Rancher Kills Pesky Bear With One Rifle Shot," *The Seattle Daily Times*, 9 May 1956; "Marauder Killed," AP wire-photo [no date], [clipping in KFC].

42. On what can only be described as a slow news day in Spokane, Kay made the paper with the story that she was training her two-year-old dog, Blitz. "Kathryn To Train Dogs," *Spokane Chronicle*, 22 October 1935 and *Spokesman-Review*, 23 October 1935. Kay includes two photographs of Blitz in *My Memory Book* (KFC).

43. "Pilot Visits Here," newspaper clipping

[possibly *YDR*, ca. January 1928]. *My Memory Book* (KFC); "Yakima Girl Hunter"; "Valley Personals," *YDR*, 26 October 1928.

44. For example, Kay's canoeing trip around the San Juan Islands in August and a fishing trip in the Blue Mountains in September 1937, both when she was living in Walla Walla. "Valley Personals," *YDR*, 18 August 1937; and "Many Yakima Women."

45. "Flying, That's Th' [sic] Life for Yakima Girl," *Seattle Post-Intelligencer*, 20 July 1928 [loose, originally from *My Memory Book* in KFC]. This article does not appear in on-line data bases or microfilm collections, although the article on the reverse side of the clipping, "Dedication of Airport May Draw 50,000," does. This clipping was perhaps taken from a regional edition of the *Seattle Post-Intelligencer* that has never been scanned or filmed. Kian Flynn, University of Washington Libraries, email, 20 September 2021.

46. Nelson, *We Never Got Away*, 178. Kay worked as a swimming instructor to earn extra money in the summer. She was appointed Senior Lifesaver by the Yakima Red Cross in 1928. "Senior Life Savers Named," *YDR*, 30 June 1928; "Swimmers enter contests in Portland meet: Miss Kershaw enters," *YDR*, 27 July 1933; "Valley Personals," 28 July 1933.

47. "Student License Issued For Wife of Ace Aviator," *YDR*, 27 August 1929; "Aircraft Survey Shows Increases," 28 August 1929; "Nation's Most Noted Bride Is Given Her License to Fly After Honeymoon," 29 August 1929; "Girl Clerks Get Thrill In Flying License Work," 24 September 1929.

Chapter 3

1. "The Female Pilots Who Made History: A Conversation with Keith O'Brien," *The Exchange*, New Hampshire Public Radio, 5 September 2018; McMillan Houston Johnson V, "Taking Off: The Politics and Culture of American Aviation 1920–1939," Dissertation, University of Tennessee, 2011: 22–23, 34, 44–47.

2. "Western Air Lines" [advertisement], *YDR*, 2 April 1928. Two hundred dollars in 1928 is the equivalent of around 3,546 dollars in 2024.

3. "Yakima Girl Air Pilot Will Help State Fair Show," *YDR*, 12 July 1928.

4. In 1929, the *Yakima Daily Republic* considered McMechan the "dean of local aviators" based on his accumulated total of 800 air hours. Charlie McAllister was a distant second with 620. In 1928, McMechan had raced his airplane—the one he used for flying lessons with students like Kershaw—from New York to Spokane; and from Spokane to Walla Walla. "Airport Work Is Making Progress," *YDR*, 25 May 1928; "Aviation Experts Say Yakima People Are Air-Minded," 2 August 1929; "Valley Personals," 12 July 1933; Grace Millay, "Whatever Happened To...? ... Maurice McMechan," *Yakima Valley Sun*, 6 January 1977; Charles Lamb, "Death leaves a hole in the sky," *YH-R*, 6 October 1988.

5. "Yakima Girl Handles Airplane On Cross-Country Flight While Her Family Waves From the Ground," *YDR*, 11 May 1928. McMechan's logbook registers a flight to Ellensburg with a student on 2 May 1928. *Aviation Log Book M. H. McMechan* (11 May 1925–22 September 1937). McAllister Museum of Aviation archives.

6. "Airport Work Is Making Progress," *YDR*, 25 May 1928 (in *My Memory Book*, KFC).

7. "The Pied Piper of Spring," [cartoon] *YDR*, 2 April 1928; "Marine Aviators Burned to Death in Plane Crash" and "Mexican Flier's Body Goes Home," 19 July 1928.

8. "Major Hoople by Ahern," *YDR*, 9, 11, 13, 17, and 18 April 1928.

9. The United States Department of Commerce handled the pilot licensing process until President Franklin Roosevelt established the Civil Aeronautics Authority in 1938. A written exam on air-traffic rules was also mandatory. "Air Commerce Regulations, Department of Commerce Aeronautics Branch, Effective December 31, 1926," in *Aircraft Year Book, 1927* (New York: Aeronautical Chamber of Commerce of America, Inc., 1927), 367–68.

10. "Flying, That's Th' Life"; "Air Thrill Lures," *Seattle Post Intelligencer*, 19 July 1928 (in *My Memory Book*, KFC); "Yakima Girl Gets License As Pilot," 22 July 1928.

11. "Initial Solo Flights Give Girl Flier Real Kick Over Experience," *YDR*, 17 July 1928.

12. "Yakima Girl Air Pilot Will Help State Fair Show"; "Air Commerce Regulations," 367; "Naches Girl to Secure License As An Air Pilot," *The Evening Record*, 18 July 1928; "Flying, That's Th' Life." In her scrapbook clipping of this article, Kershaw has crossed out "twenty" (before "hours") and written "50" in pencil.

13. "Yakima Girl Air Pilot Will Help State Fair Show."

14. "Yakima's Girl Aviator Is to Help At State Fair Aircraft Exhibition," *YDR*, 7 September 1928; "Western Airlines, Inc., Yakima, Wash. Agreement," [signed by W.O. Wikstrom, Trustee; Maurice H. McMechan, Pres[ident]; and Maud C. Bolin; dated 5 April 1928]; "Yakima State Fairgrounds 1928, Kathryn Kershaw & Maud Bolin promoting flying lessons with Western Airlines Inc., OX-5 engine & LeRhone rotary engine," [with handwritten notes by Maud Bolin]. McAllister Museum of Aviation archives. Maud Bolin (1891–1966) began flying lessons with Western Airlines in April 1928. She received her private pilot's license in August 1929 and her commercial license in July 1930. Bolin shares with Mary Riddle of the Quinault Indian Nation the distinction of being the first licensed female Native American pilot in the United States. "Indian Girl Is Full-Fledged Flyer," *Rock Valley Bee* (Rock Valley, IA), 11 July 1930.

15. "New Crop of Girl Fliers Is Ready to Take to Air So Plane Models Change," *YDR*, 24 December 1928.

16. Dean Jaros, *Heroes Without Legacy: American Airwomen, 1912-1944* (Boulder: University Press of Colorado, 1993), 100.

17. Mary Alexander, "My Experience Learning to Fly," in Sara Hillin, *Rhetorical Arts of Women in Aviation, 1911-1970* (Lanham, MD: Lexington, 2020), 108, 114.

18. Emilie Watson, "Amelia Earhart: The Flying Feminist," *Flight Paths: Purdue University Aerospace Pioneers* (13 September 2016) [https://flightpaths.lib.purdue.edu/blog/2016/09/13/amelia-earhart-the-flying-feminist/].

19. Kennedy, "But we would never talk about it," 22-25.

20. "This Trio Has Won World Renown But Unable To Pay Bills By Flying" and "Yakima Girl Flier Believes Women Can Make Air Pay," *YDR*, 5 July 1929.

21. "Robert S. Clary, "Why Not Retail Airplanes?" *Popular Aviation and Aeronautics*, January 1929: 18-21, 113-18; Erle H. Smith, "The $ Sign On The Airplane," March 1929: 68, 96-97; *Aircraft Year Book, 1929* (New York: Aeronautical Chamber of Commerce of America, Inc., 1929), 55-57. It is interesting to note that Mary Alexander told a journalist that she started flying lessons in early 1929 to add airplane sales to her Lynchburg, Virginia, car dealership. "Mary C. Alexander," *Dictionary of Virginia Biography*, Library of Virginia [https://www.lva.virginia.gov/public/dvb/bio.php?b=Alexander_Mary_C].

22. "Yakima Girl Flier Believes Women Can Make Air Pay." In the next decade, Jesse W. Lankford advanced to the position of Secretary Chief of the Air Safety Section at the Bureau of Air Commerce, United States Department of Commerce. It is worth noting that at the time of his interview with the *Yakima Daily Republic*, Lankford was receiving a moderate salary for his occupation in aviation: in 1929, he earned 3,200 dollars, the equivalent of around 57,403 dollars in 2024. See "Jesse W. Lankford, Chief, licensing section, Aeronautics Branch, Department of Commerce," *Official Register of the United States 1929: containing a list of persons occupying administrative and supervisory positions in each executive and judicial department of the government including the District of Columbia* (Washington, D.C.: Government Printing Office, 1929), 90. Lankford's salary was on the low end of the pay scale at the Department of Commerce, perhaps reflecting aviation's low priority there. He received less compensation than both Anne Cross, librarian at the Office of the Secretary, and Emily Farnum, appointment clerk at the Bureau of the Census.

23. Nelson, *We Never Got Away*, 178; "Local Girl Aviator Makes Parachute Jump on Field At Walla Walla On Air Tour and Landing is Perfect," *YDR*, 29 April 1929; "Makes Successful Jump," [clipping in KFC: possibly a Walla Walla newspaper, 29 April 1929]; "Yakima Girl Believes Women Can Make Air Pay"; "Valley Personals," *YDR*, 6 May 1929.

24. "Maurice McMechan Takes Airplane Race From Spokane By Scant Margin Of Only Two Minutes in Derby Event," *YDR*, 16 August 1929; "Air Adventurers Smile At Memory of Hungry Start," 16 August 1929; "Army Expert Takes Trophy For Air Race," 17 August 1929; "Landing Is Made On Side of Hill" and "Air Program For Convention Ends," 19 August 1929.

25. Naming an airplane after the City of Yakima is an obvious reference to Charles Lindbergh's *The Spirit of St. Louis* which he flew across the Atlantic Ocean in 1927.

26. "Aviators' Wives Approve the Job," *YDR*, 16 August 1929.

27. Bruce Allen Murphy, *Wild Bill: The Legend and Life of William O. Douglas* (New York: Random House, 2003), 119, 269; "Wild Bill: The Legend and Life of William O. Douglas," Bruce Allen Murphy, speech before the Cato Institute, Washington, D.C., 18 March 2003, C-Span Video Library Program ID 162037-1, 1:25:45 [https://www.c-span.org/video/?162037-1/wild-bill-legend-life-william-o-douglas], 1:17:38-:51. The inaccuracies, dubious quotations, and misrepresentations throughout Murphy's book are far too numerous to list here, even though he proudly touts his incisive skill in parsing the archives while investigating every aspect of Douglas's seamier side. See Murphy, speech before the Cato Institute, 18 March 2003: 14:25-15:01, 16:56-17:35, 19:45-21:10, 1:21:06-1:25:13. In Washington State, cougars are almost always found wherever deer and elk forage, preferring dense cover such as sagebrush or forest to stalk their prey. Tom R. Hulst, *The Footpaths of Justice William O. Douglas: A Legacy of Place* (Lincoln: iUniverse, 2004), 245; Gary Koehler, biologist with Washington State Department of Fish and Wildlife, interview, 7 May 2021. Perhaps Murphy absorbed William O. Douglas's imaginative description of cougars stalking mountain goats on the heights of the Goat Rocks Wilderness. See Douglas, *My Wilderness*, 143. Critiquing Murphy's discourse on constitutional law is beyond the purview of this book: however, others have done so. See Melvin L. Urofsky, "Review of Murphy, Bruce Allen. *Wild Bill: The Legend and Life of William O. Douglas*," H-law, H-Net Reviews, June 2003. Ever since its publication, the majority of local readers who knew or studied William O. Douglas remain bemused and confounded by much of the book's contents. Murphy's slipshod reputation preceded him. In a 1989 letter to Kay Kershaw and Isabelle Lynn, Mercedes Eichholz—second wife of Justice William O. Douglas—writes: "... ever since Mr. Murphy visited you after the big Douglas-do [possibly the ceremonies surrounding the dedication of the William O. Douglas Wilderness Area in 1984] I have meant to write. I enclose a copy of a letter I wrote to him after he published the [Supreme Court Justice Abe] Fortas 'bio.' I dread to think of the Douglas one. Most of the people who know the facts on Fortas were appalled when it came out …. Needless to say he has not had the grace to ever acknowledge it. I hope you sent him on his way."

Mercedes H. Eichholz, letter to Double K's [Kay Kershaw and Isabelle Lynn], dated 27 August 1989. In her scathing letter to Murphy, Eichholz states: "The book [on Justice Fortas] is marred by a myriad of errors and misrepresentations ... you frequently misinterpret Fortas's political beliefs .... Nor do you seem to understand Abe Fortas as a person. You take him literally on occasions when anyone who knew him would realize that he was being wry and sarcastic." Mercedes H. Eichholz, letter to Professor Bruce Allen Murphy, dated 13 September 1988. Ed Kershaw recalled that Murphy's two-week stay at the Double K Ranch on 6–19 August 1989 exasperated Kay and Isabelle. Ed Kershaw, interview, 17 September 2020; corroborated by Robert H. Kershaw, Zoom meeting, 16 March 2021. Many of the quotations Murphy attributes to Cragg D. Gilbert have no basis in reality. Cragg M. Gilbert, interview, 1 August 2020; nor did Murphy comprehend Gilbert family relationships, e.g., denoting Cragg D. Gilbert as the son (rather than nephew) of Elon J. Gilbert. Murphy, *Wild Bill*, 288.

28. "Flying, Relay Riding, Music and Trade of Milliner Are Mastered By Toppenish Woman As Life Pleasures," *YDR*, 4 October 1929; "Valley Personals," 17 October 1929; "Yakima Valley Personals," 18 August 1930; "Solo Trip Holds Vivid Memories," *Toppenish Review*, 15 November 1929; "Form AB-19, Department of Commerce Aeronautics Branch, Application for Pilot's License," [Maud Bolin]; photograph of Maud Bolin in front of a Waco 10 airplane, dated 20 December 1929 with note: "I purchased from h. [sic] M. Ausmilles Sept. 16, 1929 ..." in Maud Bolin Scrapbook images, McAllister Museum of Flight.

29. "Yakima Awarded Aeronautic Club," *YDR*, 23 November 1929.

30. Photograph in KFC; *Lo-Na-Hi 1928* [Lower Naches High School yearbook]: 16, 31, 34, 38, and Autographs ["Robert Kershaw ('30—to a darn good kid)," in copy at Yakima Valley Genealogical Society]; "*Lo-Na-Hi 1930*: 4, 17. No yearbook was published in 1929. The 1928 issue has a one-page lampoon of various students, "The Scandal Sheet," including an unfortunate spoof of Robert's relationship with his girlfriend, Alma Farrar. Under the headline "Young Man Commits Suicide," the local sheriff finds Robert's body suspended with fishing line from a tree with a note attached stating "life was not worth living" after Alma performed a duet with another boy at a grange meeting. *Lo-Na-Hi 1928*: 38.

31. "Yakima Valley Personals," *YDR*, 20 September 1929; "Valley Quintets Open Hoop Season," *YMH*, 14 December 1929.

32. Leonard Lerwill, "Yakima Aviators Recall Greatest Thrill in Air," *YDR*, 14, 16–18, 20–25, 27, 28, 30, 31 January 1930; 3–8, 11–13, 15, 17, 18, 20 February 1930; "Hoop Teams To End Vacation," *YMH*, 3 January 1930.

33. Lerwill, "Yakima Aviators Recall Greatest Thrill in Air," 22 January 1930. Kay's tale about her parachute malfunction has a similar "just in the nick of time" tone to the one involving the jammed Sharps rifle during her 1928 bear encounter. See "Yakima Girl Hunter."

34. Within the medical context of the 1930s, "hemorrhaging" here refers to an acute drop in hemoglobin levels (and destruction of red blood cells) due to sepsis. Blood transfusion was the only option to save such a patient. Before the discovery of antibiotics, sepsis in the hospital was lethal. Another high school boy, Clifford Wiley, was in St. Elizabeth Hospital at the same time as Robert having battled sepsis for two weeks. Wiley succumbed four days after Kershaw. "Football Injury Critical," *YDR*, 23 January 1930; "Local News Items: Condition Remains Grave," 24 January 1930; "Obituary: Clifford Wiley," 1 February 1930; "Doubts Held For Recovery of Boy," *YMH*, 28 January 1930; Phillip I. Menashe, MD, email, 17 June 2021.

35. Also, "Katherine Kershaw, Yakima woman flier," in "Doubts Held For Recovery of Boy." "Hemorrhages Cause Death of Lower Naches Student," *YDR*, 28 January 1930; "Funeral Service for Robert Kershaw," 29 January 1930; "Funeral: Robert W. Kershaw" *YMH*, 29 January 1930.

36. "Lower Naches Victorious," *YMH*, 11 January 1930; Nelson, *We Never Got Away*, 178. Equally distressing must have been Kay's operation and three-week stay at St. Elizabeth Hospital in 1934 and brother Ron's hospitalization for an unspecified ailment in 1937. "Valley Personals," *YDR*, 30 July 1934, 6 August 1934, 14 August 1934, 20 August 1934, 1 September 1934; 8 September 1937.

37. "Briefs," *YDR*, 12 February 1930.

38. "Yakima Flier to Take Air Jaunt," 25 July 1930; "Port Expects Fifty Planes In Formation" and "Valley Personals," 29 July 1930; "Many Spectators See Air Stunts," 30 July 1930; "Miss Bolin Back From Plane Tour" and "Valley Personals," 11 August 1930.

39. Kristin Snapp and Robert H. Kershaw, Zoom meeting, 16 March 2021 (Kristin and Robert are the children of Robert C. [Bob] Kershaw); Ed Kershaw, interview 27 May 2021; Ruby Montana, email 17 June 2021; Richard F. Buscher and Paul Hart, *Bush Forester for Wilderness: The Story of Richard F. Buscher as Told to Paul Hart* (Bend, OR: Maverick Publications, 2021), 104.

40. David H. Onkst, "Wing Walkers," *U.S. Centennial of Flight Commission* [https://www.centennialofflight.net/essay/Explorers_Record_Setters_and_Daredevils/wingwalkers/EX13.htm]; Gerald A. Schiller, "Flying and Dying for Hollywood in the 1920s," *Historynet* [https://www.historynet.com/motion-picture-stunt-fliers-flying-and-dying-for-hollywood-in-the-1920s.htm].

Chapter 4

1. H.M. Gilbert, letter to Francelia Amsden Gilbert and May Gilbert, 13 April 1930 (GFC).

2. H.M. Gilbert, letter to Senator Wesley L. Jones, 18 December 1931 (GFC).

3. G.W. Hamilton, Attorney General, "Chapter 8: Emergency Relief Administration," *Session Laws of the State of Washington, Twenty-Third Session, Convened January 9, Adjourned March 9, 1933* (Olympia: O.H. Olson, 1933), 103–19; *Directory of Social and Health Agencies in the State of Washington 1936* (Olympia: State of Washington Department of Public Welfare, 1936), 121; Wayne D. Rasmussen, Gladys L. Baker, and James S. Ward, *A Short History of Agricultural Adjustment, 1933–75*. Agriculture Bulletin 391, Economic Research Service, United States Department of Agriculture (March 1976): 1–4; "Welfare Board Will Organize," *YDR* 2 March 1933; "Final Plan On County Relief Settled Soon," 10 March 1933; "Riley Selects Staff to Push Relief Plans," 1 April 1933; "Officials Discuss Relief Activities," 25 July 1933; "Welfare Meeting To Be Held Here," 4 December 1935.

4. For example, in the city of Yakima: Hannah Bittle, WERA supervisor of inspectors; Rose Seiler, social services supervisor; Mildred Dodge, assistant county charity commissioner; Helen Marion, zone supervisor for the State Department of Public Welfare. "Riley Selects," *YDR*, 1 April 1933; "Eight Offices to House WERA Staff," 7 February 1935; "Valley Personals," 10 July 1935; "Yakima Valley Personals," 13 July 1935; "Miss Helen Marion Will Take Relief Post," 19 August 1935; *Polk's Yakima City and County Directory* 32 (1936) (Seattle: R.L. Polk and Company, 1936), 136, 282.

5. Snapp and Kershaw, Zoom meeting, 16 March 2021.

6. "Dr. Charles Wempe—Importance of Horses," interview excerpt, 1:03 (Wessels Living History Farm: Farming in the 1940s) [https://livinghistoryfarm.org/farminginthe40s/movies/wempe_machines_13.html].

7. "Last Will and Testament of Edward A. Kershaw," law offices of Velikanje and Velikanje, John Moore, Jr. [six pages] dated 1 June 1953 (KFC).

8. Faderman, *Odd Girls*, 93.

9. Daniel K. Walkowitz, "The Making of a Feminine Professional Identity: Social Workers in the 1920s," *The American Historical Review* 95, no. 4 (October 1990): 1055–56, 1075; Vern Bullough and Bonnie Bullough, "Lesbianism in the 1920s and 1930s: A Newfound Study," *Signs* 2, no. 4 (Summer 1977): 901.

10. "Valley Personals," *YDR*, 13 March, 14 March, 5 July, 28 July, 21 August 1933; "Yakima Valley Personals," 22 April 1933; 12 June 1933; "Swimmers Enter 12 Contests in Portland Meet," 27 July 1933; "Yakima Flooded," *Spokane Chronicle*, 11 December 1933; "Marooned Maids Flee Flood," *Spokesman Review*, 13 December 1933. Kitty and Jack Nelson grew accustomed to skiing from Bumping Lake down to town and back. See "Valley Personals," *YDR*, 28 February 1944. Kershaw stayed in Seattle on a visit with Mildred while she was attending summer school at the University of Washington in 1934. A graduate of the nursing program at St. Elizabeth Hospital, Mildred remained in Seattle for an internship then was employed at Providence Hospital in 1935. "Valley Personals," *YDR*, 13 July and 21 September 1934; 25 November 1935.

11. "Berry Gets Big Buck in Canada: Miss Kershaw Scores" and "Temperature to Drop Greatly," *YDR*, 28 October 1935; "Growers Rush to Get Fruit Into Storage," 29 October 1935; "Growers Try to Figure Out Total of Loss," 30 October 1935; "Sixth of Apple Crop Hit By Cold Snap," 31 October 1935; "Growers Drop Hope of Much Fruit Salvage," 1 November 1935; "Growers See No Hope For Saving Fruit," 2 November 1935. Kay's last listing at the Kershaw farm rural delivery route appears in *Polk's Yakima City and County Directory* 30 (1934) (Seattle: R.L. Polk and Company, 1934), 775. Her residence appears as Lower Naches in "Valley Personals," *YDR*, 1 September 1934.

12. Nelson, *We Never Got Away*, 178; *Tyee* 1930, University of Washington Yearbook, 204, 214. A press release from Catholic Relief Services as well as an article from *Seattle Times* states that Pat did graduate studies in social work at University of Chicago. See Grace Ernestine Ray, "Women Run This Dude Ranch," *Seattle Times*, 26 June 1955; Marion S. Brown, Press Release: German Mission Headquarters Catholic Relief Services [1950] [typed, two pages] (KaFC). However, she is not listed in any of the University of Chicago Convocation Programs through 1937. See "The University of Chicago Campus Publications" [http://campub.lib.uchicago.edu/search/?f1title=University%20of%20Chicago%20Convocation%20Programs]. Pat and her sister Isabel spent the summer of 1935 in Chicago and may have attended classes at the University there. Patricia Bradley, email 17 August 2022.

13. Edgar M. Gerlach, "Social Service Resource Directory for Washington," W.P.A. Project 221, 17 November 1937; "Final Freezing Night Arrives," *Spokesman-Review*, 17 October 1934; "New Relief Set-Up," 30 May 1935; "Offices of SDPW to New Quarters," *Walla Walla Bulletin*, 1 March 1936; "Sounds Like Politics," *Spokesman-Review*, 27 April 1937; "Gets Welfare Job," 31 August 1937; "Valley Personals," *YDR*, 23 September 1937; "Jury Finds Railroad Man's Morals Illegal," 18 November 1937; "Galaxy of Democrats Polish Their Speeches," 4 December 1937; "Mayor Helps Gang of Migrant Indigents to Batter Down State's Rules," 2 March 1938; "Many Are Homeowners," 4 March 1938; "County Heads Talk Over Relief Worries," 8 April 1938; "Those At Conference," 15 June 1938; "Welfare Boss Visits," 21 June 1938.

14. Nelson, *We Never Got Away*, 179–80; "Gets Welfare Post," *Spokane Chronicle*, 4 October 1938. A photograph of Pat and Kay lounging on the beach is labeled "Woodmont 1940–41" (in *Victory Picture Album*, KFC). Woodmont is on the west side of Tukwila facing Vashon and Maury Islands. This was around eleven miles from Pat's residence at 3118 South 140th Street.

15. "Service Abroad Call Accepted," *Spokesman-Review*, 16 December 1942; State of Washing-

ton Department of Social Security Identification Card No. 17-25. Expiration date 3/31/43 (KFC).

16. *Spokesman-Review Magazine*, 29 December 1946: 8.

17. Pat Kane, letter to Isabel Kane and Jerry Kane, 17 February 1937 (KaFC).

18. Pat Kane, letter to Isabel Kane, 19 July 1937 (KaFC).

19. Dr. Joseph Patrick Kane, postcard to Pat Kane and Kay Kershaw, 17 August 1941 (KaFC); *Victory Picture Album*, two black and white photographs, "Wallowa Mountains—1937" and "Off to Minam River—Joe and Arta." In the back of the photo album, Kay filled in the "notify" section of "identification in case of accident" page with "Patricia Kane—friend."

20. Pat Kane, letter to Isabel Kane and Jerry Kane, 17 February 1937 (KaFC).

21. Maurice Helland, "Introduction to West: Guest Ranches Lure Visitors from Afar To Cascade Slopes," YSH, 27 May 1956; Warranty Deed 1090838, A.C. and Claudine A. Botsford, grantors, to Kathryn Kershaw and Patricia Kane, dated 18 May 1945, filed 7 June 1945 with Yakima County, Yakima, WA.

22. "Bullock cart, Ceylon," postcard, postmarked 16 June 1943 by Army Postal Service. Scrapbook, 16 December 1943, to October/November 1943 (KFC); *Victory Picture Album* black and white photograph "Double K—1942." The photograph features two other women and several growlers of beer: see photo on page 46; "Guest Log," 1 January 1947 to 25 October 1948/12 September 1951 (KFC); Joseph P. Kane, M.D., letter to Pat Kane, 4 May 1943 (KaFC).

23. "Not Wooden Ships!" [Cascade Lumber Company advertisement], YDR, 30 November 1942; Ben Meyer Huey, "Problems of Timber Products Procurement During World War II, 1941–1945: A Report Prepared for the U.S. Department of Defense, Army, Corps of Engineers, by the U.S. Department of Agriculture, Forest Service, 1951," Master's Thesis, University of Montana, 1951: 33, 36, 38, 44, 50, 60, 80–92.

24. "Yakima Girl to See War Front," YDR, 22 January 1943.

25. "Reaches Africa," YDR, 19 July 1943; S.I. Anthon, "Daily Mirror of Life in Yakima," 19 July 1943. "Shank's pony" refers to the act of walking or hiking.

26. Scrapbook, 16 December 1943, to October/November 1943. Inscribed "Beginning December 16, 1942. When I became a Personal Service Director Services to the Armed Forces—Overseas Unit American Red Cross" (KFC). The last item in the scrapbook (loose) is a photograph of Mt. Vesuvius from the window of an airplane inscribed "To Kay from Eunice—Nov., 1943."

27. Nelson, *We Never Got Away*, 178; "Home From Italy," *Spokesman-Review*, 19 April 1944; George W. Dillon, "Dude Rancher Patricia Kane Crosses Country to Aid Sister," *Springfield Daily News*, 19 January 1953; Isabelle Lynn, "Year 'Round in the Mountains," *The Mountaineer* 1962 55, no. 4 (March 1, 1962): 34; "Valley Personals," 18 January 1944.

28. "Local Girl Back From War Task," YDR, 18 April 1944.

29. Snapp and Kershaw, Zoom meeting, 16 March 2021; Marjorie Jane, "The Women of the Double K," *Seattle Times*, 30 September 1973.

30. Ed Kershaw, interview, 18 September and 1 October 2020.

31. Nelson, *We Never Got Away*, 178.

32. Lynn, "Year 'Round in the Mountains," 34; "Dude Rancher Patricia Kane Crosses Country to Aid Sister."

Chapter 5

1. Harry Barnes, Jr., "Amelia Earhart, Husband, Returning From Vacation, Stop Overnight in Decatur," *Decatur Herald* 31 July 1934; "Amelia, Husband on Pack Horse Trip," *San Francisco Examiner*, 27 July 1934.

2. Harl N. Andersen, "Former Nebraska Girl Hostess at Retreat Where Amelia Earhart and George Putnam Go to Forget Piloting and Publishing," *The Nebraska State Journal*, 16 February 1936. Work on the Putnam cabin at the Double D came to a halt after Earhart disappeared over the Pacific Ocean on 2 July 1937.

3. Putnam quotation in Barnes, "Amelia Earhart, Husband, Returning From Vacation." This 1934 article from the *Decatur Herald* includes seven photographs, one of which features Dunrud using his lariat to capture a polar bear.

4. *The Spokesman-Review Magazine*, 29 December 1946: 8.

5. Lynn, "Year 'Round in the Mountains," 35; Nelson, *We Never Got Away*, 178–79; "Miss Kershaw and Friend Building Mountain Resort," YMH, 26 April 1946; Peggy Post, "Ranch House Carved Out Of Wilds Through Vision of Two Girls," *Seattle Post-Intelligencer*, 1 December 1946.

6. For decades, Kay and her partners at the Double K Mountain Ranch were known as "the Double K girls." To this day, Kay Kershaw, Pat Kane, and Isabelle Lynn are still referred to as "girls," or even "gals." See Murphy, *Wild Bill*, xv, 272, 277, 489; Hulst, *Footpaths*, 238–40; Susan Summit Cyr, *Tanum: A Story of Bumping Lake and the William O. Douglas Wilderness* (self-published, 2021), 240–48, 252–58; M. Margaret McKeown, *Citizen Justice: The Environmental Legacy of William O. Douglas—Public Advocate and Conservation Champion* (Lincoln: Potomac Books, 2022), 117, 167–71, 173–74, 186. Nonetheless, I have found no evidence the three women referred to themselves in this way: thus, I have chosen not to use the moniker "Double K girls" unless in a direct quotation. One local correspondent offered this insight: "I can't tell you the number of times [we] have been referred to as 'the girls' by men. It may help them feel more comfortable thinking of us as

girls rather than sexually active women." Jane Gutting, email, 10 July 2021.

7. "Ranch House Carved Out Of Wilds"; Nelson, *We Never Got Away*, 180–81; Helland, "Introduction to West: Guest Ranches Lure Visitors"; "Double K Mountain Ranch," [Northern Pacific Railway advertisement ca. 1954] (clipping in KFC); Ed Kershaw, interview, 18 August 2020. A 1946 article about the first Thanksgiving dinner for family and friends at the Double K lists Pat Kane's father as "Dr. Anthony Kane." See "Friends Gather At Dude Ranch," *YDR*, 28 November 1946.

8. "Last Will and Testament of Edward A. Kershaw," dated 1 June 1953 (KFC).

9. Pat Kane, letter to Isabel K. Bradley, 5 December 1946 (KaFC); "Two Men Missing in Hills," *YDR*, 2 November 1946; "Hope Dims For Packer Lost In Hills," 4 November 1946; "Hope Wanes In Search," 5 November 1946; "Many Join In Search," 6 November 1946; "Searchers Halt Blackburn Hunt," 7 November 1946.

10. Kane, letter to Bradley, 5 December 1946.

11. Ed Stover, "Skull, Boots Partially Solve 19-Year Disappearance Riddle," *YDR*, 19 November 1965; "Deaths Blackburn," 29 November 1965; "In Memory of Lionel Claude Blackburn," (Wood Chapel of the Pines, Idaho Falls, ID 3 December 1965) (YVM); Nick Baldwin, "In 1946, He Rode Off Into Storm," *Des Moines Tribune*, 20 December 1965; Ed Stover, email 30 July 2022.

12. For more on skiing at American Ridge, see William D. Frank, "Skiing on the East Slope of Washington State's Cascade Range, Parts 1 and 2," *Journal of the New England Ski Museum* no. 130, Fall 2023: 17–26 and no. 131, Winter 2024; "Skiing in Washington State's Naches River Canyon," in *"Danger! Natural Snow": Aspects of Ski and Olympic History, Dedicated to E. John B. Allen*, ed. Annette R. Hofmann and Christof Thöny (forthcoming).

13. Sixteen black and white photographs in *My Memory Book* scrapbook, ca. 1920–1939; eight black and white photographs, ca. 1920–1925, loose (KFC).

14. "Flying, That's Th' Life."

15. "No Snap To Make Trip to Rimrock at Present Time Game Warden Drolet Says," *YDR*, 7 January 1928; "Birthday Mountain Climb Causes Death of Tacoman," 9 January 1928; "One Below Zero Reported From Bumping Lake Today," 16 January 1928; "Bumping Lake Temperature Slides to Two Below Zero," 23 January 1928; "Valley Personals," 24 January 1928.

16. "Cascadians clippings 1930 and 1931" (YVM archives, Cascadians Box 14). A newspaper advertisement for train tickets to the 1931 Northwest Ski Tournament shows that the roundtrip from Yakima to Cle Elum and back—two hours each way—cost $2.50, including "fun both ways—special vaudeville returning" (*YDR*, 9 February 1931).

17. The courses for the downhill competitions probably included a number of obstacles to negotiate. E. John B. Allen, email correspondence, 2 May 2021. For newspaper coverage of the Cle Elum Ski tournament, see *Miner-Echo*, 7 December 1923; 18 December 1925; 19 February 1926; 23 February 1928; 24 and 31 January 1929; 14 and 21 February 1929; 21 February 1930; 6 and 20 February 1931; 5, 12, and 19 February 1932; *The Evening Record*, 17 February 1930; 15 February 1932; 20 February 1933; *YDR*, 15 January 1929; 9 February 1929; 12 and 17 February 1930; 15 February 1932; 20 February 1933; *YMH*, 18 February 1930. On Cascadians attending by train, see *Miner-Echo*, 24 and 31 January 1929; *YDR*, 15 and 18 February 1929. On Kay's first place finish, see *YDR*, "Kathryn Kershaw Places First for Devil's Dive at Cle Elum Ski Tournament," 16 February 1931; *YMH*, "Yakima Girl Takes Ski Tourney Event," 17 February 1931; "Results Feb 16–1930 [typed sheet]," in *Cle Elum Ski Club Scrapbook*, Central Washington University Archives and Special Collections, MS-019 Box 2. Also: "Cle Elum [photograph]," in "My Memory Book [scrapbook]" (KFC); "Cle Elum Ski Club Tournament Programs 1928–1933" file, Central Washington University Archives and Special Collections, MS-019 Box 3.

18. "Cascadians Look for Fine Outing on Skis Sunday," *YDR*, 19 January 1923; "Yakimans ski 22 miles on outing," 3 February 1923; "52-foot ski jump taken by Eggleston Sunday near the Nile post office," 5 February 1923; "Cascadian Club Enjoys Winter Sports Program Entertaining Over 500 Jumping at Selah Hill," 9 January 1928; "20-mile Trip on Skis Planned," 23 April 1929.

19. "Valley Personals," 18 March and 1 April 1933; Tom Lyon, "The Gold Hill Outdoor Club," in *Let's Take the Sporting Route*, 101–2.

20. "Lodge Replaces Lean-To at Skiing Course" and "Ski Lodge is Big Boost to Sport," *YDR*, 1 January 1936. Photos accompanying the articles show the newly-constructed CCC lodge and Winter Sports Club leaders W. E. Kershaw and George Rankin reclining in the old lean-to.

21. Two black and white photographs, loose (KFC). In one labeled "Gold Hill—1939," Kay and Pat stand with three friends by their cars parked along Highway 410 at the start of the trail to Gold Hill. See photo on page 55. In another labeled "Blue Mountains 1937," eleven unidentified skiers (seven women and four men) stand in front of a building ("Hotel") with skis.

22. Two black and white photographs, loose (KFC). Black and white photograph labeled "Sun Valley—1939–40–41," in *Victory Picture Album* fifteen pages, double-sided (KFC).

23. "Ski Club Gets Tournament," *YDR* 21 December 1938; "Ski Tow Arranged," 24 December 1946; Gossett, *Beyond the Bend*, 419; Helland, "Introduction to West: Guest Ranches Lure Visitors."

24. "Resourceful Women Outwit Rough Bumping Road Route," *YMH*, 7 March 1948; Lynn, "Year 'Round in the Mountains," 35; Double K brochure and price list, 1947.

25. Lynn, "Year 'Round in the Mountains," 35; "Guest Log," 1 January 1947 to 25 October 1948/12 September 1951.

26. Basil Woon, "There's a Bright Side To Things Even When 3 Mexican Aliens Make Off With Your Auto: Flying M-E and Highway 50 Prove Compensations," *Nevada State Journal*, 11 April 1954; Geoff Dornan, "Couple Works to Preserve History of Old 'Dude Ranch,'" *Nevada Appeal*, 19 December 2001.

27. Douglas, *Go East*, 159–75, 257–64, 281, 457–70.

28. Harvey Manning, "End of an Era: Kay Kershaw and Isabelle Lynn of the Double K," *Wild Cascades* (Summer/Fall 1996): 15.

29. Douglas, *Go East*, 181, 236. Douglas made his first trip to the Wallowa Mountains in 1939.

30. Murphy, *Wild Bill*, 269–70. In this section, Murphy gives the wrong year—1948 (rather than 1947)—for the opening of the Double K Ranch. Cyr incorporates Murphy's story wholesale. Cyr, *Tanum*, 233.

31. Gossett, *Beyond the Bend*, 135, 163, 268; *Metsker's Atlas of Yakima County Washington* February 1959: center of 11, Township 15N, Range 15 E.W.M. (page 34); *Polk's Yakima City Directory* 36 (1940) (Seattle: R.L. Polk and Company, 1940), 221; "Valley Personals," *YDR*, 7 August 1929; S.I. Anthon, "Daily Mirror of Life in Yakima," *YDR*, 20 June 1947. W. Douglas Holt had an office on the fourth floor of the Liberty Building in downtown Yakima in the 1940s. During that era, the Holt brothers opened the Yakima Osteopathic Hospital located east of Portia Park on Yakima Avenue.

32. S.I. Anton, "Daily Mirror of Life in Yakima," *YDR*, 31 May and 8 September 1947; "Douglas Spurns Candidacy Talk," 10 July 1947; "Dedication Date Accepted," 29 July 1947; "Bar to Honor Justice Douglas," 5 September 1947; "Unity of Purpose Set As Hospital Theme" and "Justice Douglas Honored Guest At Reception," 8 September 1947; "Supreme Court Justice Sends Message to Newspaper Carriers," 4 October 1947; "Story Picture Recalls Earlier Douglas Visit," *YMH*, 4 September 1947; "Douglas Heads Local Events For Weekend," 7 September 1947; "Justice Douglas Tells High Court Activities," "'Illness' Report Reaches Douglas At Hearty Dinner," and "Justice Douglas Urges Health Fund Increase," 9 September 1947; Jane Gargas, "Wash. Ranch Helping Troubled Boys for 50 Years," *Seattle Times*, 14 July 2012.

33. Murphy, *Wild Bill*, 270. Murphy does not include Watkins's name in his text.

34. "Artists Marry," *Baltimore Sun*, 5 July 1942; "C. L. Watkins Dies, Noted Art Scholar," *Hartford Courant* (Hartford, CT), 4 March 1945; "Maryland Historical Trust, Determination of Eligibility Form. Lyddane/Bradley Farm M:26–20, Section 8 Significance," September 1979: 4–5. Mary Watkins may have accompanied Douglas to the Double K in 1948 to investigate a potential site for a family summer vacation, not, as Murphy insinuates, to serve as "his Washington mistress." Murphy, *Wild Bill*, 270–71. She returned to the ranch from the east coast in late September 1948 and then twice in 1949: once on her own in July, then with her five-year-old son, Law, in September. She repeated the trip to the Double K with her son in 1953 (under her re-married name, Thackara) and in 1955 (divorced) and returned on her own in 1975. In 1976, Law brought his own family to Goose Prairie. "Guest Log," 31 August 1948 to 17 October 1953 (KFC); Double K Mountain Ranch [Guest Book], 14 May 1954 to 31 December 1976 (KFC). Watkins accompanied William and Mercedes Douglas on a 7,000-mile automobile trip from Karachi to Istanbul in 1957: she appears throughout Douglas's 1958 book, *West of the Indus*. Watkins published her own works on Afghanistan in the 1960s, acknowledging Douglas's help and influence. See William O. Douglas, *West of the Indus* (Garden City, NY: Doubleday, 1958), vii, 4, 7, passim; Mary Bradley Watkins, *Afghanistan: An Outline* (New Paltz: World Study Center, State University College, 1962); *Afghanistan: Land in Transition* (Princeton: Van Nostrand, 1963), vi.

35. "High in Saddle Aim of Douglas," *Los Angeles Examiner*, 14 May 1950; Dorothy McCardle, "Douglas Trains for Horseback Trek Over Himalayan Range," *Seattle Times*, 15 May 1950.

36. Published as *Of Men and Mountains* two years later.

37. "Mountains Lure Justice Douglas," *YDR*, 22 June 1948; "Guest Log," 1 January 1947 to 25 October 1948/12 September 1951, entry dated "June 19–21, 1948."

38. "Justice Douglas of Supreme Court Pays Visit to Yakima," *YMH*, 22 June 1948.

39. Douglas's signature appears in the Double K guest registers on 19–21 June 1948; 21–22 June 1952; 22 June 1955; 22 June 1957; 23 July 1960; 26–30 August 1960; 30 August–2 September 1961; 28 July 1963; 9–18 September 1963; 21–22 September 1963; 22 June–2 October 1964; 16–29 September 1965; 2 September 1970; April [no date] 1972. Mildred and Millie Douglas, his first wife and daughter, signed the guest book on 8–9 July 1950. His brother, Arthur, with his first wife, Florence, and their daughters Florence (Fluff), Nancy, and Mary registered on 15–16 July 1950. Arthur's stay made the local newspaper. "Yakima Sunday Herald Society," *YSH*, 16 July 1950. On Prairie House, see Douglas, *Go East* 240–41.

40. Jeanie Senior, "Where History Was Made," *Klickitat PUD Ruralite* (November 2007): 4–5; William O. Douglas, letter to Mercedes Hester Douglas in *The Douglas Letters: Selections from the Private Papers of Justice William O. Douglas*, ed. Melvin I. Urofsky (Bethesda: Adler and Adler, 1987), 337–38; "Douglas Mum On Politics, To Climb Peak," *YDR*, 20 August 1949; Elon H. Gilbert, interview with Cragg M. Gilbert, 31 July 2020. Elon H. is the nephew and Cragg M. Gilbert the great-nephew of Elon James Gilbert (1897–1978), William O. Douglas's boyhood friend. Cragg M. Gilbert, email, 12 October 2020.

41. Hu Blonk, "Jack Nelson Gate Tender," *Reclamation ERA* 32, no. 12 (December 1946): 263–65; William O. Douglas, "Recording #1, 12 April 1950

Banquet Yakima, Washington," Digital File 37 of 7½-inch reel approx. 25 minutes, WOD Box 32-4 Tapes and Recordings, YVMWOD: 10:30–11:30; Douglas, *My Wilderness*, 125, 136-37.

42. "Byrnes, Douglas to Address Bar," *YDR*, 16 August 1948; "Valley Personals," 17 August 1948; "Justice Douglas Makes Brief Visit," 21 August 1948; "Justice Douglas Writing Book," 1 September 1948; "Valley Personals," 2 September 1948; "Douglas Just Another Autoist," 10 September 1948.

43. "Sage of Bumping Lake and Wife Feted at Dinner," *YDR*, 16 September 1948. The moniker "sage of Bumping Lake" also appears in Douglas's chapter on Jack Nelson. Douglas lists many of the books in Jack Nelson's library, among them the presentation copy of the Lewis and Clark journals. See Douglas, *Of Men and Mountains*, 217.

44. Murphy, *Wild Bill*, 270-71.

45. Elon H. Gilbert, interview with Cragg M. Gilbert, 31 July 2020.

46. Brad Patterson, interview 9 August 2020; Ed Kershaw, interview 18 September 2020; Tim Franklin, interview 19 September 2020; Mary Ann (Kershaw) and Dale Robinson, interview 28 April 2021.

47. Elon H. Gilbert, interview with Cragg M. Gilbert, 31 July 2020.

48. "Newest Douglas Book Will Have April Premiere Here," *YDR*, 24 January 1950.

49. "Home Building Booms on Yakima's West Side," *YDR*, 6 April 1950; "Douglas Banquet Tickets All Sold," 7 April 1950; "Many Await Douglas' Book," 11 April 1950; S.I. Anton, "Douglas Book Will Lift Eyes Unto Hills," 12 April 1950; "Friends Help Launch Book," [two photographs with captions]; "Rotarians Hear Review of Book" and "Justice Douglas Revisits Yakima," [nine photographs with captions] 13 April 1950; S.I. Anton, "Mirror of the Yakima Valley," 12 June 1950; "The Uplands," 5 July 1950 [advertisement]; "Justice Douglas Here Today For World Premiere of Book," *YMH*, 12 April 1950; "Yakima Throng Fetes Douglas" and "Justice Hints Not Candidate," *YMH* 13 April 1950; "The Uplands," *YSH* 16 July 1950 [advertisement]; "The Uplands Approvals/Dedication/Acknowledgment," 9 June 1950, [Yakima County]; and "The General Plan of The Uplands A Suburban Residential District of the City of Yakima, Washington June 14, 1950" [Robert L. Worener, Landscape Architect]. YVMGF Box 3; "'Peanuts' is home: Yakima Rolls Out Welcome Mat For Favorite Son Justice Douglas," *The Dalles Chronicle* (The Dalles, OR), 12 April 1950. According to Yakima newspaper columnist S.I. Anton, Douglas acquired the nickname as a schoolboy in Yakima because of his fondness for peanuts as a snack. Anton, "Daily Mirror of Life in Yakima," 8 September 1947.

50. Douglas, "Recording #1, 12 April 1950 Banquet Yakima, Washington," Digital File 37, YVMWOD, 19:28–22:22. The wild mountain huckleberry (*Vaccinium membranaceum*) grows profusely on the eastern slopes of Washington's Cascade range at elevations between 3,000 and 7,000 feet. Pat may have acquired her huckleberry pie skills from Kitty Nelson who, for decades, was considered a regional "authority" on the pastry. "Mrs. Jack Nelson Who Is Famed for Cooking Gives Few of Recipes," *YDR*, 16 August 1929.

51. Photograph and caption, *YDR* 13 April 1950.

52. "Colorful Decorations Prepared for Douglas Dinner Thursday," *Evening Observer* (La Grande, OR), 12 April 1950; "La Grande Hails Justice Douglas," *YMH*, 14 April 1950.

53. "Justice Hints Not Candidate"; "Friends Help Launch Book." Douglas is referring to Chief Justice John Marshall (1755-1835) who was appointed to the court in 1801 at the age of 45, serving 34 years until his death. However, Stephen Johnson Field held the longevity record on the Supreme Court prior to Douglas's tenure, serving 44 days longer than Chief Justice Marshall from 1863 to 1897. Two decades later, in answer to Eric Sevareid's direct question, Douglas denied that he ever had any ambition to become the longest serving Supreme Court Justice: "No, I had no such idea. Longevity has never been part of my plans." See "Tape #28: 6 September 1972. Eric Sevareid interviews William O. Douglas at Goose Prairie, 3¾-inch tape, one hour (of two hours of interviewing)," 48:27–48:45. WOD Box 32-4 Tapes and Recordings, YVMWOD.

54. "Justice Douglas to Dedicate Snowcap in Memory of Boyhood Yakima Friend," *YDR*, 19 August 1949; "Douglas Heads For Mountains," 20 August 1949; "Douglas Dedicates High Cascade Peak," 22 August 1949; "Cascade Climbers Name Peak for Curtiss Gilbert," 24 August 1949; Douglas, *Of Men and Mountains*, 209. The *YDR* article published August 24 featured several photographs taken by staff photographer Willard Hatch who accompanied Douglas on the trip. One of these photographs appears in McKeown's book, the location misidentified as Mount Gilbert in the Sierra Nevada. See McKeown, *Citizen Justice*, illustration 17 between pp. 106 and 107.

55. "Douglas Rallies From Injuries: Doctors Expect Justice to Ward Off Pneumonia," *YDR*, 3 October 1949; "Kin Hurries To Bedside," 3 October 1949; "Friends on Picnic Ready When Justice Needed Help," 3 October 1949; "Douglas Only Judge Absent," 3 October 1949; "Calls Swamp Switchboard," 3 October 1949; "Rare Blood Available Here Quickly," 3 October 1949; Douglas, *Of Men and Mountains*, xii–xiv; *Go East*, 198–200. Elon J. Gilbert gave his detailed version of the accident to the local paper. See "Douglas-Gilbert Bound For Crystal Peak Area," *YDR* 3 October 1949.

56. "Douglas-Gilbert Bound For Crystal Peak Area." Douglas had driven up to Yakima from Pendleton, Oregon, in August for the dedication of Gilbert Peak then back to Lostine for another horse pack trip. He returned to Yakima to ride with Elon to Crystal Mountain and planned to return to La Grande, Oregon, for a hunting trip before flying

to Washington, D.C., on 6 October. His wife, Mildred, had been waiting for him on the east coast. See "Douglas Mum On Politics, To Climb Peak," *YMH*, 20 August 1949; "Injured Justice W. O. Douglas Responds to Doctor's Efforts," 4 October 1949; "Justice's Wife Flies to Yakima," 4 October 1949; "Guest Log," 1 January 1947 to 25 October 1948/12 September 1951 (KFC).

57. The group left Goose Prairie to ascend American Ridge to first camp at Kettle Creek. The next leg followed the trail to Cougar Lakes for the second camp site. Continuing south, the riders spent the third night at Fryingpan Lake. Following the Pacific Crest Trail (PCT), the group rode to White Pass then over Hogback Mountain to camp at Shoe Lake in the Goat Rocks Wild Area. Continuing on the PCT the group traversed Tieton Pass into McCall Basin then toward Elk Pass to the fifth night's camp ("West Camp"). The next day, the riders left the PCT to cross Packwood Saddle and follow the Coyote Ridge trail (above Packwood Lake) to camp at Lost Lake. Crossing Coyote Ridge, the route turned to the east, crossing west of White Pass and ascending to Cortright Point and camp number seven at Sand Lake. From here, the riders crossed Cowlitz Pass skirting Tumac Mountain to camp in Blankenship Meadows. On the final day, the group passed Twin Sister Lakes then on to Copper City and home to Goose Prairie. See Bob H. Hansen, "Trail Riders Thrilled With Beauties of Mountain Wonderland," *YSH*, 11 September 1949, text, map, and four photographs.

58. "W.O. Douglas On Trail Ride," *YDR*, 6 August 1948; "Valley Personals," *YDR*, 3 July 1930; 9 July 1930; 29 July 1930; 11 August 1930; 10 September 1932; 14 September 1932; 21 August 1933. In August 1933, Kay and Mildred Bridgeford spent two weeks travelling on horseback through the Goat Rocks, the Tumac and Blankenship Meadows region, and the Bumping River drainage.

59. "Wilderness Evening," *American Forests* 54, no. 7 (July 1948): cover; "Guest Log"; Bill Wright, "Cascade Ridges Lure Easterners Into Goat Rocks Primitive Area," *YDR*, 19 August 1948; E.V. Seaman, "Double K Mountain Ranch: Snoqualmie National Forest, Washington Trail Ride—Expedition No. 8 August 20—August 31" [no date] [mimeographed journal corresponding to entries in Double K guest book for "Trail Riders of the 'Pioneer' Cascade Crest Wilderness Trip," August 31, 1948 [twenty-three pages] (KFC).

60. Byron Fish, "Pack Trip in Cascades Unsurpassed in Scenery, By Fish Finds," *Seattle Times*, 11 September 1958; Hansen, "Trail Riders Thrilled With Beauties of Mountain Wonderland"; Helland, "Introduction to West: Guest Ranches Lure Visitors"; "Trail Riders End Long Trek Through Rugged Cascades," *Seattle Post-Intelligencer*, 28 August 1950; Shirley W. Allen, "Trail Rides Provide Zest In Pacific Northwest Area," [unknown: originally in *The Christian Science Monitor*] [no date] May 1951; "Able Riders Turn Love of Saddle, Mountains Into Picturesque Ranch," *Grit*, 18 September 1955 (clippings in KFC).

61. *The Spokesman-Review Magazine*, 29 December 1946.

62. Joyce Murdoch and Deb Price, *Courting Justice: Gay Men and Lesbians v. The Supreme Court* (New York: Basic Books, 2001), 130.

63. Cragg D. Gilbert, eulogy at William O. Douglas Memorial, First Presbyterian Church, Yakima, WA, 16 October 1980 (GFC).

64. Brad Patterson, interview, 9 August 2020; Adrienne Rose Johnson, "Romancing the Dude Ranch, 1926–1947," *Western Historical Quarterly* 43, no. 4 (winter 2012): 438, 451; "Trail Riders Thrilled With Beauties of Mountain Wonderland"; "The 'Dude Is a Vital Part of Northwest," *Inland Empire Magazine, The Spokesman-Review*, 8 November 1953: cover and 3; Grace Ernestine Ray, "Women Run This Dude Ranch," *Seattle Times*, 26 June 1955; "Kay Kershaw, Double K Mountain Ranch" Christmas card, 1956; Bob and Ira Spring, "Goat Rocks Trail Ride," *Seattle Times Pictorial*, 4 October 1959: 4; Ruby Montana, interview, 28 October 2020.

65. Brad Patterson, interview, 9 August 2020.

66. "Resourceful Women Outwit Rough Bumping Road Route"; Sara Kincaid, "High in the Mountains on a Pack Trip," *Cascades* 11, no. 3 (June 1970): 31.

67. Ed Kershaw, interview, 8 July 2023; Tim Franklin, interview, 19 September 2020. A Bob and Ira Spring photograph from 1958 shows Kay rolling a cigarette astride her horse. See "Goat Rocks Trail Ride," 4.

68. Douglas, *Of Men and Mountains*, 145, 222, 226, 278.

69. Douglas, *Of Men and Mountains*, 199–202, 207. By the 1950 publishing date of Douglas's book, Gilbert Peak had been renamed. Slipper Lake does not appear on any USGS map of the White Pass/Hogback Mountain area dating from 1890 to the present. This is probably a name Kay used for Miriam Lake located north of Shoe Lake. West Camp refers to an area west of McCall Basin on the ridge leading to the summit of Old Snowy. See Douglas, *My Wilderness*, 135, 141. Johnny Glenn was a longtime local rodeo rider and horseman. "Local riders to Compete Rodeo at Packwood," *YDR*, 3 July 1935.

70. "W.O. Douglas On Trail Ride." A series of letters from 1959 illustrates how Douglas deferred to Kay's knowledge of the area between Bumping Lake and Goat Rocks while he was writing *My Wilderness The Pacific West*. See Kay Kershaw, letters to William O. Douglas, 8 December [handwritten note, no year]; [handwritten note, no date]; William O. Douglas, letters to Kay Kershaw, 23, 24, and 25 February 1959; 4, 5, 27, and 28 March 1959; 23 and 28 September 1959; 2 and 5 October 1959; 27 November 1959; 12 December 1959. William O. Douglas Papers, Box 1011, file: Kay Kershaw (LOC).

71. Beckey, *Guide*, 44–46; Douglas, *Of Men and Mountains*, 312–29.

72. Lynn, "Year 'Round in the Mountains," 37; Nelson, *We Never Got Away*, 180; Ruby Montana, interview, 28 October 2020.

73. Kodaslide Mounted Color Transparencies," from Kodak Processing Laboratory Chicago, IL, postmarked 10 May 1954 (to Elaine Cohen, 4127 40th NE, Seattle 5, Wn); "Kodaslide Mounted Transparencies," from Kodak Processing Laboratory Los Angeles, CA, postmarked 28 February 1955 (to Isabelle Lynn, PO Box 11, Yakima, Wash.); "Pavelle Color Print on Ansco Printon," [no date] (KFC); Quit Claim Deed 1593475, signed by Patricia Kane, dated 18 October 1955. Washington Title Insurance Company, Seattle. Elaine Cohen's name and address also appear in Isabelle's "Addresses" book. Cohen signed into the guest book on the same trip to the Double K Ranch on 23 May 1954 as Frances Rummell and Isabelle. At this point, Rummell and Lynn were still living together in Olympia. Cohen may be the photographer of the 1954 picture of Kay, Pat, and Isabelle: a woman who is not Rummell stands in the same position between Kay and Pat in an identical photo at the Yakima airport, presumably taken by Isabelle.

74. Maria Centrella, email, 27 April 2023.

75. Dr. Joseph Patrick Kane, letter to Isabel Kane, 14 November 1955 (KaFC).

76. Dr. Joseph Patrick Kane, letter to Pat Kane, 11 November 1955 (KaFC).

77. Maria Centrella, email to Ed Kershaw, 1 and 8 July 2022; Helland, "Introduction to West: Guest Ranches Lure Visitors."

78. Maria Centrella, email, 27 April 2023.

79. Nelson, *We Never Got Away*, 180; Joseph P. Kane, letters to Pat Kane, 12 November 1955 and 26 January 1956 (KaFC).

80. "Bosses of the Double K," *The Cincinnati Pictorial Enquirer*, 26 March 1961.

81. S.I. Anthon, "Yakima Valley Mirror: Jack Nelson Shares Life Experiences in His Book," *YDR*, 8 November 1965.

82. "Isabel Bradley, 76, was accident victim," *Springfield Union* [Springfield, MA], 2 April 1987; "Patricia Kane, Social Worker," *Peninsula Times Tribune*, 23 September 1992; "Charlotte Centrella," *Monterey County Herald*, 1 September 2015; Centrella, email, 1 March 2022.

83. Elizabeth K. Osterman, M.D., letter to Kay Kershaw, dated 10 December 1989. Isabelle Lynn's address book includes an entry for "Betty Osterman" with an address in San Francisco.

84. Maria Centrella, emails, 3 December 2021 and 1 March 2022.

85. Pat Kane, letter to Maria Centrella, 4 December 1987 (KaFC).

86. Simon Wendt, "Defenders of Patriotism or Mothers of Fascism? The Daughters of the American Revolution, Antiradicalism, and Un-Americanism in the Interwar Period," *Journal of American Studies* 47, no. 4 (November 2013): 945. Isabelle Lynn's earliest known ancestors in America were Mathew Brown, born in 1732 near the present site of Middletown, Pennsylvania, and Hugh McCormick, born in Ireland in 1756. Hugh purchased 1,300 acres in White Deer Valley, Pennsylvania, in 1770. Isabelle Lynn, handwritten notes [no date] (KFC).

87. "Williamsport High School Class of 1934 40th Anniversary Reunion, October 26, 1974 [photo]" (KFC); Lynn, "Year 'Round in the Mountains," 37. Isabelle's obituary lists Syracuse College in New York as her alma mater. "Isabelle Lynn," *YH-R*, 27 March 1996. However, the Special Collections Research Center at Syracuse University Libraries finds no trace of her in its yearbook, file clippings, or commencement reference folders. Tiffany Miller, reference assistant, Special Collections Research Center, Syracuse University, email 30 March 2021.

88. "Isabelle Lynn Certificate No. 3848, United States Power Squadrons Women's Certificate of Qualification, U.S.P.S. Piloting Examination," 4 March 1949; photograph inscribed "Jane and Izzy Sept 1, 1946" (KFC); Lynn, "Year 'Round in the Mountains," 36–37; Manning, "End of an Era," 15; Nelson, *We Never Got Away*, 181; Ed Kershaw, interview, 18 August 2020; Brad Patterson, interview, 28 September 2020; email, 14 June 2021.

89. Lynn, "Year 'Round in the Mountains," 37.

90. Guest Book, 14 May 1954 to 31 December 1976. Frances and Isabelle had lived together at 8421 Woodcliff Court and 23 Wessex Road in Silver Spring, Maryland. They only provide a post office box for their address in Olympia, Washington.

91. Helland, "Introduction to West: Guest Ranches Lure Visitors." From mid-1954 to late 1955, Isabelle resided at St. Helen's Court, a recently-constructed brick apartment building at 1509 Summitview Avenue. *Polk's Yakima City Directory* 50 (1949) (Seattle: R.L. Polk and Company, 1949), 899; *Polk's Yakima City Directory 1954–55* (Seattle: R.L. Polk and Company, 1955): 433, 984.

92. P.L.B. 10 v6, handcolored. [Valentine card, no date] (KFC).

93. Ambassador Cards 100KV 959E 99–02 [Valentine card, no date] (KFC).

94. Lynn, "Year 'Round in the Mountains," 37; Wazeka, "Crusade for Cougar Lakes," 28.

95. Helland, "Introduction to West: Guest Ranch Lures Visitors."

96. William O. Douglas, "Wilderness Trails of the Pacific Northwest," *Mademoiselle* (April 1955): 140–41, 194–97; Isabelle Lynn, "Pack Trip to the Goat Rocks," *The Dude Rancher* 27, no. 2 (April 1958): 12–13, 24, 32–34; William O. Douglas, letter to Kay Kershaw, 28 March 1959. William O. Douglas Papers, Box 1011, file: Kay Kershaw (LOC); William O. Douglas, letter to Isabelle Lynn, 14 December 1971 (KFC); E.V. Seaman, Guest Book 14 May 1954 to 31 December 1976. For the week 7–17 September 1957, Eileen writes: "Double K gets 'A' for this trip!" Eileen Ryan continued to work and visit, logging into the guest book no less than thirty times, her last on 29 August 1988. In a pre–1956 black and white portrait featuring the Kershaw family and Double K staff, Eileen Ryan sits next to Kay on the corral fence rail, far right; Pat Kane is perched far left. See photo on page 53. From the same photo series, another image shows

Eileen and Pat watching from behind and Ed and Bob Kershaw watching from the left, as Kay, an unidentified Double K wrangler, and Kay's mother and father ride out of the corral. Helland, "Introduction to West: Guest Ranches Lure Visitors from Afar To Cascade Slopes [photograph]." Ryan (1923-2011) was also an environmental activist, serving as a board member of NCCC from 1967 to 1969. See Eileen Ryan, "Our Man in the Cabinet," *Wild Cascades*, July 1961: 2.

97. Isabelle Lynn, "Busman's Holiday at the Double K," *The Dude Rancher* 30, no. 3 (July 1959): cover, 6, 12, 30-31. The cover of this issue of *The Dude Rancher* featured a color photograph by Dan Spuler of Kay Kershaw and an unidentified rider on American Ridge. Kay was quite proud of this placement, writing to Justice Douglas: "Incidently [sic] be sure and look at your copy [of *The Dude Rancher*] that comes out in July—we have contrived to have one of our color pictures of Mt. Rainier taken from American Ridge on the front of it. The first one to be used of the Cascade Mts. we hope!" Kay Kershaw, letter to William O. Douglas [no date], William O. Douglas Papers, Box 1011, file: Kay Kershaw (LOC). The same color photograph had appeared previously on the front page of the *Yakima Sunday Herald* on 7 June 1959. The C.P. Johnston Company published a 3.5" by 5.5" postcard of Spuler's photograph (probably funded by Kay and Isabelle) for sale at the Double K Ranch: cropping the image to include the summit of Mt. Rainier, the bottom of the postcard cut off Kay's foot and the legs of both horses. "Mt. Rainier," Mike Roberts postcard C8135, Berkeley, California, published for C.P. Johnson Company, Seattle.

Chapter 6

1. David K. Johnson, *The Lavender Scare: The Cold War Persecution of Gays and Lesbians in the Federal Government* (Chicago: University of Chicago Press, 2004), 15-30; Simon Hall, "Americanism, Un-Americanism, and the Gay Rights Movement," *Journal of American Studies* 47, no. 4 (November 2013): 1110; Bérubé, *Coming Out*, 265-70.

2. "Perverts Called Government Peril," *NYT*, 19 April 1950; "More Confusion," 30 April 1950; "Red Sabotage Plan Revealed," *YDR*, 19 May 1950.

3. "Doubts Raised About Charges," *YDR*, 1 May 1950.

4. "Loyalty and Security," *YDR*, 5 May 1950.

5. Faderman, *Odd Girls*, 119; *Gay Revolution*, 93; James Kirchick, *Secret City: The Hidden History of Gay Washington* (New York: Henry Holt, 2022), 6-7.

6. Murdoch and Price, *Courting Justice*, 32; David A. Moskowitz, Gerulf Rieger, and Michael E. Roloff, "Heterosexual Attitudes Towards Same-Sex Marriage," *Journal of Homosexuality* 57, no. 2 (2010): 326 [https://www.ncbi.nlm.nih.gov/pmc/articles/PMC5065072/pdf/nihms-821201.pdf]; Bullough and Bullough, "Lesbianism in the 1920s and 1930s," 901; Faderman, *Odd Girls*, 122-23.

7. "A Modern Genie," *YDR*, 18 January 1943. Other newspapers used the title "Letting the genie out of the bottle."

8. Elizabeth Lapovsky Kennedy and Madeline D. Davis, *Boots of Leather, Slippers of Gold: The History of a Lesbian Community* (New York: Routledge, 2014), 4, 10, 31, 38-40; Bérubé, *Coming Out*, 29, 228-30, 270-71; Faderman, *Odd Girls*, 126.

9. Bérubé, *Coming Out*, 257-60; Faderman, *Odd Girls*, 130-32.

10. Faderman, *Odd Girls*, 145-46; Yvonne Keller, "'Was It Right to Love Her Brother's Wife So Passionately?': Lesbian Pulp Novels and U.S. Lesbian Identity, 1950-1965," *American Quarterly* 57, no. 2 (June 2005): 401-2.

11. Linda McCarthy, "Poppies in a Wheat Field: Explaining the Lives of Rural Lesbians," *Journal of Homosexuality* 39, no. 1 (2000): 82; Jerry Lee Kramer, "Bachelor Farmers and Spinsters: Gay and Lesbian Identities and Communities in Rural North Dakota," in *Mapping Desire: Geographies of Sexualities*, ed. David Bell and Gill Valentine (New York: Routledge 1995), 209; Faderman, *Odd Girls*, 138; Johnson, *Just Queer Folk*, 118-20.

12. Robert I. Ford, *The History of Goose Prairie and the Ira Ford Family* (self-published, 2003), 154. Ford writes that the population of Goose Prairie ranged from ten to 100 in the summer and from six to eight in the winter. Some authors have based their population figure on William O. Douglas's tongue-in-cheek line from *Go East, Young Man*: "In my speeches, I often refer to Goose Prairie as composed of eight people—Kay, Isabelle, two Fords [Ira and Bess], Bob and Bennie Bosler, and the two Douglases [William O. and his fourth wife, Cathy]." Here Douglas is obviously exaggerating since he rarely spent time during the less-populated winter season at Goose Prairie. Douglas, *Go East*, 240; Murdoch and Price, *Courting Justice*, 129; Mark Funk, "Douglas loved Goose Prairie," *Everett Herald*, 21 January 1980.

13. Quotation from guestbook entry by Maite Wall, 3 August 1974; "Double K House Party Oct 16-18 1959," "Double K House Party Oct 21-23 1960," "Double K House Party Oct 20-22 1961," "Double K House Party Oct 4-6 1963," "House Party Oct 28 4," and "Rites of Fall Party Oct 15 1967" in "Double K Mountain Ranch [guest book]," 14 May 1954 to 31 December 1976; "Double K Mountain Ranch [guest book]," September 1977 to 16 July 1990; "Double K Holiday 74 75 76" [inscribed: And So It Begins (summer 1974) A Great Friendship!] [116 photographs with handwritten comments]; "Photo Album" [inscribed: To Kay and Isabel [sic] a few records of the great 1976 September! From Lil & Shirl [39 photographs with handwritten comments]; "Meeting of 'The Clan' at the Double K Mountain Ranch, July 1984" [inscribed: To Kay and Isabelle—from your "candid" photographer Lil and your friendly assembler, Shirl] [44 photos with comments]; "Kay Kershaw

and Isabelle Lynn At the Double K 1961–1984" [48 photographs] (KFC).

14. Urofsky, "Review of Murphy," 4.

15. Douglas, *Go East*, 104.

16. *Osborn v. United States*: (1966) 385 U.S. 342; Douglas, *Go East*, 105.

17. Murdoch and Price, *Courting Justice*, 108; "Madison Ave. Queens and the PTA," *The Ladder* 10, no. 6 (March 1966): 7.

18. Murdoch and Price, *Courting Justice*, 129.

19. Hazel Rowley, *Franklin and Eleanor: An Extraordinary Marriage* (New York: Farrar, Straus and Giroux, 2010), 155, 183, 185; Doris Faber, *The Life of Lorena Hickok E.R.'s Friend* (New York: William Morrow, 1980), 86–87, 91; Faderman, *To Believe in Women*, 85–93; Douglas, *Go East*, 317–18, 359, 370; Murphy, *Wild Bill*, 255–56, 259.

20. William O. Douglas, "56: William O. Douglas at dinner honoring Mrs. Franklin D. Roosevelt, National Council of Jewish Women 15 March 1948" (WOD Speeches Binder #2, nos. 40–69 11/21/45–5/11/49 YVMWOD); Eleanor Roosevelt, "My Day, March 19, 1948" [https://www2.gwu.edu/~erpapers/myday/displaydoc.cfm?_y=1948&_f=md000918]; "My Day, June 2, 1948" [https://www2.gwu.edu/~erpapers/myday/displaydoc.cfm?_y=1948&_f=md000982], *The Eleanor Roosevelt Papers Digital Edition* (The George Washington University, 2017); *The Douglas Letters*, ed. Urofsky, 268–69.

21. Murdoch and Price, *Courting Justice*, 41–45.

22. *Roth v. United States*: 354 U.S. 508–14 (1957); *The Douglas Letters*, ed. Urofsky, 198–99, n. 2.

23. Murdoch and Price, *Courting Justice*, 80.

24. Murdoch and Price, *Courting Justice*, 90–93, 95; *Rosenberg v. Fleuti*: 374 U.S. 449 (1963). The determination in *Rosenberg v. Fleuti*, however, turned on a point of immigration law concerning what constituted illegal entry into the United States.

25. Murdoch and Price, *Courting Justice*, 35–36, 124, 128; *Boutilier v. Immigration and Naturalization Service*: 387 U.S. 125–35 (1967); David Abrahamsen, *Crime and the Human Mind* (New York: Columbia University Press, 1944), reprint (Montclair, NJ: Patterson Smith, 1969), 117–18.

26. "Introduction," *Douglas Letters*, ed. Urofsky, xvii; Murphy, speech before the Cato Institute, 18 March 2003: 10:07–10:22.

27. *Griswold v. Connecticut*, 483–84; William O. Douglas, "291: Points of Rebellion," 1966 Harvey T. Reid Lectures, Arcadia University, Wolfville, Nova Scotia, 30 and 31 January, 1 February 1967: 102–3 (WOD Speeches Binder #9 nos. 265–301 10/9/64–5/28/67, YVMWOD); Douglas, "300: The Computerized Man," American Civil Liberties Union, San Francisco, California, 20 May 1967: 2–3 (WOD Speeches Binder #9, YVMWOD); William O. Douglas, "The Attack on the Right to Privacy," *Playboy*, December 1967: 192; Lori Ann Brass, "An Arrest in New Haven, Contraception and the Right to Privacy," *Yale Medicine* (Spring 2007): 16–17.

28. *United States v. Classic*: 313 U.S. 299 (1941), 331–32; *General Committee of Adjustment of Brotherhood of Locomotive Engineers for Missouri-Kansas-Texas Railroad v. Missouri-Kansas-Texas Railroad Co.*: 320 U.S. 323 (1943), 336; *General Box Co. v. United States*: 351 U.S. 159 (1956), 169; *Textile Workers Union v. Lincoln Mills*: 353 U.S. 448 (1957), 457; *Smith v. Sperling*: 354 U.S. 91 (1957), 97; *Panama Canal Co. v. Grace Line, Inc.*: 356 U.S. 309 (1958), 317; *Wilson v. Schnettler*: 365 U.S. 381 (1961), n. 2/5; *Federal Power Commission v. Texaco, Inc.*: 377 U.S. 33 (1964), 39. See also Louis J. Sirico, Jr., "Failed Constitutional Metaphors: The Wall of Separation and the Penumbra," *University of Richmond Law Review* 45, no. 2 (2011): 477–87.

29. Plato, *Politeia* Book VII 514a–515a. In *Go East, Young Man*, Justice Douglas writes: "I was a lover of Latin and gained such proficiency that I could converse or orate in that tongue by the time I was a senior" (56). As a devoted classicist he would have been familiar with Plato's most famous work, *The Republic* (Politeia), a treatise on the ideal state. See William O. Douglas, "48: 15th Annual New York Herald-Tribune Forum on Current Problems, 28 October 1946": 8 (WOD Speeches Binder #2 nos. 40–69, 11/21/45–3/11/49, YVMWOD); Douglas, letter to Andrea Stone in *The Douglas Letters*, ed. Urofsky, 158; Douglas, "291: Points of Rebellion," 75; Douglas, "300: The Computerized Man," 2–3 (WOD Binder #9). For a more detailed discussion of Plato, Douglas, and the penumbra metaphor see William D. Frank, "Of *Women*, Men and Mountains: Kay Kershaw, Isabelle Lynn and the Double K Mountain Ranch," in *Rotary Mtg 2021 09 16* [https://www.youtube.com/watch?v=1nq0fo_VES4&t=1270s&ab_channel=yakimarotaryclub], 38:27–54:17.

30. "How Far Out Can We Go?" *The Ladder* 5, no. 4 1961 (January 1961): 4–5; "The QUA's Have It!" 10, no. 6 (March 1966): 11–13; Herbert Donaldson, "An Empirical Study—The Law vs. Private Morality," 10, no. 11 (August 1966): 10–12; Helen M. Hacker, "Homosexuals: Should They Have Equal Rights?" 14, no. 1–2 (October–November 1969): 14–16; Ocie Perry, "KQED Report on Symposium," 14 no. 3–4 (December–January 1969–70): 39–40. William O. Douglas hints at the connection between the penumbra of privacy in *Griswold* and the rights of homosexuals in "291: Points of Rebellion," 84–133; and "300: The Computerized Man." The Daughters of Bilitis is an obscure name, but laden with meaning. In 1894, the French poet Pierre Louÿs published *The Songs of Bilitis*, a series of pseudo-translations inspired by the ancient Greek poetry of Sappho of Lesbos. His purported author is Sappho's fictional contemporary, Bilitis. By attaching "daughters" to her name, the San Francisco women hoped to "hide behind the name believing that only lesbians would understand the reference to *Songs of Bilitis*, and that straight people would assume it was an organization like the [Daughters of the American Revolution]." Lillian Faderman, email, 10 July 2021; Faderman, *Gay Revolution*, 77.

31. Writing for the majority in 1973, Justice

Harry Blackmun cited *Griswold v. Connecticut* eleven times and used the penumbra metaphor three times.

32. *Lawrence v. Texas*: 539 U.S. 595 (2003).
33. *Obergefell v. Hodges*: 576 U.S. 644 (2015).
34. "Justice Douglas Dies," *YH-R*, 20 January 1980.
35. Melissa Brown, "Sen. Marsha Blackburn criticizes 1965 Supreme Court ruling on birth control access," *Nashville Tennessean*, 21 March 2022; Dave Boucher, "Michigan GOP AG candidates criticize case that nixed law banning use of birth control," *Detroit Free Press*, 21 February 2022; Adam Liptak, "Justice Jackson Joins the Supreme Court, and the Debate Over Originalism," *NYT*, 10 October 2022.
36. Murdoch and Price, *Courting Justice*, 129, 131.

Chapter 7

1. Lynn, "Year 'Round in the Mountains," 38.
2. Adam M. Sowards, "William O. Douglas's Wilderness Politics: Public Protest and Committees of Correspondence in the Pacific Northwest," *Western Historical Quarterly* (Spring 2006): 22.
3. Ed Kershaw, interview, 18 August 2020; Brock Evans, email, 22 July 2021.
4. Kristin Jackson, "Rooted in the Prairie," *Seattle Post-Intelligencer*, 19 July 1989.
5. David Louter, *Contested Terrain: North Cascades National Park Service Complex: An Administrative History* (Seattle: National Park Service, 1979), 11; Paul W. Hirt, *A Conspiracy of Optimism: Management of the National Forests Since World War Two* (Lincoln: University of Nebraska Press, 1994), xvii–xix, 31–34.
6. Gerald W. Williams, *The USDA Forest Service—The First Century FS-650* (Washington, D.C.: USDA Forest Service Office of Communication, 2005), 8; Louter, *Contested Terrain*, 14–15; "Wonderland: An Administrative History of Mount Rainier National Park. III: Establishment of Mount Rainier National Park" [https://www.nps.gov/parkhistory/online_books/mora/adhi/chap3.htm].
7. Williams, *USDA Forest Service*, 59, 76–77; Louter, *Contested Terrain*, 17, 19.
8. Washington State Planning Council, *Cascade Mountains Study* (Olympia: Washington State Planning Council, 1940), 44; Louter, *Contested Terrain*, 19. Acreage numbers sometimes lose their meaning in relation to western regions. As points of comparison: Chicago comprises 149,760 acres; New York City, 193,920 acres; Los Angeles, 321,920 acres; the State of Rhode Island, 776,960 acres; the State of Washington, 45,671,680 acres.
9. Harlan D. Unrau and G. Frank Williss, "Chapter Six: The National Park Service, 1933–1939," in *Administrative History: Expansion of the National Park Service in the 1930s* (September 1983) National Park Service, Denver Service Center [https://www.nps.gov/parkhistory/online_books/unrau-williss/adhi.htm]; Louter, *Contested Terrain*, 20–22.
10. *Establishment and Modification of National Forest Boundaries and National Grasslands: A Chronological Record 1891–2012 FS 612* (United States Department of Agriculture Forest Service, Lands and Realty Management Staff, Washington, D.C., 2012), 51.
11. "Cascade Ice Peaks National Park and Other Past Park Proposals," *Wild Cascades*, February 1963: 5–14; Unrau and Williss, "Chapter Four: New Initiatives in the Field of Recreation and Recreational Development," in *Administrative History*; "Chapter 3: the New Deal Years 1933–1941," in *America's National Park System: Critical Documents*, ed. Lary [sic] M. Dilsaver (Lanham, MD: Rowman and Littlefield, 1994) [https://www.nps.gov/parkhistory/online_books/anps/anps_3.htm]; Louter, *Contested Terrain*, 20–22.
12. *Cascade Mountains Study*, 7–9; "Revival of Crusade for Cascades National Park," *NCCC News* 4, no. 7 (July 1960): 2–5.
13. Williams, *USDA Forest Service*, 55.
14. Louter, *Windshield Wilderness*, 105–7, 113–14; Hirt, *Conspiracy of Optimism*, 36–39, 50–53, 126, 168–69, 178–81; Richard E. McArdle, "The Concept of Multiple Use of Forest and Associated Lands—Its Values and Limitations" (Fifth World Forestry Conference, Seattle, WA 29 August to 10 September 1960), in Elwood R. Maunder, *Dr. Richard E. McArdle: An Interview with the Former Chief, U.S. Forest Service 1952–1962* (Santa Cruz, CA: Forest History Society, 1979), Appendix C, 225–31.
15. John B. Oakes, "Conservation: Fight For Parks—The White House Must End Battle Between Two Federal Services," *NYT*, 2 October 1960; "Conservation: The Parks Issue—The Forest Service's Policy on the Use of Public Lands Is Analyzed," 13 November 1960.
16. This prompted one of William O. Douglas's earliest letters opposing Forest Service practices in the Snoqualmie District: "I know that country well. I travelled it as a boy and as a man and have written quite a lot about it in my book *Of Men and Mountains*." William O. Douglas, letter to Laurence Barrett, 12 June 1954 (Manuscripts Division, LOC). In 1940, the Forest Service had expanded the Goat Rocks to 82,680 acres and designated it a Wild Area. *NCCC News* 4, no. 4 (April 1960): 9.
17. "The Universe of the Wilderness is Vanishing," *Cascadians Annual Club Bulletin 1937*: 6; "A National Park Creed," *The Cascadian 1941*: 11 (YVM archives, Cascadians Box 3a 1937–1964).
18. Lex Maxwell, "To Our Mountaineering Friends," *Cascadians Annual 1958*: 1; Louis Ulrich, "To Our Mountaineering Friends," *Cascadians Annual 1959*: 1 (YVM archives, Cascadians Box 3a 1937–1964); William O. Douglas, letter to Cragg D. Gilbert, 4 June 1959; Cragg D. Gilbert, letter to William O. Douglas, 15 September 1961 (GFC).
19. "Valley Personal," *YDR*, 29 November 1943; Lyon, "The Gold Hill Outdoor Club," 101–2;

"Charles D. Hessey," *Cascadian Annual 1989*: 7; "Charles D. Hessey," *YH-R*, 12 January 1990.

20. Lowell Skoog, *Written in the Snows: Across Time on Skis in the Pacific Northwest* (Seattle: Mountaineers Books, 2021), 177–81.

21. Charles Hessey, "Club Purpose" and "Greetings to Our Mountaineering Friends," *Cascadian Annual 1956*: iii–iv (YVM archives, Cascadians Box 3a 1937–1964).

22. *NCCC News* (October 1957): 13; Charles Hessey, "The North Cascades Primitive Area," 2, no. 10 (October 1958): 1–3; 2, no. 12 (December 1958): 3; 4, no. 1 (January 1960): 3–4; 4, no. 4 (April 1960): 7; 5, no. 5 (May 1961): 16; Charles Hessey, "To Our Mountaineering Friends," *Cascadian Annual 1957*: 1; and "Americans? Si! Oui! Aye! Ja!" 84–86; "Cascadians and Conservation—1958," 69–70; "Cascadians and Conservation—1959," *Cascadian Annual 1959*: 52–53; "Report From Hoot Owl Canyon," 55–58; "Conservation—1961," *Cascadian Annual 1961*: 1; "Cascadian Conservation," *Cascadian 1963*, 57; "Cascadian Conservation [preface, two pages]," *Cascadian 1964*; "Cascadian Conservation" and "The Bumping Lake Enhancement Proposal," *The Cascadian 1965–1966–1967*, 5–8; "Conservation" and "Hessey Tracks," *Cascadian 1969*, 3–4; Charles Hessey, letter to J. Herbert Stone, 12 October 1959 (YVMCDH papers).

23. Charles D. Hessey, Jr., "Skis on the Cascades," in *The Cascades: Mountains of the Pacific Northwest*, ed. Roderick Peattie (New York: Vanguard Press, 1949), 389–94; Charles Hessey, "What Did the Hessey's [sic] do in 1958?" *Cascadian Annual 1958*: 79–82; "Charles and Marion Hessey Films, circa 1939–1971," *Archives West Orbis Cascade Alliance* [http://archiveswest.orbiscascade.org/ark:/80444/xv37585]; *NCCC News* 2, no. 3 (March 1958): 7; 2, no. 4 (April 1958): 3; 3, no. 12 (December 1958): 3; "Wilderness Film Wins Award," 5, no. 1 (January 1961): 2; 5, no. 5 (May 1961): 16.

24. Reverend Jesse Boyd, "If we must use force to attain equal rights—so be it," *YMH*, 13 January 1968; Charles Hessey, "Blacker hearts," *YMH* [letter to the editor], 21 January 1968; Hessey, rough draft ["Blacker hearts"], letter to the editor [undated] (YVMCDH papers).

25. "YVC offers course," *YH-R*, 13 April 1978; Peg Wells, Jim Dixon, and Gordon Howard, [letters to the editor], 17 July 1982; Terry Martin and Jane Schwab, "On censorship," [letter to the editor], 22 January 1989; Charles Hessey, "The Clubs," [letter to the editor], 9 July 1982; [letter to the editor], 31 July 1982; "German policy," [letter to the editor], 3 February 1985; "Communist threat," [letter to the editor], 4 August 1986; "On apathy," [letter to the editor], 2 October 1988; "Libel effort," [letter to the editor], 5 February 1989.

26. Bill Hassell, "Ski Trails for the Year," *Cascadian Annual Club Bulletin 1940*: 8 (YVM archives, Cascadians Box 3a 1937–1964).

27. Frank, *Everyone to Skis*, 28.

28. Charles Hessey, "Food for Wondering Minds," [fourteen-page typed manuscript, no date] (YVMCDH papers); Hessey, letter to Karen Degenhart, 27 October 1984, in YVM archives, Cascadians Box 10. Around the time that the fabricated *Protocols of the Elders of Zion* emerged from Russia, novelist Thomas Dixon conjoined the rites and bloodlines of the legendary Scottish clans with those of the late nineteenth-century Ku Klux Klan. Thomas Dixon, *The Clansman: A Historical Romance of the Ku Klux Klan* (New York: A. Wessels, 1907), dedication [no page number], 266, 324; Baker, *Gospel According to the Klan*, 74–75, 79.

29. Charles Hessey, letter to Cragg D. Gilbert [no date, ca. 1980]; Garner Ted Armstrong, letter to Charles D. Hessey, Jr., 23 May 1975 (YVMCDH papers).

30. Charles D. Hessey, letter to H.M.S. Richards [no date, ca. July 1978]. See also Dale Thomas, letter to Charles D. Hessey, Jr. [no date, letterhead "Broadway Christian Church"], four pages; Charles D. Hessey, Jr., letter to Dale Thomas [no date], six pages (YVMCDH papers).

31. Charles Hessey, letter to Hattie Rosencranz [no date] (YVMCDH papers).

32. Eckard V. Toy, Jr., "The Right Side of the 60s: The Origins of the John Birch Society in the Pacific Northwest," *Oregon Historical Quarterly* 105, no. 2 (Summer 2004): 262; "Second Party Forms," *Yakima Eagle*, 22 June 1966; "New Conservative Party Continues to Grow," 27 July 1966; "Hey ... That's Our Money!" [advertisement] 19 October 1966; "What does Floyd Paxton think about the war in Viet Nam?" [advertisement], *YMH*, 28 October 1966; "What does Floyd Paxton think about foreign aid to communist countries?" [advertisement], 1 November 1966; "What does Floyd Paxton think about inflation?" [advertisement,] 4 November 1966; "'Paxton, the Spoiler, Aids Bansmer,'" [reprint from *Lewiston Morning Tribune*], 5 November 1966; "Hey ... That's our money!" [advertisement], 8 November 1966; Mike Merritt, "Politics to feel loss of Paxton," *YH-R*, 12 December 1975; Jim Gosney, "John Birch Society 'is growing steadily,'" 16 May 1976; Gary Nelson, "John Birchers: 'now we just muddle along,'" 9 March 1980; "Freeze Folly," [advertisement], 12 June 1982. Paxton's *Yakima Eagle* claimed a total circulation of 25,000 copies in Yakima (and 1,000 to 1,500 out of town) during its first eight months of publication. See "Slightly to the right!" *Yakima Eagle*, 8 June 1966; "Attention Eagle Readers!" 12 October 1966.

33. "Congressional Race in Fourth District Has Two Seeking to Unseat the Incumbent," *YSH*, 6 November 1966. Paxton also headed Yakima's "Committee of 1000" that opposed funding from the federal urban renewal program.

34. Jim Gosney, "Larry Richey: He's a 'Bircher' and he's proud of it," *YH-R*, 30 June 1978; Matthew Dallek, *Birchers: How the John Birch Society Radicalized the American Right* (New York: Basic Books, 2022), 190–96.

35. "Abzug charge," *YH-R*, 27 October 1977; Dallek, *Birchers*, 152, 157, 213–15.

36. Daniel O. Haney, "Birch Society enjoying

boom in membership," *YH-R*, 16 May 1976; Chris Stirewalt, "Populism, fake news, and racist rhetoric—it's all happened before in the 1968 presidential campaign," *Business Insider*, 6 October 2018; Toy, "The Right Side of the 60s," 270.

37. William O. Douglas, *The Court Years 1939-1975: The Autobiography of William O. Douglas* (New York: Random House, 1980), 363; *Dennis v. United States*: 341 U.S. 581-91 (1951); "Do Newspapers Have a Moral Responsibility?" *Yakima Eagle*, 27 July 1966; 'Inferior Court Justice," 31 August 1966; Matthew Rosenberg, "A Teacher Marched to the Capitol. When She Got Home, the Fight Began," *NYT*, 10 April 2021.

38. Guest Book, 14 May 1954 to 31 December 1976, 21-22 September 1963. "Committee on Correspondence on the North(ern) Cascades."

39. Douglas, *Of Men and Mountains*, 290. Douglas refers to Chuck as "Charles Hussey," a misspelling that should have been apparent. Harvard-educated Elon J. Gilbert, who knew both Hessey and Justice Douglas well, edited the galley proofs for *Of Men and Mountains* and would have pointed out the mistake: "I used a great many of your suggestions and but for the painstaking care which you took, I would have been caught in some egregious errors." William O. Douglas, letter to Elon J. Gilbert, 20 January 1950; Phil Parrish [editor, *The Oregonian*], letter to Elon J. Gilbert, 28 October 1949 (GFC).

40. "[Charles Hessey was] always a hero among us westsiders despite his strong far-right views." Brock Evans, email, 22 June 2023. A "westsider" in this context refers to the more liberal and environmentally-minded residents of Washington State's Puget Sound region.

41. Brock Evans, email, 12 December 2020.

42. "Timber Group Against Wilderness Area Plan," *Spokesman-Review*, 12 September 1957, in *NCCC News* 1, no. 3 (October 1957): 6-7.

43. Brock Evans, email, 28 June 2021. Brock Evans served as Pacific Northwest representative of the Sierra Club and FWOC from 1967 to 1973, then as head of the Sierra Club's office in Washington, D.C., from 1973 to 1981. He subsequently worked with the National Audubon Society from 1981 to 1996.

44. Isabelle Lynn, "Cougar Lakes: Do-It-Yourself Wilderness," *National Parks & Conservation Magazine* 46, no. 6 (June 1972): 25; Kay Kershaw and Isabelle Lynn, letter to Karl Onthank, 5 July 1958; Onthank, letter to Kershaw and Lynn, 15 July 1958; Kershaw and Lynn, letter to Onthank, 30 July 1958; Marion Hessey, letter to Kershaw, 23 July 1958, Double K Papers, files 1-4 and 2-2. In September 1958, Carmelita Lowry sent copies of her letter addressed to District Ranger F.H. Armstrong to William O. Douglas, Charles Hessey, Karl Onthank, and Howard Zahniser. Carmelita Lowry, letter to District Ranger [F.H.] Armstrong, 27 September 1958. Double K Papers, file 1-7. Karl Onthank (1890-1967) was an administrator at the University of Oregon in Eugene for forty years and an early conservationist. In addition to the Friends of the Three Sisters Wilderness, Onthank and his wife were instrumental in founding the Save the McKenzie River Association, the Federation of Western Outdoor Clubs (FWOC), the Oregon Roadside Council, the Nature Conservancy, and the Northwest Wilderness Conference.

45. Charles Hessey, letter to Office of the District Ranger, Chelan and Twisp, 10 September 1962; Charles Hessey, letter to H.C. Chriswell, 14 November 1963; H.C. Chriswell, letter to Charles Hessey, 2 December 1963; Mary Fries, letter to Charles Hessey, 25 April 1966 (YVMCDH papers); "Horses and Trails," *Wild Cascades*, October-November 1964: 8-10; "Appendix A: History of R2 wilderness group size limit," in *Rocky Mountain Region Minimum Requirement Decision Guide for Group Size Limits in Wilderness* [https://www.fs.fed.us/r2/recreation/wilderness/training/2011-winter-meeting/wilderness-group-size/groupsize-guide-120810.pdf]; letters and permits in Double K Papers, file 2-20.

46. Charles Hessey, note to Pat Goldsworthy [stamped 19 May 1961] (NCCC records, 1732-015 Box 2).

47. Kathryn Kershaw and Isabelle Lynn, "Statement on the 'National Wilderness Preservation Act,'" 7 November 1958. Double K Papers, file 2-2.

48. "The Trek to Bend Was Worth It!" *NCCC News* 2, no. 12 (December 1958): 3; "A statement in favor of the Wilderness Bill from the Cascadians of Yakima, delivered at McCall, Idaho, October 30, 1961," typed manuscript, two pages (YVMCDH papers).

49. According to contemporaneous USFS regulations, a Wild Area referred to a tract of land between 5,000 and 100,000 acres. A Wilderness Area was larger than 100,000 acres; only the Secretary of Agriculture could eliminate or modify them.

50. Katherine [sic] Kershaw and Isabelle Lynn, "Plea made For Public Support Of Wilderness Bill," *YDR*, 9 February 1960.

51. "The Wilderness Act," *The Wilderness Society* [https://www.wilderness.org/articles/article/wilderness-act]; "Excerpts From 'Keep the Wilderness Wild,'" *NCCC News* 2, no. 5 (May 1958): 1-3; Hirt, *Conspiracy of Optimism*, 164-66, 176-77, 180, 229-32.

52. "Glacier Peak Wilderness Attacked," *NCCC News* 2, no. 1 (January 1958): 10.

53. "What the Seattle Times Forgot," *NCCC News* 3, no. 6 (June 1959): 6-7; "Spokesman-Review Editorial Takes a Crack at the Wilderness Bill," 3, no. 7 (July 1959): 4-5; "Wilderness Bill Opponent, Bert Cole, Washington's Commissioner of Public Lands, Sounds Off," 3, no. 8 (August 1959): 8 "Wilderness Backers Now In Propaganda's Big Leagues," 4, no. 6 (June 1960): 7-8.

54. James F. Simon, *Independent Journey: The Life of William O. Douglas* (New York: Harper and Row, 1980), 329; Margaret McKeown, "Justice Takes a Side," *The Seattle Times Pacific NW*, 19

August 2018: 12–17; Murphy, *Wild Bill*, 330–35; Hirt, *Conspiracy of Optimism*, 228.

55. William O. Douglas, letter to David Seymour, 11 January 1960; Douglas, letter to Edgar Wayburn, 1 October 1962; Edgar Wayburn, letter to William O. Douglas, 6 November 1962. (Binder no. 1, LOC Manuscripts Correspondence/Environmentalism, YVMWOD).

56. See Ansel Adams, Nancy Newhall and David Brower, *This Is the American Earth* (San Francisco: Sierra Club, 1960); Henry David Thoreau and Eliot Porter, *In Wildness Is the Preservation of the World* (San Francisco: Sierra Club, 1962); Henry Gilliam and Philip Hyde, *Island in Time: the Point Reyes Peninsula* (San Francisco: Sierra Club, 1962); Harvey Manning, Ansel Adams, Philip Hyde, David Simons, Bob and Ira Spring, et al., *Wild Cascades Forgotten Parkland*, introduction by William O. Douglas, ed. David Brower (San Francisco: Sierra Club, 1965).

57. Douglas, *Of Men and Mountains*, 15, 327–28; Douglas, letter to Laurence O. Barrett, 12 June 1954.

58. Patrick D. Goldsworthy, letter to William O. Douglas, 17 March 1962 (Binder no. 1, LOC Manuscripts Correspondence/Environmentalism, YVMWOD).

59. Hulst, *Footpaths*, 239; McKeown, *Citizen Justice*, 169–70; Mike Hiler, email correspondence, 8 November 2020 and 10 March 2021.

60. Isabelle Lynn, note to Patrick Goldsworthy, 29 January [1966] (NCCC records, 1732–011 Box 6); Isabelle Lynn, letters to Don [R. Campbell], 13 January 1972 and 9 February 1972 (KFC).

61. William O. Douglas, letter to David R. Brower, 3 October 1960 (Binder no. 1, LOC Manuscripts Correspondence/Environmentalism, YVMWOD).

62. William O. Douglas, letter to Pauline Dyer, 3 October 1960 (Binder no. 1, LOC Manuscripts Correspondence/Environmentalism, YVMWOD).

63. William O. Douglas, letter to Senator Henry M. Jackson, 17 October 1960 (Binder no. 1, LOC Manuscripts Correspondence/Environmentalism, YVMWOD). Reports in the *Yakima Daily Republic* indicated otherwise. See Carmelita Lowry and Eileen Ryan, "Cougar Lakes and the Eastside Press," *Wild Cascades* 5, no. 11 (November 1961): 6.

64. William O. Douglas, letter to Senator Henry M. Jackson, 15 November 1960 (Binder no. 1, LOC Manuscripts Correspondence/Environmentalism, YVMWOD). The road into the Goat Rocks Douglas refers to here is the one from Clear Lake up the North Fork of the Tieton completed in 1954.

65. William O. Douglas, letter to David Brower, 2 November 1960 (Binder no. 1, LOC Manuscripts Correspondence/Environmentalism, YVMWOD). By October 1960, Charles Hessey had joined Kay and Isabelle to oppose Barrett and USFS. Kay Kershaw and Isabelle Lynn, letter to William O. Douglas, 26 October 1960 (Double K Papers, file 1–42).

66. Adam M. Sowards, *The Environmental Justice: William O. Douglas and American Conservation* (Corvallis: Oregon State University Press, 2009), 83–91; Sowards, "William O. Douglas's Wilderness Politics," 21–22; Brock Evans, *Endless Pressure Endlessly Applied: The Autobiography of an Eco-Warrior* (La Grande, OR: Wake-Robin Press, 2020), 313–15.

67. Jeff Weathersby, "The Making of a Wilderness," *YH-R*, 18 February 1979.

68. "Flailing Around In The Sagebrush Of The Editorial Mind," *Wild Cascades* 5, no. 6 (June 1961): 5; Charles Hessey, "Wilderness Bill," [letter to the editor] *YMH*, 5 April 1962; "Stumped," [letter to the editor] *YDR*, 27 June 1963.

69. Kay Kershaw and Isabelle Lynn, letters to the editor, 19 October and 6 February 1960; 17 and 30 April 1962; 14 October 1962; 28 June 1963; 26 February 1966; 25 October 1970 (Double K Papers, Box 1–41).

70. Kershaw and Lynn, "Plea Made For Public Support Of Wilderness Bill."

71. Kathryn Kershaw and Isabelle Lynn, "Wilderness," [letter to the editor] *YMH*, 27 April 1962 (clipping in KFC); "Northwest Wilderness Conference," *Wild Cascades* 6, no. 3 (March 1962): 2.

72. "Statement of Kathryn Kershaw and Isabelle Lynn, Double K Mountain Ranch, Goose Prairie," 7 May 1962, in *Wilderness Preservation System Hearings Before the Subcommittee on Public Lands of the Committee on Interior and Insular Affairs House of Representatives Eighty-Seventh Congress First Session* (Washington, D.C.: Government Printing Office, 1962): 1437.

73. See map 4; and *Wild Cascades*, November 1962: 8–9. Howard Zahniser, letter to Kay Kershaw and Isabelle Lynn, 30 January 1961 (Double K Papers, file 1–32).

74. Charles Hessey, note to Pat Goldsworthy [stamped 1 June 1961] (NCCC records, 1732–015 Box 2); William O. Douglas, letter to Kay Kershaw, 24 January 1966; Isabelle Lynn, letter to Pat Goldsworthy, 30 March 1974; NCCC draft copy "Historical Background" [1977] [margin comment to: 'In February 1961 a proposal to establish a Cougar Lakes Wilderness Area was presented to the Forest Service by members of the Mountaineers']: "[…] might want to put in actual [?] of the 'Double [K] Girls' here since it was their proposal" (NCCC records, 1732–011 Box 6). After reading this section of my manuscript, Brock Evans acknowledged: "I never knew before now that [Kershaw and Lynn] were [first] drafters of the [Cougar Lakes] Proposal." Brock Evans, email, 22 June 2023.

75. Hessey, note to Goldsworthy [stamped 19 May 1961]; Hessey, note to Goldsworthy [stamped 1 June 1961]; Lynn, "Year 'Round in the Mountains," 38–39; Kay Kershaw and Isabelle Lynn, "A Proposal to Establish a Cougar Lakes Wilderness Area," *Wild Cascades* (July 1961): 3–5; Carmelita Lowry, "Call to Action: Cougar Lakes in Congress," December 1970–January 1971: 2; Lynn, "Do-It-Yourself Wilderness," 25.

76. William O. Douglas, "Memorandum to the

Secretary of Agriculture," 28 April 1961 (Binder no. 1, LOC Manuscripts Correspondence/Environmentalism YVMWOD).

77. Lynn, "Year 'Round in the Mountains," 39–40; Carmelita Lowry, "Report on Cougar Lakes," *Wild Cascades* 5, no. 10 (October 1961): 6–7; Guest Book, 14 May 1954 to 31 December 1976.

78. Isabelle Lynn, "Status of the Proposed Cougar Lakes Wilderness Area As Of February 1966," *Wild Cascades*, April–May 1966: 25–26.

79. Douglas had requested a year earlier that Barrett join him on a trip to Copper City and other locations to view USFS logging operations. William O. Douglas, letter to L.O. [Laurence] Barrett, 22 December 1960 (Double K Papers, file 1–42).

80. Lowry, "Call to Action," 4. In 1962, Isabelle Lynn quoted Laurence Barrett who had remarked in 1957: "Timber is a crop, like apples." Isabelle Lynn, letter to Patrick Goldsworthy, 26 January 1962 (NCCC records, 1732–015 Box 2). Using the terms "harvest" or "harvesting" in relation to logging in ancient, old-growth stands of timber in the Pacific Northwest was a "great PR stroke" unveiled at a forestry conference in British Columbia in 1968: "… sounds so like *logging's* scenic and ecological impact are no big deal, right? … sort of like mowing the lawn or cropping wheat?" Brock Evans, email, 16 June 2021.

81. Robert Wolf, "Report on Copper City Logging Snoqualmie National Forest," attachment to Senator Henry M. Jackson, 7 November 1961: 2; Henry M. Jackson, letter to William O. Douglas, 22 November 1961 (Binder no. 1, LOC Manuscripts Correspondence/Environmentalism, YVMWOD).

82. Henry M. Jackson, letter to Orville Freeman, 11 December 1961; William O. Douglas, letter to Henry M. Jackson, 3 January 1962; Frank J. Welch, letter to Henry M. Jackson, 24 January 1962; Henry M. Jackson, letter to William O. Douglas, 6 February 1962 (Binder no. 2, LOC Manuscripts Environmental articles, Supreme Court cases, YVMWOD).

83. Charles Hessey, letter to Laurence O. Barrett, 17 October 1962 (YVMCDH papers).

84. William O. Douglas, letter to David Brower, 7 September 1961 (Binder no. 1, LOC Manuscripts Correspondence/Environmentalism, YVMWOD).

85. "North Cascades Council Conservation Board Holds Meeting," *NCCC News* 1, no. 3 (October 1957): 1.

86. "Riley Again," *NCCC News* 2, no. 9 (September 1958): 3; "Wilderness Talk," 3, no. 5 (May 1959): 5.

87. W.D. Hagenstein, "To: Subscribers, Industrial Forestry Association—November 22, 1960," in *NCCC News* 5, no. 1 (January 1961): 7.

88. "In Congress," *NCCC News* 5, no. 3 (March 1961): 7; "Park Bill, Park Bill—Who's Got The Park Bill?" *Wild Cascades* 5, no. 7 (July 1961): 12; "The Forest Service In Wonderlands," 6, no. 5 (May 1962): 2; "People Who Know Wilderness Value Wilderness," September 1962: 4; "The North Cross-State Parkway," December 1962: 10; "Truth About Facts," March–April 1963: 13: J. Michael McCloskey, "North Cascades Study Team," August–September 1963: 19; Patrick D. Goldsworthy and J. Michael McCloskey, "Public Hearings on North Cascades," October–November 1963: 3–6.

89. *The Wilderness Act*, Public Law 88–577, 3 September 1964: Section 3 (d)(1)(B); Section 3 (e) [page 3].

90. Sowards, "William O. Douglas's Wilderness Politics," 37; Sowards, *Environmental Justice*, 87.

91. Cragg D. Gilbert, letter to William O. Douglas, 15 September 1961 (GFC).

92. William O. Douglas, letter to Henry M. Jackson, 1 December 1961 (Binder no. 1, LOC Manuscripts Correspondence/Environmentalism, YVMWOD). The Region 6 Regional Forester was responsible for the administration of all USFS grasslands and forests in Washington and Oregon.

93. William O. Douglas, letter to Henry M. Jackson, 3 January 1962 (Binder no. 1, LOC Manuscripts Correspondence/Environmentalism, YVMWOD).

94. Carmelita Lowry, letters to [Kay and Isabelle], 12 September 1961, and 30 September 1961 (Double K Papers, file 1–7).

95. *Wild Cascades* 5, no. 10 (October 1961): 3. By 1960, Isabelle considered Lowry a valuable ally. Isabelle Lynn, letter to William O. Douglas, 22 November 1960 (Double K Papers, file 1–42). Maps from 1961, 1962, and 1963 (Double K Papers, file 2–17).

96. Carmelita Lowry, letter to District Ranger [F.H.] Armstrong, 28 September 1958 (Double K Papers, file 1–7); "Statement of Miss Carmelita Lowry, St. Louis, Mo.," 9 May 1962, in *Wilderness Preservation System Hearings Before the Subcommittee on Public Lands of the Committee on Interior and Insular Affairs House of Representatives Eighty-Seventh Congress First Session* (Washington, D.C.: Government Printing Office, 1962): 1400; Carmelita Lowry, letter to John P. Saylor, 6 March 1966 (Double K Papers, file 1–8); Isabelle Lynn, "Carmelita Lowry January 11, 1974," *Wild Cascades*, June–July 1973 [published April 1974]: 28.

97. Entry on 30 August–2 September 1961. Lowry signed into the guest book on many other occasions including 6 September 1957; 11 October 1959; 5–15 September 1962; 29 July 1965; 22 August 1966; 28 August 1967; 9 and 25 August 1968; 27 August 1969; 3 September 1970; 24–25 April 1971; 28 August 1971; and 29 August 1973. Based solely on two letters exchanged between Justice Douglas and conservation pioneer Mardy Murie at the end of March 1966 and one letter she received two weeks later from Senator Henry M. Jackson, Margaret McKeown makes the untenable claim that Murie "played a vital role"—listing her by name along with Douglas, Lynn, and Kershaw—in establishing the Cougar Lakes Wilderness. See McKeown, *Citizen Justice*, 171–72, 174, 232 n 74, 75, 77.

98. William O. Douglas, letters to Carmelita

Lowry, 22 and 24 February 1971 (Double K Papers, file 1-1).

99. Carmelita Lowry, Double K Mountain Ranch guestbook entry, [30] August 1971.

100. Chapter 237-990 WAC, "Appendix-Determination of Geographic Names, Washington State Legislature"; Isabelle Lynn, letter to Don Campbell, Forest Supervisor Mt. Baker-Snoqualmie National Forest, 14 April 1975; George Larsen, Transportation Planner, Mt. Baker-Snoqualmie National Forest, letter to Don Campbell, Forest Supervisor, 2 April 1975; Roger R. Chamard, Assistant Director, Engineering Region 6, letter to Mt. Baker-Snoqualmie [sic], 2 April 1975 (KFC); Lynn, "Carmelita Lowry," *Wild Cascades*, June-July 1973: 28; "The Return of the Irate Birdwatcher," Fall 1984: 26. Carmelita Basin (formerly Horseshoe Camp) is located due east of Copper City and just northwest of Bismarck Peak. Its waters drain northwest into Copper Creek.

101. J. Herbert Stone, letter to Kay Kershaw and Isabelle Lynn, 27 March 1962, in *Wild Cascades* 6, no. 4 (April 1962): 13.

102. William O. Douglas, letter to Kay Kershaw, 28 April 1962 (Binder no. 1, LOC Manuscripts Correspondence/Environmentalism, YVMWOD).

103. Laurence O. Barrett, letter to Kay Kershaw, 26 September 1961 (Binder no. 1, LOC Manuscripts Correspondence/Environmentalism, YVMWOD); George Marshall and Harvey Broome, "Report of Proposed Cougar Lakes Wilderness Area," *The Wilderness Society*, 26 March 1962: 3-4; "Wilderness Protection Urged For Cougar Lakes Area In Washington," *Wild Cascades*, April 1962: 6; "The Proposed Cougar Lakes Wilderness Area," November 1962: 10.

104. William O. Douglas, letter to Henry M. Jackson, 28 February 1962 (Binder no. 1, LOC Manuscripts Correspondence/Environmentalism, YVMWOD). A collection of Pat Goldsworthy's photographs documents the road excavation and extensive logging around Copper City ca. October 1962 (NCCC records 1732-015 Box 6, file: Copper City).

105. Laurence O. Barrett, letter to Kay Kershaw, 27 June 1963; Kay Kershaw and Isabelle Lynn, letter to Henry M. Jackson, 30 June 1963; Kershaw and Lynn, letter to Barrett, 2 July 1963; Edward F. Cliff, letter to Henry M. Jackson, 22 July 1963; Kershaw and Lynn, letter to Jackson, 4 August 1963 (NCCC records, 1732-011 Box 6).

106. Orville Freeman, letter to Henry M. Jackson, 16 May 1962, in *Wild Cascades* 6, no. 7 (July 1962): 4; J. Michael McCloskey, "The Product of An Appeal: The New High Mountain Policy," 6 no. 6 (June 1962): 6-7.

107. Patrick D. Goldsworthy, letter to Henry M. Jackson, 24 July 1962, in *Wild Cascades* 6, no. 8 (August 1962): 5.

108. Lynn, "Do-It-Yourself Wilderness," 26.

109. Isabelle Lynn, "Status of Cougar Lakes Wilderness Proposal," *Wild Cascades*, May 1970: 8. Other than a brief mention of the Copper City sale in July 1961, no other reference occurs in the NCCC newsletters until Lynn's 1970 piece. See *Wild Cascades* 5, no. 7 (July 1961): 12.

110. Edward C. Crafts, recorded interview by William H. Moss, 17 November 1969 (John F. Kennedy Oral History Program): 6-7. [https://www.jfklibrary.org/sites/default/files/archives/JFKOH/Crafts%2C%20Edward%20C/JFKOH-ECC-01/JFKOH-ECC-01-TR.pdf]; "Interior Agriculture North Cascades Study Team," *Wild Cascades*, March-April 1963: 3-4, 13-14; "The New Strategy: Summer 1963," *Wild Cascades*, May-June-July 1963: 2; J. Michael McCloskey, "North Cascades Study Team," August-September 1963: 3.

111. Sowards, "William O. Douglas's Wilderness Politics," 32; Sowards, *Environmental Justice*, 2-3, 83, 85; William O. Douglas, "239: Address," National Civil Liberties Clearing House, Washington, D.C., 28 March 1963: 8; Douglas, "246: Education on the Bill of Rights," 18 June 1963: 8; and "247: Education on the Bill of Rights," New Jersey Education Association, 5 October 1963: 9 (WOD Speeches Binder #8).

112. Brock Evans, email, 22 July 2021.

113. William O. Douglas, note to Pat Goldsworthy, 25 August [1963]; Douglas, note to Goldsworthy [stamped 7 September 1963]; Douglas, note to Goldsworthy, 31 August 1963 (NCCC records, 1732-011 Box 6); Guest Book, 14 May 1954 to 31 December 1976. The title "Committee on Correspondence on the North(ern) Cascades Sept. 21-22, 1963" as well as the names of Justice William O. and Joanie Douglas appear at the top of the page in Joanie's handwriting.

114. "The New Strategy: Summer 1963," 2. The North Cascades Wilderness was a proposal for the re-designation of the North Cascades Primitive Area. This region subsequently was included in the North Cascades National Park. See Patrick D. Goldsworthy, "North Cascades Primitive Area Trip," *NCCC News* 4, no. 9 (September 1960): 8-11; "The North Cascades," map produced by North Cascades Conservation Council (San Francisco: Sierra Club, 1965) in Manning, *Wild Cascades*, insert.

115. William O. Douglas, "Introduction," *Wild Cascades Forgotten Parkland*, 15; Louter, *Windshield Wilderness*, 118, 121-23.

116. An online version of the NCCC newsletter, *Wild Cascades*, May 1970, contains a map comparing Kershaw and Lynn's original Cougar Lakes proposal (at this point subsumed by NCCC) with the 1965 reduced Mt. Aix Wilderness proposal of USFS. A dotted line indicates the previously existing boundaries of the Cougar Lakes Limited Area established in the 1940s. See [http://npshistory.com/newsletters/the-wild-cascades/may-1970.pdf]: 7.

117. The North Cascades Study Team, *The North Cascades Study Report: A Report to the Secretary of the Interior and the Secretary of Agriculture* (October 1965): "Introduction: conclusions" and "Appendix B: Position Statement by Forest Service:

III. What is multiple use," [https://www.nps.gov/parkhistory/online_books/noca/study_report/appb.htm]; J. Michael McCloskey, "The Future of the Cougar Lakes Limited Area (Washington)," *Wild Cascades*, October–November 1964: 6.

118. Owen S. Stratton, letter to Edward C. Crafts, 27 September 1965. *The North Cascades Study Report*: "Individual Views of Team Study Members." [https://www.nps.gov/parkhistory/online_books/noca/study_report/sec4.htm].

119. "At Last! The North Cascades Study Team Report," *Wild Cascades*, December–January 1965–1966: 6; Patrick D. Goldsworthy, "Reactions to Study Report," February–March 1966: 2. Stratton was in communication with Carmelita Lowry and sympathetic to the Cougar Lakes Wilderness campaign. Owen Stratton, letter to Carmelita Lowry, 22 February 1966; Carmelita Lowry to [Kay Kershaw and Isabelle Lynn], 6 March 1966 (Double K Papers, file 1–8).

120. Walt Woodward, "Cole Favors 'Multiple-Use' in North Cascades," *Seattle Times*, 15 June 1965.

121. "Forestry Official Airs Cougar Lakes Proposition," *YMH*, 15 February 1966.

122. Isabelle Lynn, [letter to the editor] *YDR*, 26 February 1966; Lynn, "Status of the Proposed Cougar Lakes Wilderness Area As Of February 1966," 26.

123. Isabelle Lynn, letter to William O. Douglas, 1 March 1966 (Double K Papers, file 1–42).

124. William O. Douglas, letter to Orville Freeman, 14 April 1966 (Binder no. 1, LOC Manuscripts Correspondence/Environmentalism, YVMWOD).

125. Orville Freeman, letter to William O. Douglas, 8 April 1966 (Binder no. 1, LOC Manuscripts Correspondence/Environmentalism, YVMWOD). In June, Freeman reiterated the urgency of resolving the North Cascades prior to tackling Cougar Lakes. Orville Freeman, letter to William O. Douglas, 16 June 1966 (Binder no. 2, LOC Manuscripts: Environmental articles, Supreme Court cases, YVMWOD collection).

126. Douglas, *Of Men and Mountains*, 279–91.

127. A.W. Greeley, letter to William O. Douglas, 21 July 1966 (Binder no. 1, LOC Manuscripts Correspondence/Environmentalism, YVMWOD); Lyon, "The Gold Hill Outdoor Club," 101–2.

128. Patrick D. Goldsworthy, "The Eye of the Storm," *Wild Cascades* (October–November 1966): 2.

129. "Outdoor Group Plans," *YDR*, 21 October 1966; "Yakiman Elected Head of Group Opposing Park," *YMH*, 23 October 1966; "Opposition to National Park gets teeth at Yakima confab," *Fishing and Hunting News*, 29 October 1966 in *Wild Cascades*, October–November 1966: 5; Goldsworthy, "Eye of the Storm"; Charles Hessey, letter to Paul Brooks, 2 November 1966 (YVMCDH papers). In 1957, Cascade Lumber Company of Yakima merged with Boise Payette Lumber Company of Boise, Idaho, to form Boise-Cascade.

130. William O. Douglas, "Draft" [no date; three pages] (Binder no. 1, LOC Manuscripts Correspondence/Environmentalism, YVMWOD); William O. Douglas, "Cougar Lakes Hearings," *Wild Cascades*, December 1967–January 1968: 21. Although this document relates to hearings held in 1966, it is possible Douglas compiled his findings to accompany Isabelle Lynn's "Bumping Boondoggle" article in the same issue.

131. Walt Woodward, "Wilderness Park in Cascades Asked," *Seattle Times*, 20 March 1967; Patrick D. Goldsworthy, "The Bases Are Loaded!" *Wild Cascades*, February–March 1967: 2.

132. The Rev. R. Riley Johnson, "Dear Friend": form letter [no date] in *Wild Cascades*, October–November 1967: 15.

133. "Quotations From S.1321 Hearings before the Subcommittee on Parks and Recreation of the Committee on Interior and Insular Affairs United States Senate Ninetieth Congress April 24 and 25, 1967, Washington, D.C.," in *Wild Cascades*, June–July 1967: 9.

134. Stephen Ponder, "Jackson sees Cascade park in three to four years; favors blocking Kennecott," *Skagit Valley Herald* [Mt. Vernon, WA], 30 May 1967.

135. Lowry, "Report on Cougar Lakes," 4.

136. Lynn, "Status of Cougar Lakes Wilderness Area Proposal," 6; Lynn, "Do-It-Yourself Wilderness," 26; Brock Evans, "The Alpine Lakes: Stepchild of the North Cascades," *Wild Cascades*, October–November 1967: 5; Evans, *Endless Pressure*, 163–64.

137. Freeman, letter to Douglas, 8 April 1966.

138. Isabelle Lynn, "For Cascadian Dam," [letter to the editor] *YSH*, 30 October 1966; Ed Stover, "Proposed Dam Would Enlarge Bumping Lake 13-Fold," *Yakima Herald*, 1 March 1966.

139. Isabelle Lynn, "Bumping Boondoggle," [no date, double-spaced typed manuscript, five pages] (KFC); *Wild Cascades*, December–January 1967–1968: 8–11; William Gough, "Bumping Lake is the issue" and "Water or wilderness—battle forces grouping," *YSH*, 14 January 1968; "Bumping Lake plan gets heavy backing," 19 January 1968. From its completion in 1951 through the mid-1970s, the Chinook Hotel was the premier downtown venue for meetings, conferences, and rooms for VIPs. The Yakima Chamber of Commerce had offices in the hotel and the Red Lion bar on the first floor was the preferred local watering hole for the well-connected.

140. Cragg [D.] Gilbert, "Escapeland," *Wild Cascades*, December–January 1967–1968: 2–5; Patrick Goldsworthy, "Congress Needs More Help To Decide North Cascades Issue," 6–7; Evans, *Endless Pressure*, 153–57; Brock Evans email, 14 June 2023. Charles Hessey kept a copy of Gilbert's speech in his papers and must have provided NCCC with a copy of his remarks. "Address to local chapter of the Society of American Foresters," [no date] (YVMCDH papers).

141. "Aspinall's Snit," *Seattle Post-Intelligencer*,

23 April 1968. Evans booked a suite of rooms at the Benjamin Franklin Hotel stocked with typewriters and paper to accommodate those he had convinced to appear before the hearings. Evans, *Endless Pressure*, 153–57.

142. Patrick Goldsworthy, "Our Troops Victorious At House Hearings," *Wild Cascades*, February–March 1968: 2. By 1970, Outdoors Unlimited had disappeared from the scene.

143. Brock Evans, email, 28 June 2021.

Chapter 8

1. Don McKeehen, "Promoting Small Outdoor Recreation Business," paper presented at the North Cascades Outdoor Recreation Conference, Sun Mountain Lodge, Winthrop, Washington, 1–2 October 1974, in *Conference Notes on the Development, Operation, and Management of Private Outdoor Enterprises* E.M. 3920, May 1975 (Cooperative Extension Service, College of Agriculture, Washington State University).

2. Ed Kershaw, interview, 1 May 2023. Several iterations of Lucky lived at the Double K over the course of three decades.

3. "Clear Air, Thrills at Dude Spots," *Spokesman-Review*, 21 May 1961.

4. Joseph Parker Sullivan, "A Description and Analysis of the Dude Ranching Industry in Montana," Master of Science Thesis (University of Montana, 1971), 17, 101; Robert G. Athearn, *The Mythic West in Twentieth-Century America* (Lawrence: University Press of Kansas, 1986), 136–40.

5. Helland, "Introduction to West: Guest Ranches Lure Visitors."

6. Jim Gosney, "'DoubleK [sic] Girls' The good life is worth the fight," *YH-R*, 5 May 1978.

7. Wazeka, "Crusade for Cougar Lakes," 28.

8. Jim Gosney, "Double K combats 'progress,'" *YH-R*, 18 September 1987.

9. Gosney, "'DoubleK Girls.'"

10. Manning entries on 17 February 1968, 24–25 April 1971, 26 October 1980. Harvey Manning (1925–2006) is best known for his book *Mountaineering: The Freedom of the Hills*, first published in 1960. He also authored a series of best-selling Pacific Northwest hiking guides published by The Mountaineers. Entries for Broome: 18 August 1961, 5–15 September 1962, 17 August 1964, 30 August to 6 September 1965, 25 August 1968, 27 August 1969, 3 September 1970, 27 August 1971, 29 August 1973; Alexander: 21 August 1981; Brower: 21–22 September 1963. Guest Book, 14 May 1954 to 31 December 1976; "Double K Mountain Ranch Guest Book," September 1977 to 16 July 1990 (KFC).

11. Charles Reich, *The Greening of America* (New York: Random House, 1970), 398-99; William O. Douglas, "337: American University 21 May 1972": 3 (WOD Speeches Binder #11, YVMWOD); Sam Roberts, "Charles Reich, Who Saw 'The Greening of America,' Dies at 91," *NYT*, 17 June 2019. Reich's guest book entries include 18 August 1956, 27 June 1961, 31 July 1964, 12–18 August 1968, 6 August 1969, 1–17 July 1970, 19 July 1972, 28 September 1975. On the shared interest in the craft of writing, see Appendix.

12. Eric Sevareid, letter to Isabelle Lynn, 11 September 1972; Burton Benjamin, letter to Kay Kershaw, 3 October 1972; Cathleen Douglas, letter to Isabelle Lynn and Kay Kershaw, 23 July 1976; Eric Sevareid, letter to Kay Kershaw and Isabelle Lynn, 13 December 1977 (KFC). Guest book entries include Sevareid, 30 June 1972; Benjamin, 30 June and 4 August 1972, 29 September 1984.

13. Gerry Weir, entry, 14 August 1972. "Guest Book," September 1977 to 16 July 1990.

14. Seth McCormick Lynn, Jr., email, 28 June 2021. Seth and his parents were visiting the week of 5 July 1965.

15. Entries on 22 June 1955 and 22 June 1957.

16. Selincourt: 16–22 August 1951; Mary Anne Smith: 13 June 1958; Koht: 15 June 1962; Myron Smith: 15 June 1962; Kazemi: 17 September 1963; Etukudo: 6–10 July 1964; Kuhlman: 14 August 1973; Kiyomiya and Kojima: 5 July 1976; Deeb: 26 June 1983.

17. Mort Cathro, "Travelin' Light in Washington State: Spinsters Run Isolated Dude Ranch," *Oakland Tribune*, 8 September 1968. Cathro visited the Double K the week of 12–18 August 1968. Charles Reich was on vacation for the week during Cathro's visit. He gets a nod in the article: "On my recent overnight stay the other guests were a young Yale professor ..." At the time, Reich's *The Greening of America* was still over a year away from publication.

18. Double K guest book entries: Koht and Gilbert, 15 June 1962; Kazemi and Douglas, 17 September 1963; Thomas P. Ferguson, Jr., Head of Global Network Outreach, Eisenhower Fellowships, interview, 27 September 2020; M. Kazemi, transcript of taped interview [no date, four pages], Eisenhower Fellowships archives; Isabelle Lynn, letter to Marty Bagby Yopp, 2 June 1976 (WOD Box 19 file #101 Misc. Letters, YVMWOD). Isabelle writes: "This [slide image] is the Justice's former interpreter, Mohammed [sic] Kazemi, with the Justice in the Hindoo." See also acknowledgment to "M. Kazemi" in William O. Douglas, *Strange Lands and Friendly People* (New York: Harper and Brothers, 1951), xv.

19. "Greetings from the two ..." Double K Christmas card, 1969 (KFC). See photo on page 115.

20. "Request for Statement of Earnings," postcard, postmarked, 23 January 1968; J.L. Fay, Director Bureau of Data Processing & Accounts, Social Security Administration Form OAR 7014a (11–65) [1937 thru Jun 1967]; William E. Hanna, Jr., Director, Bureau of Data Processing Form OAR 7014a (2–71) [1937 thru Mar 1974] (KFC).

21. Seth McCormick Lynn, letter to Isabelle Lynn, 21 November 1975 (KFC).

22. Isabelle Lynn, letter to Northern Central Bank, 25 November 1975 (KFC).

23. Isabelle Lynn, letter to Seth McCormick Lynn, 25 November 1975. Isabelle addresses her brother as Jim, and he addresses her as Sister in their correspondence. He signs as Jim, she as Isabelle. Seth McCormick Lynn, letter to Isabelle Lynn, 15 October 1975; Isabelle Lynn, letter to Seth McCormick Lynn, 20 October 1975; Seth McCormick Lynn, letter to Isabelle Lynn, 28 October 1975; Isabelle Lynn, letter to Seth McCormick Lynn, 2 November 1975; Seth McCormick Lynn, letter to Isabelle Lynn, 4 December 1975 (KFC).

24. Ed Kershaw, interview, 1 May 2023; Seth McCormick Lynn, Jr., email, 28 June 2021.

25. William O. Douglas, letter to Robert S. McNamara, 3 July 1967; Robert S. McNamara, letter to William O. Douglas, 15 July 1967 (Binder no. 2, LOC Manuscripts Environmental articles, Supreme Court cases, YVMWOD).

26. William O. Douglas, letter to Robert S. McNamara, 28 July 1967 (Binder no. 2, LOC Manuscripts Environmental articles, Supreme Court cases, YVMWOD); Urofsky, *The Douglas Letters*, 250.

27. William O. Douglas, letters to Lyndon Baines Johnson, 12 August and 7 September 1967; Urofsky, *The Douglas Letters*, 250–51; Douglas, letter to Warren G. Magnuson, 21 August 1967 (Binder no. 2, LOC Manuscripts Environmental articles, Supreme Court cases, YVMWOD).

28. Harold Brown, letter to William O. Douglas [no date, stamped 22 September 1967] (Binder no. 2, LOC Manuscripts Environmental articles, Supreme Court cases, YVMWOD).

29. William O. Douglas, letter to Henry M. Jackson, 1 February 1968 in Urofsky, *The Douglas Letters*, 251.

30. Henry M. Jackson, letter to William O. Douglas, 12 March 1968; William O. Douglas, letter to [Henry M.] "Scoop" [Jackson], 2 May 1968 (Binder no. 2, LOC Manuscripts Environmental articles, Supreme Court cases, YVMWOD).

31. Henry M. Jackson, letter to William O. Douglas, 24 May 1968; Harold Brown, letter to Henry M. Jackson, stamped 23 and 24 May 1968 (Binder no. 2, LOC Manuscripts Environmental articles, Supreme Court cases, YVMWOD).

32. Gosney, "'DoubleK Girls.'"

33. Isabelle Lynn, "Do We Let the Knuckledraggers Take Over?" [typewritten manuscript, no date ten pages]: 2 (KFC).

34. William O. Douglas, letter to David Brower, 3 October 1960; letter to Polly Dyer, 3 October 1960; letter to Henry M. Jackson, 17 October 1960; letter to Henry M. Jackson, 15 November 1960 (Binder no. 2, LOC Manuscripts Environmental articles, Supreme Court cases, YVMWOD).

35. Lynn, "Do We Let the Knuckledraggers Take Over?" 3.

36. William O. Douglas, letter to David Brower, 7 September 1961 (Binder no. 2, LOC Manuscripts Environmental articles, Supreme Court cases, YVMWOD); "Cougar Lakes Wilderness Recommendations," *The Mountaineer 1965* 58, no. 4 (15 March 1965): 67; William O. Douglas, "269: The Campfire Club of America, New York, NY, 21 January 1965": 3 (WOD Speeches Binder #9 nos. 265–301 10/9/64–5/28/67, YVMWOD).

37. Lynn, "Do We Let the Knuckledraggers Take Over?" 3; "Irate and His Friends," *Wild Cascades* (October–November 1965): 12–13; Gilbert, "Escapeland," 5; "Trail Bike Trips in Wenatchee National Forest," *Wild Cascades* (October–November 1969): 6; "Irate and His Friends," *Wild Cascades* (May 1970): 9–11.

38. William O. Douglas, letter to Isabelle Lynn, 29 November 1971 (KFC).

39. Isabelle Lynn, letter to Don R. Campbell, 13 January 1972 (KFC).

40. John A Biggs, letter to Kay Kershaw, 25 February 1972 (KFC). A black and white photograph inscribed by Kay Kershaw: "Jan. 1974 At the front door of Double K—4 snomos trespassing by no tresp. signs- [sic]." The image shows Isabelle in a defensive stance confronting a group of snowmobilers. Photo album "Kay Kershaw and Isabelle Lynn at the Double K 1961-1984)" [86 black and white and color photographs with handwritten comments] (KFC). Kay and Isabelle continued to push for snowmobile regulations right up until their final years at Goose Prairie. Isabelle Lynn, letter to Mike Hiler, 4 January 1987 (Mike Hiler, personal correspondence file).

41. Isabelle Lynn, "Dammed If You Do," *National Parks & Conservation Magazine* 46, no. 1 (January 1972): 14–20; "Do-It-Yourself Wilderness," 23–27; Jan Schaeffer, letter to Isabelle Lynn, 28 February 1972; Isabelle Lynn, letter to Jan Schaeffer [no date, attached to Schaeffer's 28 February letter]; Isabelle Lynn, letter to Jack Kessie, 5 May 1972 (KFC).

42. Isabelle Lynn, letter to Council on Environmental Quality, 11 March 1972; letter to William D. Ruckleshaus, 11 March 1972 (KFC).

43. Hilda S. Brooks, letter to Isabelle Lynn, 31 March 1972 (KFC).

44. Isabelle Lynn, letter to Jan [Schaeffer], 30 March 1972 (KFC).

45. Lynn, "Do We Let the Knuckledraggers Take Over?" 1–2. *A Clockwork Orange* is a 1971 film by Stanley Kubrick featuring a cast of disturbing, anti-social thugs bent on an ultra-violent crime spree.

46. Lynn, "Do We Let the Knuckledraggers Take Over?" 9.

47. Isabelle Lynn, letter to Jack Kessie, 5 May 1972 (KFC).

48. "Tape #28: 6 September 1972. Eric Sevareid interviews William O. Douglas," 21:45–22:00. William O. Douglas's *Playboy* articles include "The Attack on the Right to Privacy," December 1967; "Civil Liberties: The Crucial Issue," January 1969; "The Public Be Dammed," July 1969; "An Inquest on Our Lakes and Rivers," June 1968; "Points of Rebellion," January 1970. Douglas also had another article prepared for *Playboy* that went unpublished: "A Task Force for Ecology," [manuscript, 45 pages] (Binder no. 1, LOC Manuscripts Correspondence/Environmentalism, YVMWOD).

49. William O. Douglas, letter to Isabelle Lynn, 28 April 1972 (KFC).

50. Eleanor Dienstag, "Looking for An Agent? Watch Out!" *NYT* 9 February 1969; Lawrence Van Gelder, "Candida Denadio, 71, Handled 'Catch-22' Dies," *NYT* 25 January 2001.

51. William O. Douglas, letter to Isabelle Lynn, 3 May 1972 (KFC).

52. Judy Sisson, letter to Isabelle Lynn, 9 May 1972; Isabelle Lynn, letter to Judy Sisson, 12 May 1972 (KFC).

53. Hy Cohen, letter to Isabelle Lynn, 14 June 1972 (KFC).

54. Hy Cohen, letter to Isabelle Lynn, 28 June 1972; Isabelle Lynn, "Large and Small Bores in the National Lands," typed manuscript, no date, nine pages (KFC). Isabelle had submitted this article (or one similar to it) to another magazine in late 1971, but it had been rejected: "I can't understand why Tony's magazine won't touch a gun article," Douglas writes. "Go ahead and write your gun piece. You, by the way, should be selling these pieces, not giving them away." William O. Douglas, letter to Isabelle Lynn, 14 December 1971 (KFC).

55. Hy Cohen, letter to Isabelle Lynn, 30 September 1972 (KFC).

56. Cohen, letter to Lynn, 14 June 1972; Isabelle Lynn, letter to Hy Cohen, 21 June 1972 (KFC).

Chapter 9

1. Henry M. Jackson, letter to William O. Douglas, 15 December 1971 (Binder no. 1, LOC Manuscripts Correspondence/Environmentalism, YVMWOD); "Alpine Wilderness Hearings Still Two Years Away," *Seattle Times*, 28 October 1971; "Area for Recreation: Jackson Bill designates 265,000 acres," *Seattle Post-Intelligencer*, 11 December 1971; Patrick D. Goldsworthy, letter to Congressman Thomas M. Pelly, 7 October 1972, in *Wild Cascades* (December 1972–January 1973): 11–12.

2. "A Cougar Lakes Bill Now In Congress," *Wild Cascades* (October–November 1971): 20.

3. Perhaps reflecting on his own close encounter with a Presidential nomination, Douglas wrote to Isabelle in 1976: "I ran into some of Scoop's friends, and they think it is quite a letdown to run for the Presidency and then for the Senate." William O. Douglas, letter to Isabelle Lynn, 28 July 1976 (KFC).

4. William O. Douglas, letter to Henry M. Jackson, 25 February 1971 (Binder no. 2, LOC Manuscripts Environmental articles, Supreme Court cases, YVMWOD); Douglas, letter to Carmelita Lowry, 24 February 1971.

5. Charles F. Wilkerson and H. Michael Anderson, "Land and Resource Planning in the National Forests," *Oregon Law Review* 64, nos. 1 and 2 (1985): 33 [https://scholar.law.colorado.edu/articles/1038].

6. Don R. Campbell, letter to William O. Douglas, 15 August 1972 (Binder no. 2, LOC Manuscripts Environmental articles, Supreme Court cases, YVMWOD); Wilkerson and Anderson, "Land and Resource Planning," 33 *n* 149.

7. Isabelle Lynn, letter to William O. Douglas, 19 February 1971 (Binder no. 2, LOC Manuscripts: Environmental articles, Supreme Court cases, YVMWOD).

8. William O. Douglas, letter to Isabelle Lynn, 15 January 1972 (Binder no. 2, LOC Manuscripts Environmental articles, Supreme Court cases, YVMWOD).

9. William O. Douglas, letter to Isabelle Lynn, 15 May 1971; Nan Burgess, typed note to Isabelle Lynn [no date, attached to Douglas's letter 15 May 1971] (KFC).

10. William O. Douglas, letter to Isabelle Lynn, 12 May 1971 (KFC).

11. Simon, *Independent Journey*, 446–48; "Douglas steps down;—pain is too much," *YH-R*, 13 November 1975; Mike Murphey, "Reflecting on a prairie home," 7 October 1979; Funk, "Douglas loved Goose Prairie."

12. "NCCC minutes—Board of Directors Meeting," 3 June 1972; "NCCC minutes—Board of Directors Meeting," 4 November 1972 (NCCC Records, 1732-001 Box 1 file "Correspondence, 1972–1973, Hessey, Charles").

13. Betty Lagergren, "An Announcement of the Formation of The Cougar Lakes Wilderness Alliance," *Wild Cascades* (October–November 1972): 13; Isabelle Lynn, "Review/Preview The Cougar Lakes," *Wild Cascades* (Spring 1977): 27–28. Lagergren misspells Representative Saylor's name as "Snyder." John P. Saylor appears on the letterhead of the CLWA. See YVMCDH papers, folder: Identity Correspondence; "Cougar Lakes Wilderness," [pamphlet of Cougar Lakes Wilderness Alliance, no date] (YVM archives, Cascadians Box 14).

14. These included the Seattle, Tacoma, Everett, and Olympia chapters of the Mountaineers; the Intermountain Alpine Club of Richland, Washington; the Seattle, Tacoma, and Yakima chapters of the Audubon Society; the FWOC, the Sierra Club; the Wilderness Society; and the Friends of the Earth.

15. Isabelle Lynn, letter to Harvey Manning, 8 December 1970 (NCCC records, 1732-015 Box 2); Harvey Manning, letter to Isabelle Lynn, 12 December 1970 (Double K Papers, file 1–11); Lynn, letter to Douglas, 19 February 1971.

16. Mike Galvin, Washington Environmental Council, letter to Isabelle Lynn, President CLWA, 20 November 1975 (YVM archives, Cascadians Box 10); Jennifer Sprague, "Making Waves: A Classic Boondoggle," *Pacific Search* (July–August 1977): 18.

17. Lynn, "Review/preview," 28; Galvin, letter to Lynn, 20 November 1975; "Wilderness backers preparing campaign," *YH-R*, 9 November 1975; Joe Walicki, letter to Brock Evans, 29 May 1976 (Brock Evans Papers).

18. Carmelita Lowry, letter to [Kay Kershaw and Isabelle Lynn], 10 December [1971?]: [page

4, handwritten]. Also: "Don't fret about Chuck Hessey. What can you expect of a man who eschews booze?" Lowry, letter to [Kay Kershaw and Isabelle Lynn], 15 January 1971 (Double K Papers, file 1–8).

19. "North Cascades Conservation Council Board of Directors Meeting May 5, 1973," *Wild Cascades* (April–May 1973): 9–10; "Long Live The Old! Bring On The New!" *Wild Cascades* (Spring 1977): 5; NCCC, letter to Charles and Marion Hessey with handwritten note from Patrick Goldsworthy, 20 November 1984 (YVMCDH papers); "Memo to Board of Directors: Nomination and Election of Board Members (Term 1972–1975)" [no date]; Patrick Goldsworthy, assorted handwritten comments on letters cc'd to Hessey: 27 April 1972; 5 May 1973; 1 October 1973; 17 July 1974 (NCCC records 1732-001 Box 1 in file "Correspondence, 1972–1973 Hessey, Charles"). Hessey's draft letters on CLWA stationary include: partial letter to "Bruce Ritter, Covenant House New York, NY" [no date]; partial letter to "Brother Clyde" [no date]; partial letter to "Dear Mr. Reed" [no date]; partial letter to "Fr. [Father] Stewart" with typed valediction "Your Israelite brother, in Christ" [no date]; partial letter to "David Webber" [no date: ca. 1977]. The earliest date is on Hessey, letter to Garner Ted Armstrong, 23 May 1975 (YVMCDH papers).

20. James Morton Turner, *The Promise of Wilderness: American Environmental Politics Since 1964* (Seattle: University of Washington Press, 2012), 112–15.

21. Brock Evans, "Environmental Campaigner: From the Northwest Forests to the Halls of Congress," oral history conducted by Ann Lage in *Building the Sierra Club's National Lobbying Program 1967–1981* (Berkeley: Regional Oral History Office, Bancroft Library University of California, 1985), 281–86; Dennis M. Roth, *The Wilderness Movement and the National Forests: 1964–1980* (Washington, D.C.: U.S. Department of Agriculture, Forest Service, 1984), 55–59; Robert D. Baker, Larry Burt, and Robert S. Maxwell, et al., *The National Forests of the Northern Region—Living Legacy November 1993* (College Station: Intaglio, 1993): 269–70; Williams, *The USDA Forest Service—The First Century*, 121; Doug Scott, "RARE II Roadless Area Review and Evaluation Program: 1977," *Wild Cascades* (Summer 1977): 25–30; Patrick Goldsworthy, "One Last Big Push for the Cougar Lakes, Washington's Next Wilderness," *The Wild Cascades* (Fall 1977): 17, 20; "Rare-II: A Citizen's Handbook for the National Forest Roadless Area Review and Evaluation Program: 1977–1978," Winter 1978: 16–22; Joel Connelly, "Forest Service in Middle of Timber Industry, Ecology Fight," *Seattle Post-Intelligencer*, 12 February 1978; M. Rupert Cutler, email, 30 June 2021.

22. "RARE-II: A Citizen's Handbook," 16; Turner, *The Promise of Wilderness*, 186–91.

23. Goldsworthy, "One Last Big Push," 14, 20; "Naches-Tieton-White River Land Use Study," Snoqualmie and Gifford-Pinchot National Forest, 1974 (YVM archives, Cascadians Box 11); Buscher and Hart, *Bush Forester for Wilderness*, 107.

24. Jeff Weathersby, "The Making of a Wilderness," *YH-R*, 18 February 1979.

25. Evans, "Environmental Campaigner," 69, 101; Goldsworthy, "One Last Big Push," 14. See maps in Wazeka, "Crusade for Cougar Lakes," 27, and "Cougar Lakes Wilderness Proposal of Conservation Coalition January 1978," *The Wild Cascades* (Fall 1977): 18–19.

26. William O. Douglas, letter to Isabelle Lynn, 12 May 1971 (KFC). Carmelita Lowry, letter to Brock Evans, 16 January 1971; Evans, letter to Lowry, 21 January 1971; Lowry, letter to [Kay Kershaw and Isabelle Lynn], 29 January 1971 (Double K Papers, file 1–8); Brock Evans, letter to David Osterholt, 30 May 1973 (Brock Evans Papers).

27. "Cougar Lakes Wilderness Hearings Yakima: February 4 Tacoma: February 11 [flyer insert, five pages]," in *Wild Cascades* (Fall 1977); Brock Evans, interview, 14 December 2020.

28. Rob Tucker, "4-Wheel Drive Group Opposes Proposal for Cougar Lakes, Vows Court Fight," *YH-R*, 30 December 1977.

29. Fred Fishback, "Wilderness: Lumber firm opposes Forest Service proposal for Bumping Lake region," *YH-R*, 17 November 1977; "Cougar Lakes Wilderness Area Compromise to be Sought," 20 December 1977; Ken Wilcox, "Cougar Lakes Doubts Aired," 3 January 1978.

30. Joseph Turner, "Cougar Lakes Committee Wants Wilderness Shelved," *YH-R*, 24 January 1978.

31. "Cougar Lakes Hearings: Yakima Phase," *Wild Cascades* (Winter 1978): 24.

32. Joseph Turner, "Cougar Lakes: Majority At Hearing Want to Double The Size of Proposed Wilderness Area," *YH-R*, 5 February 1978; Turner, "Wilderness Backed: Ex-Supreme Court Justice William Douglas Supports Forest Service's Cougar Lakes Plan," 9 March 1978.

33. "Cougar Lakes Hearings: Tacoma Phase," 25–26; Joel Connelly, "Bigger Wilderness Backed in Hearing," *Seattle Post-Intelligencer*, 12 February 1978. Mike Ruby was very active in the Sierra Club and a personal friend of Brock Evans, director of the organization's Washington, D.C., office at the time of the Tacoma Cougar Lakes hearing. Evans, "Environmental Campaigner," 56. Evidently, Ruby came up with this suggestion on his own. Brock Evans, email, 11 August 2021.

34. K.K. [Kay Kershaw], "Dixy's Version of Cougar Lakes," *Wild Cascades* (Winter 1978): 28. See page 130.

35. Joel Connelly, "The Battle For National Forests ... And Jobs," *Seattle Post-Intelligencer*, 13 February 1978; Hirt, *Conspiracy of Optimism*, 263–65.

36. Joel Connelly, "Washington State's Battle Over Timber," *The Living Wilderness* 42, no. 143 (October/December 1978): 4–6.

37. Joel Connelly, "Wilderness? A Tale of Two Forests," *Seattle Post-Intelligencer*, 14 February 1978.

38. "N3C Annual Board Meeting," *Wild Cascades* (Spring 1978): 11.

39. Mike Murphey, "Cougar Lakes Wilderness: Only one of 10 options listed would preserve it," *YH-R*, 16 June 1978; Murphey, "Wilderness: Roadless area views vary at open house," 15 July 1978.

40. Jeff Weathersby, "The Making of a Wilderness," *YH-R*, 18 February 1979.

41. Mike Murphey, "RARE II: Study trims Cougar Lakes wilderness plan," *YH-R*, 4 January 1979.

42. Mike Murphey, "Wilderness area: Wood products industry can 'live with' smaller proposal, but Cougar Lakes backers vow fight," *YH-R*, 5 January 1979.

43. Weathersby, "Making of a Wilderness."

44. C. Peter Sorenson, email, 9 December 2020. Sorenson served as an assistant to Cutler during his tenure as Assistant Secretary of Agriculture; Brock Evans, email, 12 December 2020; Evans, interview, 14 December 2020; Evans, "Environmental Campaigner," 270–73.

45. Paul O. Wilson, "Cougar Lakes: Park Service recommends more wilderness" and map, *YH-R*, 8 April 1979.

46. M. Rupert Cutler, interview and email, 7 December 2020. On Cutler and Worthington, see Evans, "Environmental Campaigner," 283–84.

47. Isabelle Lynn, letter to Henry M. Jackson, 22 January 1979; Brock Evans, letter to Isabelle Lynn, 5 June 1979 (YVM archives, Cascadians Box 10); Murphey, "Wilderness Area: Wood products"; Kristine Rodine, "Wilderness: Commissioners oppose an increase in area," *YH-R*, 9 September 1978; Weathersby, "Making of a Wilderness"; Murphey, "RARE II: Study trims."

48. Jeff Weathersby, "Wilderness: Park Service reportedly would leave more in Cougar Lakes than Forest Service wants," *YH-R*, 6 April 1979; Wilson, "Cougar Lakes."

49. Jeff Weathersby, "Cougar Lakes request: Carter wants 5 times more wilderness," *YH-R*, 16 April 1979; "Cougar Lakes plan: Seattle congressmen prevailed on wilderness," 17 April 1979.

50. Joel Pritchard, packet to Philip E. Johnson containing Cougar Lakes Wilderness Act HR 4528 (19 June 1979) with maps (YVM archives, Cascadians Box 11).

51. Jeff Weathersby, "Wilderness: 270,000 acres pushed in Cougar Lakes bill," *YH-R*, 21 June 1979.

52. Myron Strick, "A House divided: Split likely to delay Cougar Lakes Wilderness action," *YH-R*, 5 July 1980; Sen. Warren G. Magnuson, letter to Cragg D. Gilbert, 13 March 1980 (GFC).

53. Lyn Watts "Wilderness: Multi-use section may draw lawsuit," *YH-R*, 15 July 1980; Joel Pritchard and Mike Lowry, letter to Donald H. Smith, Forest Supervisor Wenatchee National Forest, 12 November 1980 (YVM archives, Cascadians Box 10).

54. Isabelle Lynn, letter to Denny Miller, 10 January 1981 (YVM archives, Cascadians Box 10).

55. Nick Provenza, "Deadline for deciding Cougar Lakes' fate endorsed," *YH-R*, 23 April 1981.

56. Mike Lowry, letter to Phil Johnson, 10 March 1981; Mike Lowry, letter to Douglas Peters, 27 July 1981; Henry M. Jackson, letter to Douglas Peters, 6 August 1981; Eric Pryne, "Lowry sold on protecting wilderness area," *Seattle Times*, 31 August 1981 (YVM archives, Cascadians Box 10).

57. Gary E. Nelson, "Morrison ready to tackle new term," *YH-R*, 30 December 1984; "Morrison offers real gubernatorial material," 24 October 1991; Lynn, letter to Miller, 10 January 1981.

58. Lynn, letter to Miller, 10 January 1981; Isabelle Lynn, letter to Jim Blomquist, 13 October 1981; Jim Blomquist, letter to Isabelle Lynn, 15 October 1981 (YVM archives, Cascadians Box 10).

59. David Lester, "White Pass, Cougar Lakes in wilderness debate," *YH-R*, 17 February 1984.

60. Sid Morrison, email, 22 December 2020.

61. "Administration would open Cougar Lakes Area not in wilderness proposal," *YH-R*, 8 May 1981; Thomas Korosec, "Testimony offered in wilderness bills," 9 May 1981; "Cougar Lakes plan renews controversy," 10 May 1981.

62. "Cougar Lakes logging: Forest Service making plans for timber sales," *YH-R*, 5 February 1982; Steve Woodruff, "Logging plans in proposed wilderness area may spur Congress," 6 February 1982.

63. Dave Lester, "Cougar Lakes Wilderness: Timber sale plan fuels 20-year-old debate," *YH-R*, 23 May 1982; "Congressional action stalled: Delays are stifling hopes for Cougar Lakes Wilderness Area," 23 May 1982.

64. See Frank, "Skiing on the East Slope of Washington State's Cascade Range, Part 2."

65. Cragg D. Gilbert, Charles Rankin, and Frank Ditter represented White Pass Corporation shareholders at the 1957 meeting. S.B. Olsen, USFS file report, 7 November 1957; Charles D. Hessey, letter to Lawrence [sic] O. Barrett, 31 August and 26 September 1960; L.O. Barrett, Snoqualmie National Forest Advisory Council Meeting report, 13 October 1960; C.G. Jorgensen, letter to Laurence O. Barrett, 24 May 1961 (KFC).

66. Lyn Watt, "Support predicted for a compromise on Cougar Lakes," *YH-R*, 4 July 1981; Gordy Holt, "Boundary shifts in wilderness area considered," *YH-R*, 1 February 1983; "Expansion of ski area pushed by Rep. Morrison," *YH-R*, 30 January 1983; Phil Baechler, "Plan to expand White Pass pits skiers vs. Sierra Club," 24 February 1983; "Wilderness bill," [editorial], *Seattle Post-Intelligencer*, 13 February 1984.

67. Isabelle Lynn, letter to Andy Weisner, 20 January 1984 (YVM archives, Cascadians Box 10); Kay Kershaw and Isabelle Lynn, letter to Slade Gorton and Henry M. Jackson, 16 May 1983, in *Washington State Wilderness Act of 1983: Hearings Before the Subcommittee on Public Lands and Reserved Water of the Committee on Energy and Natural Resources United States Senate Ninety-Eighth Congress First Session on S 837 Bill to Designate Certain National Forest System Lands in the State of Washington for Inclusion in the National Wilderness Preservation System, and for Other Purposes Part 2 Appendix* (Washington, D.C.: Government Printing Office, 1984), 2017. Slade Gorton

(1928–2020), a Republican, served in the Senate from 1981 to 1987 and 1989 to 2001.

68. Isabelle Lynn, letter to Bob Kershaw, 5 January [1984; handwritten]; Phillip E. Johnson [President, CLWA], letter to Sid Morrison, 11 January 1984; Cragg D. Gilbert and Bob Kershaw, letter to Sid Morrison, 17 January 1984; Kay Kershaw and Isabelle Lynn, letter to John F. Seiberling, 18 January 1984; Isabelle Lynn, letter to Slade Gorton, 2 February 1984; Lynn, letter to Jean Durning [The Wilderness Society], 1 February 1984; Charles D. Hessey, letter to Cragg D. Gilbert, 7 February 1984; Kay Kershaw and Isabelle Lynn, letter to Bob Kershaw, 24 February [1984; handwritten]; John Bloxom, letter to Thomas Foley, 16 February 1984; Thomas Foley, letter to John Bloxom, 17 February 1984; Marvin Sundquist, letter to Sid Morrison, 10 March 1984 (KFC).

69. Kay Kershaw and Isabelle Lynn, letter to John F. Seiberling, 18 January 1984 (YVM archives, Cascadians Box 10).

70. In the early 1980s, fifty-one affiliated groups organized under an umbrella consortium—the Goat Rocks Emergency Committee—to oppose any deletion from the Goat Rocks Wilderness Area. See Susan Saul, [co-chair, Goat Rocks Emergency Committee], letter to Charles Flower, 15 September 1983 [letterhead] (KFC).

71. David Lester, "White Pass, Cougar Lakes in wilderness debate," *YH-R*, 17 February 1984. Some thirty-six years later, Morrison stated: "I don't remember all the give and take of the wilderness debate in Congress. I am guessing that I introduced the 2,400 acre [sic] expansion to get something on the table because it had to start somewhere, knowing that it would be enthusiastically opposed by conservation groups." Morrison, email, 22 December 2020.

72. David Lester, "A compromise, finally," *YH-R*, 8 March 1984.

73. For the Henry M. Jackson Wilderness, see description and map in *The Wild Cascades* (Fall 1984): 12–13, 20–21.

Chapter 10

1. Charlotte Mayerson, letter to Isabelle Lynn and Kay Kershaw, 31 January 1980 (KFC).

2. "Justice Douglas Dies," *YH-R*, 20 January 1980; Doris Grunebaum, letter to Kay Kershaw and Isabelle Lynn, 22 January 1980 (KFC).

3. William O. Douglas, letter to Kay Kershaw and Isabelle Lynn, 12 May 1970 in Urofsky, *The Douglas Letters* 403–4.

4. Murphy, *Wild Bill*, 420–22; Robert Roth, "The Years of Douglas," *The Sunday Bulletin* (Washington, D.C.), 28 October 1973; "Impeach move made twice," *YH-R*, 13 November 1975; "Justice Douglas dies," 20 January 1980; William O. Douglas, letter to Jim DeWitt Bowmer, 25 May 1970 in Urofsky, *The Douglas Letters*, 405–6; "Recording #25: 16 April 1970 TV commentary from three networks [ABC, CBS, NBC] on impeachment," 3¾-inch tape 15 minutes; "Recording #26: 16 December 1970 TV comments: reaction to House Select Committee's finding of innocence of William O. Douglas," 3¾-inch tape, ten minutes (WOD Box 32-4 Tapes and Recordings, YVMWOD). Douglas had been the subject of two earlier impeachment resolutions: in 1953, over his temporary stay of execution for convicted atomic spies Julius and Ethel Rosenberg; and in 1966, questioning his moral standards after his fourth marriage to Cathleen Heffernan, then a twenty-three-year-old college student who was forty-four years his junior.

5. Charles Reich, letter to Isabelle Lynn, 8 August 1975 (KFC).

6. Rob Tucker, "Douglas Brings Court to Valley," *YH-R*, 12 December 1975; Don Duncan, "Justice Douglas dies at 81; A mix of Solomon, Huck Finn," *Seattle Times*, 20 January 1980; Murphy, *Wild Bill*, 490–91; Simon, *Independent Journey*, 450–51.

7. Charles Reich, 28 September 1975 in "Guest Book, 14 May 1954 to 31 December 1976"; Murphy, *Wild Bill*, 491–93; Simon, *Independent Journey*, 450–51.

8. William O. Douglas, letter to Isabelle Lynn, 14 November 1975 (KFC).

9. Charlotte Mayerson, letter to Isabelle Lynn and Kay Kershaw, 18 November 1975 (KFC). A decade later, Isabelle Lynn referred to Cathy Douglas as "mindless Cathy." Isabelle Lynn, letter to Carolyn and Betty Langergren, 20 October 1989 (YVM archives, Document Box 222).

10. "Douglas to Stay a Month in Stroke Unit," *NYT*, 18 November 1975.

11. William O. Douglas, letter to Isabelle Lynn, 16 December 1975 (KFC).

12. William O. Douglas, letter to Isabelle Lynn, 1 October 1975 (KFC).

13. Marty Bagby Yopp, letters to Isabelle Lynn, 16 March and 7 July 1976 (KFC).

14. William O. Douglas, letter to Isabelle Lynn, 28 July 1976 (KFC).

15. William O. Douglas, letter to Isabelle Lynn, 9 August 1976 (KFC).

16. Douglas, letter to Lynn, 28 July 1976.

17. Marty Bagby Yopp, letter to Isabelle Lynn, 12 August 1976 (KFC).

18. William O. Douglas, letter to Kay Kershaw, 29 November 1977 (KFC).

19. Mike Murphey, "Reflecting on a prairie home," *YH-R*, 7 October 1979.

20. Mike Murphey, "Yakima friends remember 'a man you could count on,'" *YH-R*, 20 January 1980.

21. Funk, "Douglas loved Goose Prairie."

22. Kay Kershaw and Isabelle Lynn, letter to Robert F. Utter, 24 January 1980 (KFC).

23. Ron Graham, "Cougar Lakes show best of Douglas Wilderness: Compromise key to bill's success," *YH-R*, 4 October 1984.

24. Ron Graham, "Preservation champion: William O. Douglas fought to preserve Cougar

Lakes area," *YH-R*, 30 September 1984. Retired USFS Ranger Richard Buscher makes the incredible claim that it was his idea—expressed to Morrison—to name the Cougar Lakes Wilderness for Justice Douglas. Buscher and Hart, *Bush Forester for Wilderness*, 111.

25. Cougar Lakes Hearings: Tacoma Phase" *Wild Cascades* (Winter 1978): 26.

26. Isabelle Lynn, letter to Don [?], 20 January 1980 (KFC). "Baldy" refers to Baldy Peak, a high point on Nelson Ridge halfway between Nelson Peaks and Buffalo Hump, four miles southeast of Goose Prairie and five miles north of Mt. Aix. See map "Cascade Mountains, Washington" on front endpapers of *Of Men and Mountains*. Douglas mentions Baldy along with Old Scab Mountain and Buffalo Hump as peaks he could see looking south from Prairie House. Douglas, *Go East*, 240.

27. Isabelle Lynn, letter to Betty Fletcher, 24 January 1980 (KFC). See also William O. Douglas, "338: Seattle-King County Bar Association, Seattle, Washington 27 June 1972" (WOD Speeches Binder #11, YVMWOD). Betty Binns Fletcher (1923–2012) was a prominent attorney in Washington State prior to her appointment to the Ninth Circuit. She was a friend and admirer of William O. Douglas. See Walt Lowe, "William O. Douglas: A Life On the High Court," third draft [script for television documentary on KYVE-TV, 563 pages], 15 August 1988: 22; "Fletcher Tape 72," [KYVE-TV documentary raw footage for William O. Douglas: A Life On the High Court] (YVM archives).

28. Philip E. Johnson, letter to Cathleen C. [sic] Douglas, 28 January 1980 (YVM archives, Cascadians Box 10).

29. June [Remillard?], letter to Isabelle Lynn, 1 February 1980 (KFC).

30. Monty J. Podva, letter to Isabelle Lynn, 15 February 1980 (KFC).

31. Monty J. Podva, letter to Jimmy Carter, 6 February 1980 (KFC).

32. Monty J. Podva, letter to Isabelle Lynn and Kay Kershaw, 14 February 1980 (KFC).

33. Douglas W. Scott and Brock Evans, "Fitting Memorial," *Washington Post*, 2 February 1980; Evans, *Endless Pressure*, 189–203, 313–15.

34. Isabelle Lynn, letter to Brock Evans, 20 February 1980 (KFC).

35. Isabelle Lynn, letter to James G. Deane, 20 February 1980 (KFC).

36. Isabelle Lynn, letter to Bob Kershaw, 7 March [1984] (KFC).

37. Ron Graham, "Officials to dedicate William O. Douglas Wilderness Area," *YH-R*, 27 September 1984; "Wilderness Area: Bumping Lake ceremony pays tribute to Douglas," 30 September 1984; "The New William O. Douglas Wilderness," *Outdoors West* [FWOC newsletter] 7, no. 2 (Winter 1984): 12; sixteen color photographs on two album sheets [29 September 1984] (KFC).

38. Double K Mountain Ranch Guest Register, "Dedication of the William O. Douglas Wilderness Sept. 29, 1984" [three pages]; three loose photo album pages with twenty-three photographs of the William O. Douglas Wilderness dedication ceremony (KFC).

39. Kay Kershaw and Isabelle Lynn, "William O. Douglas Wilderness," *Wild Cascades* (Fall 1985–Spring 1987): 14.

40. Various Double K Mountain Ranch Christmas cards, dated 1956–59; 1961–62; 1964; 1968–70; 1972–73; 1981; 1984–85; [nine undated]; two Christmas cards, Kay and Isabelle 1993 and [one undated ca. 1990]; Kay Kershaw Christmas card [undated ca. 1944] (KFC).

41. William O. Douglas, letter to Kay Kershaw, 28 March 1974 (KFC). Chester "Chet" Huntley (1911–1974) was a newscaster for NBC Television from 1956 to 1970. His Big Sky project envisioned a 5,800-acre ski area southeast of Bozeman, Montana. Ray Ring, "Big Sky, big mess in Montana," *High Country News*, 31 March 1997.

42. Brad Patterson, interview, 9 August 2020. The Double K Drifter or Driftpan was the signature drink concocted by Kay and Isabelle: a vodka martini with bitters kept in the freezer. Tim Franklin, interview, 17 September 2020.

43. "Draft White Paper: National Forest William O. Douglas Wilderness Institute, Naches Ranger District, January 24, 1989," [eleven pages]; Kristin Jackson, "Rooted in the Prairie," *Seattle Times*, 9 July 1989; "Non-profit group to buy Douglas retreat," *YH-R*, 12 August 1989.

44. Mike Hoge, email, 25 January 2021. Hoge is the current owner of Prairie House.

45. "Draft Environmental Statement: Proposed Bumping Lake Enlargement Supplemental Storage Division Yakima Project, Washington," Regional Office, Pacific Northwest Division Bureau of Reclamation Boise, Idaho (10 February 1977), 126 pages with appendices; Rob Tucker, "Bumping enlargement plan opposed," *YH-R*, 10 April 1977; Tucker, "Bumping Valley disaster feared," 19 April 1977; Isabelle Lynn, letter to *YH-R*, 1 July 1977; Lynn, letter to Water Resources Council, 9 August 1977 (KFC).

46. "Enhancement plan will favor wildlife," [editorial] *YH-R*, 13 December 1985; Isabelle Lynn, "Bumping Lake," [letter to the editor], 18 December 1985.

47. "Statement of Loren Strain, Citizens for Responsible Water Projects, Inc.," and "Written Statement: Citizens for Responsible Water Projects, Incorporated," in *Umatilla Basin Project and the Yakima River Basin Water Enhancement Project Hearing before the Subcommittee on Water and Power of the Committee on Energy and Natural Resources One Hundredth Congress United States Senate Second Session on S1613 [...] and S2322 [...] June 28, 1988* (Washington, D.C.: United States Government Printing Office, 1989), 150–55: "Yakima River Basin Storage Study: Wymer Dam and Reservoir Appraisal Report," Technical Series No. TS-YSS-16, United States Department of the Interior Bureau of Reclamation Pacific Northwest Region September 2007, 2; "Yakima

River Basin Study: Bumping Lake Enlargement Planning Design Summary Update United States Bureau of Reclamation Contract No. 08CA10677A ID/IQ, Task 48," United States Department of the Interior Bureau of Reclamation Pacific Northwest Region Columbia-Cascades Area Office March 2011, 1–3; Melissa Hansen, "Integrated Water Plan Moves Forward," *The Good Fruit Grower*, 1 April 2014 [https://www.goodfruit.com/integrated-water-plan-moves-forward/].

48. "Local water conservation efforts face another test," *YH-R*, 21 June 2023; Charlie de La Chapelle, interview, 28 March 2023; de La Chapelle, email, 29 March 2023; and De La Chapelle, letter to Talmadge L. Oxford, 16 June 2022 [attached].

49. "Douglas Wilderness a fitting memorial," *YH-R*, 8 March 1984.

50. "Testimony of Rep. Mike Lowry on S. 837, the Washington Wilderness Act, June 7, 1984," in *Additions to the National Wilderness Preservation System Hearings Before the Subcommittee on Public Lands and National Parks of the Committee on Interior and Insular Affairs House of Representatives Ninety-Eighth Congress Second Session Serial No.98-3 Part XI* (Washington, D.C.: U.S. Government Printing Office, 1985), 527.

51. Patrick D. Goldsworthy, "One More Milestone Along the Wilderness Road: The Washington State Wilderness Act of 1984," *Wild Cascades* (Fall 1984): 20.

52. See Map 8.

53. Craig Troianello, "Ski area expansion debate a bit rocky," *YH-R*, 10 November 1988.

54. Kevin McCarthy, email, 16 January 2021.

55. Craig Troianello, "Hogback Basin: controversy ensnarls peaceful mountain area," *YH-R*, 9 April 1989; Philip E. Johnson, letters to Sid Morrison, 3 February and 27 March 1989 (YVM archives, Cascadians Box 10).

56. David Lester, "A bigger White Pass? Forest Service gives preliminary OK to expansion," *YH-R*, 28 June 1989.

57. Ron Graham, "Crest Trail threatened by ski plan," *YH-R*, 10 August 1989.

58. McCarthy, email, 16 January 2021.

59. Lynn and Kershaw, letter to Gorton and Jackson, 16 May 1983.

60. *Record of Decision White Pass Expansion Master Development Plan Proposal Final Environmental Impact Statement Gifford Pinchot National Forest Amendment No. 19* (Forest Service, United States Department of Agriculture, Pacific Northwest Region, June 2007): 2. Kay and Isabelle contributed money to the Hogback Basin Preservation Association in the late 1980s and early 1990s. Erik Splawn, interview, 27 April 2022.

61. Kevin McCarthy, "Expansion when? The ball is in their court," *Ski White Pass Magazine*, 1987–88: 8–9; Wes Nelson, "Yakima tribe joins appeal of ski expansion," *YH-R*, 30 September 1990; "Attention Skiers: White Pass Extension Update," [advertisement by WPSC], *YH-R*, 17 December 1991; *Hogback Basin Preservation v. U.S. Forest Service*, 577 F. Supp. 2d. 1139, No. C07–1913JLR. 10 September 2008; Mark Lawler, "Ski Area Mania Trashes Backcountry," *Wild Cascades* (Winter 2007–2008): 19; Adam Pearson, "White Pass Ski Resort will double in size," *Seattle Times*, 5 March 2010; Craig Hill, "Long-awaited White Pass ski area expansion opens today," 4 December 2010.

Epilogue

1. William O. Douglas, letter to Kay Kershaw, 29 November 1977 (KFC); Gosney, "Double K combats 'progress'"; "Non-profit group to buy Douglas retreat."

2. Kay Kershaw, letters to Kay Lagergren, 8 and 13 November 1987; Isabelle Lynn, letter to Kay Lagergren, 30 November [1987] (YVM archives, Document Box 222); John S. Barany, MD, interview, 17 February 2022.

3. Pat Kane, letter to Centrella.

4. Kathleen Tresham Anderson, *Birds, Bats and Baling Wire* [self-published 2009], 11–14; Cragg M. Gilbert, email, 27 January 2021; Ed Kershaw, interview, 4 February 2021.

5. Ed Kershaw, interview, 18 August 2020.

6. A 1,200 square foot brick house located at 114 North 45th Avenue in Yakima.

7. Kay Kershaw, letters to Carolyn and Betty Lagergren, 7 November 1989, 29 December 1989, and 12 January 1990 (YVM archives, Document Box 222); Ruby Montana, interview, 28 October 2020; Anderson, *Birds, Bats*, 21–22; Kathryn Kershaw and Isabelle Lynn, Statutory Warranty Deed, Yakima County 2900013, to Thomas T. Anderson and Kathleen Tresham Anderson, dated 21 August 1990; Thomas T. Anderson and Kathleen Tresham Anderson, Statutory Warranty Deed, Yakima County 3102570, to Dennis Richardson and Kay Richardson, dated 31 July 1995.

8. Snapp and Kershaw, Zoom meeting, 16 March 2021.

9. President William J. Clinton, letter to Isabelle Lynn and Kay Kershaw, 15 October 1993 (KFC).

10. Ed Kershaw, interviews, 18 August 2020 and 4 February 2021; James J. Haven, MD, interview, 18 March 2021.

11. Barany, interview, 17 February 2022.

12. Ed Kershaw, interview, 18 August 2020; Manning, "End of an Era: Addendum by H.M.," 16; Snapp and Kershaw, Zoom meeting, 16 March 2021; Seth McCormick Lynn, Jr., email, 28 June 2021.

13. Tripp Robinson, interview, 2 May 2021 (Tripp is the son of Mary Ann [Kershaw] Robinson).

14. Gosney, "'DoubleK Girls'"; "Double K combats 'progress.'"

15. Ed Kershaw, interview, 18 August 2020.

16. Brad Patterson, interview, 9 August 2020; Mary Ann (Kershaw) Robinson, interview, 28 April 2021.

17. Ginger Hislop, interview, 8 August 2020.

18. Anderson, *Birds, Bats*, 27–28; Buscher and Hart, *Bush Forester for Wilderness*, 105; John Baule, interview, 20 July 2020; Larry Frank, interview, 19 August 2020; Noel Kelley, interview, 20 August 2020.

19. Ruby Montana, interview, 28 October 2020.

20. Murphey, "Yakima never sure about Douglas."

21. Hislop, interview, 8 August 2020.

22. "Weather History for Palo Alto, CA," *The Old Farmer's Almanac* [https://www.almanac.com/weather/history/zipcode/94301/1992-09-24].

23. "Harold and Maude—If you want to sing out, sing out—Ruth Gordon," YouTube, 1:56 [https://youtu.be/EKGze_1DWbE]. Music and Lyrics, Cat Stevens, 1971.

Appendix

1. Royston Ellis in Palash R. Ghosh, "The Beatles in 1960s Liverpool: Royston Ellis Remembers," *International Business Times*, 8 January 2013 [https://www.ibtimes.com/beatles-1960-liverpool-royston-ellis-remembers-996876].

2. Amanda Shaver, "Segal, Erich: Love Story,"*20th Century American Bestsellers* (University of Virginia, Department of English) [https://bestsellers.lib.virginia.edu/submissions/23]; Jack Doyle, "The Love Story Saga, 1970–1977," *PopHistoryDig.com*, 29 June 2011.

3. Thomas Meehan, "The Yale Faculty Makes the Scene," *The New York Times Magazine*, 7 February 1971: 50.

4. Meehan, "The Yale Faculty," 48–50.

5. Keller, "Was It Right," 403–4; Adrienne Raphel, "What Happened to the Harlequin Romance?" *The New Yorker*, 8 May 2014 [https://www.newyorker.com/business/currency/what-happened-to-the-harlequin-romance/amp].

6. Bérubé, *Coming Out*, 272; Faderman, *Odd Girls*, 146–47; Keller, "Was It Right," 386, 388; Ghosh, "Royston Ellis Remembers."

7. Marijane Meaker [Vin Packer], in Keller, "Was It Right," 390; "Writer Marijane Meaker," Terry Gross interview, *Fresh Air*, 25 August 2003 (19:53) [https://www.npr.org/templates/story/story.php?storyId=1407163].

8. *The Ladder* 1, no. 7 (April 1957): 14; 5, no. 1 (October 1960): 24–26; 5, no. 4 (January 1961): [28]; 5, no. 7 (April 1961): [28]; 5, no. 10 (July 1961): [28]; 7, no. 8 (May 1963): [28]; 8, no. 4 (January 1964): [31]; 8, no. 6 (March 1964): [28]; 11 no. 12 (October–November 1967): 30.

9. *The Ladder* 6, no. 5 (February 1962): 9; 7, no. 2 (November 1962): 23; 7, no. 4 (January 1963): 9; 7, no. 6 (March 1963): 25; 7, no. 10 (July 1963): 15; 8, no. 2 (November 1963): 9; 8, no. 7 (April 1964): 24; 8, no. 12 (September 1964): 19, 26; 11, no. 7 (May 1967): 11; 11, no. 11 (September 1967): 12; 13, no. 9–10 (June–July 1969): 18–23.

10. *Memoirs v. Massachusetts*: 383 U.S. 413 (1966).

11. Gene Damon, "The Lesbian Paperback," *The Ladder* 13, no. 9–10 (June–July 1969): 18.

12. Gene Damon, "Lesbiana," *The Ladder* 15, nos. 1–2 (October–November 1970): 36.

13. Faderman, *Odd Girls*, 224–26; Keller, "'Was It Right,'" 393. Bannon's entire five-book series, *The Beebo Brinker Chronicles*, was republished in the mid-seventies by Arno Press, an imprint of *The New York Times*. Naiad Press reissued them again in 1983; and Cleis Press for a third time at the turn of the twenty-first century. Stephanie Foote, "Deviant Classics: Pulps and the Making of Lesbian Print Culture," *Signs* 31, no. 1 (Autumn 2005): 178–81.

14. Franklin Banner, letter to Isabelle Lynn, 30 April 1934 (KFC).

15. Two typewritten manuscripts of *Crucifixion Land* are extant. One is an eighty-five page, single-spaced typewritten manuscript, undated and untitled. The prose is stilted and awkward in places. The other is a 173-page, double-spaced typewritten copy of the former with edits, corrections, re-writes, and queries in a variety of handwriting (KFC).

16. Isabelle Lynn, [*Crucifixion Land*] untitled typewritten manuscript (173 pages), 89, 100, 173. Isabelle is quoting Heinrich Heine, *Buch der Lieder* "Die Heimkehr 46." On page 89, Lynn also includes a stanza from Heine's *Neue Gedichte* "Verschiedene—Seraphine 9: Was wir lieblich fest besessen/ Schwindet hin, wie Träumerein/ Und die Herzen, die vergessen/ Und die Augen schlafen ein" (What we hold the dearest disappears like daydreams/ and hearts forget and eyes close in sleep).

17. "Nazi Troops March in Heidelberg Fete," *NYT*, 28 June 1936.

18. Lynn, *Crucifixion Land*, 53–54. The German Christian Movement of the mid–1930s was an attempt to reconcile Nazism with Christianity. The group's symbol was a Christian cross superimposed on a swastika. See the cover of Gerhard Hahn, *Christuskreuz und Hakenkreuz* [The Cross of Christ and the Hooked Cross], Schriftenreihe der "Deutschen Christen" Hannovers Nr. 1 (1934), Bibliothek des Landeskirchenamts, Hannover, GER (pdf).

19. Lynn, *Crucifixion Land*, 173.

20. John W. Chambers, 2nd, "Quiet on Set, for Elusive Butterfly of War," *NYT*, 5 January 1997; "The Butterfly—All Quiet on the Western Front (10/10) Movie Clip (1930) HD" 2:26 [https://www.youtube.com/watch?v=nMlDPsRwZE4].

21. "Whit Burnett, Founder of Story Magazine, Dies," *NYT*, 24 April 1973.

22. Whit Burnett, letter to Isabelle Lynn, 29 November 1937 (KFC).

23. Whit Burnett, letter to Isabelle Lynn, 8 December 1937 (KFC).

24. "Books—Authors," *NYT*, 6 September 1946; Steve Perry, "Another Stray Memory," 12 June 2011 [Old Enough to Know Better] [http://

themanwhonevermissed.blogspot.com/2011/06/another-stray-memory.html].

25. Isabelle Lynn, letter to A.L. Fierst, 20 November 1949 (KFC).

26. Isabelle Lynn, "Structure of Grief," double-spaced typed manuscript [nine pages, November 1949] (KFC).

27. Orville Prescott, "Books of The Times," *NYT*, 23 June 1948.

28. "Erotica for Women," *Newsweek*, 27 December 1971 (clipping in KFC).

29. Henry Popkin, "The Famous and Infamous Wares of Monsieur Girodias," *NYT*, 17 April 1960; "Olympia Press Head May Relocate Here," 3 March 1965; "Publisher Turns New (Clean) Leaf," 5 May 1966; Clyde C. Farnsworth, "2 Publishers End 'Sex Fiction' Pact," 24 August 1967; Israel Shenker, "Girodias Sees Rich View of Erotic Interest in U.S.," 16 October 1968; Maurice Girodias, *The Frog Prince* (New York: Crown, 1980), 1–5; "Maurice Girodias, A French Publisher and an Author, 71," *NYT*, 5 July 1990; "Maurice Girodias, 'Lolita' Publisher," *Los Angeles Times*, 5 July 1990.

30. "Erotica for Women."

31. Elisabeth Newbold, *The City Within* (New York: Maurice Girodias Associates, 1973), 28, 107, 120, 197.

32. Joseph A. von Bradish, "Deutsche Romantik und Schellings Religionsphilosophie," *Monatshefte für Deutschen Unterricht* 35, nos. 3–4 (March–April 1943): 176; Ulrike Jureit, "Lebensraum," in *Online Lexikon zur Kultur und Geschichte der Deutschen im östlichen Europa*, 2016 [https://ome-lexikon.uni-oldenburg.de/begriffe/lebensraum].

33. Isabelle Lynn, letter to William O. Douglas, 6 May 1962; Lynn to Douglas, letter, 24 January 1966 (Double K Papers, file 1–42).

34. Newbold, *The City Within*, 2, 17, 23, 50, 70, 101, 132, 158, 170, 183, 185.

35. Newbold, *The City Within*, 35, 178, 191.

36. Newbold, *The City Within*, 43.

37. Newbold, *The City Within*, 43, 105, 141.

38. Newbold, *The City Within*, 135–43; Faderman, *Odd Girls*, 175; Kennedy and Davis, *Boots of Leather*, 68, 151–83.

39. Isabelle Lynn, letter to Maurice Girodias, 25 May 1972; Isabelle Lynn, letter to Scott Meredith, 5 November 1973; "Scott Meredith Literary Agency, Inc. Service and Terms," [mailer, no date]; "Agreement between Isabelle Lynn and Capito N.V. Amsterdam," contract dated 25 May, signed by Isabelle Lynn (KFC).

40. Lynn, letter to Girodias, 25 May 1972.

41. Isabelle Lynn, letter to Maurice Girodias and typewritten single page biographical sketch, 4 June 1972; Isabelle Lynn, double-spaced single page document [biographical sketch, rough draft, no date] (KFC).

42. Isabelle Lynn, letter to Maurice Girodias and "Structure of Grief by Elisabeth Newbold" [double spaced typewritten document, eight pages], 11 July 1972 (KFC).

43. Marcia M. Gallo, "Introduction: The Ladder: A Lesbian Review, 1956–1972. An Interpretation and Document Archive," Alexander Street [https://documents.alexanderstreet.com/d/1003268047].

44. Segal's *Love Story* and Reich's *Greening of America* simultaneously held the number one spots on the *New York Times* lists of bestsellers in fiction and non-fiction on 27 December 1970; 17, 24, and 31 January 1971; 7 and 14 February 1971. The conjunction of the two books at the pinnacle of the bestseller lists was a point of pride for the Yale community and especially pleasing for Segal and Reich who also happened to be close friends. Meehan, "The Yale Faculty," 50.

45. Charles Reich, letter to Isabelle Lynn, 10 April 1973 (KFC).

46. Charles Reich, letter to Isabelle Lynn, 27 May 1973 (KFC).

47. Charles Reich, letter to Isabelle Lynn and "Comment on *The City Within*—from Charles A. Reich," handwritten review [four pages], 12 June 1973 (KFC). Reich was averse to using a typewriter, so unless he dictated a letter to a typist (see his letter to Lynn, 10 April 1973), all his correspondence was handwritten: "I don't type, so you'd best make a couple of carbons [carbon copies] before sending [the commentary] to the publishers."

48. Isabelle Lynn, letter to Maurice Girodias, 14 June 1973 (KFC).

49. Lynn, letter to Girodias, 14 June 1973.

50. Lynn, letter to Girodias, 14 June 1973.

51. Caroline Wright, letter to Isabelle Lynn and two dust jacket proofs, 15 May 1973 (KFC).

52. Susan A. Sueyres, letter to Isabelle Lynn, 20 June 1973 (KFC).

53. Isabelle Lynn, letter to Susan Sueyres, 26 June 1973 (KFC).

54. Seth McCormick Lynn, Jr., email, 28 June 2021. Isabelle also mentioned working on a cookbook to Harvey Manning. Isabelle Lynn, letter to Harvey Manning, 15 November 1970 (NCCC records, 1732-015 Box 2).

55. Charlotte Leon Mayerson, letter to Isabelle Lynn, 14 August 1973 (KFC). Mayerson stayed at the Double K when she came to Goose Prairie in the summer to work with Justice Douglas, signing into the guest register on 10 August 1973; 28 August and 22 September 1974; and 2 September 1975. She had planned on returning to the Double K to resume working on the manuscript with Douglas in August 1976. William O. Douglas, letter to Kay Kershaw and Isabelle Lynn, 16 April 1976; Charlotte Mayerson, letter to Kay Kershaw and Isabelle Lynn, 10 August 1976 (KFC).

56. "A Conversation with Jim Brogan," College of Health and Social Sciences, San Francisco State University, 14 June 2016 [https://chss.sfsu.edu/news-announce/conversation-professor-jim-brogan]; Charles Reich, letter to Isabelle Lynn, 21 April 1973; Reich, letter to Lynn, 12 June 1973 (KFC). In the latter half of the twentieth century, Berkeley boasted an extraordinary number of bookstores south of the University of California campus.

57. "A Listing of Recently Published Books," *NYT*, 30 June 1973.
58. "Elisabeth Newbold, *The City Within*," *The New York Times Book Review* [advertisement], 9 September 1973 (clipping in KFC).
59. Shenker, "Girodias Sees Rich Vein."
60. Marcia Seligson, "Bad Boy of Publishing: Lyle Stuart," *The New York Times Book Review*, 30 November 1969: 34, 36; Matt Schudel, "Controversial Publisher Lyle Stuart, 83," *Washington Post*, 28 June 2006.
61. American Arbitration Association, "Demand for Arbitration," to Maurice Girodias Associates, Inc., 26 November 1974: 1–2; American Arbitration Association, "Respondent's Reply to Demand For Arbitration," 11 December 1974: 1–4 (KFC).
62. Lynn, letter to Meredith, 5 November 1973.
63. Scott Meredith, letter to Isabelle Lynn, 15 November 1973 (KFC).
64. Caroline Wright, letter to Isabelle Lynn, 30 January 1974 (KFC). Wright mistakenly gives the end-of-year date as "December 31, 1974."
65. "Respondent's Reply," 4–6.
66. "Respondent's Reply," 5.
67. Isabelle Lynn, letter to Jeffrey Laytin, 18 December 1974; Maurice Girodias, letter to Jeffrey Laytin, 5 February 1975 (KFC); Isabelle Lynn, letter to Brock Evans, 28 October 1974 (Brock Evans Papers); Seth McCormick Lynn, Jr., email, 28 June 2021.
68. Maurice Girodias, letter to Isabelle Lynn, 13 December 1974 (KFC).
69. Lynn, letter to Laytin, 18 December 1974; Isabelle Lynn, letter to Charlotte Mayerson, 19 December 1974 (KFC). At the time of Isabelle's letter, Jeffrey Laytin (JD 1969) was working at the law offices of Machat and Kronfeld in New York City. Laytin went on to establish his own practice specializing in trademark enforcement, licensing, and branding.
70. Lynn, letter to Mayerson, 19 December 1974.
71. Lynn, letter to Laytin, 18 December 1974; Jeffrey Laytin, letter to Isabelle Lynn, 31 December 1974; Isabelle Lynn, letter to Jeffrey Laytin, 7 January 1975; Jeffrey Laytin, letter to Isabelle Lynn, 10 January 1975; Isabelle Lynn, letter to Jeffrey Laytin, 14 January 1975 (KFC); "Would You Pay Two Dollars for a Cake of Soap?" [advertisement for Good Earth soap by Lyle Stuart, Inc.] *The New York Times Magazine*, 29 December 1974: 29.
72. Jeffrey Laytin, letter to Maurice Girodias Associates, Inc., 21 January 1975; Maurice Girodias, letter to Jeffrey Laytin, 5 February 1975; Jeffrey Laytin, letter to Isabelle Lynn, 14 February 1975; Isabelle Lynn, letter to Jeffrey Laytin, 19 February 1975 (KFC).
73. "Publisher of Book on Kissinger Told to Leave U.S.," *NYT*, 30 May 1974; Eric Pace, "Novel on Kissinger Held Up by Dispute Over Two Passages," 12 June 1974; "Notes on People," 27 June 1974; "Notes on People," 5 June 1975.
74. Jeffrey Laytin, letter to Lyle Stuart, Inc., 25 March 1975 (KFC).
75. Lillian Faderman, email, 23 September 2021.
76. Ruby Montana, interview, 28 October 2020.

Bibliography

Newspapers, Magazines, Newsletters

Baltimore Sun (Baltimore, MD)
Cascadians (Yakima, WA)
The Cincinnati Pictorial Enquirer (Cincinnati, OH)
Crystal Mountain Tracks (Crystal Mountain, WA)
The Dalles Chronicle (The Dalles, OR)
Decatur Herald (Decatur, IL)
Des Moines Tribune (Des Moines, IA)
The Dude Rancher (Billings, MT)
The Evening Observer (La Grande, OR)
The Evening Record (Ellensburg, WA)
Everett Herald (Everett, WA)
Hartford Courant (Hartford, CN)
Inland Empire Magazine (Spokane, WA)
The Ladder (San Francisco, CA)
Los Angeles Examiner (Los Angeles, CA)
Los Angeles Times (Los Angeles, CA)
Miner-Echo (Cle Elum, WA)
Monterey County Herald (Monterey, CA)
The Morning Oregonian (Portland, OR)
The Mountaineer (Seattle, WA)
Nebraska State Journal (Lincoln, NE)
Nevada Appeal (Carson City, NV)
Nevada State Journal (Reno, NV)
New York Times (New York, NY)
New York Times Book Review (New York, NY)
New York Times Magazine (New York, NY)
North Cascades Conservation Council News (Seattle, WA)
The Northwest Magazine (St. Paul, MN)
The Oregon Daily Journal (Portland, OR)
The Oregon Statesman (Salem, OR)
The Oregonian (Portland, OR)
Peninsula Times Tribune (Palo Alto, CA)
Popular Aviation and Aeronautics (New York, NY)
Reno Gazette-Journal (Reno, NV)
Rock Valley Bee (Rock Valley, IA)
San Francisco Examiner (San Francisco, CA)
Seattle Post-Intelligencer (Seattle, WA)
Seattle Times (Seattle, WA)
Skagit Valley Herald (Mt. Vernon, WA)
Spokane Chronicle (Spokane, WA)
Spokesman-Review (Spokane, WA)
Spokesman-Review Magazine (Spokane, WA)
Springfield Daily News (Springfield, MA)
Springfield Union (Springfield, MA)
Sunday Bulletin (Washington, D.C.)
Toppenish Review (Toppenish, WA)
Walla Walla Bulletin (Walla Walla, WA)
Washington Post (Washington, D.C.)
Washington State Evergreen (Pullman, WA)
Wild Cascades (Seattle, WA)
Yakima Daily Republic (Yakima, WA)
Yakima Eagle (Yakima, WA)
Yakima Herald (Yakima, WA)
Yakima Herald-Republic (Yakima, WA)
Yakima Morning Herald (Yakima, WA)
Yakima Sunday Herald (Yakima, WA)
Yakima Valley News (Yakima, WA)
Yakima Valley Sun (Yakima, WA)

Collections

Brock Evans Papers. Special Collections, University of Washington, Seattle, WA.
Charles D. Hessey, Jr., Papers. Yakima Valley Museum, Yakima, WA.
Cle Elum Ski Club Collection. Archives and Special Collections, Central Washington University, Ellensburg, WA.
Double K Mountain Ranch Records. Special Collections, University of Washington, Seattle, WA.
Eisenhower Fellowships Archives. Philadelphia, PA.
Gilbert Family collection. Yakima, WA. Privately held.
Gilbert Family collection. Yakima Valley Museum, Yakima, WA.
Kane Family collection. Auburn, CA, and Berea, OH. Privately held.
Kershaw Family collection. Yakima, WA. Privately held.
McAllister Museum of Aviation Archives. Yakima, WA.
North Cascades Conservation Council Records. Special Collections, University of Washington, Seattle, WA.
William O. Douglas Collection. Yakima Valley Museum, Yakima, WA.
William O. Douglas Papers. Library of Congress. Washington, D.C.
Yakima Valley Genealogical Society Library. Yakima, WA.

Books, Manuscripts, Articles, Recordings, Ephemera

Additions to the National Wilderness Preservation System Hearings Before the Subcommittee on Public Lands and National Parks of the Committee on Interior and Insular Affairs House of Representatives Ninety-Eighth Congress Second Session Serial No.98-3 Part XI. Washington, D.C.: U.S. Government Printing Office, 1985.

"Air Commerce Regulations, Department of Commerce Aeronautics Branch, Effective December 31, 1926." *Aircraft Year Book, 1927*: 359–72. New York: Aeronautical Chamber of Commerce of America, Inc., 1927.

Aircraft Year Book, 1929. New York: Aeronautical Chamber of Commerce of America, Inc., 1929.

America's National Park System: Critical Documents. Ed. Lary [sic] M. Dilsaver. Lanham, MD: Rowman and Littlefield, 1994 [https://www.nps.gov/parkhistory/online_books/anps/anps_3.htm].

Anderson, Kathleen Tresham. *Birds, Bats, and Baling Wire*. [Self-published], 2009.

Athearn, Robert G. *The Mythic West in Twentieth-Century America*. Lawrence: University Press of Kansas, 1986.

Baker, Kelly J. *Gospel According to the Klan: The KKK's Appeal to Protestant America, 1915–1930*. Lawrence: University of Kansas Press, 2011.

Baker, Robert D., Larry Burt, and Robert S. Maxwell, et al. *The National Forests of the Northern Region—Living Legacy November 1993*. College Station: Intaglio, 1993.

Baskin, R.N. *Reminiscences of Early Utah*. Salt Lake City: [Baskin?], 1914.

Beckey, Fred. *Cascade Alpine Guide: Climbing and High Routes, Columbia River to Stevens Pass*. Seattle: The Mountaineers, 1973.

Bérubé, Allan. *Coming Out Under Fire: The History of Gay Men and Women in World War Two*. New York: The Free Press, 1990.

Blonk, Hu. "Jack Nelson Gate Tender." *Reclamation ERA* 32, no. 12 (December 1946): 263–65.

Brass, Lori Ann. "An Arrest in New Haven, Contraception and the Right to Privacy." *Yale Medicine* (Spring 2007): 16–17.

Brown, Rebecca A. *Women on High: Pioneers of Mountaineering*. Boston: Appalachian Mountain Club Books, 2002.

Bruce, Ben. "The Rise and Fall of the Ku Klux Klan in Oregon in the 1920s." *Voces Novae* 11, article 2 (2019) [https://digitalcommons.chapman.edu/vocesnovae/vol11/iss1/2/].

Bullough, Vern, and Bonnie Bullough. "Lesbianism in the 1920s and 1930s: A Newfound Study." *Signs* 2, no. 4 (Summer 1977): 895–904.

Buscher, Richard F., and Paul Hart. *Bush Forester for Wilderness: The Story of Richard F. Buscher as Told to Paul Hart*. Bend, OR: Maverick Publications, 2021.

"The Butterfly—All Quiet on the Western Front (10/10) Movie Clip (1930) HD." 2:26 [https://www.youtube.com/watch?v=nMlDPsRwZE4].

Canaday, Margot. *The Straight State: Sexuality and Citizenship in Twentieth-Century America*. Princeton: Princeton University Press, 2009.

The Cascades: Mountains of the Pacific Northwest. Ed. Roderick Peattie. New York: Vanguard Press, 1949.

"Catalogue 1925–1926: Announcements 1926–1927." University of Oregon Bulletin 23, no. 7 (June 1926). University of Oregon Libraries Scholars' Bank [http://hdl.handle.net/1794/11276].

Cathro, Mort. "Travelin' Light in Washington State: Spinsters Run Isolated Dude Ranch." *Oakland Tribune*, 8 September 1968.

Chalmers, David. *Notes on Writing the History of the Ku Klux Klan*. Gainesville: University Press of Florida, 2015.

"Charles and Marion Hessey Films, circa 1939–1971." *Archives West Orbis Cascade Alliance* [http://archiveswest.orbiscascade.org/ark:/80444/xv37585].

"Chinook 1927" [Sate College of Washington Yearbook]. Washington State University Libraries Digital Collections [https://content.libraries.wsu.edu/digital/collection/chinook/id/15721/rec/28].

Cogswell, Phil. "Decision Left on Stump: Lawyers Hike 6 Miles in Woods to Find Justice Douglas." *Oregonian*, 1 September 1970: 6.

"A Conversation with Jim Brogan." College of Health and Social Sciences, San Francisco State University, 14 June 2016 [https://chss.sfsu.edu/news-announce/conversation-professor-jim-brogan].

Crafts, Edward C. Recorded interview by William H. Moss, 17 November 1969. John F. Kennedy Oral History Program [https://www.jfklibrary.org/sites/default/files/archives/JFKOH/Crafts%2C%20Edward%20C/JFKOH-ECC-01/JFKOH-ECC-01-TR.pdf].

Cyr, Susan Summit. *Tanum: A Story of Bumping Lake and the William O. Douglas Wilderness*. [Self-published], 2021.

Dallek, Matthew. *Birchers: How the John Birch Society Radicalized the American Right*. New York: Basic Books, 2022.

"David Evans Company (1850)." *Pioneer Data Base 1847-1868 The Church of Jesus Christ of Latter-Day Saints* [https://history.churchofjesuschrist.org/overlandtravel/companies/114/david-evans-company].

Directory of Social and Health Agencies in the State of Washington 1936. Olympia: State of Washington Department of Public Welfare, 1936.

"Dr. Charles Wempe—Importance of Horses." Interview excerpt 1:03. Wessels Living History Farm: Farming in the 1940s [https://livinghistoryfarm.org/farminginthe40s/movies/wempe_machines_13.html].

"Double K Mountain Ranch [Guest Book]." 14 May 1954 to 31 December 1976. Kershaw Family collection.

———. September 1977 to 16 July 1990. Kershaw Family collection.

"Double K Mountain Ranch, Goose Prairie, Washington." Brochure. With "Price List, Season 1947."

Douglas, William O. "The Attack on the Right to Privacy." *Playboy*, December 1967: 191–92, 244–45.

———. "Civil Liberties: The Crucial Issue." *Playboy*, January 1969 [https://www.iplayboy.com/issue/19690101].

———. "Cougar Lakes Wilderness Recommendations." *The Mountaineer 1965* 58, no. 4 (15 March 1965): 66–67.

———. *The Court Years 1939-1975: The Autobiography of William O. Douglas*. New York: Random House, 1980.

———. *The Douglas Letters: Selections from the Private Papers of Justice William O. Douglas*. Ed. Melvin I. Urofsky. Bethesda: Adler and Adler, 1987.

———. "56: William O. Douglas at dinner honoring Mrs. Franklin D. Roosevelt, National Council of Jewish Women 15 March 1948." Yakima Valley Museum William O. Douglas Collection, WOD Speeches Binder #2, nos. 40–69 11/21/45–5/11/49.

———. "48: 15th Annual New York Herald-Tribune Forum on Current Problems, 28 October 1946." Yakima Valley Museum William O. Douglas Collection, WOD Speeches Binder #2 nos. 40–69 11/21/45–5/11/49.

———. *Go East, Young Man the Early Years: The Autobiography of William O. Douglas*. New York: Random House, 1974.

———. "An Inquest on Our Lakes and Rivers." *Playboy*, June 1968: 96–98, 177, 180–81. Yakima Valley Museum William O. Douglas Collection Binder no. 1, Library of Congress Manuscripts Correspondence/Environmentalism.

———. *My Wilderness: The Pacific West*. Garden City, NY: Doubleday, 1960.

———. *Of Men and Mountains*. New York. Harper and Row, 1950.

———. "Points of Rebellion." *Playboy*, January 1970 [https://www.iplayboy.com/issue/19700101].

———. "The Public Be Dammed." *Playboy*, July 1969 [https://www.iplayboy.com/issue/19690701].

———. "Recording #1, 12 April 1950 Banquet Yakima, Washington." 7½-inch reel approx. 25 minutes. Yakima Valley Museum William O. Douglas Collection, WOD Box 32-4 Tapes and Recordings.

———. Scrapbook and photos of "Men and Mountains [sic]" book release 1950. Yakima Valley Museum William O. Douglas Collection Box 34.

———. *Strange Lands and Friendly People*. New York: Harper and Brothers, 1951.

———. "A Task Force for Ecology." [Manuscript, 45 pages]. Yakima Valley Museum William O. Douglas Collection Binder no. 1, Library of Congress Manuscripts Correspondence/Environmentalism.

———. "300: The Computerized Man." American Civil Liberties Union, San Francisco, California, 20 May 1967. Yakima Valley Museum William O. Douglas Collection, WOD Speeches Binder #9 nos. 265–301 10/9/64–5/28/67.

———. "338: Seattle-King County Bar Association, Seattle, Washington 27 June 1972." Yakima Valley Museum William O. Douglas Collection, WOD Speeches Binder #11, nos. 332–365-D, 2/9/72–1979.

———. "339: Houston, Texas, State Bar of Texas, 6 July 1972." Yakima Valley Museum William O. Douglas Collection, WOD Speeches Binder #11, nos. 332–365-D, 2/9/72–1979.

———. "337: American University 21 May 1972." Yakima Valley Museum William O. Douglas Collection, WOD Speeches Binder #11, nos. 332–365-D, 2/9/72–1979.

———. "291: Points of Rebellion." 1966 Harvey T. Reid Lectures, Arcadia University, Wolfville, Nova Scotia, 30 and 31 January, 1 February 1967. Yakima Valley Museum William O. Douglas Collection, WOD Speeches Binder #9, nos. 265–301 10/9/64–5/28/67.

———. "269: The Campfire Club of America, New York, NY, 21 January 1965." Yakima Valley Museum William O. Douglas Collection, WOD Speeches Binder #9, nos. 265–301 10/9/64–5/28/67.

———. "261: The Guidance Center New Rochelle, NY 23 May 1964." Yakima Valley Museum William O. Douglas Collection, WOD Speeches Binder #8, nos. 224–264 10/14/62–7/26/64.

———. *West of the Indus*. Garden City, NY: Doubleday, 1958.

———. "Wilderness Trails of the Pacific Northwest." *Mademoiselle* (April 1955): 140–41, 194–97.

"Draft White Paper: National Forest William O. Douglas Wilderness Institute, Naches Ranger District, January 24, 1989."

Dyreson, Mark. "Icons of Liberty or Objects of Desire? American Women Olympians and the Politics of Consumption." *Journal of Contemporary History* 38, no. 3 (July 2003): 435–60.

Establishment and Modification of National Forest Boundaries and National Grasslands: A Chronological Record 1891–2012 FS 612. United States Department of Agriculture Forest Service, Lands and Realty Management Staff, Washington, D.C., 2012.

Evans, Brock. *Endless Pressure Endlessly Applied: The Autobiography of an Eco-Warrior*. La Grande, OR: Wake-Robin Press, 2020.

———. "Environmental Campaigner: From the Northwest Forests to the Halls of Congress." Oral history conducted by Ann Lage in *Building the Sierra Club's National Lobbying Program 1967–1981*. Berkeley: Regional Oral History Office, Bancroft Library University of California, 1985.

Faber, Doris. *The Life of Lorena Hickok: E.R.'s Friend*. New York: William Morrow, 1980.

Faderman, Lillian. *The Gay Revolution: The Story of the Struggle*. New York: Simon & Schuster, 2015.

———. *Odd Girls and Twilight Lovers: A History of Lesbian Life in Twentieth-Century America*. New York: Columbia University Press, 1991.

———. *To Believe in Women: What Lesbians Have Done for America—A History*. Boston: Houghton Mifflin, 1999.

"The Female Pilots Who Made History: A Conversation with Keith O'Brien." *The Exchange*, New Hampshire Public Radio, 5 September 2018.

"Fletcher Tape 72." [Raw footage for KYVE-TV documentary "William O. Douglas: A Life on the High Court"]. Yakima Valley Museum archives.

Foote, Stephanie. "Deviant Classics: Pulps and the Making of Lesbian Print Culture." *Signs* 31, no. 1 (Autumn 2005): 169–90.

Ford, Robert I. *The History of Goose Prairie and the Ira Ford Family*. [Self-published], 2003. Yakima Valley Museum archives.

Frank, William D. *Everyone to Skis! Skiing in Russia and the Rise of Soviet Biathlon*. DeKalb: Northern Illinois University Press, 2013.

———. "Of *Women*, Men and Mountains: Kay Kershaw, Isabelle Lynn and the Double K Mountain Ranch." *Rotary Mtg 2021 09 16 21:18-54:17* [https://www.youtube.com/watch?v=1nq0fo_VES4&t=1270s&ab_channel=yakimarotaryclub].

———. "Skiing on the East Slope of Washington State's Cascade Range, Parts 1 and 2," *Journal of the New England Ski Museum* no. 130, Fall 2023: 17-26 and no. 131, Winter 2024 (forthcoming).

Gallo, Marcia M. "Introduction: The Ladder: A Lesbian Review, 1956-1972. An Interpretation and Document Archive." Alexander Street [https://documents.alexanderstreet.com/d/1003268047].

Gerlach, Edgar M. "Social Service Resource Directory for Washington." W.P.A. Project 221, 17 November 1937.

Ghosh, Palash R. "The Beatles in 1960s Liverpool: Royston Ellis Remembers." *International Business Times*, 8 January 2013 [https://www.ibtimes.com/beatles-1960-liverpool-royston-ellis-remembers-996876].

Gilbert, Cragg D. Eulogy at William O. Douglas Memorial, First Presbyterian Church, Yakima, WA, 16 October 1980. Gilbert Family collection.

Gilbert, Curtiss. Scrapbook (1898-1912), ninety-one pages. Gilbert Family collection.

Gill-Peterson, Julian. *Histories of the Transgender Child*. Minneapolis: University of Minnesota Press, 2018.

Girodias, Maurice. *The Frog Prince*. New York: Crown, 1980.

Gossett, Gretta Petersen. *Beyond the Bend: A History of the Nile Valley in Washington State*. Fairfield, WA: Ye Galleon Press, 1979.

———. "Naches All Because of Water 9 July 1963." Typewritten manuscript [26 pages]. Naches file, Yakima Valley Museum archives.

———. [Notes typewritten, no date]. Naches file, Yakima Valley Museum archives.

Graham, Billy. *Blow, Wind of God! Selected Writings of Billy Graham*. Ed. Donald E. Demaray. New York: Signet, 1977. Reprint of Baker Book House, 1975.

———. *World Aflame*. Garden City, NY: Doubleday, 1965.

Graham, Patricia Albjerg. "Expansion and Exclusion: A History of Women in American Higher Education." *Signs* 3, no. 4 (Summer 1978): 759-773.

"Guest Log." 1 January 1947 to 25 October 1948/12 September 1951. Kershaw Family collection.

———. 31 August 1948 to 17 October 1953. Kershaw Family collection.

Hahn, Gerhard. *Christuskreuz und Hakenkreuz*. Schriftenreihe der "Deutschen Christen" Hannovers Nr. 1 (1934), Bibliothek des Landeskirchenamts, Hannover, Germany.

Hall, Simon. "Americanism, Un-Americanism, and the Gay Rights Movement." *Journal of American Studies* 47, no. 4 (November 2013): 1109-1130.

Hamilton, G.W, Attorney General. "Chapter 8: Emergency Relief Administration." *Session Laws of the State of Washington, Twenty-Third Session, Convened January 9, Adjourned March 9, 1933*. Olympia: O.H. Olson, 1933.

Hansen, Melissa. "Integrated Water Plan Moves Forward." *The Good Fruit Grower*, 1 April 2014 [https://www.goodfruit.com/integrated-water-plan-moves-forward/].

"Harold and Maude—If you want to sing out, sing out—Ruth Gordon." YouTube, 1:56 [https://youtu.be/EKGze_1DWbE]. Music and Lyrics, Cat Stevens, 1971.

Heine, Heinrich. *Buch der Lieder* [https://www.gutenberg.org/cache/epub/3498/pg3498.html].

———. *Neue Gedichte* [https://www.staff.uni-mainz.de/pommeren/Gedichte/NeueGedichte/].

Heuterman, Thomas H. "Bifurcation: How the Wapato, Washington *Independent* Covered Japanese in the Yakima Valley, 1920-1942." Paper presented at the Annual Meeting of the Association for Education in Journalism and Mass Communication. San Antonio, Texas, 3 August 1987 [45 pages].

Hillin, Sara. *Rhetorical Arts of Women in Aviation, 1911-1970*. Lanham, MD: Lexington, 2020.

Hirt, Paul W. *A Conspiracy of Optimism: Management of the National Forests Since World War Two*. Lincoln: University of Nebraska Press, 1994.

Hogback Basin Preservation v. U.S. Forest Service, 577 F. Supp. 2d. 1139, No. C07-1913JLR. 10 September 2008.

Huey, Ben Meyer. "Problems of Timber Products Procurement During World War II, 1941-1945: A Report Prepared for the U.S. Department of Defense, Army, Corps of Engineers, by the U.S.

Department of Agriculture, Forest Service, 1951." Master's Thesis, University of Montana, 1951.

Hulst, Tom R. *The Footpaths of Justice William O. Douglas: A Legacy of Place.* Lincoln: iUniverse, 2004.

An Illustrated History of Klickitat, Yakima and Kittitas Counties: With an outline of the early history of the State of Washington. Ed. William S. Schiach and Harrison D. Averell. Chicago: Interstate, 1904.

"In Memory of Lionel Claude Blackburn." Wood Chapel of the Pines, Idaho Falls, Idaho, 3 December 1965.

Jaros, Dean. *Heroes Without Legacy: American Airwomen, 1912-1944.* Boulder: University Press of Colorado, 1993.

"John Russell Homestead (Circa 1885)" [http://www.cowichecalls.com/stories.asp?storyID=7].

Johnson, Adrienne Rose. "Romancing the Dude Ranch, 1926-1947." *Western Historical Quarterly* 43, no. 4 (Winter 2012): 437-61.

Johnson, Colin R. *Just Queer Folk: Gender and Sexuality in Rural America.* Philadelphia: Temple University Press, 2013.

Johnson, David K. *The Lavender Scare: The Cold War Persecution of Gays and Lesbians in the Federal Government.* Chicago: University of Chicago Press, 2004.

Johnson, Lloyd Phillip. *Where's Frank? An Intrepid Leader, 18 Boy Scouts, 10,000 Miles in an Open Truck.* Virginia Beach: Koehler Books, 2016.

Johnson, McMillan Houston, V. "Taking Off: The Politics and Culture of American Aviation 1920-1939." Dissertation, University of Tennessee, 2011.

Jureit, Ulrike. "Lebensraum." *Online Lexikon zur Kultur und Geschichte der Deutschen im östlichen Europa*, 2016 [https://ome-lexikon.uni-oldenburg.de/begriffe/lebensraum].

Katz, Johnathan Ned. *The Daring Life and Dangerous Times of Eve Adams.* Chicago: Chicago Review Press, 2021.

Kazemi, M. Transcript of taped interview [no date, four pages]. Eisenhower Fellowships archives.

Keller, Yvonne. "'Was It Right to Love Her Brother's Wife So Passionately?': Lesbian Pulp Novels and U.S. Lesbian Identity, 1950-1965." *American Quarterly* 57, no. 2 (June 2005): 385-410.

Kennedy, Elizabeth Lapovsky. "'But we would never talk about it': The Structures of Lesbian Discretion in South Dakota, 1928-1933." *Inventing Lesbian Cultures in America.* Ed. Ellen Lewin. Boston: Beacon Press, 1996. 15-39.

Kennedy, Elizabeth Lapovsky, and Madeline D. Davis. *Boots of Leather, Slippers of Gold: The History of a Lesbian Community.* New York: Routledge, 2014.

Kershaw, Kay. *The Ideal* [Scrapbook 16 December 1942-November 1943]. Kershaw Family collection.

_____. *My Memories* [Scrapbook ca. 1925-1935]. Kershaw Family collection.

_____. *My Victory Album* [Pocket-sized photo album]. Kershaw Family collection.

Kincaid, Sara. "High in the Mountains on a Pack Trip." *Cascades* 11, no. 3 (June 1970): 30-33.

Kirchick, James. *Secret City: The Hidden History of Gay Washington.* New York: Henry Holt, 2022.

Kramer, Jerry Lee. "Bachelor Farmers and Spinsters: Gay and Lesbian Identities and Communities in Rural North Dakota." *Mapping Desire: Geographies of Sexualities.* Ed. David Bell and Gill Valentine. New York: Routledge, 1995, 200-13.

"Lesson Thirteen: Cities and Hinterlands: The Modern Northwest." In John Findlay, "History of Washington State and the Pacific Northwest." Center for the Study of the Pacific Northwest, University of Washington [https://www.washington.edu/uwired/outreach/cspn/Website/Classroom%20Materials/Pacific%20Northwest%20History/Lessons/Lesson%2013/13.html].

Let's Take the Sporting Route: Mountaineering in Central Washington 1949-1970. Ed. William D. Frank. Yakima: Yakima Valley Museum, 2022.

Lo-Na-Hi 1930 [Lower Naches High School Yearbook 1930]. Yakima Valley Museum archives.

Lo-Na-Hi 1928 [Lower Naches High School Yearbook 1928]. Yakima Valley Genealogical Society Library.

Lo-Na-Hi 1925 [Lower Naches High School Yearbook 1925]. Yakima Valley Museum archives.

Lo-Na-Hi 1924 [Lower Naches High School Yearbook 1924]. Yakima Valley Museum archives.

Long, Michael G. *Martin Luther King, Jr., Homosexuality, and the Early Gay Rights Movement: Keeping the Dream Straight?* New York: Palgrave Macmillan, 2012.

Louter, David. *Contested Terrain: North Cascades National Park Service Complex: An Administrative History.* Seattle: National Park Service, 1979.

_____. *Windshield Wilderness: Cars, Roads, and Nature in Washington's National Parks.* Seattle: University of Washington Press, 2006.

"The Love Story Saga, 1970-1977." *PopHistoryDig.com*, 29 June 2011 [https://www.pophistorydig.com/topics/love-story-saga-1970-1977/].

Lowe, Walt. "William O. Douglas: A Life On the High Court." KYVE-TV script, third draft, 53 pages, 15 August 1988. Yakima Valley Museum archives.

Lyman, William Dennison. *History of the Yakima Valley, Washington Comprising Yakima, Kittitas and Benton Counties.* Vols. 1 and 2. Chicago: S.J. Clarke, 1919.

Lynn, Isabelle. "Busman's Holiday at the Double K." *The Dude Rancher* 30, no. 3 (July 1959): 12, 30-31.

_____. "Cougar Lakes: Do-It-Yourself Wilderness." *National Parks & Conservation Magazine* 46, no. 6 (June 1972): 23-27.

_____. *Crucifixion Land.* [Untitled double-spaced typed manuscript, 85 pages, ca. 1937]. Kershaw Family collection.

———. *Crucifixion Land*. [Untitled typed manuscript, 173 pages, ca. 1937]. Kershaw Family collection.

———. "Dammed If You Do." *National Parks & Conservation Magazine* 46, no. 1 (January 1972): 14-20.

———. "Do We Let the Knuckledraggers Take Over?" [Typewritten manuscript, no date, ten pages]. Kershaw Family collection.

———. "Large and Small Bores in the National Lands." [Typed manuscript, no date, nine pages]. Kershaw Family collection.

———. "Pack Trip to the Goat Rocks." *The Dude Rancher* 27, no. 2 (April 1958): 12-13, 24, 32-34.

———. "Structure of Grief." [Double-spaced typed manuscript, nine pages]. November 1949. Kershaw Family collection.

———. "Year 'Round in the Mountains." *The Mountaineer 1962* 55 no. 4 (March 1, 1962): 33-40.

Manning, Harvey, Ansel Adams, Philip Hyde, David Simons, and Bob and Ira Spring, et al. *Wild Cascades Forgotten Parkland*. Introduction by William O. Douglas, ed. David Brower. San Francisco: Sierra Club, 1965.

Marsden, George. *Fundamentalism and American Culture*. 2nd ed. New York: Oxford University Press, 2006.

———. *Understanding Fundamentalism and Evangelicalism*. Grand Rapids: William B. Eerdmans, 1991.

"Maryland Historical Trust, Determination of Eligibility Form. Lyddane/Bradley Farm M:26-20, Section 8 Significance." September 1979.

McArdle, Richard E. "The Concept of Multiple Use of Forest and Associated Lands—Its Values and Limitations." Fifth World Forestry Conference, Seattle, Washington, 29 August to 10 September 1960. In Elwood R. Maunder, *Dr. Richard E. McArdle: An Interview with the Former Chief, U.S. Forest Service 1952-1962*. Santa Cruz, CA: Forest History Society, 1979, Appendix C, 225-31.

McCarthy, Kevin. "Expansion when? The ball is in their court." *Ski White Pass Magazine*, 1987-88: 8-9.

McCarthy, Linda. "Poppies in a Wheat Field: Explaining the Lives of Rural Lesbians." *Journal of Homosexuality* 39, no. 1 (2000): 75-94.

McCormick, Henry A. *An X-Ray on the Yakima Valley: A Typical Illustration of Rural Life in the valleys of Yakima with Naches Avenue of North Yakima, supplementary*. North Yakima: Republic, 1911.

McKeehen, Don. "Promoting Small Outdoor Recreation Business." Paper presented at the North Cascades Outdoor Recreation Conference, Sun Mountain Lodge, Winthrop, Washington, 1-2 October 1974. *Conference Notes on the Development, Operation, and Management of Private Outdoor Enterprises* E.M. 3920 May 1975. Cooperative Extension Service, College of Agriculture, Washington State University.

McKeown, M. Margaret. *Citizen Justice: The Environmental Legacy of William O. Douglas—Public Advocate and Conservation Champion*. Lincoln: Potomac Books, 2022.

———. "Justice Takes a Side." *The Seattle Times Pacific NW*, 19 August 2018: 12-17.

Metsker's Atlas of Yakima County Washington. February 1959. Yakima Valley Museum archives.

Moskowitz, David A, Gerulf Rieger, and Michael E. Roloff. "Heterosexual Attitudes Towards Same-Sex Marriage." *Journal of Homosexuality* 57, no. 2 (2010): 325-336 [https://www.ncbi.nlm.nih.gov/pmc/articles/PMC5065072/pdf/nihms-821201.pdf].

"Mount Rainier History." National Park Service [https://www.nps.gov/mora/learn/historyculture/mount-rainier-history.htm].

"Mt. Rainier." Mike Roberts Postcard C8135, Berkeley, California, published for C.P. Johnson Company, Seattle.

Murdoch, Joyce, and Deb Price. *Courting Justice: Gay Men and Lesbians v. the Supreme Court*. New York: Basic Books, 2001.

Murphy, Bruce Allen. *Wild Bill: The Legend and Life of William O. Douglas*. New York: Random House, 2003.

———. "Wild Bill: The Legend and Life of William O. Douglas." Speech before the Cato Institute, Washington, D.C., 18 March 2003. C-Span Video Library Program ID 162037-1, 1:25:45 [https://www.c-span.org/video/?162037-1/wild-bill-legend-life-william-o-douglas].

Nelson, Jack. *We Never Got Away*. Yakima: Franklin Press, 1965.

"The New William O. Douglas Wilderness." *Outdoors West* 7, no. 1 (Winter 1984): 12.

Newbold, Elisabeth. *The City Within*. New York: Maurice Girodias Associates, 1973.

———. "Structure of Grief." [Double-spaced typewritten manuscript, eight pages]. July 1972. Kershaw Family collection.

The North Cascades Study Team. *The North Cascades Study Report: A Report to the Secretary of the Interior and the Secretary of Agriculture*. October 1965 [https://www.nps.gov/parkhistory/online_books/noca/study_report/appb.htm].

Official Register of the United States 1929: containing a list of persons occupying administrative and supervisory positions in each executive and judicial department of the government including the District of Columbia. Washington, D.C.: Government Printing Office, 1929.

Onkst, David H. "Wing Walkers." *U.S. Centennial of Flight Commission* [https://www.centennialofflight.net/essay/Explorers_Record_Setters_and_Daredevils/wingwalkers/EX13.htm].

Oregana 1926. [University of Oregon Yearbook]. University of Oregon Libraries Scholars' Bank [http://hdl.handle.net/1794/12019].

Parker, Patsy. "The Historical Role of Women in Higher Education." *Administrative Issues Journal* 5, no. 1 (Spring 2015): 3-14.

Perry, Steve. "Another Stray Memory," 12 June 2011 [Old Enough to Know Better] [http://themanwhonevermissed.blogspot.com/2011/06/another-stray-memory.html].

Polk & Company Directory Yakima 1918. Seattle: R.L. Polk and Company, 1918.

Polk's Yakima City and County Directory. Volume 32 (1936). Seattle: R.L. Polk and Company, 1936.

Polk's Yakima City and County Directory 1924. Seattle: R.L. Polk and Company, 1924.

Polk's Yakima City Directory 36 (1940). Seattle: R.L. Polk and Company, 1940.

_____. 50 (1949). Seattle: R.L. Polk and Company, 1949.

Polk's Yakima City Directory 1954–55. Seattle: R.L. Polk and Company, 1955.

Quit Claim Deed 1593475. Signed by Patricia Kane, dated 18 October 1955. Washington Title Insurance Company, Seattle.

Raphel, Adrienne. "What Happened to the Harlequin Romance?" *The New Yorker*, 8 May 2014 [https://www.newyorker.com/business/currency/what-happened-to-the-harlequin-romance/amp].

Rasmussen, Wayne D., Gladys L. Baker, and James S. Ward. *A Short History of Agricultural Adjustment, 1933–75.* Agriculture Bulletin 391. Economic Research Service, United States Department of Agriculture. March 1976.

Ray, Verne F. "Native Villages and Groupings of the Columbia Basin." *Pacific Northwest Quarterly* 27, no. 2 (April 1936): 99–152.

Record of Decision White Pass Expansion Master Development Plan Proposal Final Environmental Impact Statement Gifford Pinchot National Forest Amendment No. 19. Forest Service, United States Department of Agriculture, Pacific Northwest Region, June 2007.

"Recording #25: 16 April 1970 TV commentary from three networks [ABC, CBS, NBC] on impeachment," 3¾-inch tape 15 minutes. WOD Box 32-4 Tapes and Recordings, Yakima Valley Museum William O. Douglas collection.

"Recording #26: 16 December 1970 TV comments: reaction to House Select Committee's finding of innocence of William O. Douglas," 3¾-inch tape, ten minutes. WOD Box 32-4 Tapes and Recordings, Yakima Valley Museum William O. Douglas collection.

Richards, Kent D. *Isaac Stevens: Young Man in a Hurry.* Provo: Brigham Young University Press, 1979.

Roosevelt, Eleanor. "My Day, June 2, 1948." *The Eleanor Roosevelt Papers Digital Edition.* The George Washington University, 2017 [https://www2.gwu.edu/~erpapers/myday/displaydoc.cfm?_y=1948&_f=md000982].

_____. "My Day, March 19, 1948." *The Eleanor Roosevelt Papers Digital Edition.* The George Washington University, 2017 [https://www2.gwu.edu/~erpapers/myday/displaydoc.cfm?_y=1948&_f=md000918].

Roth, Dennis M. *The Wilderness Movement and the National Forests: 1964–1980.* Washington, D.C.: U.S. Department of Agriculture, Forest Service, 1984.

Rowley, Hazel. *Franklin and Eleanor: An Extraordinary Marriage.* New York: Farrar, Straus and Giroux, 2010.

"Rules for Field Ball." *American Physical Education Review* 24, no. 35 (1929): 304–7.

Rusk, C.E. *Tales of a Western Mountaineer: A Record of Mountain Experiences on the Pacific Coast.* Boston: Houghton Mifflin, 1924.

Schiller, Gerald A. "Flying and Dying for Hollywood in the 1920s." *Historynet* [https://www.historynet.com/motion-picture-stunt-fliers-flying-and-dying-for-hollywood-in-the-1920s.htm].

Seaman, E.V. "Double K Mountain Ranch: Snoqualmie National Forest, Washington Trail Ride—Expedition No. 8 August 20—August 31" [no date, mimeograph]. Kershaw Family collection.

Senior, Jeanie. "Where History Was Made." *Klickitat PUD Ruralite* (November 2007): 4–5.

Sevareid, Eric, and William O. Douglas. "Tape #28: 6 September 1972. Eric Sevareid interviews William O. Douglas at Goose Prairie, 3¾-inch tape, one hour (of two hours of interviewing)." WOD Box 32-4 Tapes and Recordings, Yakima Valley Museum William O. Douglas Collection.

Shaver, Amanda. "Segal, Erich: Love Story." *20th Century American Bestsellers.* University of Virginia, Department of English [https://bestsellers.lib.virginia.edu/submissions/23].

Simon, James F. *Independent Journey: The Life of William O. Douglas.* New York: Harper and Row, 1980.

Sirico, Louis J., Jr. "Failed Constitutional Metaphors: The Wall of Separation and the Penumbra." *University of Richmond Law Review* 45, no. 2 (2011): 459–89.

Skoog, Lowell. *Written in the Snows: Across Time on Skis in the Pacific Northwest.* Seattle: Mountaineers Books, 2021.

Sowards, Adam M. *The Environmental Justice: William O. Douglas and American Conservation.* Corvallis: Oregon State University Press, 2009.

_____. "William O. Douglas's Wilderness Politics: Public Protest and Committees of Correspondence in the Pacific Northwest." *Western Historical Quarterly* (Spring 2006): 21–42.

Splawn, A.J. *Ka-Mi-Akin: The Last Hero of the Yakimas.* 3rd ed. Caldwell, ID: Caxton, 1958.

Stirewalt, Chris. "Populism, fake news, and racist rhetoric—it's all happened before in the 1968 presidential campaign." *Business Insider* 6 October 2018.

Sullivan, Joseph Parker. "A Description and Analysis of the Dude Ranching Industry in Montana." Master of Science Thesis, University of Montana, 1971.

"Supplementary Listing Record: James Gleed Barn," United States Department of the Interior, National Register of Historic Places [https://npgallery.nps.gov/GetAsset/4f490584-08fd-4082-809a-2828dce6bbd9].

Thirty-fifth Annual Catalogue of the State College of Washington for 1926 Pullman, Washington June, 1926. Olympia: Jay Thomas, Public Printer, 1926.

"Thomas T. Anderson and Kathleen Tresham Anderson, Statutory Warranty Deed Yakima County 3102570, to Dennis Richardson and Kay Richardson." 31 July 1995.

Turner, James Morton. *The Promise of Wilderness: American Environmental Politics Since 1964.* Seattle: University of Washington Press, 2012.

"*Tyee* 1930." University of Washington Yearbook. University of Washington Libraries Digital Collection [https://digitalcollections.lib.washington.edu/digital/collection/uwdocs/id/17313].

Umatilla Basin Project and the Yakima River Basin Water Enhancement Project Hearing before the Subcommittee on Water and Power of the Committee on Energy and Natural Resources One Hundredth Congress United States Senate Second Session on S1613 [...] and S2322 [...] June 28, 1988. Washington, D.C.: United States Government Printing Office, 1989.

"University of Oregon Faculty and Student Directory 1925–1926." Associated Students University of Oregon Graduate Manager's Office. University of Oregon Libraries Scholars' Bank [http://hdl.handle.net/1794/11905].

Unrau, Harlan D., and G. Frank Williss. *Administrative History: Expansion of the National Park Service in the 1930s* (September 1983) National Park Service, Denver Service Center [https://www.nps.gov/parkhistory/online_books/unrau-williss/adhi.htm].

"The Uplands Approvals/Dedication/Acknowledgment," 9 June 1950 [Yakima County]. Yakima Valley Museum Gilbert Family Collection, Box 3.

Urofsky, Melvin L. "Review of Murphy, Bruce Allen. *Wild Bill: The Legend and Life of William O. Douglas.*" H-law. H-Net Reviews, June 2003 [https://networks.h-net.org/node/16794/reviews/17004/urofsky-murphy-wild-bill-legend-and-life-william-o-douglas].

Von Bradish, Joseph A. "Deutsche Romantik und Schellings Religionsphilosophie." *Monatshefte für Deutschen Unterricht* 35, no. 3–4 (March–April 1943): 174–79.

Wade, Jean E. *Schools of Yakima County.* Unpublished manuscript. 2006–07. Yakima Valley Museum archives.

Walkowitz, Daniel K. "The Making of a Feminine Professional Identity: Social Workers in the 1920s," *The American Historical Review* 95, no. 4 (October 1990): 1051–075.

Washington State Planning Council. *Cascade Mountains Study.* Olympia: Washington State Planning Council, 1940.

Washington State Wilderness Act of 1983: Hearings Before the Subcommittee on Public Lands and Reserved Water of the Committee on Energy and Natural Resources United States Senate Ninety-Eighth Congress First Session on S 837 Bill to Designate Certain National Forest System Lands in the State of Washington for Inclusion in the National Wilderness Preservation System, and for Other Purposes Part 2 Appendix. Washington, D.C.: Government Printing Office, 1984.

Watkins, Mary Bradley. *Afghanistan: An Outline.* New Paltz: World Study Center, State University College, 1962.

———. *Afghanistan: Land in Transition.* Princeton: Van Nostrand, 1963.

Watson, Emilie. "Amelia Earhart: The Flying Feminist." *Flight Paths: Purdue University Aerospace Pioneers* (13 September 2016) [https://flightpaths.lib.purdue.edu/blog/2016/09/13/amelia-earhart-the-flying-feminist/].

Wazeka, Bob. "The Crusade for Cougar Lakes," *The Living Wilderness* 42, no. 143 (October/December 1978): 26–33.

"Weather History for Palo Alto, CA." *The Old Farmer's Almanac* [https://www.almanac.com/weather/history/zipcode/94301/1992-09-24].

Weeks, Jeffrey. Interview on "London Weekend Television, Gay Life," London Minorities Unit, 1981 ["Being Gay in the Thirties (Gay Life)" 34:46 https://www.youtube.com/watch?v=FzPzb3exfVc].

Wendt, Simon. "Defenders of Patriotism or Mothers of Fascism? The Daughters of the American Revolution, Antiradicalism, and Un-Americanism in the Interwar Period." *Journal of American Studies* 47, no. 4 (November 2013): 943–69.

"Wilderness Evening." *American Forests* 54, no. 7 (July 1948): cover.

Wilkerson, Charles F., and H. Michael Anderson. "Land and Resource Planning in the National Forests," *Oregon Law Review* 64, nos. 1 and 2 (1985) [https://scholar.law.colorado.edu/articles/1038/].

Williams, Gerald W. *The USDA Forest Service—The First Century* FS-650. Washington, D.C.: USDA Forest Service Office of Communication, 2005.

Woerner, Robert L. "The General Plan Of The Uplands A Suburban Residential District of the City of Yakima, Washington June 14, 1950." Yakima Valley Museum Gilbert Family Collection, Box 3.

"Wonderland: An Administrative History of Mount Rainier National Park. III: Establishment of Mount Rainier National Park" [https://www.nps.gov/parkhistory/online_books/mora/adhi/chap3.htm].

"Writer Marijane Meaker." Terry Gross interview. *Fresh Air* 25 August 2003 (19:53) [https://www.npr.org/templates/story/story.php?storyId=1407163].

"Yakima River Basin Storage Study: Wymer Dam and Reservoir Appraisal Report." Technical Series No. TS-YSS-16, United States Department of the Interior Bureau of Reclamation Pacific Northwest Region September 2007.

"Yakima River Basin Study: Bumping Lake Enlargement Planning Design Summary Update

United States Bureau of Reclamation Contract No. 08CA10677A ID/IQ, Task 48." United States Department of the Interior Bureau of Reclamation Pacific Northwest Region Columbia-Cascades Area Office March 2011.

Supreme Court Cases

Boutilier v. Immigration and Naturalization Service: 387 U.S. 118 (1967).
Dennis v. United States: 341 U.S. 414 (1951).
Dobbs v. Jackson Women's Health Organization: 597 U.S. 215 (2022).
Eisenstadt v. Baird: 405 U.S. 438 (1972).
Federal Power Commission v. Texaco, Inc.: 377 U.S. 33 (1964).
General Committee of Adjustment of Brotherhood of Locomotive Engineers for Missouri-Kansas-Texas Railroad v. Missouri-Kansas-Texas Railroad Co.: 320 U.S. 323 (1943).
Griswold v. Connecticut: 381 U.S. 479 (1965).
Lawrence v. Texas: 539 U.S. 558 (2003).
MANual Enterprises, Inc. v. Day: 370 U.S. 478 (1962).
Memoirs v. Massachusetts: 383 US 413 (1966).
Obergefell v. Hodges: 576 U.S. 644 (2015).
ONE, Inc. v. Olesen: 355 U.S. 371 (1958).
Osborn v. United States: 385 U.S. 323 (1966).
Panama Canal Co. v. Grace Line, Inc.: 356 U.S. 309 (1958).
Roe v. Wade: 410 U.S. 113 (1973).
Romer v. Evans: 517 U.S. 620 (1996).
Rosenberg v. Fleuti: 374 U.S. 449 (1963).
Roth v. United States: 354 U.S. 476 (1957).
Skinner v. Oklahoma ex rel. Williamson: 316 U.S. 535 (1942).
Smith v. Sperling: 354 U.S. 91 (1957).
Textile Workers Union v. Lincoln Mills: 353 U.S. 448 (1957).
United States v. Classic: 313 U.S. 299 (1941).
Wilson v. Schnettler: 365 U.S. 381 (1961).

Index

Numbers in **_bold italics_** indicate pages with illustrations

Abrams, Lester 18, **_18_**
Abzug, Bella 92
acreage 60, 85, 128, 132, 134, 138, 191*n*8
Adams, Ansel 97
Adams, Eve 177*n*20
aeronautics (aviation) 30–39, **_33_**, 49, 117, 180*n*22
agriculture 3, 8–13, 15, 40–41, **_42_**, 114, 139, 148, 151
Agriculture Adjustment Act (Federal, Washington State) 41
Ahtanum (WA) 9, 12, 17–19, **_18_**
airplane dealerships 34, 180*n*21
Alexander, Mary 32, 180*n*21
All Quiet on the Western Front 159
all-terrain vehicles (ATV) 116–19
Alpine Lakes 95, 104–6, 108, 126
American Civil Liberties Union 124
American Forestry Association (AFA) 65–68
American Legion 16
American Opinion bookstore 91
American Psychiatric Association 77
American Red Cross 44, 46–47, 71–72
American Ridge 2, 5, 52–53, 55–58, 63, **_69_**, 83, 93, 135, **_135_**, 187*n*57, 189*n*97
American River 4, 5, 13, 43, 44, 55, 65
American River Run *see* American River Ski Bowl
American River Ski Bowl 55–57, **_57_**
ancient forests 93, 152, 195*n*80
Anderson, Garrett 55
Anderson, Kathleen 152
Anderson, Tom 152

Anti-Alien Act (Oregon) 16
Anti-Alien Land Law (Washington State) 17
anti-Semitism 90, 158–59
Anton, S.I. 60, 186*n*49
Armstrong, F.H. (Spike) 100
Armstrong, Garner Ted 90–91
Arnold, June 171
Aspinall, Wayne 110, 124–25
aviation *see* aeronautics

Backcountry Horsemen of Washington 128–29
backpacking 28, 88
Baldy Peak 145, 204*n*26
Bannon, Ann 156–57, 206*n*13
Barany, John 152
barnstorming 30, 34, 38
Barrett, Laurence O. **_95_**, 97–98, 100–104
Beckey, Fred 68, 173*n*3
The Beebo Brinker Chronicles 206*n*13
Benjamin, Burton 113, 146
Benjamin Franklin Hotel 110, 197–98*n*141
Berkeley (CA) 207*n*56
Bill of Rights 1, 80–82
Black, Sir Cyril 171
Black, Hugo 112
Blackburn, Lionel Claude (Joe) 51–53
Blackmun, Harry 190–91*n*31
Blankenship Meadows 4, 5, 13, **_66_**, 96–98, 100, 102, 187*n*57, 187*n*58
Bledsoe, Stewart (Stu) 130
"blister sisters" 97
The Blue Book 91
Blue Mountains 44, 56
board feet 101, 104, 130–31, 137
bohemianism 178*n*34
Boise-Cascade 108, 128, 134, 135, 197*n*129
Bolin, Maud (Lillie) 32, 36, 38, 179*n*14
Bolshevism 14

book release 62–65, **_65_**, 70; *see also Of Men and Mountains*
Botsford, A.C. 45
Botsford, Claudine A. 45
Boutilier v. Immigration and Naturalization Service 79–80
Boy Scouts 6, 7, 55, 89, 174*n*11
Bridgeford, Mildred 43, 182*n*10, 187*n*58
Broad's Stationary 63, 64
Brogan, Jim 166–67
Broome, Harvey 100, 112
Brower, David 90, 93, 98, 101, 102, 105, 112
Brown, Harold 116
Brown, Rita Mae 171
Buck Creek Pass 28
Bumping Lake 4, 12, 36, 38, 43, 54, 66, **_66_**, 68, 83, 93, 98, 101, 108, 112, 116–18, **_123_**, **_133_**, **_135_**, 138; enlargement 109–10, 125–26, 145, 148
Bumping River 4, 5, 12–13, 55, **_66_**, 96, 103, 131, **_139_**
Bureau of Mines 125
Bureau of Reclamation 11, 109, 125–26
Burnett, Whit 159
Buscher, Richard 203–4*n*24

Camp Fife 53
Camp Roganunda 21
Campbell, Don 97, 118
Capito N.V. 168, 171
Capitol Theatre 17, 176*n*41
Carlton Pass 5, 12–13
Carmelita Basin 103, 196*n*100
Carnival Bill 15
Carson, Rachael 97
Carter, Jimmy 134–35, 145
Cascade crest 3–5, 8, 12–13, 86, 96, 118
Cascade Lumber Company 88, 101, 197*n*129; *see also* Boise-Cascade
Cascade Mountains 54, 86

219

Index

Cascadians 5–6, 23, 28, 43, 54–55, 87–89, 93, 95, 101, 178*n*37
Castro, Fidel 167
Catholic Charities 44, 50
Catholic Relief Services 69
Cathro, Mort 113
Chelan (WA) 43, 93, 108; *see also* Lake Chelan
Chesapeake & Ohio Canal 96
Chinook (yearbook) 26
Chinook Hotel 110, 197*n*139
Chinook Pass 3–5, 13, 43, 56, 65, **66**, 88, 95, **123**, 128, 133, **133**, **135**, 137, 139–40
Christmas cards 115, **115**, 146, **147**
Church, Frank 117
churches 9, 10, 12, 14–17, 19, 71, 108, 154, 175*n*31, 175*n*34
cigarettes 23, 63, 67, 187*n*67
cisgender 176*n*2
Citizens for Responsible Water Projects 148
The City Within 161–71, **166**
Civil Aeronautics Authority 179*n*9
civil rights 122
Civilian Conservation Corps (CCC) 55, 57, **57**
Cle Elum (WA) 54
Cle Elum Dam 17
Cle Elum Lakes 148
Cle Elum Ski Club 54
Cle Elum Ski Tournament 38, 184*n*17
Clear Lake 5, 11, **66**, 87, 194*n*64
Cleman, Ted 28, 178*n*40
Cleman Mountain 178*n*40
Cliff, Edward 108
Cliffdell (WA) 23, 28, 43, 44, 54
A Clockwork Orange 120, 199*n*45
cocktails 2, 163, 173*n*7
Cohen, Elaine 188*n*73
Cohen, Hy 121, 163
Cole, Bert 96, 106
Commercial Hotel 63, **64**
Committee for Reasonable Wilderness 139–40
Committees of Correspondence 105
Communism 2, 74–76, 91–92, 163
Confederated Tribes and Bands of the Yakama Nation 4, 8, 11, 17, 32, 148, 150, 174*n*14, 175*n*24
conservation 84–85, 95–98, 131, 136, 148; *see also* environmentalism
Conservative Party 91; *see also* John Birch Society; Paxton, Floyd

Constitution 14, 27, 80, 82, 180–81*n*27
Copper City 13, **66**, 96–98, 100–4, 195*n*79, 196*n*104, 196*n*109
Corpron, Dr. Douglas 62, **64**
Cougar Lakes 5, **66**, **123**, **133**
Cougar Lakes Conservation Coalition 126
Cougar Lakes Limited Area 92, 99, 102, 104, 106, 109, 196*n*116
Cougar Lakes Wilderness 83–84, 99–104, 108, **100**, 110, 122–139, **123**, **133**, **135**, 144–46, 194*n*74, 195*n*97, 197*n*119
Cougar Lakes Wilderness Alliance (CLWA) 103, 125–26, 129, 133–34, 139, 145–46, 149, 200*n*13
cougars 36, 180–81*n*27
Cowiche Canyon 59, 61
Cowlitz Pass 5, 28, 178*n*38, 187*n*57
Crafts, Edward C. 109
Crucifixion Land 157–60, 206*n*15, 206*n*16, 206*n*18
Crystal Mountain 58, 65, 112, 138, 186–87*n*56
Curtis, the Rev. C.C. 17
Cutler, M. Rupert 127, 132–34, **133**, 202*n*44

Darwinism 14
Daughters of Bilitis (DOB) 81, 156, 164, 190*n*30
Daughters of the American Revolution 190*n*30
Deitz, Bob 143
discrimination 16, 19, 75, 78; *see also* racism
disturbed sexuality 76
Dixon, Thomas 192*n*28
Dobbs v. Jackson Women's Health Organization 173*n*6
dogs 22, 111, 178*n*38, 178*n*42; *see also* Lucky
Donadio, Candida 120–21
Double D Dude Ranch 49–50, 58, 62, 183*n*2
Double K Drifter 147, 204*n*42
"Double K Girls" 50, 77, 153, 183–84*n*6
Double K Mountain Ranch 5, 36, 45, 49–73, **46**, **51**, **52**, **53**, 92, 105, 111–12, **115**, 116–19, 125, 154
Douglas, Joan (Martin) 60, 105, 196*n*113
Douglas, Mercedes (Eichholz) 61, 100, 180–81*n*27, 185*n*34
Douglas, Mildred (Riddle) 185*n*39, 186–87*n*56
Douglas, William (Jr.) 142–43

Douglas, William O. 1, 5, 15–16, 58–64, **64**, 77–81, **81**, 83–84, 92, 105, 122–25, **124**, 128, 141–44, 175*n*34, 180–81*n*27, 185*n*56, 186*n*49, 186*n*53, 186–87*n*56, 187*n*70, 189*n*12, 190*n*29, 193*n*39, 203*n*4; *see also* Kershaw, Kay; Lynn, Isabelle; *Of Men and Mountains*; Supreme Court
Draft Environmental Impact Statement (DEIS) 127, 132
dude ranch industry 2, 49–50, 53, 58, 67, 69, 77, 111–12, 114
The Dude Rancher 73, 99, 189*n*97
Dunrud, Carl 49–50, 183*n*3
Dyer, Pauline 98

Earhart, Amelia 32–34, 49, 58, 62, 183*n*2
Economy Act of 1933 86
Eisenstadt v. Baird 81–82
Ellensburg (WA) 28, 30, 148, 179*n*5
Enchantment Wilderness 106, 108
Environmental Impact Statement (EIS) 123–29, 132, 134, 149
Environmental Protection Agency (EPA) 119, 134
environmentalism 84–88, 97; *see also* conservation
erotica 161–62, 171; *see also* pornography
eugenics 20
evangelicalism 13–16, 22, 175*n*31; *see also* fundamentalism
Evans, Brock 93, 105, 109, 110, 126, 128, 133, 145, 193*n*43, 194*n*74, 195*n*80, 197–98*n*141, 201*n*33
Evans, Dan 108
Evans, David 9
Evans, Dr. Hiram Wesley 19, 176*n*49

Faderman, Lillian 24, 42, 163, 190*n*30
Fairbanks, H.B. 30
farming 2, 15, 41, **42**, 114, 139, 151; *see also* agriculture
Federal Emergency Relief Administration 41
The Federation of Western Outdoor Clubs (FWOC) 88, 98, 109
femininity 21, 27
feminism 26–27, 92
Fennimore, Stephanie 143
Field, Steven Johnson 186*n*53

field ball 26, 178n29
Fierst, A.L. 160
Fish Lake 4–5, 12, 13, 101, 103, 131
fishing 8, 28, 61, 63, 179n44
Fletcher, Betty Binns 145, 204n27
Flying H Ranch 59, 61
Ford, Gerald 141,
Ford, Ira 143, 189n12
Forest Reserve Act 85
Forks (WA) 106
Fortas, Abe 180–81n27
Fourteenth Amendment 77, 80–82; *see also* Bill of Rights
Franklin, Tim 146
Freeman, Orville 99, 104, 105, 107, 109
Freud, Dr. Sigmund 20
Fryingpan Lake *66*, 67
fundamentalism 2, 14–15, 24; *see also* evangelicalism

German Christian movement 206n18
German Romantic movement 162
Germany 50, 71, 90, 157–60, 162
Gifford Pinchot National Forest (Gifford-Pinchot) *123*, 126, 131, 133
Gilbert, Bruce 88–89
Gilbert, Cragg Douglas 6–7, 13, 67, 88, 90, 102, 107–8, 110, 118, 139–40, 144, 146, 174n9, 180–81n27, 197n140, 202n65
Gilbert, Curtiss Richey 6–7, *7*, 65, 88, 174n8, 174n9, 174n10, 174n11
Gilbert, Elon H. 61, 62, 185n40
Gilbert, Elon James 6, 7, *7*, 59–63, *64*, 65–68, 88, 108, 114, 180–81n27, 185n40, 186n55, 186–87n56, 193n39
Gilbert, Horace Mark (H.M.) 6, 7, 19, 40
Gilbert, Horace N. 60–61, 65
Gilbert, Jennith 60–61, 65
Gilbert, Virginia 146
Gilbert Peak (Curtiss Gilbert Peak) 7, 65, 67–68, 186n54
Girodias, Maurice 161–71
Glacier Peak 28, 86, 87, 89, 90
Glacier Peak Wilderness 87, 89, 93, 94, 101, 106, 108, 140
Gleed (WA) 9, 10, *10*, 21, *22*, *42*, 43, 91, 176–77n5
Gleed, James 176–77n5
Glenn, Johnny 67–68, 187n69
Goat Rocks Emergency Committee 203n70
Goat Rocks Wilderness 3–5, 7, 11, 43, 65–68, *66*, 86–88, 90, 97–98, *123*, 127, 131, 133, 138–39, *139*, 149–50, 187n57–58, 191n16, 194n64; *see also* Gilbert Peak
Gold Hill 8, 13, 43, 55–56, *55*, 58, 90, 92, 94, 184n21; cabin 55–56, 88, 94, 107–8; ski club 107–8
Goldman, Emma 24
Goldsworthy, Patrick 97, 104, 105, 110, 122, 126, 128, 149
Goldwater, Barry 91
Good Earth soap 170
Good Samaritan Hospital 142–43
Goose Prairie (WA) 4–5, 23, 36, 44–46, 50–53, 57–58, 60–61, *66*, 67, 77, 83, 93–95, 100, 109, 113, 116–19, 124, 141–44, 146–48, 151–53, 166, 187n57, 189n12, 204n26
Gorton, Slade 138–39, 150, 202–3n67
Graham, Billy 15, 171, 175n35
Great Depression 40–43, 75, 86
The Greening of America 112, 165, 167, 198n17, 207n44; *see also* Reich, Robert
Griswold v. Connecticut 1–2, 80–82, 173n6, 190n30, 190n31

Hagenstein, W.D. 102
Hakenkreuz 158, 206n18
Hallauer, Wilbur 129
Hammond, R.A. (Chuck) 50–51
Harlequin Romance 156
Harrison, Benjamin 84–85
Harrison, Mary 9
Hart, Louis 17
Hartley, Roland 40
harvesting (timber) 101, 107, 195n80; *see also* logging
Hatch, Willard 186n54
Hayakawa, S.I. 136
Heidelberg 71, 157–58; *see also* Germany
Heine, Heinrich 157–59, 206n16
hemorrhaging 38, 181n34
Henry M. Jackson Wilderness 140
Hessey, Charles D., Jr. 88–94, *89*, 98–99, 101, 105, 108–9, 112, 118, 120, 125–26, 146, 193n39, 193n40, 194n65, 197n140, 200–1n18, 201n19
Hessey, Marion (Monter) 88–90, 92, 93, 105
heterosexuality 21, 77, 79, 156
Hickok, Lorena 78
High Cascades National Park 86–87
Highway 12 5, 57–58, 91, *123*, 128, *133*, *135*
Highway 410 5, 45, *55*, 59, 65, 94, *95*, 119, *123*, 127–28, 135, 138, 184n21
Hislop, Ginger 153
Hitler, Adolf 158
Hogback 138, 149, 187n57
Hogback Basin Preservation Association 205n60
Holt, W. Douglas 59, 185n31
homosexuality 15, 20–24, 74–82, 91, 163–66, 175n35, 177n16; *see also* lesbianism
Hoover, Herbert 40–41, 136
Hoover Dam 114
horses 3, 21, 26, 29, 41, 43–44, *45*, 47–48, 52, 60, 64–65, *69*, 70, 94, 117, 142; horse-packing 2, 6, 7, 12, 28, 38, 43, 44, 49, 52, 60, 94, 153, 178n37
House Judiciary Committee 141
huckleberry 63, 186n50
hunting 8, 28, 37, *37*, 52–53, 63, 112, 118, 178n40
Huntley, Chet 147, 204n41
Hutchinson, Lydia 22
Hyde, Philip 93, 97

impeachment 141, 203n4
Initiative 49 18–19, *18*, 176n48
Invisible Empire 15, 17; *see also* Ku Klux Klan
irrigation 8, 10–12, 109, 114, 148

Jackson, Henry M. (Scoop) 2, 7, 92, 98, 101–4, 108–9, 117, 122–23, *123*, 126, 128, 131, 140, 145, 150, 195n97, 200n3
Jackson, Ketanji Brown 82
Japanese-Americans 16–17, 176n43
jeeps 2, 98, 116–18, 129
Jenkins, Walter 78
John Birch Society 2, 19, 91–92, 163
Johnson, Lyndon B. 78, 95, 116–17
Johnson, Phil 145, 149
Johnson, the Rev. Robert Riley 93, 108–10
Jones, Wesley L. 40

Kachess Dam 11, 148
Kane, Isabel 44–45, 68, 71, 182n12
Kane, Dr. Joseph Patrick 45, 51, 68–69, 71, 184n7
Kane, Patricia (Pat) 2, 43–47, *45*, *46*, 50–53, *53*, 55–59, *55*, 62–63, *64*, 65–72, *70*, 75, 77–78, 115, 151–54, 178n40, 182n12, 182n14, 183–84n6, 188–89n96

Index

Kazemi, Manoutchehr 114, 198*n*18
Keechelus Dam 4, 11, 148
Kennedy, Anthony 81–82
Kennedy, John F. 91
Kershaw, Edward (Ed) Ronald **53**, 115, 151–53, 180–81*n*27, 188–89*n*96
Kershaw, Edward (Edwin) Ambrose 6, 8, 9–10, **9**, 22, 51
Kershaw, Elizabeth (Betty) Ann (Boone) **53**
Kershaw, Kay: athletics 27–29, 178*n*38, 179*n*44, 179*n*46; aviation 29, 30–39, **33**, 180*n*25; and Bruce Allen Murphy 36, 59, 180–81*n*27; Bumping Lake 109–10, 148; and Charles Hessey 92–94, 126, 194*n*65; college 25–27, 177*n*26; Cougar Lakes 93–110, 122–40, 194*n*74; Double K 45–46, **46**, 49–53, **53**, 65–68, **69**, 77, 111–21, 183–84*n*6; farming 40, 41, **42**, 43; hunting 28, 178*n*40; and Isabelle Lynn 68, **70**, 71–73, 83, 151–52; and the Kershaw family 37, **37**, 41, 51, 115, 139, 146, 151–53, 181*n*36; and Pat Kane 44–46, **46**, 68–71, **70**, 151, 182*n*14; Red Cross 46–48, **47**; and Sid Morrison 137–39, 146; skiing **4**, 54–58, **55**, **56**; social services 41–43, 44; United States Forest Service 97, 99, 100–4, 107, 119; and William O. Douglas 58–64, **64**, **81**, 82, 83, 94, 96–99, 107, 125, 128, 141–44, 153–54, 187*n*70; William O. Douglas Wilderness 144–47, **147**; youth 3, 7, 9–10, **10**, **11**, 14, 19, 20, 21–25, **22**; *see also* Douglas, William O.; Kane, Pat; lesbianism; Lynn, Isabelle
Kershaw, Ora (Whitmore) 9–10, **9**, **11**, 174*n*18
Kershaw, Robert (Bob) Chester **53**, 139, 181*n*39, 188–89*n*96
Kershaw, Robert Whitmore 10, **10**, 37–39, **37**, 181*n*30, 181*n*34
Kershaw, Ronald Edward 10, **10**, 26, **37**, **53**, 181*n*36
Kershaw, W.E. 43, 184*n*20
Kershaw Drive **42**, 174*n*13
Kettle Creek **66**, 187*n*57
King, Mary V. 23
Kinsey, Alfred 80
Kittitas County 3, 4, 11, 28
Kloochman Rock 5, 68
Koht, Paul Gruda 114
Krag the Kootenay Ram 6, 174*n*9

Ku Klux Klan 2, 14, 15–19, **18**, 22, 92, 175*n*39, 176*n*43, 176*n*49, 192*n*28

The Ladder 156–57, 164
Lake Chelan 93, 105
Langston, Connie 152
Lankford, Jesse W. 34, 180*n*22
Lantz, Robert 120–21
Lawrence v. Texas 1, 81
Laytin, Jeffery 170–71, 208*n*69
League of Women Voters 27
Lebensraum 162–63
Lerwill, Leonard 37–38
lesbianism 23–24, 42, 75, 92, 156, 162–63, 165, 175*n*35; *see also* homosexuality
Lewis, Robert 132
Lewis and Clark Expedition 4, 61, 186*n*43
Lewis County 13, **133**
LGBTQ+ 80, 82, 83, 152; *see also* homosexuality; lesbianism
Lindbergh, Charles 29, 30, 35, 180*n*25
Lo-Na-Hi 21, 181*n*30
logging 13, 40, 84–88, 93, 101, 104, 116, 118, 129, 130, 134–36, 138, 195*n*80
Lost Lake **66**, 187*n*57
Lostine (OR) 59–63, 186–87*n*56
Love Story 155–56, 161, 165, 207*n*44
Lower Naches High School 21, **22**, 25, 37, 38, 59
Lowry, Carmelita 100, **100**, 102–3, 109, 125, 126, 193*n*44, 195*n*97, 197*n*119
Lowry, Mike 134–38, 146, 149
Lucas, Robert W. 74–75
Lucky **53**, 111, 146, **147**, 198*n*2
Lyle Stuart Publishers 167–171
Lyman Lake 28, 89–90
Lyng, Richard E. 136–37
Lynn, Isabelle: and Bruce Allen Murphy 36, 59, 180–81*n*27; Bumping Lake 109–10, 148; and Charles Hessey 92–94; and Charles Reich 112–13; Cougar Lakes Wilderness 83–84, 93, 99–104, 105–7, 128, 134, 136–37, 194*n*74; Cougar Lakes Wilderness Alliance 125–26; Double K 66–67, 72, 77, 111–21, 183–84*n*6; and family 113–15, 152, 188*n*86, 199*n*23; and Frances Rummell 72, 188*n*73, 188*n*90; in Germany 157–58, 206*n*16; and Kay Kershaw 2, 68, 70, **70**, 72, 83, 91, 151–53; and the Kershaw family 115, 153; North Cascades Conservation Council 105; and Ruby Montana 68, 151, 171; and Sid Morrison 137–38; United States Forest Service 94, 97–98, 101, 103, 107; White Pass 138–39, 150; and William O. Douglas 60, 72, 82, 92, 96, 124–25, 141–44, 146–47, 197*n*130; William O. Douglas Wilderness 144–46, **147**; as a writer 72–73, 98–99, 109, 118–121, 148, 157–171, 200*n*54, 207*n*54; youth and college 71–72, 188*n*87; *see also* Cougar Lakes Wilderness Alliance; *The City Within*; *Crucifixion Land*; Douglas, William O.; Kershaw, Kay; lesbianism; Newbold, Elisabeth; Reich, Charles; *Structure of Grief*
Lynn, Seth McCormick 113–15, 199*n*23
Lynn, Seth McCormick, Jr. 113, 115, 198*n*14
Lyon, Tom 107

Magnuson, Warren G. 108–9, 116
Major Hoople 31
Manashtash Lake 28
Manning, Harvey 59, 112, 125, 126, 198*n*10, 207*n*54
MANual Enterprises, Inc. v. Day 79
marriage 14–15, 23, 35, 42, 59, 62, 69, 71, 79, 82
Marshall, George 100
Marshall, John 64, 186*n*53
martinis 2, 163, 173*n*7, 204*n*42
Maxwell, Lex 55, 88
May, Catherine 109
Mayerson, Charlotte 141–42, 166, 170, 207*n*55
The Mazamas (Portland) 88, 95
McAllister, Charlie 30, **33**, 179*n*4
McAllister Meadow 5, 11
McArdle, Richard 87, **95**, 96
McCall Basin 11, 88, 187*n*57, 187*n*69
McCarthy, Joseph R. 74–75, 92
McCarthy, Kevin 149–50
McCloskey, J. Michael 105
McCormack, Mike 122, 125–26, 135–36, **135**
McGrady, Mike 167
McGuire, John R. 127, 132–33
McKinley, William 85
McMechan, Maurice 30–34, **33**, 179*n*4, 179*n*5
McNamara, Robert 116–17

Memoirs v. Massachusetts 157
Mercy Theatre *see* Capitol Theatre
Meredith, Scott 168
Miller, Denny 145
Miller, Isabel 157; *see also* Routsong, Alma
Minam River 44
mining 12–13, 49, 54, 84–86, 107, 125, 136
Miriam Basin 138, 187*n*69
Miya'wax 11; *see also* Confederated Tribes and Bands of the Yakama Nation
Montana, Ruby 68, 151, 153, 171
Morrison, Sid 136–40, 144, 146, 203*n*71, 203–24*n*24
Morse Creek 8, 138
motorcycles 118–20, *130*; *see also* Tote Goat
Mount Adams 1, 3–5, 6, 28, 61, 63, 81, 83, 86, 131
Mount Aix 5, 99, 100, 106–8, 122, *123*, 130, *130*, 135, *135*, 196*n*116, 204*n*26
Mount Hood 5, 28
Mount Rainier 2–6, 13, 28, 54, *69*, 85–86, 105, 189*n*97
Mount Rainier National Park 6, 12–13, 22, *66*, 83–85, 95, 105–6, *123*, 127, 133–34, *133*, *135*, *139*
Mount Shuksan 28
Mount Stuart 5, 23, 28, 178*n*37
mountaineering 5–8, 23, 27–28, 88–89, 90, 178*n*34
The Mountaineers (Seattle) 87–88, 95, 112, 194*n*74, 198*n*10, 200*n*14
multiple use 85–87, 93, 96, 99, 106, 129, 132, 134, 136
Murie, Olaus and Mardy 96, 195*n*97
Murphy, Bruce Allen 36, 39, 59, 62, 80, 124, 180–81*n*27, 185*n*30, 185*n*34

Naches (WA) 3–6, 9–10, 12, 14, 21–22, 25, 28, 175*n*24, 176–77*n*5, 178*n*40
Naches Pass 3, 4, 8, 13, 128
Naches Ranger District 97, 100, 145
Naches River 4, 12, 23, 55–56, 91, 93, 95, 148
Naches-Tieton-White River Land Use Plan 127, 129
Naked Came the Stranger 167
Natchez 12–13, 175*n*24; *see also* Naches
National Environmental Protection Act (NEPA) 123, 124, 149, 150

National Forest Management Act 131
National Park Service 85–87, 96, 102, 105–6, 124, 134
National Parks and Conservation Association 119–21, 169
National Trust for Historic Preservation 147
National Wilderness Protection Act (Wilderness Bill of 1964) 94
Nature Conservancy 147, 193*n*44
Nazism 206*n*18
Nelson, Jack *4*, 20, 21, 34, 38, 43, 45, 47–48, 60–62, *64*, 69–70, 182*n*10, 186*n*43, 186*n*50
Nelson, Kitty *4*, 20, 21, 34, 38, 43, 45, 47–48, 60–62, *64*, 69–70, 182*n*10, 186*n*43, 186*n*50
Nelson Ridge 5, 57, 99, 100, 103, 204*n*26
neurosis 76, 77
Newbold, Elisabeth 164, *166*, 170
Nile Valley (the Nile) 59, 61
Nineteenth Amendment 26
Nixon, Richard 91, 119, 120, 141
Norse Peak Wilderness 128, 135, *139*, 140, 149
North Africa 46–47
North Cascades 90, 95
North Cascades Conservation Council (NCCC) 88–89, 93–106, 109–10, 118, 122, 125–26, 129–31, 133, 145
North Cascades National Park 90, 92, 105–10, 196*n*114
North Cascades Primitive Area 86, 104, 196*n*114
North Cascades Study Team 106, 108, 122
North Yakima 6, 8, 10, 12
North Yakima and Valley Railroad 12
Northwest Forest Plan 150
Northwest Ski Tournament 54–55, 184*n*16

Obergefell v. Hodges 1, 82, 173*n*6
Of Men and Mountains 1, 62–68, 71, 96, 108, 186*n*43, 191*n*16, 193*n*39, 204*n*26; *see also* Douglas, William O.
old-growth forests 83, 93, 131, 138, 195*n*80; *see also* ancient forests
off-road vehicles (ORV) 112, 118, 120, 129; *see also* all-terrain vehicles; motorcycles; Tote Goat

Old Scab Mountain *135*, 204*n*26
Olympia (WA) 15, 44, 72, 144, 188*n*73, 188*n*90, 200*n*14
Olympia Press 161, 164, 165, 168
Olympic Hotel 91
Olympic National Park 97
Olympic Peninsula 106
ONE, Inc. v. Olesen 79
Onthank, Karl 93–94, 193*n*44
Oregana 26
Orlando Press 161–63
Osborn v. United States 78, 163
Osterman, Elizabeth 188*n*83
Outdoors Unlimited 108–10

Pacific Crest Trail 28, 65, 83, *123*, 131, 133, 135, *135*, 139, 178*n*38, 187*n*57
Pacific Forest Reserve 85
Pacific Northwest 1–2, 5, 14, 19, 54, 58, 72, 84, 86–87, 89–90, 91, 93, 96, 104, 111, 116
Pacific Northwest Four-Wheel Drive Association 128
Packer, Vin 156
Packwood Lake *66*, 187*n*57
Palouse 26, 44
paperback novels 155–57, 161, 164, 166, 168, 171
Paquet, Joseph 142–43
parachute jump 34, 36–38, 181*n*33
Park, Parkway, and Recreational Area Study Act 86
Pasayten Wilderness 90, 108
Passage, Mike 151
Patterson, Brad 67, 72, 147, 153
Paxton, Floyd 91, 192*n*33; *see also* the Conservative Party; *Yakima Eagle*
Peck, Annie Smith 28
penumbra 1, 81, 173*n*4, 190*n*29, 190*n*30, 190–91*n*31
Perkins, Frances 78
pilot's license 30–32, 36, 179*n*9, 179*n*14; *see also* aeronautics
Pinchot, Gifford 85
Plato 190*n*29
Playboy 120–21, 199*n*48
Podva, Monty 145
pornography 157, 16–62, 170–71; *see also* erotica
Porreca, A. (Tino) 50–51
Prairie House 60, 62, 142–43, 146–48, 185*n*39, 204*n*26, 204*n*44; *see also* Douglas, William O.
President Kissinger 170
primitive areas 86–87, 89, 92, 104, 123, 127, 196*n*114
Pritchard, Joel 134–38, 146

Prohibition 14, 16, 19, 24
Protocols of the Elders of Zion 90, 192*n*28
public hearings 101–2, 105, 122, 128, 144
pulp novels 77, 156–57; see also paperback novels
Putnam, George Palmer 33, 49–50, 58, 62

Q-Anon 92

racism 16, 17, 155; see also discrimination
railroads 8, 12, 13, 176–77*n*5, 184*n*16
Rattlesnake Creek 8, 103, 104, 137
Ray, Dixy Lee 129, **130**
Reagan, Ronald 136–38, 144
recipes 2, 166, 173*n*7, 186*n*50, 204*n*42, 207*n*54
Reconstruction Finance Corporation 40
Red Cross 1, 44, 46–47, 71, 72, 179*n*46
Region 6 102–4, 107, 132, 195*n*92
Rehnquist, William 113
Reich, Charles 112–13, 142, 165–67, 198*n*17, 207*n*44, 207*n*47
The Rich and the Super-Rich 167
Rimrock Lake 5, 11, 54, 66, **66**, 87, **123, 139**, 148
Roadless Area Review and Evaluation (RARE I) 127; (RARE II) 127–28, 131–36
Robertson, W.W. 17, 176*n*43
Robinson, Tripp 153
Roe v. Wade 81; see also *Dobbs v. Jackson Women's Health Organization*
Rogers, John 132
Romer v. Evans 152
Roosevelt, Eleanor 78
Roosevelt, Franklin D. 41, 58, 78, 86, 179*n*9
Roosevelt, Theodore 85, 99
Roosevelt Elementary School 72
Rosenberg v. Fleuti 79, 190*n*24
Ross Lake National Recreational Area 108
Rotell, Don 149
Roth v. United States 79
Routsong, Alma 157; see also Miller, Isabel
Rovig, R.D. 17
Roza Irrigation District 129
Ruby, Mike 129–30, 144, 201*n*33
Rubyfruit Jungle 171
Ruckleshaus, William 119
Rummell, Frances 72, 188*n*73, 188*n*90

Rusk, Claude Ewing 5
Russia 5, 99, 113, 174*n*5, 192*n*28
Ryan, Eileen **53**, 73, 102, 126, 188–89*n*96

sailing 28, 71, 178*n*38
St. Elizabeth Hospital 37, 38, 181*n*34, 181*n*36, 182*n*10
St. Michael's Episcopal Church 108
St. Thomas Aquinas Church 71, 154
San Francisco (CA) 24, 31, 76, 81, 145, 165, 166, 169, 188*n*83, 190*n*30
sanitation cutting 106
Saylor, John 103, 122, 126, 200*n*13
Schanbel, Gary 143
Scott, Doug 133, 145
Seawell, John 14, 34, 38
Segal, Erich 155–56, 207*n*44; see also *Love Story*
Sehnsucht 162
Seiberling, John 134, 136, 139
Selah (WA) 8, 10, 12, 92, 176–77*n*5
Senate Committee on Energy and Natural Resources 123, 138; Insular and Interior Affairs 123
sepsis 38, 181*n*34
Sevareid, Eric 113, 186*n*53
sexology 20
shank's pony 47, 183*n*25
Shoe Lake **66**, 138, 187*n*57, 187*n*69
The Sierra Club 87, 88, 90, 93, 96, 97, 100, 101, 105, 109, 112, 127–28, 137, 139, 145, 193*n*43, 200*n*14, 201*n*33
Simmons, Bessie 23
Sister Gin 171
skiing **4**, 6, 27, 44, 54–58, **55, 56, 57**, 88–90, 117, 120, 149–50, 178*n*34, 182*n*10, 184*n*12, 184*n*17, 184*n*20
Skinner v. Oklahoma 77
Slipper Lake 67, 187*n*69; see also Miriam Basin
Snoqualmie National Forest 83, 86, **95**, 97–98, 100, 102, 105, 107, 118, **123**, 125, 131, 191*n*16
Snoqualmie Pass 69
Snow Mountain Ranch 59, 63
snowmobiles 112, 118–20, 199*n*40
sodomy laws 78–79
sonic booms 116–18
Sorenson, C. Peter 202*n*44
Soviet Union 50, 74, 90, 92, 122; see also Russia

Sowards, Adam 102
spinster 24, 77, 114, **115**
Spuler, Don 189*n*97
State College of Washington (SCW) 25–26, 27, 88
Stehekin 86, 87, 89, 90, 105
Stone, Cathy (Cathleen Heffernan) Douglas 67, 78, 189*n*12, 203*n*4, 203*n*9
Stone, J. Herbert **95**, 102, 103
Story Press 159
Stratton, Owen 106, 107, 197*n*119
Structure of Grief 160–61, 164–65
Stuart, Lyle see Lyle Stuart Publishers
Sueyres, Susan 166
Sun Valley (ID) 44, 56, 117
Supreme Court 1, 58, 64, 65, 77–82, 125, 142, 157, 186*n*53; see also Black, Hugo; Douglas, William O.; Field, Steven Johnson; Jackson, Ketanji Brown; Kennedy, Anthony; Marshall, John; Rehnquist, William; Thomas, Clarence
swimming 26, 29, 32, 43, 179*n*46
Syracuse College 188*n*87

Thanksgiving 115, 184*n*7
Thomas, Clarence 173*n*6
Thomas, Gertrude 41
Three Sisters Primitive Area 87, 89, 93, 193*n*44
Tieton High School 38
Tieton Pass 187*n*57
Tieton Reservoir **66**; see also Rimrock Lake
Tieton River 4–7, 11–13, 87–89, 97, **139**, 194*n*64
Timberwolf Mountain **123, 135, 135**
Tipsoo 6, 13, 65
tomboy 20
Torrès, Tereska 156
Tote Goat 118, 130; see also motorcycles
Trail Riders of the West 65, 94
trams 130, **130**, 138
transgender 176*n*2
Treaty of the Potomac 105
the Triangle 5–6, 66, 85–86, 127
Truitt, Clarence 5, 55, 88, 93, 107–8
Tumac Mountain 4–5, **66**, 135, **135**, 187*n*57, 187*n*58
Twin Sisters Lakes 5, 100, 102, **133**
Tydings, Millard 74

Udall, Stewart 97, 105
Ulrich, Louis 88
Underhill, Miriam O'Brien 28
United States Department of Agriculture 26, 85, 127; see also United States Forest Service
United States Department of Commerce 34, 179n9, 180n22
United States Department of the Interior 85; see also Bureau of Mines; Bureau of Reclamation
United States Forest Service (USFS) 2, 13, 52, 58, 73, 78, 83, 85–89, 92–110, 118–120, 122–25, 127–38, 147–50, 194n65, 195n79, 195n92, 196n116
United States Geological Survey 125
United States Reclamation Service 11, 12; see also Bureau of Reclamation
United States Securities and Exchange Commission (SEC) 58, 78
University of Chicago 43, 182n12
University of Heidelberg 158
University of Oregon 25, 177n23, 177n26, 193n44
Up Haste 167, 207n56
The Uplands 63
Utter, Robert 144

Vance, Joe B. 17–18, *18*
Victorian era 23–24, 27
Vietnam War 116, 155
Voice of Prophecy 91
voting rights 26, 152, 176n43, 178n30

Wagen, Alma 22–23
Walla Walla (WA) 34, 37, 39, 43–44, 78, 179n44
Wallowa Mountains 44, 59, 185n29
Walter Reed Hospital 48, 125, 141
Wapato (WA) 12
Washington Emergency Relief Administration (WERA) 41–43, 182n4
Washington Forest Protection Association 130
Washington State Department of Ecology 119, 120, 129, 134
Washington State Department of Public Welfare (WSDPW) 41, 43, 182n4

Washington State Planning Council 86
Washington Wilderness Bill 138, 140, 144, 149–50
Watkins, Mary Bradley 60, 65, 185n34
Welch, Robert 91, 163; see also *The Blue Book*; John Birch Society
West Camp *66*, 67, 187n57, 187n69
Western Air Lines 30, 32, 179n14
"westsider" 193n40
Whalen, William J. 134
White House Office of Management and Budget (OMB) 134
White Pass 3, 5, 13, 57–58, 66, *66*, 89, 105, 112, *123*, 128, 133, *135*, 138, 187n57, 187n69
White Pass Corporation 138, 202n65
White Pass ski area expansion 138–39, *139*, 149–50, 203n71
White Pass Ski Company (WPSC) 138–40, *139*, 149–50
White River 13, 127, *139*
Whiteside, Jim 146
Whitman College 78
Wilcox, Ken 128
wild area 191n16, 193n49; see also wilderness area
Wilderness Alps of the Stehekin 90
wilderness area 84, 88, 92, 94–96, 100, 105–7, 108, 122, 124, 127, 129, 145, 149, 193n49; see also Alpine Lakes; Cougar Lakes Limited Area; Cougar Lakes Wilderness; Enchantment Wilderness; Glacier Peak Wilderness; Goat Rocks Wilderness; Henry M. Jackson Wilderness; Mount Aix; Norse Peak Wilderness; Pasayten Wilderness; William O. Douglas Wilderness
Wilderness Attribute Rating System (WARS) 132
Wilderness Society 87, 88, 95–97, 99–100, 104, 112, 133, 139, 147, 200n14
William O. Douglas Wilderness 2, *139*, 140, 144–46, *147*, 149, 180–81n27
wing-walking 36, 39; see also barnstorming
women's athletics 26–29

women's colleges 23, 25
Workman, Fanny Bullock 28
World War I 6, 7, 13, 14, 23, 24, 30, 32, 157–58, 159
World War II 1, 6, 19, 44, 47–48, 70, 74, 75, 77, 87, 88, 159, 162, 174n11
World Wide Church of God 90
Worthington, Dick 132–33

An X-Ray on the Yakima Valley 6–9

the Y 5, 54
Yakama Indian Reservation 4, 17, 176n43; see also Confederated Tribes and Bands of the Yakama Nation
Yakima (WA) 1–4, 15–19, 28, 30–39, 44, 45, 54, 58–65, 68, 84, 88, 99, 108–9, 114, 128–30, 141, 143, 151–53, 166, 180n25, 182n4, 184n16, 185n31, 186–87n56, 188n91, 192n33, 205n6
Yakima Airport 31, *33*, 34, 37–38, 62, 68, *70*, 143, 188n73
Yakima Chamber of Commerce 53, 63, *64*, 67, 74, 107, 108–9, 128, 197n139
Yakima County 1, 3–19, 40–43, 53, 87, 91–92, 108–9, 128–29, *133*, 135, 146, 152–53, 163, 176–77n5, 177n20
Yakima County Bar Association 59
Yakima County Courthouse 142
Yakima County Washington State Fair 14, 15, 17, 32
Yakima Eagle 91, 192n32; see also Paxton, Floyd
Yakima Federal Courthouse 153
Yakima High School 59, 63
Yakima, Natchez and Eastern Railway Company 12
Yakima River 4, 10–11, 109, 148
Yakima Ski Club 55–57
Yakima War 8, 174n14
Yakima Winter Sports Club 55, 184n20
Yale University 2, 58, 80, 112–13, 155–56, 165, 198n17, 207n44
Yellow Submarine 156
Yellowstone National Park 49, 83–84
Yosemite National Park 84

Zahniser, Howard 95–96, 99, 193n44

www.ingramcontent.com/pod-product-compliance
Ingram Content Group UK Ltd.
Pitfield, Milton Keynes, MK11 3LW, UK
UKHW051850210426
5322IPUK00025B/641